THE GOALS OF PSYCHOTHERAPY

THE CENTURY PSYCHOLOGY SERIES

Richard M. Elliott, Gardner Lindzey, & Kenneth MacCorquodale
Editors

THE GOALS OF PSYCHOTHERAPY

Edited by

Alvin R. Mahrer

Director, Laboratory of Psychopathology and Director, Psychological Training, Veterans Administration Hospital, Denver, Colorado University Park Psychological Center

New York

APPLETON-CENTURY-CROFTS

Division of Meredith Publishing Company

ACKNOWLEDGMENTS

Page 59. From "Goals of Psychotherapy" by John C. Whitehorn.
In *Research in Psychotherapy: Proceedings of a Conference.* Copyright © 1959, by American Psychological
Association, Inc. Reprinted by permission of the pub-
lisher and the author.

Page 59. From "Therapeutic Goals and Their Significance for
Therapeutic Strategy" by John C. Whitehorn. In *Psychiatric Treatment*, Vol. 31, Proceedings of the Association for Research in Nervous and Mental Disease.
Baltimore: Williams and Wilkins, 1953. Reprinted by
permission of the Association for Research in Nervous
and Mental Disease and by permission of the author.

Preface

THE purpose of this book is to provide a forum of answers to the question, What are the goals of psychotherapy? Like most fundamental issues, that of psychotherapeutic goals is most difficult to study. Our purpose is to open up this issue, to study the nature of these goals and the matters with which they are concerned, and to try to understand, appreciate, and articulate the similarities and differences in the several approaches found in this book.

Each of the contributors undertook the most difficult task of honestly and openly investigating the foundations of his own psychotherapeutic goals. I am indebted to these colleagues for their willingness to join me in this venture and for their candor in confronting the issues at hand. I must also express appreciation to my patients; they allow me the opportunity to confront the raw realities of psychotherapy, of which goals is certainly one.

Students and colleagues deserve thanks for helping to develop the theoretical framework. I want especially to thank Drs. Peter Grossman, Robert Southard, Robert Fenner, John Means, Michael Projansky, Seymour Opochinsky, Peter Weiss, and Larry Brittain. Appreciation is also extended to Dr. John R. Thompson for his help in the initial administrating of the book, and to Dr. Fred H. Herring for providing the necessary working milieu. Personal thanks are extended not only to Dr. Herring but also to Dr. E. Ellis Graham, Lee Sparkman, and Maya Oughtred.

A. R. M.

Contents

THE GOALS OF PSYCHOTHERAPY

1

Introduction

Alvin R. Mahrer, Ph.D.

PROBLEM

THE literature on psychotherapy has relatively little to offer on the goals of psychotherapy—their identification, significance, and organization. On this point, clinicians, researchers, and theoreticians have been curiously inarticulate. This book is an attempt to deal with such issues. It is intended, however, that our conclusions and proposed categories of psychotherapy be catalytic rather than final, and that they provide a stimulus rather than a solution to resolving the problem of psychotherapeutic goals.

In contrast to the paucity of literature on goals, two bordering areas of investigation have attracted considerable attention, namely, methods and techniques of psychotherapy, and indices of improvement. However, the methods and techniques are only working subgoals which point the way toward the ultimate goals without telling us a great deal about them. Nor is the understanding of goals furthered by progress in identifying indices of improvement, for the study of indices is tangential to the study of the ultimate goals themselves. The essential goals of psychotherapy remain inadequately explored.

In this book, we will propose an outline of general psychotherapeutic goals, as contrasted with the goals of any particular school or approach to psychotherapy. In addition to this major purpose, the book has many secondary purposes. One deals with similarities and differences among therapeutic approaches. A challenging assertion often heard is that therapeutic approaches are essentially similar once they are stripped of differences in vocabulary and once it is recognized that they may use different means in attempting to attain similar goals. Our study of ultimate goals should provide some data on the essential similarity or difference among approaches.

It is often contended that some kinds of psychotherapy are more ambitious than others in their attempt to bring about deep and sweeping alterations in personality and character structure. Other kinds of psychotherapy, it is im-

1

plied, have more limited goals—more supportive, palliative, and superficial. Another secondary purpose of our investigation, then, is to inquire into the meaningfulness of this dimension.

To understand different kinds of psychotherapy and to investigate similarities and differences among them, a number of category systems are available. However, no such system is based upon differences in aims, purposes, or goals, even though this dimension may well hold promise as a worthwhile and meaningful method of categorizing our contemporary array of therapeutic approaches. An additional secondary purpose is, therefore, to consider a functional taxonomy of psychotherapies based on their functions or goals.

For research purposes, a list of goals would be of value. It would provide a basis for deriving criteria of improvement, for assessing various kinds of psychotherapeutic change, and for comparing between and within varying approaches. Too often, therapeutic aims are not organized and systematized, and studies include therapists aiming toward conflicting and sometimes contradictory goals. It would also be possible to study the relationships between goals and various approaches; conceivably, one approach may be better than another to achieve certain goals. By drawing attention to long-range goals a broader perspective could be given to the mass of working operations, subgoals, and therapeutic techniques. In addition, weak spots would be revealed in, and guidelines provided for, the improvement of working therapeutic techniques and operations.

A further purpose is to inquire into the assumptions about personality which underlie a given cluster of ultimate goals. Beginning with a set of ultimate goals, and investigating the underlying personality notions, assumptions, and models, the expectation is that this approach will uncover kinds of psychotherapeutic personality models which depart from the traditional categories of psychoanalytic, client-centered, ego analytic, learning theory, and others.

Still another purpose is to inquire into the specific nature of the long-range psychotherapeutic goals. Is psychotherapy essentially a means of reducing distress, alleviating problems, and curing an illness, or is it essentially a means of attaining growth, development, maturity, and a higher plane of adjustment? Does psychotherapy increase conformity, or does it enhance individual differences? Does it facilitate or destroy creativity?

Such a list could also clarify the relationship between psychotherapeutic theories and systems of sociophilosophical values. Are psychotherapeutic theories inseparable parts of larger value systems? Do they contain their own value systems? Are they independent of value systems?

It is presumed that psychotherapeutic goals refer almost exclusively to patients or clients, yet the conceptualization of healthy, optimal functioning may go beyond patients, and apply to society in general. A further secondary purpose is to inquire into the extent to which these goals bear implications for society in general, over and above the class of patients or clients.

METHOD

Selection of Contributors

Our method bypasses the study of psychotherapeutic schools and approaches, and concentrates, rather, on the ideas of individual psychotherapists. The various therapeutic schools, systems, and approaches may be well organized along certain theoretical dimensions, but it would be begging the question to presume that any given therapeutic school possesses a set of identifying goals, and that the goals of any one school are different from the goals of all other schools. In actual operation, goals are held by individual psychotherapists rather than by a particular school or system of psychotherapy.

On the other hand, our aim is to select a broad sample of psychotherapists. Two considerations were relevant here. Psychotherapists were selected from a variety of working settings, atmospheres, and situations (e.g., private practice, psychoanalytic institutes, hospitals, university psychology departments, medical schools). Individual psychotherapists were also selected from a variety of theoretical backgrounds (e.g., Freudian psychoanalytic, behavior therapies, client-centered, Adlerian, existential, rational-emotive, direct analytic).

Individual Psychotherapy

A common thread is the emphasis upon individual treatment. Thus, "psychotherapy" refers primarily to a single therapist and single patient rather than implying multiple-therapist techniques, group therapy, milieu treatment, or other kinds of therapeutic procedures. Furthermore, the emphasis is upon therapy with adult patients rather than with children or adolescents.

Psychotherapeutic Goals

For the individually treated adult, "psychotherapeutic goals" refers to the long-range, ultimate aims and purposes, directionalities, and outcomes of therapy. The focus is not upon the working techniques of psychotherapy (orienting the patient, interpretation, the development of transference, etc.). These are methods, operations, and subgoals which serve only as pathways toward the ultimate or long-range goals. Nor do "therapeutic goals" refer here either to the particular "goals" such as "bolstering her defenses," tailored to fit a given patient, or to the body of considerations which help determine such goals. That goal-setting process calls for proper consideration of the patient's age, ego strength, the acuteness and severity of the disturbance, the motivation for treatment, and so forth. Once again, this is tangential to our meaning of psychotherapeutic goals.

Instructions

Each contributor was given essentially the above description of what psychotherapeutic goals are and are not. The question, then, was, What are his particular, general, long-range, and ultimate goals? There were no formal guides or suggested outlines for approaching the problem, nor was any contributor placed in the position of being the spokesman for a school or any particular psychotherapeutic approach. The intent was to maximize each contributor's freedom of expression.

Limitations

Our method of investigating therapeutic goals rests upon the representativeness of this sample of therapists. It must be acknowledged that the sample is inadequate. Furthermore, it would have been better, in order to study individual therapists, to present samples from their actual therapeutic exchanges rather than their polished public statements.

The proposed organization of psychotherapies into families is based, of course, upon the particular sample of psychotherapists represented in the book. The purpose is to suggest a method of organizing psychotherapies on the basis of goals or functions rather than to propose a fixed or final set of categories. The particular three families of psychotherapy which are proposed here should therefore be taken as a first approximation of a functional analysis of psychotherapies.

2

Goals in Psychotherapy: Mediating and Ultimate

Morris B. Parloff, Ph.D.

An Introduction to the Person

by Jerome D. Frank, M.D.

Morris Parloff is exceptionally well qualified by training, experience, and ability to write on the goals of psychotherapy. After graduation from Western Reserve, he obtained a master's degree in social work from the University of Chicago, then spent four years in Military Intelligence where he prepared himself for his professional career by extensive experience in interviewing. He then joined the Veterans Administration in Washington, D.C. as a psychiatric social worker. His obvious talents and interests soon led to his employment in a research project on group therapy from 1947 to 1949. Here he became intimately acquainted with group therapy of hospitalized patients, leading to a continuously fruitful interest in the hospital milieu.

Feeling the need for a broader base in theory and scientific method, he returned to his alma mater to obtain a doctorate in clinical psychology. In 1951 he joined the psychotherapy research project at Johns Hopkins and, while making highly significant contributions to it, also carried out for his Ph.D. thesis a research study on the effect of the relationship offered by the group therapist on the outcome of treatment.

Seeking a wider scope, he joined the National Institute of Mental Health in 1953, where he is now Chief of the Section on Personality.

Dr. Parloff is with the Section on Personality, Laboratory of Psychology, National Institute of Mental Health, National Institutes of Health, U.S. Public Health Service, Department of Health, Education and Welfare.

During the past decade he has conducted penetrating and ingenious research on aspects of psychotherapy. This includes a study of the impact of ward milieu philosophies on nursing role concepts, and of the communication of values between therapist and patient. In recent years his major research interest has been in creativity, an attribute that he himself possesses.

His theoretical and programmatic contributions include many papers on psychotherapy, combining his clinical and research orientations. He was coorganizer of the first American Psychological Association Research Conference on Psychotherapy and coeditor of the proceedings of that conference.

While all this was going on, he somehow found time to obtain a thorough grounding in psychoanalytic theory and is now a Research Associate Candidate of the Washington Psychoanalytic Institute. This has not, however, narrowed his theoretical orientation; he continues to roam freely among interpersonal theories, skillfully appropriating and building on the conceptualizations that best meet his needs. He does not, however, confine himself to study and the laboratory but also participates in professional and community activities. He is a member of the Maryland Board of Examiners in Clinical Psychology and of the Executive Board and faculty of the Washington School of Psychiatry.

Dr. Parloff combines the sensitive, compassionate human understanding and practical common sense of the social worker with the disciplined research skills of the psychologist. His readers, like his friends, can be confident that they will come away from a contact with him stimulated and enlightened.

THE question, "What are the goals of the practicing psychotherapist?" has a disturbingly familiar ring. It is reminiscent of the now classic plaint of some middle-class, middle-aged, seemingly successful individuals who present themselves for therapy because they have become unsure of their aims and uncertain of their accomplishments. Perhaps psychotherapy has reached a comparable stage of perplexity in its professional development.

If you will accept the analogy, then we may adopt the role of the therapist. In this capacity it is easier to resist the temptation to offer reassurances to the clinician-patient who presents this problem. One is inclined to point out that the very fact of his having raised the question is evidence of the commendable soundness of his ego and the essential integrity of other of his vital hypothetical constructs. As we listen to this patient's recital of his basic convictions, attitudes, and behavior, we find ample evidence, however, that unfortunately he does have a problem. For example, the clinician-patient reports that he has grave doubts regarding his ability even to identify the pathology which he seeks to treat, is unable to predict outcome, is unable to specify goals until they have been attained, and believes that the undefined basic changes he wishes to effect are essentially unmeasurable. He is, however, certain of the validity of his particular theory and the efficacy of his techniques. In brief, he appears to be in the remarkable position of having a cure in search of a definable disease.

In my view, the contributors to this volume have been placed in the untenable position of being clinician-patient and clinician-therapist simultaneously. We are asked to be both questioner and answerer. It may be apropos, therefore, to remind ourselves of the observation, "A man who steps outside and rings his own doorbell should not be astonished to find nobody home" (Malcolm, 1961, p. 34).

How does it come about that a field which, although young by many standards, has had some 50 or 60 years of apparently increasing success and recognition, now finds itself preoccupied about the "real" meaning of its existence? Is the problem that the clinician brings to us to be regarded basically as a reality problem or can we infer some deeper dynamic significance? In either case, what are the resistances which prevent him from coping with this problem more effectively?

Shall we accept the clinician's question regarding his goals as a straightforward plea for direct suggestion as to what they should be? This appears highly unlikely since the patient does not appear to have found much comfort in earlier readings of the literature, which abounds with lists of all the things which are good and desirable. Watson, in a survey of outcome literature, found that more than 100 criteria had been used singly and in combination by investigators up to 1952 (Watson, 1952). No matter how exhaustive a list we might be able to present, it is doubtful whether any clinician reviewing the list would express either pleasure or chagrin at finding that we had included some goals which had previously escaped his notice. It is not very likely that the clinician would say to himself, "I wonder why I hadn't thought of that. I must remember to do that with my patients from now on." I do not believe that the question can be resolved by our pontificating what the true goals of therapy are or should be.

It is probably also safe to assume that no matter how ambitious or limited are the goals which the therapist avows, they are chosen with the expectation that they will be helpful to the patient and most certainly not injurious. The changes which he effects are not to result in the crippling of important psychological functions or the limiting of the patient's potential for significant life experiences. If a therapist were free to choose the goals of either (1) effecting temporary alteration of superficial, trivial variables, which would also result in further constricting the individual, or (2) producing permanent change of deep and dynamically meaningful variables in such a manner as to facilitate the growth and development of the personality, then, all other things being equal (i.e., time, effort, money, accessibility, etc.), the therapist would undoubtedly select the latter goals.

As a researcher it is my conviction that sound research can be performed only after thorough observation and analysis of the phenomena have permitted the differentiation between real and pseudo issues. If we accept the view that the clinician's problem does not lie in his having overlooked some important goals, and that he does not deliberately choose to be ineffective or injurious, then we may consider some issues which appear to underlie the confusion regarding clinical goals.

In this paper I shall deal with six factors which represent areas of apparent confusion and complexity regarding the clinician's choice of goals: (1) mediating vs. ultimate goals; (2) the therapist; (3) schools of therapy; (4) the patient; (5) concepts of mental health; and (6) moral values.

MEDIATING vs. ULTIMATE GOALS

Stepping out of the therapist's role, I propose at the outset to offer a formulation which I believe is central to the analysis of the remaining five factors. I suggest that the problem of goals of therapy can be better understood if we divide goals into two categories: mediating and ultimate. The mediating goals involve the clinician's assumptions regarding the necessary steps and stages which a patient must achieve if the treatment is to be effective. These then are the enabling or mediating conditions which lead to the accomplishment of the ultimate goals.

The most readily verbalized goals deal with the mediating processes of therapy. Thus there is little hesitation on the part of the therapist of a particular school to enunciate as his goals such things as making the unconscious conscious, recall of the repressed, deconditioning, counterconditioning, strengthening or weakening of the superego, development and analysis of transference neurosis, promoting insight and flexibility, increasing capacity for symbolization, increasing self-acceptance, and others. These *mediating* goals are of particular value to the therapist in that they give him some indication that he and the patient are traveling the correct road. He believes that they provide a basis for judging the pervasiveness, depth, and permanence of the ultimate change he will effect.

Mediating goals are held to be signposts of progress. They are not usually believed to be in themselves the final destination. But it is in regard to the *ultimate* goals that the clinician is least verbal. To specify ultimate goals is to express value judgments, and this many therapists are loath to do. It is, however, the ultimate goal that is the principal concern of the therapist in fulfilling his contract with the patient and the community.

Granted that the clinicians of various schools hold quite different concepts regarding the mediating processes, does it follow that their ultimate goals are also different? I propose that the ultimate goal of all therapy is to reduce discomfort and increase effectiveness of the patient in his biological and social functioning. A fuller elaboration of this idea has been published and will not be repeated here (Parloff, Kelman, and Frank, 1954). We may argue that these goals do not go far enough in achieving "positive" mental health, or that changes produced by one method are transitory or perhaps even limit further development.

We recognize that unfortunately there are no reliable instruments which give a *direct* reading of the degree of personality reorganization, depth of change, creativity, or self-actualization. The evidence from projective tests that significant structural personality changes are effected in therapy is unimpressive, no matter what the form of therapy investigated. Judgments of relevant change are made on the basis of the observed behavior and expressed attitudes of the patient. The clinician interprets these data in the context of his total understanding of the patient. Altering the observed behavior and expressed attitudes is the goal of all therapists.

What follow-up research there is indicates that some of the superficial therapies have produced remarkably robust and enduring effects (Frank, 1961; Rogers and Dymond, 1954). It is theoretically possible that even limited psychotherapy which helps free some of the energy involved in maintaining defenses might enable the patient to deal more adequately with other problems. This process could, under fortunate circumstances, snowball in its effect.

Mediating goals appear to differ from one theory of psychotherapy to another. However, if the therapist accepts his responsibility to be primarily that of psychotherapist rather than educator, investigator, philosopher, or ally, then the differences in the stated ultimate goals will in all likelihood be small.

THE THERAPIST

The formulation of goals for a given patient may in part be a reflection of the therapist's personality and values. His value systems affect not only the particular methodology employed but also the appraisal of what changes are desirable. I believe it is necessary to accept as a reality factor that the clinician, regardless of his training and the state of his personal analysis, is probably never totally free from the influence of his own needs, attitudes, and cultural values in the conduct of psychotherapy.

It is widely accepted that the therapist's personality and the relationship he is able to establish with the patient are basic to the outcome of therapy. For this reason, training institutions are concerned about the selection of suitable prospective therapists. There is also some evidence that the particular training and intellectual information possessed by a therapist may be considerably less important than his ability to relate to and understand people. Such abilities may be distressingly resistant to improvement by formal training (Betz and Whitehorn, 1956; Rogers, 1956).

Although therapists may differ in their concepts of the necessary mediating goals, it does not follow that their concepts and achievement of ultimate goals differ. For example, Whitehorn reported that the group of therapists who were found to be most successful in their treatment of schizophrenics included some who viewed treatment as helping patients to conform and other therapists who preferred to stress freedom and independence. The effectiveness of the therapist in assisting the patient to recover from his psychotic episode and to be discharged from the hospital was independent of mediating goals, but did appear to be related to the therapist's willingness to lead his patients in one or the other direction in a consistent fashion (Whitehorn, 1959).

SCHOOLS OF THERAPY

The clinician is quick to point out that the various schools have different goals. This belief, incidentally, permits the schools to tolerate each other and therefore has become a necessary, if untested, part of the folklore of psychotherapy. It is "well known" that brief psychotherapy has modest and restricted goals whereas intensive psychoanalytic therapies have grander and more sweeping goals. It is equally "well known" that brief psychotherapies are content with amelioration whereas the depth therapies are satisfied with nothing less than cure by elimination of the dynamic causes of psychopathology. It appears that the pervasiveness of change which one reportedly seeks and hopefully obtains is directly related to the complexity of the personality theory to which one subscribes. Whitehorn has suggested that the greater one's conviction regarding the correctness of his "understanding of pathogenesis," the more inclined he is "towards the perfectionistic formulation of goals; [whereas] skepticism and humility incline one towards melioristic formulation of goals" (Whitehorn, 1959, p. 9). If we interpolate the observation that reality rarely keeps theories' promises, then it is clear why Grinker should have found that the goals of the younger rather than the more experienced therapists include "uncovering significant dynamic processes during long-term treatment with desire for cure or so-called complete reorganization of the personality" (Grinker, 1959, p. 134).

Although psychoanalysis continues to be viewed as the most powerful and most ambitious form of psychotherapy, there has been a growing deemphasis within the ranks of psychoanalysts on the necessity of achieving the "cures" consisting of extensive personality reorganization. Analysts such as Knight disclaim any extraordinarily lofty goals for psychoanalysis. He stated that the patient and his family must be prepared for the fact that the patient will not "become a paragon of all the virtues and accomplishments, without flaw, defect, or any anxiety and capable of behaving in every possible situation like a superman" (Knight, 1941, p. 437). Knight believes instead that a more reasonable expectation is that "The patient will remain essentially the same person after the best analysis—rid of his disabling symptoms, perhaps, or able to handle what ones are still left more adaptably, be more productive, happier in his relationships, but still the same person as to native endowment, appearance, and basic temperament" (Knight, 1941, p. 437).

According to Redlich, the goal of psychoanalysis has been successively modified from cure to improving adjustment and now to a technique principally for personality exploration—albeit the best one available (Redlich, 1960). We need not assume that this position is universally accepted among analysts but merely that some highly trained and experienced therapists have found reason to lower their sights. To this degree the gap between schools in terms of ultimate goals has been narrowed.

If the various schools of therapy take seriously the notion that they have different ultimate goals, then in diagnosing a patient's needs they must decide which school of therapy would be most appropriate. If this is the case, one must conclude that a great underground traffic of cross-referrals from one school to another exists, but remains remarkably unobtrusive. The fact remains that as far as can now be determined from the research literature, despite divergences of theory and of methods, the ultimate results of therapy appear to be similar (Frank, 1961).

THE PATIENT

Most clinicians accept as axiomatic that psychotherapy begins with a diagnosis in order that the psychotherapy provided may be designed to meet the patient's needs. Some notable dissenters from this view include the client-centered therapists and existential therapists. Their assumption is that emotional disorders have a common general etiology and therefore a single form of therapy can be applied to a fairly wide range of patients. Diagnosis in the sense of understanding the patient's dynamics is, however, viewed as a continuing process throughout the course of therapy. The diagnostic function, then, is inseparable from treatment.

Few therapists today find the current diagnostic classificatory schema very helpful in determining the form of treatment, except perhaps on the grossest level. There is little evidence that these classification systems have a high level of reliability, validity, or prognostic value. My experience coincides with that of Knight, who concluded, "Far too often in current practice the type of psychotherapy used with the patient is determined solely by the limited training and ability of the psychotherapist rather than by either the type of illness the patient has or type of patient that has the illness" (Knight, 1954, p. 58). Despite dissatisfaction with current classification systems, most therapists feel more comfortable operating on the assumption that the form and course of therapy offered is not independent of the patient.

Psychotherapists, particularly psychoanalysts, are quite frank to report that the range of patients suitable for their services is quite restricted. Obviously, they do not see as their professional goal the capacity to treat every harried patient who chooses to present himself. The assessment of the patient's assets and liabilities is conscientiously undertaken, with particular concern for intelligence, age, capacity to verbalize and introspect, degree of anxiety, and, most important, a sufficiently intact personality to withstand the rigors of the treatment form. In addition to the personality assets which a patient must have in order to do well in therapy, he is often required to have adequate financial assets.

It appears that therapists who require that their patients demonstrate great ego strength at the outset of therapy, aim at effecting more extensive change in patients than that contemplated by their less demanding colleagues. Why it should be that the best "put-together" patients should require the greatest amount of reorganization is not immediately clear. It does, however, imply a rather impressive dissatisfaction on the part of the analyst with the personality of even the best-functioning patients available. Such therapists must view the treatment needs of the less fortunate patients who do not qualify for their deep therapy as being extravagantly grim.

The goals may be determined in reference to the therapist's assessment of a given patient's usual level of performance. Thus a decision may be (1) to restore a patient to his earlier level of functioning, or (2) to raise the individual to new levels of functioning, never previously achieved. The decision to restore may be based on one of the following evaluations: (a) the level of previous functioning was good so that this is all that is required of therapy; (b) the investment of time and energy necessary to do more than strengthen and reestablish the defense system is prohibitive; or (c) restoration of ego-functioning is all that is safely possible since the removal of defenses may be dangerous to the patient (Gill, 1951). The second—and grossly ambitious—goal is similarly based on the assessment of the needs and strengths of the patient. This goal is presumably achieved not by strengthening defenses but by analyzing them.

Such formulations regarding psychodynamics rather than symptoms give the appearance of offering a set of categories upon which to base one's goal decisions that is superior to the usual diagnostic categories. The major problem which remains, however, is that it is yet to be demonstrated that therapists can make such assessments with any degree of reliability. There *is* considerable evidence that our current knowledge of psychodynamics is not sufficient to permit us to be accurate in the prediction of results of therapy. Alexander has noted that "patients who according to a textbook should recover, stubbornly refuse to improve and others with initial bad prognosis unexpectedly do recover. One of the most baffling facts in the rapid 'transference cures' which often persist even if no further treatment is administered . . . not only do 'transference cures' sometimes persist but marked personality changes take place in the following years" (Alexander, 1955, p. 326).

The relationships among the assessment of a patient's capacities and needs, the intermediate goals selected, and the ultimate goals achieved appear to be far from established.

CONCEPTS OF MENTAL HEALTH

The clinician speaks enthusiastically, but not without a trace of anxiety, regarding his goal of assisting his patients to achieve "positive mental health." The usual therapist's dictum that treatment should be based on what is required and what is possible appears now to have been converted to: "If it is possible, then it is required."

There appear to be at least three main views regarding the concept of mental health. The first is that it represents the highest level of functioning of which *mankind* is capable. This concerns the fullest utilization of capacities which are presumed to be innately characteristic of man, as distinct from other animals. The referent is the capacities of man rather than their unique representation in a given individual. Although mental health and mental illness may be viewed as distributed along a continuum in the poulation, the cutoff point for designating the mentally healthy is very high. A clinician who seriously entertains this view believes that man is characterized by an infinite capacity for growth and that it is in the nature of man to be creative and to use fully his cognitive powers. The clinician's task, therefore, is to continue working with the patient until he gives evidence of having achieved the desired state of maturity. I find it puzzling that the clinician who holds this goal of mental health for his patients should devote so much of his energy to working with the emotionally disturbed, rather than the emotionally stable individual. It suggests that these therapists may believe that the "sick and deviant" among us are the more likely candidates for realizing the aim of functioning at the highest level of which mankind is capable. This assumption would be consistent with the formerly fashionable view that creativity and emotional disturbance are highly correlated.

A second concept of mental health has as its criterion the full utilization of the *individual patient's unique capacities*. Such a concept of mental health makes no more claim to unity than does the concept of mental illness. An individual may be effective in some areas and limited in others. It suggests that the term mental health may be applied with equal accuracy to a well-functioning genius and to a well-functioning moron. This view of mental health requires that we be able accurately to assess the capacities of patients. Although clinicians who hold this view believe that mental health is not merely the absence of conflict or illness, they make clear that the concept need not encompass all the high values of our culture. Unlike the first group of theorists, they finesse the sticky problems of attempting to define the ultimate values for this culture, in the present and in the future, and for all civilizations (Jahoda, 1958, p. 79).

A third and less popular view represents the class or discontinuity hypothesis. This is described by Korner, who believes that health and illness are not matters of degree within an individual: a man is either mentally healthy or mentally ill. The mentally healthy experience stress and psychic injury but have the resiliency to recover. The mentally ill may function well until stressed but lack the capacity to recover spontaneously. There is no overlap between these groups, and the goal of making an individual of the mentally ill class "mentally healthy" is therefore an idle one (Korner, 1958).

One of the major resistance values of the overall mental health concept is that it implies that the clinician has successfully solved the problems of dealing with mere "negative" mental health and may now go on to the happier task of accentuating the positive.

When the clinician attempts to go beyond the goal of removing the pathological condition, he is inevitably expressing some value judgment regarding "the good life." An increasing number of therapists are willing to accept the responsibility of advocating particular values as being those that foster mental health, and they maintain that they are in a good position to have such values. Who, they ask, is in a better position to have developed useful concepts regarding the prevention of mental illness and the promotion of mental health (Wolpe, 1958; Herzberg, 1945; Phillips, 1956; Frankl, 1955; Thorne, 1950; Ellis, 1958)?

There remains, however, a large group of therapists who claim that they are not interested in tampering with the value systems of their patients. Many, following the precedent of Freud, disclaim interest in influencing the values of patients, on the basis that as scientists they are concerned with reality and facts and do not presume to be in a position to provide the patient with a philosophy of life (Hartmann, 1960).

This discrepancy in the clinicians' attitudes toward values may, for some, reflect differences in their basic philosophy regarding the nature of man. For example, therapists who subscribe to the view that man's natural state is to mature, grow, and to express his innate goodness, may view the requirements of therapy as simply the removal of the blocks, fixations, and regressions which interfere with such natural development. These therapists have the confident expectation that this treatment will permit the individual to select his own goals and that these will be valid for the individual and, ultimately, valuable for society. Therapists whose theories do not permit such a sanguine view of man's inevitable growth in the direction of morality require of themselves that in addition to dealing with blocks they provide the patient with fairly specific information and training regarding behavioral techniques, values, etc. Some therapists view man's highest good as the achievement of inner peace and equanimity, others believe that labor is man's highest aspiration, and still others suggest that pleasure is the ultimate goal of man (Pruyser, 1958).

There is an undeniable aesthetic satisfaction in being able to formulate one's concepts of mental health in elegant and dynamically sophisticated terms. The value to the field of having lofty aims is also undeniable. However, when clinicians interpret the capacity to formulate these ideals as evidence of their own capacity to attain such goals, they are indulging in magical thinking. The value of goals lies not merely in the ability to state them, but rather in the ability to achieve them.

The proponents of "mental health" state that their goals differ from those of other therapists not merely in degree but in kind. However, no matter how much we may admire the faith and the level of aspiration of the "mental health" devotees, we still find no evidence that their ultimate achievements with comparable patients differ from those attained by others.

MORAL VALUES

Although the moral values issue arises in relation to one's concept of mental health, it exists on an even broader basis. Some therapists believe that a patient's pathology lies in his existing attitudes and values. It remains an open question, however, whether mental health may be achieved by adopting "the right values," aligned in the proper hierarchy, or whether mental health is the condition from which the good values are spontaneously generated. Although the preponderant number of clinicians do not set as their goal training the patient to adopt specific attitudes and behavior patterns, there can be little question that some of the therapist's values are communicated to the patient wittingly or unwittingly. At least three studies report that patients who are judged by their therapists to have improved are the ones who in the course of therapy moved in the direction of accepting the therapist's values (Rosenthal, 1955; Schrier, 1953; Parloff, 1960).

Quite apart from whether we succeed in keeping our values from the patient the question remains: Should we try? Goodwin Watson points out that even the decision to permit the patient self-direction in the selection of his values is in itself a moral choice on the part of the therapist. It assumes that self-direction outweighs any possible losses that might derive from the patient's "unenlightened pursuit of less rewarding or even damaging courses of action" (Watson, 1958).

I do not propose to review again the issues of whether therapists should communicate their values, and—since they apparently do—what values they should communicate. Instead, let us recognize that in a very real sense all of present-day therapy may be said to be based on the therapists' values. In the absence of knowledge, we can only express preferences, biases, and value judgments. In the absence of information, therapists behave on the basis of faith. We have no other choice, since to postpone action until the "true facts" are in would immobilize us all.

If the best method of treating a patient were known, it would be unethical for a therapist to use any technique less effective. I accept James's (1890) observation that "An act has no ethical quality whatever, unless it be chosen out of several all equally possible." I would no more propose to argue with a man's therapeutic faith than with his religious dogma. I request only that articles of faith be presented as such and not be introduced as scientific fact.

Thus, in reviewing with our clinician-patient his presenting complaints, we have heard some of the issues which he experiences as making the question of goals overwhelmingly complex. I have, in analyzing the complaints, suggested that some of the problems may be greatly simplified by recognizing a distinction between mediating goals and ultimate goals.

Unlike the researcher, the clinician, in fulfilling his primary function, cannot be content to remain at the level of mediating goals. The clinician's responsibility lies in achieving the ultimate goals for which therapy was undertaken, namely, to relieve distress and to enhance the effectiveness of the patient's biological and social functioning. There is ample evidence that the statements of mediating goals are quite different, depending on the therapist, school, evaluation of patient's needs, concepts of mental health, and moral values; however, there is a reasonable basis for the speculation that there may be relatively little difference in the goals regarding ultimate change. Such differences as exist regarding the ultimate goals appear to concern not the nature of the changes but rather their durability and their extent. It appears that some forms of therapy assert as their goal the achievement of extensive reorganization and enduring changes which they believe other therapies cannot offer. This, then, becomes a matter for research rather than debate. Research studies may attempt to assess the relationship between mediating and ultimate goals, and to compare, across forms of therapy, the achievement of both types of goals with comparable patients over comparable treatment and post-treatment intervals.

Although patients as a group can hardly be called poor sports, as their tolerance of our various ministrations will attest, I believe they would join me in urging the therapists to adopt the pragmatic philosophy that it's not so much how you play the game that counts, but whether you win or lose.

EPILOGUE

The clinicians' devotion to the principle of reality-testing requires that this discussion take cognizance not only of hypothetical "ideal" goals but also of actual goals currently achieved. It is important that we know whether discrepancies exist between such *ideal* and *actual* goals. Are there, for example, goals which can be attained only under specified treatment conditions, and goals which are not yet obtainable under any known set of conditions?

The clinician is coming increasingly under attack for his failure to demonstrate in a convincing way that a meaningful relationship exists between his theory, his methods, his statement of goals, and what he ultimately achieves. The hundreds of evaluation studies currently available—including those by this writer—have unfortunately provided little guidance either to the researcher or to the clinician. The failure of our research literature to build up any reliable body of knowledge must be recognized. The principal failing of these studies is frequently not in the design or in any lack of research skills but is found instead in limitations of scope and lack of comparability of important variables. Perhaps the clearest evidence of the inadequacy of our literature is that the defense against such critics as Eysenck and Levitt maintains that those authors made the pitiful mistake of taking seriously our published "outcome" reports. These critics are accused of having made the cynical assumption of comparability among the evaluation studies where none had been intended.

A field which must resort to the defense that no one can prove that what it does is harmful or merely ineffective is in an appallingly vulnerable state. A field that appears unable to distinguish between the results obtained by psychotherapeutic efforts of the charlatan and those obtained by the well-trained ethical practitioner is inviting disaster.

I urge that as clinicians we undertake to monitor ourselves, for if we do not anticipate and remedy the situation, we will become increasingly subject to attack, some of which has already begun. We must adopt a positive approach and seek to demonstrate that what we do is indeed useful. We also have a moral obligation to be clear about what the patient receives from us and what he does not receive. Just as we insist that the patient's goals be realistic, so we must insist that the clinician's goals and his assessment of their achievement be realistic.

It is no surprise that the therapist's suggested solution to these problems is to do more therapy, and the researcher's solution is, inevitably, to do more research. The therapist frequently appears to believe that the individual who insists on the importance of more research must himself need more therapy because of the inordinate naïveté of his faith that he has but to provide facts and they will be accepted and utilized. My concern at the moment, however, is with obtaining the facts rather than with their final implementation.

I do not propose that the solution lies in urging once again that the clinician conduct systematic research. I frankly do not believe that the clinician should be burdened with the task of research in addition to the job of therapy. Moreover, the clinician may not be particularly well suited by temperament or by the fact of his personal stake in the treatment to undertake rigorous and systematic research. I do believe, however, that he has an obligation to participate even more fully in research by making his work accessible for study.

I suggest, therefore, that a responsible representative group of clinicians seek the services of a competent research agency, public or private, to undertake a large-scale evaluation study which cuts across schools of therapy and types of patients. The aim of such a study would be to obtain data which would permit us to move toward the goal of determining the nature, degree, and durability of change specifically attributable to a particular form of therapy for a particular type of patient for a specified unit of time. Criteria and measures must be worked out in collaboration with representatives of the various major schools of psychotherapy and these measures should be applied to *all* patients included in the study, independent of the form of therapy to which they are exposed. Without attempting to suggest a research design, I believe it would be necessary to obtain sufficient data regarding the patients to permit the researcher to follow the course of comparable patients in different forms of therapy. Measurements should be obtained before and at set intervals during and subsequent to therapy.

This field has sometimes managed to insulate itself from the impingement of reality by the indiscriminate invocation of such notions as these: the patient's negative reactions to the therapist are merely manifestations of transference; and individuals who urge that we demonstrate rather than assert our competence reveal only their own resistances. Frieda Fromm-Reichman, in referring to these and similar devices, stated in a lecture in 1948 that these defensive maneuvers may permit us to ". . . err with impunity." I believe we must recognize that the price for this privilege is that we run the risk that we may also be "impugned with verity."[1]

REFERENCES

Alexander, F. Discussion. In P. H. Hoch, Aims and limitations of psychotherapy. *Amer. J. Psychiat.*, 1955, **112**, 326-327.

Betz, Barbara J., and Whitehorn, J. C. The relationship of the therapist to the outcome of therapy in schizophrenia. In N. S. Klein (Ed.), *Psychiatric research reprints.* Washington, D.C.: Amer. Psychiat. Ass., 1956. Pp. 89–105.

Ellis, A. Rational psychotherapy. *J. gen. Psychol.*, 1958, **59**, 35–49.

Frank, J. D. *Persuasion and healing: a comparative study of psychotherapy.* Baltimore: Johns Hopkins Press, 1961.

Frankl, V. *The doctor and the soul.* New York: Knopf, 1955.

Gill, M. M. Ego psychology and psychotherapy. *Psychoanal. quart.*, 1951, **20**, 62–71.

Grinker, R. R. A transactional model for psychotherapy. *A.M.A. Arch. gen. Psychiat.*, 1959, **1**, 133–148.

Hartmann, H. *Psychoanalysis and moral values.* New York: International Universities Press, 1960.

Herzberg, A. *Active psychotherapy.* New York: Grune & Stratton, 1945.

Hoch, P. H. Aims and limitations of psychotherapy. *Amer. J. Psychiat.*, 1955, **112**, 321–327.

Jahoda, Marie. *Current concepts of positive mental health.* New York: Basic Books, 1958.

James, W. *Principles of psychology.* London: Macmillan, 1890.

Knight, R. P. Evaluation of the results of psychoanalytic therapy. *Amer. J. Psychiat.*, 1941, **98**, 434–446.

Knight, R. P. A critique of the present status of the psychotherapies. In R. P. Knight and C. R. Friedman (Eds.), *Psychoanalytic psychiatry and psychology.* New York: International Universities Press, 1954. Pp. 52–64.

Korner, I. J. Mental health vs. mental illness. *Ment. Hyg.*, 1958, **42**, 315–320.

Malcolm, D. *The New Yorker*, 1961, **37**, 234.

[1] I am indebted to my colleague, Dr. Donald S. Boomer, for this epigrammatic restatement of Fromm-Reichman's observation.

Parloff, M. B. Communication of values and therapeutic change. *A.M.A. Arch. gen. Psychiat.*, 1960, **2,** 300–304.

Parloff, M., Kelman, H., and Frank, J. Comfort, effectiveness, and self-awareness as criteria of improvement in psychotherapy. *Amer. J. Psychiat.*, 1954, **3,** 343–351.

Phillips, E. L. *Psychotherapy.* Englewood Cliffs, N.J.: Prentice-Hall, 1956.

Pruyser, P. W. Is mental health possible. *Bull Menn. Clin.*, 1958, **22,** 58–66.

Redlich, F. C. Psychoanalysis and the problem of values. In J. H. Masserman (Ed.), *Science and psychoanalysis.* Vol. 3. *Psychoanalysis and human values.* New York: Grune & Stratton, 1960.

Rogers, C. R. Training individuals to engage in the therapeutic process. In C. R. Strothers (Ed.), *Psychology and mental health.* Washington, D.C.: American Psychological Association, 1956. Pp. 76–92.

Rogers, C. R., and Dymond, R. (Eds.) *Psychotherapy and personality change.* Chicago: University of Chicago Press, 1954.

Rosenthal, D. Changes in some moral values following psychotherapy. *J. consult. Psychol.*, 1955, **19,** 431–436.

Schrier, H. The significance of identification in therapy. *Amer. J. Orthopsychiat.*, 1953, **23,** 585–604.

Thorne, F. C. *Principles of personality counseling. J. clin. Psychol.*, 1950. Pp. 336–346.

Watson, R. I. Measuring the effectiveness of psychotherapy: problems for investigation. *J. clin. Psychol.*, 1952, **8,** 60–64.

Whitehorn, J. C. Goals of psychotherapy. In E. A. Rubinstein and M. B. Parloff (Eds.), *Research in psychotherapy.* Washington, D.C.: American Psychological Association, 1959. Pp. 1–9.

Wolpe, J. *Psychotherapy by reciprocal inhibition.* Stanford: Stanford University Press, 1958.

3

The Goals and Responsibilities
of the Psychotherapist:
Some Problematic Issues

Milton Greenblatt, M.D., and
Daniel J. Levinson, Ph.D.

An Introduction to the Persons

by Gerald L. Klerman, M.D.

In recent years, collaboration between clinical psychiatrists and social scientists has proven highly successful. Examples include Alfred Stanton, M.D., and Morris Schwartz, Ph.D., who wrote the now classic monograph, *The Mental Hospital*; and Fritz R. Redlich, M.D., and A. B. Hollingshead, Ph.D., whose collaboration resulted in *Social Class and Mental Illness*. The close friendship and active collaboration between Milton Greenblatt, M.D., and Daniel J. Levinson, Ph.D., in Boston, is very much in this pattern. Although of different professional backgrounds, they bring to the areas of mental health and psychotherapy research their strong humanitarian devotion to patient care, coupled with their capacity to translate complex and abstract theoretical formulations into ideas with immediate practical usefulness.

Milton Greenblatt was born in 1914 in Boston, Massachusetts. Raised and educated in the Boston area, he graduated *summa cum laude* from

Dr. Greenblatt is Superintendent of Boston State Hospital and Professor of Psychiatry, Tufts University School of Medicine.

Dr. Levinson is Professor of Psychology in the Department of Psychiatry, Yale University, and Director, Research Unit for Social Psychology and Psychiatry, Connecticut Mental Health Center.

Tufts College in 1935 and *cum laude* from Tufts College School of Medicine in 1939. During this period, he became actively engaged in research in physiology, with particular interest in thyroid metabolism. After an internship in general medicine at the Beth Israel Hospital in Boston, he decided to explore the possibility of a career in neurology and psychiatry.

From 1941 to 1963, he was closely associated with the Boston Psychopathic Hospital, now known as the Massachusetts Mental Health Center. He began his residency in psychiatry in 1941 and soon became actively involved in research, particularly in electroencephalography. He rapidly rose in responsibility, from Senior Physician to Director of Research and Laboratories and Assistant Superintendent. Concurrently, he was active in the Department of Psychiatry at Harvard Medical School, where he became Associate Clinical Professor. He was very closely associated with Harry C. Solomon, M.D., then Superintendent of the Massachusetts Mental Health Center and Professor of Psychiatry at Harvard Medical School. This association resulted in their oustanding studies on lobotomy which culminated in 1951 in the award of the Hofheimer prize of the American Psychiatric Association to Dr. Greenblatt (with Dr. Robert Arnot and Miss Beatrice Talbot).

Soon after the investigations of lobotomy, Dr. Greenblatt shifted his interest to research in social psychiatry. Supported by grants from the Russell Sage Foundation, he and his associates undertook an extensive program of "action research" attempting the transformation of mental hospitals from traditional custodial orientations to active therapeutic environments. It was during this period that he became associated with Dr. Levinson.

Daniel J. Levinson was born May 28, 1920, in New York City, but was raised and educated in Southern California. He received a B.A. degree from the University of California at Los Angeles in 1940 and then went to the University of California at Berkeley for graduate study in psychology. During this time, he became a member of the research team —which also included T. W. Adorno, Else Frenkel-Brunswik, and Nevitt Sanford—investigating the social psychology of prejudice and authoritarianism. From this endeavor, the group produced its famous book, *The Authoritarian Personality*. Dr. Levinson came to Harvard in 1950 as a member of the Department of Social Relations. Soon after moving to Massachusetts, he began to apply the concepts and techniques of social psychology to studies of the attitudes and role performance of professional personnel and patients in a mental hospital.

He held a Career Investigator Award from the NIMH from 1955 to 1960, and a faculty research award from the Foundations Fund for Research in Psychiatry, 1960 to 1965. His recent books include *Patienthood in the Mental Hospital* (with E. B. Gallagher), and *The Executive Role Constellation* (with R. C. Hodgson and A. Zaleznik).

Drs. Greenblatt and Levinson have been colleagues since 1950. Their collaboration has resulted in a number of articles written together on the role of therapeutic attitudes, hospital change, professional identity, and role performance as these factors influence clinical care, social change in the hospital, and drug therapy. With R. Williams, they edited *The Patient and the Mental Hospital,* and with G. L. Klerman, they edited *Mental Patients in Transition.*

Currently, Dr. Greenblatt is the Superintendent of the Boston State Hospital and Professor of Psychiatry at Tufts University School of Medicine. Dr. Levinson is Professor of Psychology in the Department of Psychiatry, Yale University, and Director, Research Unit for Social Psychology and Psychiatry, Connecticut Mental Health Center.

Both men bring to their work a keen sensitivity to the needs of patients as human beings and a profound interest in the subtle influences of organizational life and social patterns upon the individual's freedom and personal development and upon the development of science.

OVER 2000 years ago, Hippocrates laid down principles of medical care that remain valid to this day. The Hippocratic Oath announces as a first principle the goal of dedication to the patient's welfare, saving him from harm and wrong, and avoiding mortal drugs even if demanded by the patient or family.

I swear ... so far as power and discernment shall be mine, I will carry out regimen for the benefit of the sick, and will keep them from harm and wrong. To none will I give a deadly drug even if solicited. ... Into whatsoever home I shall enter I will go for the benefit of the sick.

Hippocrates was conscious of the special authority and power of the physician and the need to regulate that power in accord with the rights of the individual and with his own responsibility to society. He brought about the separation of medicine from religion, establishing the principle that disease had natural causes and could be cured by natural means. The responsibility of the physician to be scientist as well as healer, and to pass on his new knowledge without personal aggrandizement, were embodied in his life and works. In his dictum, "nature heals, the physician is only nature's assistant," we have a statement of humility that should be remembered by all who use specialized knowledge or skills in the service of their fellow man.

Healing by means of the spoken word, or, more strictly, through a relationship between two people is, of course, as old as history. Psychiatry applies relationship therapy in many forms, some of which are customarily grouped under the rubric "psychotherapy." Two features of the current practice of psychotherapy are relevant in this discussion: the effort to bring psychotherapy

within the orbit of scientific medicine; and the fact that the domain of psychotherapy is being entered by a host of practitioners other than physicians—
from fields as diverse as psychology, social work, nursing, and theology. In
view of the enormous need for such help and the fact that the psychotherapeutic art can be mastered without the medical degree, this trend toward the diffu-
sion of training and practice in psychotherapy is of great potential value to
society.

The literature abounds with discussions of psychotherapeutic orientation
and technique. At the same time, there is some evidence—and a growing impression—that the specific techniques of the therapist may be of less importance than the quality of his general wisdom and experience in dealing respon-
sibly with the individual patient. It is to the latter problem that this paper is
addressed. We are concerned, in other words, not with psychotherapy as a
method, but with the psychotherapist—the goals, responsibilities, and problematic decisions with which he must continually grapple as he intervenes in
the lives and fortunes of those who seek his help.

We shall discuss four major goals that have stood the historical test of
medical practice and that have, as we shall try to show, equal relevance for
the practice of psychotherapy. They constitute the primary valuational impera-
tives in therapeutic work. Each goal can be stated simply enough, but the nature and timing of its application often pose difficult problems for the psychotherapist. There are alternative ways of pursuing each, and the pursuit of one
may hinder the fulfillment of another. The ultimate test of "sound clinical
judgment" in the therapist is his capacity to weigh them in balance and to
orchestrate them variously over the course of his efforts with every patient.
The goals are, in the order of their priority:

1. As far as possible, do no harm.
2. Relieve suffering.
3. Assist natural healing processes toward recovery.
4. Prolong life.

The order of priorities is important. Note that the prolongation of life—
perhaps the most obvious and most dramatized goal—is not necessarily the
first consideration of the healer. It is often more important to avoid doing
harm and to relieve suffering than to prolong life. It should also be noted
that furthering the patient's recovery is by no means the only goal, and indeed
it is given third rather than first priority. Novice psychotherapists are sometimes given the idea—and it is one to which they are highly receptive—that
their sole task as therapist is to bring the patient to a previously unattained
state of mental health. They are then unprepared for the more mundane and
narcissistically less gratifying efforts that are so often necessary with patients
for whom more limited goals are required. We wish further to emphasize the
wording of this third injunction: the healer, medical or other, can only assist

the healing processes given in the nature of the organism. He does not *cure;* he does not destroy illness or create health; at best he furthers the curative powers of nature. He must always be ready to consider that nature might heal without his intervention, and he must continually be careful lest he retard nature's benign course or accelerate its malignant direction.

We shall discuss each goal in turn.

AS FAR AS POSSIBLE, DO NO HARM

The first concern of the therapist is to decide realistically whether the skills at his disposal will benefit the patient. We must avoid the easy assumption that our intervention is necessarily helpful. It is customary in the healing trades to honor all modes of intervention with the name "treatment," but history readily yields the lesson that "treatment" is not always therapeutic. Prediction of clinical course is always difficult, and it is even harder to predict how our efforts will affect the natural history of the disorder. If in the long run we make no significant addition to the patient's satisfaction or personal growth, can we justify the large investment of time, money, and work usually involved in psychotherapy?

It is all too easy to assume that our psychotherapeutic skills, on whose refinement we have lavished so much time and energy, are applicable to a broader range of human problems than is actually the case. Psychiatry may well have promised more than it can deliver, especially in the treatment of obsessive-compulsive neurosis, character disorder, and chronic schizophrenia. We should be sharply cognizant of the fact that there is as yet no final agreement as to the value of psychotherapy. Indeed, not a few studies have failed to demonstrate convincingly that such intervention alters significantly the course of illness (Frank, 1959; Frank, 1961; Frank, Gleidman, Imber, Stone, and Nash, 1959). Let us admit that we are richer in conviction for and against various therapeutic modalities than we are in demonstrated truth.

The lack of an imposing literature of controlled studies indicating the efficacy of psychotherapy has led some investigators to attempt "therapy without therapist," so to speak (DiMascio and Brooks, 1961). In such studies the therapist is replaced by an automaton or tape recorder. Yet one finds that if the patient talks, he may make symptomatic gains as impressive as when a therapist is participating. We are forced to consider the "toxicity" of the therapist as well as his positive influence. Therefore, let us not intervene unless there is reasonable assurance that the patient can be benefited, or unless the imperative need to relieve suffering is, by itself, a sufficient goal.

What harm can we do? Strong emotions are released by psychotherapy. If we miscalculate, the patient may commit suicide; if stresses are prolonged, psychosomatic disease may be precipitated; if impulse control is weak, psychopathic acting-out may ensue; and during the uncovering process of self discovery, love affairs may be broken, marriages torn asunder, and innocent families and children forced to suffer the brunt of a patient's turmoil.

However, there is a dilemma here, not a simple rule. The injunction reads, *"as far as possible*, do no harm." All therapeutic intervention is a calculated risk. An apparently innocuous drug may produce anaphylaxis. One must weigh the hazards of intervention against the perils of restraint. The therapist is forced to make a decision, and he must accept responsibility for the consequences. In this latter respect society distinguishes the physician-psychotherapist from the lay psychotherapist; the responsibilities of the former have been defined by tradition and law. The lay psychotherapist is a newcomer to the field, and a fabric of laws based on a history of cases in litigation has not as yet developed around him. The education of nonmedical therapists in various disciplines might well be enriched by greater emphasis on and understanding of the therapist's grave risks and responsibilities in fostering the welfare of his patients.

RELIEVE SUFFERING

It is the natural impulse of the therapist (and of all men of good will who identify with the sufferer) to try to relieve pain and distress wherever it is found. Once again, however, a seemingly obvious goal raises problematic questions. Clearly, the immediate relief of suffering is not always to the patient's ultimate benefit.

When, for example, the patient presents an acute abdomen and the diagnosis is in doubt, the physician does not immediately prescribe analgesics to relieve pain. He may choose to defer action until the condition asserts itself with greater force and the signs become clear. After another day, perhaps, nature localizes a migrating abdominal pain in one abdominal quadrant, the white count climbs, and fever appears; now the probabilities of appendicitis are sufficiently established to plot a course of action. Thus, we justify delay in relief of suffering in order to clarify a diagnosis. Once the diagnosis is established, the patient may be subjected to surgery. The operation leaves him in a miserable state: he is prostrate; his abdomen is sore; he vomits and cannot tolerate anything by mouth; he is punctured by intravenous needles. The choice has been to render the patient acutely uncomfortable for the sake of attacking and eradicating an underlying disease which, if neglected, would endanger his life. We justify both the delay and the necessity to make the patient much sicker for the sake of specifically attainable long-range objectives.

With mental suffering as well, we have to make the choice between delay until we reach a diagnosis or can embark on a therapeutic course, and immediate intervention with ameliorative action. We must also decide whether to work primarily toward relieving the patient's distress or to get at his basic psychopathology with the possibility of greatly increasing his acute suffering. We can, of course, do both: we can give considerable support and warmth while probing old wounds; in fact, some patients cannot tolerate an approach to painful conflicts unless at the same time they receive at least some of the nurturance for which they hunger.

Difficult decisions of this kind confront the psychotherapist repeatedly, and much of the current interest in use of drugs symptomatically is based on their potential for early preventive relief of tension. Each therapist has his own subtle ways of reaching a decision based on his conception of what is best for the patient, how much he feels the patient can bear, and how much suffering he believes the patient should be asked to put up with. There is certainly a large variation in what may be done in similar circumstances by different therapists; some of the relevant determinants surely include the personality and philosophical orientation of the individual therapist (Klerman, Sharaf, Holzman, and Levinson).

Finally, we must always consider the patient in his social context. The patient does not suffer alone. At each stage of his illness those around him may be affected. Whether and how we choose to relieve suffering in the patient should be judged in the total context of his life situation and his significant others, for our responsibilities as therapists extend roughly as far as the bounds of the patient's interpersonal world. There is always both a psychodynamic and a social aspect to our therapeutic work, whether or not we acknowledge and conceptualize this. Our overriding goal is not merely to aid the patient, but if possible to increase the sum of human satisfaction in the total living network in which the patient is involved.

ASSIST NATURAL HEALING PROCESSES
TOWARD RECOVERY

Our largest and most difficult question is how to assist the patient towards recovery. There are two problems here: (1) What can this patient achieve by way of greater health and reduced vulnerability? (2) How can he be helped to achieve it?

What the patient can achieve is in part a function of time: what can he achieve within one visit? within a few visits? over an extended period of time? Our goals are constantly being revised in relation to the patient's changing status. His clinical course during therapeutic work takes some definite form: he goes from strength to strength; he has ups and downs but generally moves forward; he has large upswings and long periods of incubation before the next surge; and so on. Within a given visit, our goal may be merely to get acquainted, to assure the patient that we are human, to allay a specific sector of anxiety, to appraise the depth of a depression or the risk of suicide, or simply to find out how he happened to come to our office.

Within a short time segment, our goals again are various: to evaluate a sector of his personality, appraising strengths and weaknesses; to observe how he handles stresses; to explore a series of relationships within any given area of human activity—sex, work, play, intellectual life, family or social life. Or, temporarily casting specific goals to the winds, we may aim only to encourage him to run on—to learn more of how he thinks and feels and what makes him tick. Not infrequently we should retreat to a period of minimal activity to ascertain how our previous interventions may have interfered with the natural flow of his discourse. In this process we seek answers to various questions: How well can he endure the anxiety of talking about this or that painful issue? How much can he express at this time without being overwhelmed and disorganized? How much insight is he ready for? What should we avoid, gloss over, or buttress by supportive reactions?

We are saying, in short, that psychotherapy in its short sequences is a constant and rapid interplay between a flexible, ever-emerging series of hypotheses and a feedback of data from the patient. In this sense it is a growing experience for both parties, and functions in part like a servomechanism: constantly adjusting and readjusting, on the basis of new data, progressively developing insights and broadening awareness of the patient's nature and possibilities.

Overriding long-term goals must also be chosen from among multiple alternatives, and the choice is rarely easy. In some cases we may be content merely with supporting the patient's defenses, so as to avoid a breakdown in a fragile ego unable to take the strain of more intensive self-examination. In many such cases, where progress is slow or nonexistent, we may shift our energies to essentially *rehabilitative* goals. That is, we may seek to enhance the adaptive abilities of the individual in areas that do not require resolution of core psychological conflicts. Can the patient make gains in terms of better physical status, through elimination of handicapping illnesses, or through development of greater physical fitness? Can his work abilities be further developed by job counseling, change of situation, training towards new occupational skills? Can his educational deficits be made up by special tutoring or schooling? Can the patient derive new pleasure from intellectual interests lying fallow, wanting proper stimulation? Can his social skills be developed by encouraging him to join new groups which he would otherwise have avoided? Can he be taught to regain old and long-atrophied patterns of socialization by close association with a warm and humane companion-teacher? Or can the complicated psychosocial tangle in which the patient is enmeshed be eased by joint or individual discussions with members of his family?

These rehabilitative goals often imply the cooperation of other healing agents—the family service, the rehabilitation counselor, the school teacher, the industrial therapist or employer, the medical specialist or physical therapist. And often these more complex aims are better met within a setting like a hospital or clinic that offers an array of professionals, all cooperating in a total plan for the patient. But even in office psychotherapy it is frequently both wise and feasible to direct the energies of the patient into a variety of constructive channels, supplementing the deeper forms of psychological therapy.

In other cases, especially those with less chronic problems, the ego can better handle analytical-type therapy. Here, the anxiety or hostility are not so

massive or so deeply ingrained, and vulnerability to disorganization or frag-
mentation is perhaps less a genetic channel for the individual. In such cases
our work is directed towards keeping the patient's core problems before him,
gently insisting that he face his inner soul, that he learn to live with the frightening or repelling image of himself, that he tolerate his fantasies of exploding
or of performing mayhem on his fellow man.

As the patient slowly digests these bitter fragments, we may begin to realize some of the goals of psychotherapy directed towards *personality growth*
in the deeper sense: lessened anxiety in a variety of situations; greater enjoyment of solitude; fewer blocks against relating to other human beings, especially in intimate personal and love relationships; greater freedom in directing
energies outside the self; greater effectiveness in confronting the demands of
life; and more meaningful achievement in objective terms.

Goals may be fixed or they may be changeable. For example, it may be
considered a requirement that *conditions* of therapy be stabilized and that the
patient be required to live up to some sort of a basic contract, if only to give
structure to the relationship. This is most desirable where patients have led
chaotic lives. In such instances, the time and place may be fixed throughout
the course of therapy; also the fee; and more particularly the patient's responsibility for taking the initiative in presenting himself and his problems at
each session. Certain defenses may be ruled out immediately or discouraged
throughout. For example, the patient's attempt to obtain personal information
from the therapist in order to change the relationship from professional to
friendship; the defensive need to create anxiety in the therapist and test his
tolerance by directing at him all sorts of frightening and destructive fantasies;
or the desire to obtain the therapist's approval for infantile or pathological
forms of impulse gratification.

Almost always we try to hold constant the qualities of the interaction, the
therapeutic atmosphere. We accept everything the patient has to say; we do
not criticize; we often prefer to question rather than to make categorical statements; and when we undertake to offer analytical formulations, we present
them tentatively, asking the patient's participation in the new understanding.
Other goals may be extremely flexible, especially the day-to-day ones. We may
not attempt to explore the patient's homosexual wishes and concerns for instance, when his denial is too forceful and his underlying anxiety too strong.
We postpone it to a later time when he is more comfortable and more able to
withstand the threat. Or, we realize that further pursuit of a problem will lead
to the recognition of his homosexual interest in the therapist; unless the patient
is ready for this awareness, it can produce a break in therapy. Again, in the
case of an unhappy marriage, we may shift from exploring the possibility of
divorce to accepting the reality of a less than satisfactory domestic life, because
the patient has come to understand the depth of meaning to him of his young
children, whose lives would be disrupted and partly sacrificed to the broken
home.

How do we know what goals to start with, when to alter, modify, or relinquish them, and what new goals to adopt? First and foremost, from intensive observation and study of the patient; secondly, from clinical experience with many patients; and finally, by learning through close contact with masters of the art. Learning psychotherapy is like mastering the art of playing a difficult instrument: we benefit most from close supervision and demonstration by teachers, with a view primarily towards developing the talents nature has given us. Many teachers are needed, lest a single identification become monolithic and constraining. Each has his own specialized techniques. Together they teach us more than a bag of tricks; we learn flexibility, the ability to vary the approach to suit the patient—in a word, creative psychotherapeutics.

Throughout the procedure we must be conscious of the individual in his total context. Therapy directed only to the patient and oblivious to his surroundings is not responsible therapy. We endeavor to relieve the patient of his suffering and to facilitate his growth. However, the important individuals in his life are often threatened and hurt by the changes, whether these be release of aggressive affect, decreased or increased dependency, or removal of critical supports from those around him. If, in helping the patient to move toward health, we simultaneously push his spouse towards illness, we have hardly effected a favorable balance in the totality of human affairs. Our responsibilities, therefore, extend well beyond the limits of the therapist's office.

PROLONG LIFE

This final goal is two-headed: one is the actual prolongation of life in years; the other is making the years count, in the sense of living a full life and coming to terms with its existentially given limits.

With respect to the first, it is our responsibility to prevent suicide and to help the accident-prone patient to avoid serious traumata during the course of therapy—either to himself or against others. We must be alert to his tendency to take undue risks with his health, to woo disability, so to speak, in the service to his neurosis (Freud [1928] suggested in the case of Dostoevsky that his epilepsy was very much in the service of his neurosis, a dangerous condition under some circumstances.) We know that many patients tend to cover their sorrows with drugs to the point of addiction, or to drown them with alcohol, risking grievous consequences. Patients with predisposition to somatic disorder may suffer precipitation of a psychosomatic condition unless psychotherapy is properly graded within their tolerance limits.

The second aspect of the goal of prolonging life involves the patient's discovery of *meaning and purpose* with reference to his span of time on earth. Freed from the burdens of neurotic self-involvement, the patient learns to live more outside himself while living more richly within. He learns to be more responsible for others, and to work out some of his unresolved tension, guilt, and aggression through meaningful endeavor with others. Towards the end of therapy we often find that the patient has formed an interest in social welfare and in various forms of cultural development—inner values which he did not suspect existed. Clarification of the relationship between the new trends and the unresolved character or neurotic residues is often an issue in the last stages of treatment. Finally, a philosophical attitude towards death is a necessary part of our psychological work. In his search for answers to fundamental questions regarding life and death, the patient is interested in the psychiatrist's own feelings and attitudes. This is a newly developing area of imagination (Erikson, 1950; Feifel, 1960; Hackett, 1962; May, Angel, and Ellenburger, 1958; Weisman and Hackett, 1961), and one that merits further investigation. If we aim toward the fullest life for our patients we must help them adapt to the inevitable. To paraphrase Theodore Roosevelt: only those are ready to die who have not been afraid to live; those who have truly lived are not afraid to die.

To sum up: we have *not* presented here a rationale for a particular variety of psychotherapeutic technique. We have not tried to derive a unified therapeutic approach from a highly conceptualized theory of personality or of psychopathology. Nor have we limited ourselves to a consideration of the clinical goals therapists usually have in mind when they speak of intensive "insight-oriented" psychotherapy with relatively mature and healthy patients. Our concern, rather, is with the therapist himself, and with the wide range of problematic issues he must face if he accepts the responsibility of trying to ply his trade with the fantastic variety of persons who seek professional help. Their problems are not encompassed by any textbook of psychiatry or abnormal psychology. Their life circumstances inevitably intrude into the course of therapy, and taking account of them carries the therapist far beyond the usual boundaries of a psychotherapeutic model.

In these times of great technical specialization (in the clinic as in the university and the factory), it behooves us to keep in mind the broad array of phenomena within which particular professionals carve out their increasingly narrow sectors of theoretical and applied interest. The approach represented here has important implications for training, practice, and research. In various disciplines, students of psychotherapy are often taught in ways that lead them to neglect, or actively to avoid, many of the problems and responsibilities of actual clinical practice. Heavy emphasis is put on certain therapeutic goals to the exclusion of others. One result, commonly noted in the last few years, is the fact that professional help is highly concentrated in certain segments of society and is virtually unavailable (or even unknown) to most people. Again, research on selection and prognosis, on the course of therapy, and on the effectiveness of various treatment modalities, suffers greatly from a narrowness of vision. The effectiveness of therapy, for example, must be evaluated relative to the goals of both therapist and patient and the patient's overall life condition. Moreover, the adequate evaluation of change in the patient must involve more than the use of tests and interviews. It requires an assessment of changes in his mode of living, and to do this we must engage in direct exploration of how he lives, both before and after therapy.

The ultimate goal is to increase the psychotherapist's contribution to theory, to research, and to human welfare. Toward this end, his greatest need at present is to *broaden his professional perspective and responsibility* rather than to seek more specific techniques for the pursuit of narrower therapeutic goals with more limited clienteles.

REFERENCES

DiMascio, A., and Brooks, G. W. Free association to a fantasied psychotherapist. A case report. *Arch. gen. Psychiat.*, 1961, **4,** 513–516.

Erikson, E. H. *Childhood and society.* New York: Norton, 1950.

Feifel, H. (Ed.) *The meaning of death.* New York: McGraw-Hill, 1960.

Frank, J. D. The dynamics of psychotherapeutic relationship. Determinants and effects of the therapist's influence. *Psychiatry*, 1959, **22,** (1), 17–39.

Frank, J. D. *Persuasion and healing.* Baltimore: Johns Hopkins Press, 1961.

Frank, J. D., Gleidman, L. H., Imber, S. D., Stone, A. R., and Nash, E. H. Patients' expectancies and relearning as factors determining improvement in psychotherapy. *Amer. J. Psychiat.*, 1959, **115** (11), 961–968.

Freud, S. Dostoevsky and Parricide (1928). *Collected Papers.* Vol. 5. Chapter 21. The International Psychoanalytic Library, No. 37. London: The Hogarth Press and the Institute of Psycho-Analysis, 1950.

Hackett, T. P. Treatment of the dying patient. *Current Psychiat. Ther.*, 1962, Vol. 2.

Klerman, G. L., Sharaf, M. R., Holzman, M., and Levinson, D. J. Sociopsychological characteristics of resident psychiatrists and their use of drug therapy. *Amer. J. Psychiat.*, 1960, **117,** 111–117.

May, R., Angel, E., and Ellenburger, H. F. (Eds.) *Existence, a new dimension in psychiatry and psychology.* New York: Basic Books, 1958.

Weisman, A. D., and Hackett, T. P. Predilection to death, including psychiatric problems. *Psychosom. Med.*, 1961, **23,** 232–256.

4

Goals in Psychotherapy:
Practical Applications

Lewis R. Wolberg, M.D.

An Introduction to the Person

by Emanuel K. Schwartz, Ph.D., D.S.Sc.

Lewis R. Wolberg, a pioneer in contemporary psychotherapy, graduated from the University of Rochester and received his medical degree from Tufts College. He had internships at Vassar Bros. Hospital in Poughkeepsie, New York and at Los Angeles General Hospital, and residencies at the Boston Psychopathic Hospital and later at Kings Park State Hospital. He became a Diplomate of the American Board of Psychiatry in 1936.

His interest in dynamic psychiatry brought him to the New York Psyanalytic Institute for training. Committed to exploring the new and the different, however, he broke away from the New York Psychoanalytic Institute with Horney, Thompson, and others and completed his analytic training at the American Institute for Psychoanalysis. Since 1943 he has been a Clinical Professor of Psychiatry at New York Medical College and a member and past chairman of the Faculty of the Comprehensive Course in Psychoanalysis there.

In 1936, long before the current concern with cholesterol, Dr. Wolberg published *The Psychology of Eating*, which is still as contemporary as any of the more recent works on dieting.

There are at least four areas of psychotherapy in which Dr. Wolberg has pioneered. The first is in the use of hypnosis as a therapeutic agent. His book, *Hypnoanalysis*, and his two-volume *Medical Hypnosis*, are classics in the field.

Second, he has accepted the need for modifying therapeutic techniques to meet the needs of the largest number and varieties of persons. To this end he founded the Postgraduate Center for Mental Health, formerly a Postgraduate Center for Psychotherapy, in 1945, and is now its Medical Director and Dean. There, patients who cannot afford prevailing private fees and for whom traditional psychoanalytic techniques are inappropriate are treated. With the need for new kinds of education and training in integrating various therapeutic theories and evolving new techniques, short-term treatment methods, group therapy, and modified dynamic regimens were developed. A training center for psychiatrists, psychologists, and social workers was chartered in 1948 as part of the Postgraduate Center. Some of Dr. Wolberg's new ideas are incorporated in his monumental *Techniques of Psychotherapy*. Himself a highly gifted teacher, he utilizes extensively the still camera, the motion picture, television, tape recordings, and other audiovisual aids.

To promote interdisciplinary cooperation in preventing and treating mental illness and promoting mental health, Dr. Wolberg has brought together clinicians from the three mental health professions, other behavorial scientists, research personnel, and community workers to integrate efforts for treating, training, investigating, and applying mental health principles.

Finally, he has early been in the forefront of the current emphasis on community and social psychiatry. Low-cost treatment, preventive techniques, public mental health education, and the training of nonclinical personnel in mental health principles have benefitted from his intensive activity. He has stimulated interest in transcultural psychiatry and is instrumental in bringing together, on innumerable occasions, outstanding and stimulating contributors in the mental health field from all over the world.

Dr. Wolberg is an unusually gifted coordinator of information, creator of new ideas, and an inspiration to those who work with him.

In psychotherapy, organized psychological techniques are applied by a trained professional person for the purpose of resolving emotional difficulties and of enhancing personality growth and development. The value of any psychotherapeutic scheme must be judged by how completely it has achieved these goals. No matter how ingenious the system, or how accomplished the operation, or how deftly it validates the theoretical premises around which the techniques are organized, we cannot say that it is successful unless it satisfies a rudimentary principle—it must make the patient feel better and function better. Simple as this principle may seem, its consideration plunges us into a maze of auxiliary problems, one of which is that the patient's judgment of how much has been done for him is not the best index of the adequacy of the psychotherapeutic procedures to which he has been exposed. Thus the patient may often fail to appreciate the seriousness of his disability, or even to recognize that certain symptoms exist. In the course of therapy, he may displace his overt anxiety and develop a less obvious somatic symptom such as hypertension, which insidiously operates unknown to him at the very time that he boasts of having conquered his suffering.

Assuming that we eliminate this false measure of improvement, we must still regard with suspicion positive symptom relief. Such relief may be a by-product of adventitious forces such as spontaneous remission or cure, the placebo element, the relationship situation, and emotional catharsis. It may occur by default in that the patient makes a bargain with his neurosis, abandoning goals of mature personality fulfillment and repressing fundamental conflicts in order to avoid anxiety. Peace is gained at the expense of his adaptive integrity. These facts notwithstanding, we must accept as a basic premise the proposition that symptom amelioration or cure is a prime criterion of success in psychotherapy.

A second criterion is the individual's capacity to function better in his relationships. Here too the patient's judgment of his progress may not constitute the best index of how far he has progressed. He may assume that he is operating successfully while displaying characterologic defects that tend to alienate him from others. Thus by driving aggressiveness he may achieve material success, gaining homage from those who fear his power. By the same token, the verdicts of the patient's family and of cultural and subcultural groups to which he belongs must be carefully scrutinized, since their values may not reflect the best standards of mental health. They may regard his emerging independence as a sign of defiance and sickness, on the basis that compliance and submission to authority are tokens of adjustment. And the therapist himself may reflect fallacious cultural standards by aligning himself with neurotic cultural value systems such as ambitiousness, perfectionism, and power, which become for him indices of proper functioning.

Granting that we can circumvent these obstructions, we may say that successful therapy enables an individual to participate with others as a member of his group, to give and to receive love more fully, and to relate himself to people without undue dependency, domineeringness, submissiveness, or detachment. Implied is the facility to assume a role with authority without succumbing to destructive rage or fear, while also maintaining flexibility, and, on essential occasions, taking over leadership and acting as a constructive authority without needing to control or to wield power for power's sake.

A third criterion is an improved capability to withstand unavoidable frustrations and deprivations—organizing tendencies toward resolution of provocative stress factors instead of taking refuge in immature defenses, such as aggression, masochism, and fantasy formation.

A fourth criterion is an increased spontaneity, assertiveness, self-confidence, self-respect, self-tolerance, and creative self-fulfillment. There is a willingness to recognize past neurotic patterns and misinterpretations, which supports a liberation from strictures of one's childhood and an exposure to more constructive ways of reacting and relating.

A fifth criterion is a greater command in deriving pleasure from creature comforts and biological needs—from food, rest, relaxation, sex, work, and play. This necessitates adequate gratification in conformity with the mores and conventions of society. It also means subjecting these needs to essential reality limitations.

A sixth criterion involves an adjustment of one's life goals in line with personal limitations, scaling down ambitions, avoiding perfectionism, balancing personal with group standards, and harmonizing individual and cultural ideals.

THE PRINCIPLE OF GOAL MODIFICATION

A meritorious psychotherapy must scale its goals to conform with certain practical considerations. We may roughly classify goal gradation into three general groupings: (1) The least ambitious of objectives is to reestablish the emotional equilibrium of the individual to a point where he can function at his optimal level within the ranges of his personality limitations and the reality situation. (2) More extensive is the mission of fostering a rearrangement of present-day attitudes, values, and life purposes in line with a more realistic adjustment to the environment and to people. (3) Most extensive is the reconstructive aim of promoting growth in personality development to a point where distortions in character structure are remedied and more mature adaptive and creative potentials are achieved.

How far a particular individual will be able to progress along the road of personality reconstruction will depend upon his intrinsic capacities for growth, the skill of the therapist, and social acceptance of his changed self. Absent incentives, practical limitations of time and finances, a high degree of structuralization of his neurosis with severe warping of his personality matrix, poverty of defensive reserves, obdurate resistances to the acquisition of insight and the accepting of normality, and secondary gains which put a premium on neurotic behavior will prevent the individual from moving ahead. Damage to the personality may be so severe by virtue of the extent of trauma during the formative years as to impair capacities for change and to impose on psychotherapy insurmountable obstacles that divert it from its healing objectives.

The extent of goals achieved is also dependent upon the competence of the therapist. We assume that the latter is adequately trained and that he is not himself handicapped by so great a personality distortion as to interfere with his therapeutic functioning. Where there are any serious defects in technical competence or personality, an obstruction will be placed in the path of far-reaching goal fulfillment. Of importance also is the nature of the environment in which the patient must live; conditions may be so harsh as to jeopardize security. Vital also is a factor that is often overlooked, namely that the patient may belong to a subcultural group in which certain eccentricities or neurotic distortions have a utilitarian value; this, too, will of necessity upset the patient's thrust toward normality.

An effective psychotherapy must, therefore, accept the necessity of goal modification toward the modest objective of optimal functioning, while striving to bring the individual to the greatest degree of personality reconstruction within his grasp. Means of measuring the individual's growth potential have not yet been fully devised. Some prognostic data have been presented elsewhere in terms of the age of the patient, duration of his illness, severity of his symptoms, diagnosis, level of intelligence, definitive motivations for therapy, depth of insight, degree of secondary gain, hereditary elements, constitutional factors, early environmental influences, developmental history, the nature of current interpersonal relations, customary modes of handling stress, existing ability to gratify vital needs, precipitating environmental factors, previous adjustment, level of social maturity, current environmental situation, and past therapeutic failures (Wolberg, 1954, pp. 230–245). Irrespective of such information, the only real measure of how far the patient can go and will go in his therapeutic journey will be determined in the forge of the treatment process itself.

INDICES OF GOAL ACHIEVEMENT

Indications of the potentials of the patient in his immediate experience will become apparent to the observant therapist not too long after treatment has begun. In judging how extensively the patient has achieved ideal criteria of mental health, it is essential that we obtain, in addition to subjective data from the patient of how he feels, and estimates by the therapist of the patient's progress, some objective scales of improvement. The principle must be followed that no single index of change is in itself valid. Each index has to be related to all other factors at our disposal, in order better to interpret its meaning.

The individual's behavior in specific aspects of life functioning may serve as a provisional guide to his adjustment. Adequate scales for evaluating levels of function have not been developed, although some encouraging attempts are being made to provide us with effective yardsticks. In the main, the informational areas are these: (1) changes in the patient's immediate symptoms in comparison with the symptomatic picture at the time therapy was started; (2) changes in the manner in which he relates himself to people in general, i.e., to authority, to his peers, and to those on a lower status level; (3) changes in his character structure, particularly the dependence-independence balance, level of aggression, degree of detachment, intensity of perfectionism, self-esteem, and self-confidence; (4) changes in his ability to adapt himself to unavoidable stresses and responsibilities that are a parcel of his environment; (5) changes in his marital and sexual adaptation; (6) changes in his work adjustment; (7) changes in his social and community relationships; (8) changes in his physical condition, the quality of his general health, and habit patterns, such as those related to food intake, rest, sleep, recreation, and physical activity; (9) changes in intake of alcohol, sedatives, transquilizers, and other medicaments; (10) changes in his philosophical and religious outlook; (11) gross changes in his environment.

Some investigators have attempted to simplify the criteria which measure the effects of therapy. Thus, Parloff, Kelman, and Frank (1954) have developed three rating scale procedures to measure the patient's comfort, effectiveness, and self-awareness, procedures which they feel give satisfactory results as an evaluating tool. Rogers (1954), utilizing the Willoughby Emotional-Maturity Scale, found that increase of maturity as determined by the scale correlated positively with successful completion of therapy as rated independently by the counselors. Klein (1960) has described an interesting rating scale that deals with environmental factors.

Self-administered inventories such as the Minnesota Multiphasic Personality Inventory have been found useful by a number of investigators (Kaufman, 1950; Schofield, 1950; Leary and Harvey, 1956). While we may not agree with the existing scales and methods of scoring, the giving of an inventory at the beginning, the end, and on follow-up provides us with significant items which we can use as an objective means of comparison. The author for years has employed an extensive inventory in this way, and he has found it a useful aid toward estimating change. An expanded version of this inventory is now in the process of preparation and scoring.

The question is often asked regarding the utility of projective tests in evaluating personality change. Many contradictory reports have been published both depreciating (Berg, 1952; Murphy, 1951) and praising (Kutash, 1954; Schafer, 1955) projective tests as evaluators. Most of the criticism is the product of distrust in the sensitivity of projective instruments in giving us clues that we can use to indicate prognosis or to designate whether an individual is capable of making a good social adjustment. We must remember that we are not as interested in psychological performance as an index of adjustment as we are in comparing the changes in psychological performance at the end of therapy with that at the beginning to determine which areas of psychic functioning, if any, have been altered. The traditional modes of scoring and interpreting projective tests probably do not apply to the special task of judging the value of psychotherapy in reaching set goals. When we try to press the usual test interpretations into this usage, our results become confusing and meaningless.

Generally the qualitative aspects of Rorschach responses are more useful than the quantitative aspects, a fact emphasized by Piotrowski and Schreiber (1952). Similarly the Thematic Apperception Test (Dymond, 1954), the

Draw-a-Person Test (male and female figure drawings) (Modell, 1951; Rez-nikoff and Mundy, 1956), and handwriting samples are capable of giving us raw, tangible data that we can use as a basis for comparison studies. Here, too, the traditional interpretations do not seem to hold up when we try to apply them to evaluative research. A fertile field for experimentation lies in the re-valuation of projective tests applied to the assessing of psychotherapy.

Dreams are reflective of significant symbolic processes and may be em-ployed as another means of studying the progress of goal achievement. Changes in dream content are to be expected as therapy proceeds and after it is ter-minated. Such changes include the reduction of memories charged with pain-ful associations; the restructuring of deleterious attitudes and fantasies toward parental agencies and siblings; the shifting from immature to mature defenses, from unwholesome to constructive interpersonal strivings and attitudes; the lessening in distortion of symbols connoting unconscious repudiated impulses and needs; the diminution of images of inner conflict with decrease in anxiety manifestations; the representation of the self in less destructive terms; and the resolution of symbolizations that depict resistance and transference.

Physiological reactions may indicate how far the individual has pro-gressed in treatment. Our instruments, however, are not yet refined enough to pick up and to measure the significance of many of the nuances of physiologi-cal change associated with states of psychological unrest. Important leads have, however, become apparent in polygraph readings during psychiatric inter-views involving certain physiological functions, such as the heart rate and sweating (DiMascio, Boyd, Greenblatt, and Solomon, 1955; Boyd and DiMascio, 1954; Bexenstein, 1955). It is reasonable for us to assume that an individual exposed to a test situation of frustration and stress will react less explosively physiologically after successful psychotherapy than he did to equiv-alent stimulation prior to treatment. That this hypothesis is plausible is indi-cated by some experiments (Thetford, 1952a; Thetford, 1952b; Shagass and Malmo, 1954).

A fertile field presents itself to the researcher in studying before-and-after reactions to psychotherapy in relation to selected stimuli, such as to movies depicting provocative themes or reflective of basic problems in the individual, or to hypnotically induced conflicts. The standardization of these procedures is a matter we must relegate to the future. In the meantime we may have to content ourselves with the detection of gross physiological upsets which are dis-cernible through our present instruments. In the event an individual has a physical disorder induced or aggravated by tension which is present at the time psychotherapy is started, we may be able to determine its destiny at the end of therapy. Its resolution is one manifestation of outcome success.

On the other hand, a physical examination may reveal functional somatic disorders not present at the beginning of therapy, but induced by the repres-sion of important conflicts and their attendant anxieties. This will correct any false optimism of how much has been done for the patient, since a reduction of his psychological symptoms has been gained at the expense of his physiological functioning. It is certainly no indication of success for an individual to lose a phobia if his anxieties have been internalized in the form of hypertension.

The study and analysis of therapy interviews observed through a one-way screen, in sound movies, or from video tapings, would appear to be another fruitful way of examining variables related to goals. Unfortunately the results are restricted by the training limitations of the observers and raters, by their theoretical biases which encourage a prejudiced selection of data, and by their personal problems which enjoin them to by-pass content that stirs up anxiety. Most of the categories that are listed in current content-analytic studies tell us little about the impact of therapy on the patient's problems. They lead to interesting speculations about possible dynamisms that are responsible for shifts in content, but they do not enhance our understanding of psychological change. What actually is the meaning of decreases or increases of reference to the therapist, parental objects, or contemporaries; to the past, present, or future; to one's work, hobbies, or recreations; to physiological processes and needs; to affects, impulses, and attitudes; to insightful concepts or symptoms; and to a medley of other aspects of thinking, feeling, and behaving? The interpretation of such data, no matter how carefully collected and scored, necessitates the use of hypotheses that are so vague and nondynamic that they do not stand up under rigorous scrutiny. In spite of careful documentation, we are no further than we were when we started. This does not mean that such studies are not important. Changes in meaningful communication probably do occur as a result of therapy, but the correlation of significant aspects of the communicative process with improvement of an emotional problem has not yet been established to a point where we can identify the variables that should most carefully be noted. It behooves the therapist who is interested in research to collect samples of representative sessions fully recorded on tape or plastic records at the beginning, during the course of, and at the end of therapy, so that comparisons may be made, if not immediately after completion of treatment, then some years later after the therapeutic results are more clear. Perhaps some day, when the most important variables have been delineated, the content of these recordings can be studied with greater benefit.

REFERENCES

Berg, I. A. Measures before and after therapy. *J. clin. Psychol.*, 1952, **8,** 46–50.

Bexenstein, V. E. A case study of the use of palmar sweating as a measure of psychological tension. *J. abnorm. soc. Psychol.*, 1955, **50,** 138–143.

Boyd, R. W., and DiMasco, M. A. Social behavior and autonomic physiology: a sociophysiologic study. *J. nerv. ment. Dis.*, 1954, **120,** 207–212.

DiMascio, M. A., Boyd, R. W., Greenblatt, M., and Solomon, H. C. The psychiatric interview (a sociophysiologic study). *Dis. nerv. Syst.*, 1955, **16,** 4–9.

Dymond, R. F. Adjustment changes over therapy from Thematic Apperception Test Ratings. In C. R. Rogers and R. F. Dymond (Eds.), *Psychotherapy and personality change.* Chicago: University of Chicago Press, 1954. Pp. 109–120.

Kaufmann, P. E. Changes in Minnesota Multiphasic Personality Inventory as a function of psychiatric therapy. *J. consult. Psychol.*, 1950, **14**, 458–464.

Klein, H. R. A study of changes occurring in patients during and after psychoanalytic treatment. In *Current approaches in psychotherapy.* New York: Grune & Stratton, 1960. Pp. 151–175.

Kutash, S. B. The impact of projective techniques on basic psychological science. *J. proj. Tech.*, 1954, **18**, 453–469.

Leary, T., and Harvey, J. S. A methodology for measuring personality changes in psychotherapy. *J. clin. Psychol.*, 1956, **12**, 123–132.

Modell, A. H. Changes in human figure drawing by patients who recover from regressed states. *Amer. J. Orthopsychiat.*, 1951, **21**, 584–596.

Murphy, W. F. Problems in evaluating the results of psychotherapy. *A.M.A. Arch. neurol. Psychiat.*, 1951, **66**, 653–654.

Parloff, M. V., Kelman, H. C. and Frank, J. D. Comfort, effectiveness and self-awareness as criteria of improvement in psychotherapy. *Amer. J. Psychiat.*, 1954, **111**, 343–351.

Piotrowski, Z. A., and Schreiber, M. Rorschach percept-analytic measurement of personality changes during and after intensive psychoanalytically oriented psychotherapy. In C. Bychowski and J. L. Despert (Eds.), *Specialized techniques in psychotherapy.* New York: Basic Books, 1952. Pp. 337–361.

Reznikoff, M., and Mundy, L. Changes in human figure drawings associated with therapy: a case study. *Amer. J. Psychother.*, 1956, **10**, 542–549.

Rogers, C. R. Changes in the maturity of behavior as related to therapy. In C. R. Rogers and R. F. Dymond (Eds.), *Psychotherapy and personality change.* Chicago: University of Chicago Press, 1954. Pp. 215–237.

Schafer, R. Psychological test evaluation of personality change during intensive psychotherapy. *Psychiatry*, 1955, **18**, 175–192.

Schofield, W. Changes in response to the MMPI following certain therapies. *Psychol. Monogr.*, 1950, **64**, 311.

Shagass, C., and Malmo, R. B. Psychodynamic themes and localized muscular tension during psychotherapy. *Psychosomatic Med.*, 1954, **16**, 295–314.

Thetford, W. N. The measurement of physiological responses to frustration before and after non-directive psychotherapy. In O. H. Mowrer (Ed.), *Psychotherapy: theory and research.* New York: Ronald Press, 1952. Pp. 641–656. (a)

Thetford, W. N. An objective measurement of frustration tolerance in evaluating psychotherapy. In W. Wolff and J. A. Precker (Eds.), *Success in psychotherapy.* New York: Grune & Stratton (Personality Monographs), 1952, **3**, 26–62. (b)

Wolberg, L. R. *The technique of psychotherapy.* New York: Grune & Stratton, 1954.

5

Goals of Psychoanalytic Therapy

Leon J. Saul, M.D.

An Introduction to the Person

by Franz Alexander, M.D.

Dr. Leon Saul came to psychiatry and psychoanalysis via the natural sciences, in particular, chemistry, physics, and neurophysiology, and his interest in scientific research has never left him. Unlike the majority of those who become fascinated with the great possibilities which the psychoanalytic method opened up for the treatment of psychiatric patients, Leon Saul has remained all his life fundamentally research oriented. His first venture was a joint research with Hallowell Davis, tracing action potentials from ear to brain as an approach to the nerophysiology of hallucinations. This earned him the Massachusetts Research Prize.

After completing his training analysis he joined the Chicago Institute for Psychoanalysis and remained on its staff from 1932 to 1942. At the same time he continued his neurophysiological work with Professor Ralph Gerard at the University of Chicago. This predestined him to become one of the most productive members of the research team of the Chicago Psychoanalytic Institute.

In the psychological field he was particularly challenged by one of the basic problems, not only of psychiatry but society in general—man's hostility to man. The Chicago period, however, was only a preparation for a new phase in his career as Professor of Psychiatry and Chief of the Section of Preventive Psychiatry at the University of Pennsylvania in the

Dr. Saul is with the Section of Preventive Psychiatry, University of Pennsylvania School of Medicine. Thanks is due the Roger Williams Straus Memorial Foundation and Public Health Service Grant No. MH-07615-01.

Department of Psychiatry under Dr. Edward Strecker and then Dr. Kenneth Appel. During all these years Dr. Saul was engaged in the practice of psychoanalysis and made use of clinical observations for the further clarification of basic principles of treatment as well as of psychodynamics.

In Dr. Saul's professional profile, his never-wavering emphasis upon precise observation and clear reasoning stands out. Early scientific training has left him immune to uncritical dogmatism, with a mind always open to new ideas. A master of expressing complex psychodynamic constellations and processes in an economical and pungent style, he is an outstanding teacher and disseminator of contemporary knowledge about the human personality and its disturbances. And his deep humanitarian interest and compassion for the suffering has made him an outstanding therapist. With all these qualities, Dr. Saul is a model for a modern psychiatrist.

I

IN considering the goals of treatment, it is well to recall that historically psychoanalysis began not only as a method of therapy but also as a method of research developed by a brilliant pioneer. In fact, the main emphasis in Freud's writings was on exploration of the human mind, on the development of psychoanalysis as a science of the psyche more than as a curative procedure (Jones, 1957; Freud, 1954). In his later years he was somewhat pessimistic about humanity and also about psychoanalysis as a method of treatment. This therapeutic pessimism is reflected in his "Analysis Terminable and Interminable" (Freud, 1950).

Guntrip (1962), in his excellent review of recent evolution of psychoanalytic theory, sees pessimism in many of Freud's general formulations. An example is the view that pleasure is the goal of life but is no more than homeostatic equilibrium and, eventually, the relief of all tensions by the fulfillment of an instinct to die, the death drive. Another example is the inevitability of such conflict between instinct and civilization that expression of instinct means criminality and its repression makes neurosis. But here normally maturing instincts are not differentiated from those disordered by faulty upbringing prior to about six years of age. By about this age, Freud concluded, the base for the personality and for neurosis has for the most part been laid (Freud, 1949, p. 83).

Actually, in certain of Freud's statements, expressed with unmistakable lucidity and definitiveness, there is solid ground for views which are by no means pessimistic, and these have given direction to later advances in the basic concepts in the field. However, Freud did not develop these himself, although he stated them clearly. He was almost incredibly productive, and besides the subjects he worked on and wrote about in the main stream of his thought and development, he threw out all kinds of observations and formulations, many of them obviously fundamental (Jones, 1957).

Among these basic observations, he never elaborated his remarks throughout his work on the fundamental importance of the child's long dependence upon its parents. This he stresses in his introduction to Reik's *Ritual* (1962); in *Future of an Illusion* (in which he sees dependence as one root of man's need for religion); and in *An Outline of Psychoanalysis* (Freud, 1949). Fairbairn, Rank, Alexander, and others emphasize this dependence explicitly, but Freud, to my knowledge, never published a specific study of it. So, too, he saw the import of hostility in Dora but was then focused upon other matters and did not deal with it until decades later and then more as a philosophical generalization than as detailed clinical observation.

Another formulation is a model of succinct expression and states briefly but explicitly the rationale of psychoanalytic therapy and the goal of this treatment. Here is the passage, which is from his last major work, *An Outline of Psychoanalysis* (Freud, 1949, p. 67):

If the patient puts the analyst in the place of his father (or mother) he is also giving him the power which his superego exercises over his ego, since his parents were, as we know, the origin of his superego. The new superego now has an opportunity for a sort of *after-education* of the neurotic; it can correct blunders for which his parental education was to blame.

Take this together with his statement in the same work on p. 122:

. . . the superego continues to act the role of an external world toward the ego, although it has become part of the internal world. During the whole of a man's later life it represents the influence of his childhood, of the care and education given to him by his parents, of his dependence on them—of the childhood which is so greatly prolonged in human beings by a common family life. And in all of this what is operating is not only the personal qualities of these parents but also everything that produced a determining effect upon them themselves, the tastes and standards of the social class in which they live and the characteristics and traditions of the race from which they spring.

The implications of these statements are crystal clear. The child internalizes the parents through their attitudes and treatment of him and also by identification with them. The parents form *imagos* in the child's mind; they are *introjected* as parts of the child's superego. The child takes over in its mind the parents' attitudes, feelings, and behavior to it; and the child continues to react to these imagos as he did to his parents. Further, he projects these imagos onto other persons, and therefore reacts to these other persons in some part as he did to his parents. (Of course by the term "parents" we mean to include siblings and substitutes—all those responsible for the child, as well as close to him and emotionally important for him.)

If parents reject and depreciate a child, the child feels rejecting and depreciatory to himself and harbors toward the parents resentment which he may show openly or may repress, only to have it come out toward himself or toward others, or in the form of symptoms. The child who is treated with authoritarian, punitive harshness may be crushed psychologically or may be openly or covertly rebellious and hostile and is apt to carry this pattern over to other persons by the mechanisms described above.

In passing we may remark that as this author studies patients, it appears to him that the choice of reaction, e.g., whether the child becomes cowed or rebellious, and also the choice of symptoms seems to be the outcome of the quantitative balance of motivational forces within the personality. Heredity no doubt plays some role in this but seems to be overshadowed by the power of what Freud called the parental "blunders." This means that no baby, no matter what its heredity, can withstand gross disorder of personality if it is treated badly enough. The potential for abuse by others through omission or commission is overwhelmingly more powerful than the child's potential for resistance to such abouse.

The two quotations from Freud given above reveal a marked advance in his thinking and delineate a new conceptual model of the personality and its psychopathology and of the rationale and goals of treatment. Before sketching this model, let us note that the description in psychoanalytic terms (introjection, imago, superego, projection) can readily be recast in the terms and concepts of Freud's contemporary, Pavlov, and is consistent with studies in animal ethology such as those of imprinting (Hess, 1958, pp. 81–90).

Leaving aside discussion of whether part of the superego is a precipitate of the Oedipus complex, the basic concept of the superego as a grouping in the mind of ideals, standards, training, and identifications—an internalization of training and identifications—is entirely intelligible in terms of conditioning. Taking our first random example: If a child's mother is rejecting, then the child is conditioned by her presence to feeling rejected. When the mother appears, she is associated with rejection, just as in Pavlov's experiments, when a bell sounds, it is associated with food.

This conditioning, if it occurs early, can and often does spread. The child is conditioned by the mother to expect rejection. If this occurs early in life when the mother is almost the sole caretaker of the child, then it may spread to all women, bringing feelings of rejection and expectation of it from all women. It may even spread to all people, men as well as women. And as the mother feels toward and treats the child, so is the child conditioned to feel toward and treat itself.

If the mother is associated with rejection which is painful, frustrating, and threatening (since the small child is helpless and dependent on its mother for its very existence), then the child reacts with one of its mechanisms of adaptation—arousal for flight or fight. It cannot flee nor can it fight. The frustrated flight may stimulate regressive behavior, i.e., psychological flight to earlier patterns of behavior, perhaps those of a time when relations with the mother were better (Alexander, 1961). The fight response generates rage and hostility which come out in behavior directly or indirectly, or in symptoms, or turned against the child as a form of masochism. The child is conditioned to react to the mother with the expectation of rejection and with this fight-flight response in some form and status. If the pattern spreads, the child reacts to other women who are "mother-figures" to it in this same way, even to all women, even to all people. The result is withdrawal from human relations and hostility to other persons, plus an inner sense of being unloved and rejected. These are the effects of the conditioning, or in analytic terms, of the rejecting maternal superego. Hence also a depreciated self-image and problems in ego identity (Erikson, 1959).

We have said that Freud's later emphasis upon the effects on the child of the external world and upon psychoanalysis as a method of after-education to correct those effects which were injurious, marked a major advance in his thinking. This advance, which began many years before with *The Ego and the Id* (Freud, 1935), is clearly formulated by him in the two quotations above. The history of this evolution is interesting and significant for the goals of treatment.

Freud's very earliest investigations (Freud and Breuer, 1936) led him to the concept of psychological *trauma*. An experience that was traumatic was repressed. It was repressed chiefly just because it was so traumatic. If the therapist could bring it back to consciousness, then the intense emotion associated with it was abreacted and the symptoms which had been caused by these repressed feelings were relieved. Freud looked for the traumatic memories by hypnosis and then by encouragement and finally, with a stroke of genius, by a complete reversal of procedure—by telling the patient, rather than to seek a specific memory, to say anything and everything, to associate freely. By this method Freud was able to learn what went on in the minds and feelings of his patients, even in their dreams and even much of which they themselves were not conscious. He was immediately impressed by the conflicts in his patients over sexual impulses. From then on he gave to sexuality the most prominent place in his efforts to understand human personality and its development. In his search for the then totally unknown causes of neurotic symptoms, Freud connected them with the aftereffects of sexual trauma during childhood, reported to him by his patients. Here he introduced the concept of later neurosis resulting from traumatic experiences in early childhood. Then he found that many of these childhood experiences had never occurred to his patients but were only fantasied by them. He pursued his studies of sexuality during childhood and thereafter, but did not at that time develop either his concept of trauma, or of anything other than sexual trauma during childhood, which produced permanent neurotic aftereffects.

It is curious, as others have remarked, e.g., Bowlby (1959), that so great an observer as Freud should have neglected so important a discovery of his own. The fact is, however, that for decades thereafter Freud gave very little weight to the amount of a child's behavior which is a reaction to the ways in which it is treated. Instead there seems to be the implicit assumption that parents love their children and treat them well and therefore the problems of the children must derive from inevitable inner conflicts in the child's instinctual development. For example, neuroses could arise from excessive orality, causing a fixation at this phase of development, or from failure to resolve the Oedipus complex, which involves the child in sexual attraction to one parent, and inevitable jealousy and hostility, with consequent guilt and fear of retaliation, toward the other parent. If the child is anxious or shows other neurotic behavior the answer is to be found in the emotional problems of the Oedipus complex, and relatively little attention was paid as to whether the child's anxiety might result from, let us say, tension between the parents and a pending divorce.

There is nothing mutually exclusive in the two points of view. It is simply a matter of study to determine how much of a child's reaction can be a reaction to the ways in which it is treated. In later years, as we have seen in the quotation from Freud, he returned to this concept, saw the profound and permanent aftereffects of how the parents treated the child, and saw the goal of psychoanalysis to be the correction of the aftereffects of the early parental "blunders" in their treatment of the child.

Of course Freud never abandoned the idea of the aftereffects of trauma during childhood. It is simply that, intensely occupied with developing his other observations and ideas, he never concentrated upon it and elaborated it. How implicit it actually was in his thinking is demonstrated in *An Outline of Psychoanalysis* (1949) in his description of castration anxiety. Here he states that the mother notices her small son's interest in his genital, forbids his touching it, then threatens him eventually with cutting it off, and finally follows this up with the threat of the father's power to do this. Then when the little boy sees a girl's genitals, he is struck by the fact that such a threat could possibly become a reality. The point is that in this passage Freud derives the child's anxiety from threats by his mother. We have only to consider that mothers and fathers threaten their children in many areas in addition to the sexual. The child wakes up the parents at night, it refuses to eat, it throws its food on the floor, it pulls over a lamp, it does or fails to do any number of things which go against the grain of the parents and invoke their angry threats in the context of their efforts to discipline the child. Freud's concept, slightly extended, thus becomes the key to modern thinking in the field.

II

Meanwhile the whole field of psychodynamics has been developing primarily out of Freud's initial investigations. Not only analysts but workers in all the related fields have been interested in this problem of the roots of psychopathology, behavior, and personality. Out of this work, but also in the direct line of development of Freud's thinking, has come the following model of the personality, and its psychopathology and treatment.

Before the child is born, it does not have any psychological relationship to another person in the way that it will have later. This continues to be true immediately after birth. Studies of animals (which now include ducks, geese, cats, dogs, monkeys, sheep, and other species) show that during some period after birth, the young of the species develops an attachment to its mother or, if she is absent, to a substitute. This formation by the young of the attachment to the mother is called by the animal ethologists "imprinting." More correctly, what the ethologists call "imprinting" is roughly what the psychiatrist calls the attachment of the child to its mother. It channels other feelings, including later sexual attachments and social reactions and relations. These are not dislodged from the original object which may even be an inanimate substitute for the mother.

If the child is well treated, it forms this attachment to its mother. My impression is that in humans this certainly takes place by the age of two months. Now the child has the attachment, and the mother's love and care becomes its only safeguard of physical survival. Hence its "dependent love needs" toward the mother are the great unconditioned stimulus. The child must do anything to keep the mother's love, else it will perish. If the mother is rejecting, then we see a variety of responses such as those mentioned above. The child becomes conditioned to expect feelings of rejection and develops a pattern of emotional responses to them. The usual trauma is not a single, overwhelming experience. Rather, as we understand the term today, it usually consists of injurious attitudes and behavior over long periods by the parents or substitutes to the child. In general, (1) the younger the child and (2) the more intense the faulty attitudes, feelings, and behavior of the parents to it, and the longer this lasts, the more profound the deleterious effects upon the developing personality, in other words, the more serious and extensive is the psychopathology and the more permanent and deep seated within the person.

The essentials of our model, then, come out somewhat as follows: Each child is born with an inner potential of development and growth to maturity (and thereafter, of senescence and death—the completion of the life cycle). What kind of adult the child will develop into if he is raised with good human relationships and no blunders of any consequence can be determined in a number of ways. For example, one can observe the direction of this development and how it would have proceeded if it were not for traumatic influences during early childhood. One can see in successfully treated patients the direction in which their development actually proceeds. The therapist can compare a series of patients, each with different problems, observing how those parts of the personality which were not fixated or warped by mistreatment actually did develop. A series of patients can be compared to see the general lines of development of the healthy parts of their personalities.

Although I did not state this procedure, the results are reported in *Emotional Maturity* (Saul, 1960). I made a list of patients whom I had treated intensively over a ten-year period and whom I felt I understood fairly well. Under each name was then written a summary of the patient's major problem, comparing it with the apparently well-matured other parts of his personality. However, there is obviously great need for further systematic studies along these lines. Present material indicates strongly that *the child raised with good, free, easy, loving, understanding, secure human relations develops into a responsible, productive, and loving spouse, parent, and citizen of good will; and that not only neuroses but in general all forms of psychopathology (in the intact organism) also derive from chronic traumatic influences upon the child during its earliest years.* There is certainly general agreement among students of behavior that, as stated by Hess (1959), the early experiences of the young of all species have a profound effect upon their behavior for the rest of their lives (Saul and Wenar, 1965).

It seems useful to arrange psychopathology on a scale grading from manifestations which are chiefly internal, as certain psychosomatic symptoms (such as elevation in blood pressure) on through neuroses, psychoses, and addictions, to the very frank behavior disorders, including criminality. Such an arrangement emphasizes the essential similarity in the nature of the etiology of all of these conditions.

Opinion persists (Waelder, 1960) that the neuroses result specifically from the unsuccessful repression only and exclusively of a sexual impulse which returns in the distorted form of a symptom. Freud himself states this in *An Outline of Psychoanalysis* (1949, p. 85). However, mounting evidence seems to indicate that neuroses of all sorts can arise from a variety of emotional conflicts and are not limited in their etiology *exclusively* to sexual impulses. Sexual impulses can certainly cause conflict—of this there is no doubt—but so can other impulses also. In addition, on theoretical grounds, it has seemed to me, ever since the publication of Freud's *The Ego and the Id* (1935) that the distinction between neurosis and character disorders no longer holds theoretically. There is no disagreement, so far as I know, among analysts today that neurosis is primarily a problem of the ego and also of the superego. (Freud, 1949, p. 83). Thus the total personality is involved and from all we know of the formation of the ego and superego, as evident in the very brief quotations from Freud above, these are formed by the continuation of the overall relationship to the parents and others responsible for or close to the child. As we have said, the child internalizes these, or in other terminology, is conditioned by them.

Thus we have the conceptual model of the child born with innate drives to mature and to complete its life cycle. If the child is provided with good human relations, given love, understanding, and security during childhood, it matures into a secure, responsible, productive adult with good human relations in his or her family, intimate circles, community, and nation—the child becomes an adult.

Put in another way, the child continues into adult life the emotional patterns formed in childhood. At the core of everyone's personality there is an emotional pattern of this kind which is essentially a continuation of his reactions to the treatment he received as a child. It is determined by early conditioning, or in analytic terms, by the internalization as superego of the individuals who accorded him this treatment.

In general, the younger the child, the more vulnerable he is to the influences upon him. The basic emotional pattern of the personality is probably laid down, as Freud stated (1949, p. 83) by the time the child is approximately six years old, hence the vital importance to the child's future of the period of its life from conception to about six years of age. Of course this does not mean, however, that later experiences do not also have extremely important effects. The significance for the goals of treatment, however, is that if the child was well treated with good human relations prior to age six, he has a foundation of strength and health in his personality which can withstand a good deal of trauma later. On the other hand, if he has been badly treated prior to age six, he may never straighten out entirely no matter how favorable the circumstances later.

This also applies to the early weeks and months of life and probably while the child is still *in utero*. If the child is badly enough treated in the first few weeks of life, then it is conceivable that its capacity for imprinting, that is for forming the attachment to its mother and hence any attachment, may be permanently damaged. This has been demonstrated in monkeys by Harlow and Zimmerman (1959) and by Liddell (1956) in goats, to mention only two examples. It may well be, although it is not at the present proven, that psychotic children, in whom the capacity to form an attachment is so obviously deranged, may suffer from this because the treatment they received in the early weeks of life impaired this capacity for attaching to the mother and therefore to other persons. Once the attachment is formed, then at least there is a relationship to people, however disturbed this may be through faulty treatment.

We also have considerable information about the lines of development of the child: from dependence toward independence; from needs for love as it receives it from the mother, to the capacity to give it; from the egocentricity which goes with an organism whose job it is to grow up and with consequent inferiority feelings and excessive competition, to the capacity for social cooperation; from relative automaticity of behavior to increasing ego strength, judgment, and adaptability; from the use of the fight-flight response as a major mechanism of adaptation to capacity for social cooperation which makes possible the formation of family, circles of friends, and civilization; from sex as play to sex in the service of love, mating, reproduction, the formation of family; from a sense of reality almost completely formed by the child's emotional reactions to those close to and responsible for it to a less emotionally colored, more realistic grasp of the nature of people and the world (Saul, 1960).

Summarizing the model then, we have the following: The child is born with certain capacities for development to maturity. *The condition of good human relationships, love, understanding, and security is the ideal setting for the child to mature properly. If this setting is provided, then the child becomes a secure, responsible spouse, parent, and citizen without any appreciable psychopathology.*

An emotional pattern is formed in every one during earliest childhood, especially from conception to about age six. With good treatment the child matures as just stated. With faulty treatment, through omission or commission, it may either be deranged in its capacity to imprint so that it hardly forms any attachment at all or else, if attachments are formed, the child's patterns of response to others may be warped by later faulty attitudes, feelings, and treatment of the child.

In general, the earlier the influences upon the child, the greater their effects. However the personality matures after about age six the underlying emotional patterns formed prior to this age persist with little change for life. These patterns, as we have noted, are primarily feelings toward other human beings in response to the feelings of the important persons during the early years to the child.

It is now clear that *the goal of causal treatment of internal disorders is the correction of psychopathology—of the pathological area of the dynamics— the pathodynamics, which consists primarily of disordered emotional patterns of reactions to other persons formed especially prior to about age six.* The earlier they are formed and the more deep-seated they are, the more difficult they are to influence by any form of psychological therapy available to us today. We are speaking only of the emotional problems seen in an office practice. We are not including in this chapter the psychoses nor those conditions which are primarily reactive to traumatic situations such as the neuroses of war, in which, for example, any man, no matter how stable, if kept at the front long enough would break down (about 120 days as I remember it).

Our model is of an individual born with certain developmental trends; these trends being conditioned by the treatment he received from those responsible for and close to him as a child, especially during his earliest years, thereby shaping a pattern of emotional attitudes, feelings, and reactions toward other human beings; and this emotional pattern continuing within his personality for life, as he interacts in his particular culture and in his immediate personal psychological field, which in part he makes for himself and which in part is imposed upon him. Stated succinctly, each individual interacts with other persons with his innate drives toward development and adaptation and his persisting childhood patterns, both of which have been conditioned most powerfully during his earliest years, but also by later experiences.

If the individual comes to us for therapy because of great conflict or tension with his environment, this may be primarily because of the stresses of his current environment to which no one, however stable and flexible, could adapt; it might be from failure of his particular personality to *fit* the particular field; it may be a failure in his own capacity for adaptation; and at the extreme, the problem may arise primarily because of conflict, failures, or warpings of development *within* the individual himself which cause difficulties no matter what the environment. These disorders of development we find regularly to stem from pathological emotional problems formed during the earliest years, especially until about six years of age, by the treatment the person experienced as a child at the hands of others.

III

If this conceptual model is correct, then it becomes clear that in the predominantly internal problems arising chiefly from within the personality, the task of causal therapy is to correct the pathological emotional patterns formed in childhood. Since these patterns consist of feelings toward other persons, they can only be adequately corrected by working them through as feelings toward one or more other persons. It was one of Freud's great discoveries that patients transfer these patterns to others, including the analyst. Thus the relationship to the analyst is in effect a sample human relationship. The disordered childhood pattern repeats itself in some part and form to the therapist. The task is to work with the mature part of the patient's personality in shared responsibilities, analyzing out the pathological elements, thereby releasing the patient's potential for continuing his natural emotional development.

Freud frequently compared analytic therapy with surgery. In the quotation we have used, he specifically calls it "after-education." It has similarities to both. For example, a young girl was much criticized and restricted by her mother. The reaction she developed was rebellious hostility to the mother expressed in behavior which is meant to defy her. This behavior is in danger of bringing the child to the attention of the police and also of having her expelled from school, damaging her reputation. The surgery in this case consists of a "hostilotomy." If the analyst can make conscious, work through, show other ways of reacting, and by all other methods available to him, reduce the girl's hostility to her mother so that she can handle this relationship without the defiant, hostile, self-punitive acting out, then the danger is reduced—like lowering the basal metabolism by removing part of the thyroid to reduce its secretions. Of course this also involves helping the girl understand the other major emotional forces, specifically the mother's domination and criticalness, and the girl's self-defense against this by hostile rebellion. This opens up other ways of dealing with her mother which are less injurious to both and are more consonant with good relations and with the forces of maturing. If the defense is no longer needed, or is replaced by other, more mature reactions, then the hostility and the consequent masochistic, self-injurious behavior are undercut. This is a sort of psychological surgery.

At the same time, as after-education, the analyst comes to stand during treatment, just as Freud said, in the place of a parent and can provide the insights and the attitude of sympathetic understanding freed of those other attitudes of the mother which cause the girl's hostile reaction to her. Thus also, as Freud described, the analyst, through the patient's projecting her superego onto him, is in a position to correct the "parental blunder." The patient *learns* to distinguish between his childhood reactions to a parent and his present-day reactions as an adult to the analyst who is not his parent. Our subject is goals and not method and technic. Therefore, except for a few remarks in the following paragraph about interpretation and education, we will not discuss the procedures by which the goals can, with more or less success, be achieved. The degree of success depends upon the balance of forces in the patient and their fixity. How influenceable they are is determined by such factors as the intensity and degree of the traumatic forces, how early in the child's life they were exerted, how frequent, how consistent, and unrelieved they were, how long they continued, what balancing and compensating factors there are, and similar variables.

Apart from the balance of forces within the patient, therapeutic progress also depends upon both the skill and personality of the analyst and thus upon how well suited the analyst is to the particular personality and particular problems of the patient. There is disagreement on this point, and some analysts still believe that any analyst can treat any person with equal effectiveness. This is no place to advance empirical data, and I will only state that the conclusion from my three decades of experience is that the choice of analyst for a particular patient is of great importance in many cases. This is in part because the therapeutic results, about the dynamics of which in the individual case we have a great deal to learn, depend not only upon the depth and accuracy of the analyst's understanding and interpretations, but also upon the transference to the analyst of the neurotic, i.e., the disturbed childhood motivations and their derivatives. How these develop, the ways in which the analyst deals with them, his feelings about them, and his feelings about the patient—these all are indicative of the analyst's personality, as well as of his insightfulness and skills. His personality creates an emotional climate in which the whole treatment is conducted. Reduced to simplest terms, as Freud said, "the patient puts the analyst in the place of his father (or mother)" thereby "giving him the power which his superego exercises over his ego." Thus the analyst's personality becomes an inevitable part of the patient's new superego. Insight alone is insufficient; and equally inadequate, sometimes even dangerous, is a supportive attitude without insight (Saul, 1958). For example, a girl felt guilty because of a sexual transgression and remained depressed despite kindly reassurance from her therapist. She only improved when given insight into the sources of her exaggerated guilt in the extreme puritanism of her father. Conversely, a young man felt that there were certain things he simply could never tell the analyst. He knew this was a pattern he had had toward his mother. This insight alone did not help. He had to have the experience of testing the analyst, telling these things bit by bit, cautiously feeling his way to prove the truth of insight he already had; he had to discriminate between his conditioning by a threatening mother and the present reality of full freedom to reveal himself to the analyst with approval for progress instead of punishment from a shocked parent.

Insofar as the analyst provides the attitudes of tolerance, sympathy, and understanding, free from traumatic elements, coupled with insight for the patient into the emotional pattern, its development, history, and the way in which it operates, he is imparting insight and understanding in a fashion which justifies terming it "after-education." The procedure opens the patient's mind to much that is going on in his reactions as well as in the reactions of others. In deepening and broadening the patient's understanding, his mind is freed from some of the automaticity of the patterns of reaction which were formed in childhood and have been continued reflexively since. The patient sees the possibility of new ways of reacting; for example, the girl mentioned previously, with the overly critical, restrictive, controlling mother, can learn to handle the relationship to her mother in other ways than by hostile, self-injurious acting out. New choices are opened up, which means increases in adaptability and flexibility. Put another way, the girl is desensitized in some degree to her mother's constant interfering efforts at frustrating control so that the girl does not pain her mother and damage herself in her rebellious reactions to this. Insofar as the relationship is better understood and better handled, it no longer absorbs so much of the patient's energy. Therefore it increases the free energy and, with the diminution of tension, also increases the capacity for relaxation. The patient has been conditioned to react in a certain way, and the analytic therapeutic procedure is intelligible as a method of deconditioning and reconditioning. The patient no longer need have his life lived for him from within because of the aftereffects of the treatment he received during childhood—the way he was conditioned then, or, in psychoanalytic terms, the internalization of the parental figures and the continued reactions to these introjects as his superego. He becomes increasingly able to live his life through the judgment of his ego rather than the automaticity of his superego, and this in turn increases his capacity to learn from experience.

Since the problem is primarily a continuation of faulty human relationships, its correction also results in improved relations with other persons. With the growth of his judgment and understanding, his sense of reality improves, and he is less dominated by views of others and of himself which were imposed by the treatment he received from those responsible for him and by his interplay of feelings with them. He can see himself less as a small child and more realistically appraise his capacity as a grown adult with personality, intelligence, and physical powers for responsibility and productivity. The more realistic view of himself, the healthier self-image, or, what is similar, a mature ego identity can make an enormous difference to the patient in living his life. This is in part because how people respond to each of us is determined so largely not only by how we feel toward them, but also by how we feel toward ourselves.

With the reduction of the pathological emotional patterns, inner frustration is reduced and capacities are increased for satisfactions in real life.

Mental and emotional health is largely, in simple terms, a matter of maturity combined with adjustment. There are situations as the war showed us (Saul, 1960) in which it is easier for a childish, egocentric personality to adjust, thinking only of himself, without much sense of responsibility for others, than it is for a mature person with a well-developed sense of responsibility and reality and capacity to love, who has on his mind the welfare of the men in his command and of his wife and children at home (Saul and Pulver, 1965).

Our overall goal is to release the patient's emotional development out of the automatic pathological emotional pattern so that he can mature to his full capacity to enjoy loving and being loved, working and playing—a balanced life of maturity insofar as it is possible in the world today. Put another way, a major goal of treatment is to turn the patient from fixations in certain responses—to turn him, through reopening the development, from being on the way *in* to movement on the way *out*.

Needless to say these goals are not achieved in the office alone. Here the patient has the total analytic experience, the emotional experience of transference and countertransference, the insights and working through, and everything that he can learn from the analyst. But a vital part of the goal consists in helping the patient *make use of this experience in his living*. This, like his symptom, is a matter of the balance of forces within the patient. It is determined by all those influences upon him, especially during earliest childhood, which were in various ways traumatic and by all those which in various ways permitted him to develop properly and gave him his strengths. Finally, it is only practice in living, the patient's capacity to use the analytic experience, which will further him on his way to these goals. That, too, insofar as possible, the analyst must help him with, perhaps by what he does not do as much as by what he does.

IV

The above goals were not formulated by armchair philosophy, nor were they derived theoretically from the conceptual model presented in the previous section. They are an empirical description of what can be observed to occur in analytic treatment. These goals, and the whole of the author's *Technic and Practice of Psychoanalysis* (Saul, 1958) were formulated from notes accumulated over a period of ten years. Whatever appeared empirically and definitively in his experience with treatment was jotted down along with the name of the patient and the date and the surrounding material and dropped into a file folder. These goals, like the book, are a résumé of these empirical observations. Samples of the raw data are being selected for publication in book form.

Not every goal is included because we wish to avoid getting into the subject of procedure and technic. For example, there is the patient's dependence, which Freud repeatedly remarked upon as fateful for the human race. This dependence, originally on the parent, combined with the child's love needs usually develops very strongly toward the analyst. Goals of treatment must include properly dealing with this tendency of the patient to attach his dependent love needs to the analyst so that they never become too strong and so that they are sufficiently reduced at the end of treatment for the patient to be maturely independent. The same considerations apply to the patient's competitiveness, hostility, and guilt. The goal of dealing with such of the forces as make difficulties can be summarized as adequate resolution of the transference.

All of these goals are ideals. They are, no doubt, never fully achieved, but it is obviously of vital importance for therapy to understand them. Without them the therapist is piloting a ship without a compass or is like a surgeon operating in semi-darkness. If the patient is properly treated, then he understands his childhood pattern and its formation, and he sees how it operates in his real life and also in the transference. The after-education and surgery, insofar as they are effective, therefore include resolution of the pathological patterns in the transference as well as in life. Since the goals are ideals, perhaps it would be more correct to say *reduction* of the pathology rather than its resolution.

V

Psychotherapy is still a controversial field. The reasons for the controversy are, I think, no longer so much academic as they are historical, political, and personal. Psychodynamics is now far enough advanced for differences to be settled through facts rather than polemics, but criticisms are inevitable. Hence the following remarks.

The conceptual model herein delineated is meant to include cultural factors. These are stated clearly in the second quotation from Freud. There is no conflict in thinking between the biological and the cultural. The two are closely interrelated. Cultural customs may help, or else hinder or warp, the biological development. How an individual behaves is shaped largely by his culture. Also, each culture presents certain problems of adaptation. At the same time, if, as the facts seem to show, there is a biological course of development and a whole group of people, a whole culture, deviates from this, then we are justified, using the yardstick of biological development, in saying that this entire culture shows emotional deviation from basic biological development, that is, psychopathology. Psychopathology is no less because it is manifested in a whole culture, any more than pock-marked skin is healthy because it occurs in a culture in which small-pox is endemic. If one says that he is a god, superior to everyone else, and it matters not what he does to others in order to establish his supremacy, he is locked up; if a whole group of people say this, and therefore it becomes recognized as the idealogy of a political movement

or of a tribe or culture, this does not change its being a deviation from biological maturing. Certainly the culture effects the maturing of the children
within it and also provides the setting in which they must operate as adults.
Ideally the culture would favor maturing and the functioning in the culture
of mature adults.

The formulations we have presented derive primarily from the author's
basic training for psychotherapy, which was in Freudian psychoanalysis, and
from his own experience. It is evident that these formulations reflect conclusions of various so-called "deviationists" and "revisionists." Adler saw the
importance of inferiority feelings and power seeking, of sibling rivalry, of
childhood memories, and "life style;" Jung also questioned the exclusive significance of sexuality in the personality. Rank saw the importance of dependence and Ferenczi of the needs of love. Fromm and Horney have pointed out
the importance of cultural factors. Sullivan stressed the fact that the emotional forces with which we deal relate to persons, to ourselves and to others,
that they are feelings between persons, "interpersonal." It seems to me that
the work of these and other writers are contributions, not deviations. For
Freud himself was the greatest revisionist (Saul and Watson, 1955) questioning and changing and dissatisfied at the very end, feeling, as he told Franz
Alexander the summer before his death, that much of what he had published
was not correct and needed revision. This chapter evolved from Freud's work
and is in its line of development, and is not derived primarily from the other
contributions; I hope that those in other groups will not feel offended by the
omission of a review of the main ideas of their leaders.

Hopefully, there seems to be a trend toward the integration, synthesis, and
critical teaching of all valid contributions, testing them not against authority
but against reality, as reality is studied by careful observation of empirical
phenomena. This is, of course, essential to the development of a true science
of personality and behavior. Such a science is becoming distinguishable in
embryonic form. It is called psychodynamics. The outgrowth of Freud's work
is now so broad as to utilize the contributions, not only of analysts and dynamic psychiatrists, whatever their emphases, but also the findings of all fields
relevant to personality and behavior, such as conditioned reflexology, animal
ethology, Gestalt psychology, field and learning theories, cultural anthropology, and the like. Gradually all of these will no doubt be integrated and syn-
thesized into a true basic science of personality and behavior and their disorders.

The general goal of psychotherapy is to *understand the patient*, to understand his psychopathology and his strengths, so that methods can be improved
for reaching ever nearer to the goal of all causal, rational treatment, namely
the understanding and diminution of the sources of psychopathology.

We have been speaking of the major immediate goals of psychoanalytic
treatment in dealing with the individual patient. Two other goals of a different
nature should, I think, also be included.

The psychoanalytic treatment of patients, through the intensive study over prolonged periods of individual human beings, continues to be an extremely important source of information about the human being, about his thinking, feeling, and behavior, about his mind and heart, about his biology, about his personal and sociological behavior, and about his most primitive feelings and what he values as his highest aims. This knowledge is of utmost importance.

Human life consists chiefly of relationships with people. It is these which provide each of us with our greatest happiness and also with our most dire misery. It is these which provide what we feel to be lofty or vile and these which threaten us with extinction. The psychoanalyst deals, perhaps more directly than any other professional person, with these motivations, with what we call the human spirit. Therefore, it would seem that he has an obligation to make one of his goals the utilization of his therapeutic procedures for the purpose of increasing scientific knowledge. The patient sacrifices time and money for the help he receives and the analyst gains a livelihood for the help he gives. Because of the special nature of this field, however, it would seem that a particular responsibility falls upon the analyst just because of the direct way in which he deals with the human motivations and their sources. It is a responsibility to use his therapeutic method as Freud did, as a research tool also—not merely to help each patient but to learn from the patient something which will further the science of the understanding of man.

This knowledge, we hope, can be used for *prevention*, and this would seem to be the greatest and ultimate goal. From what the analyst learns in helping the few can he not make some contribution which will point the way toward helping the many? Has our field not already shown the truth of the old adage that as the twig is bent the tree is inclined? If this is the case, should it not be a primary goal to discover and formulate what it is that bends the twig so that these injurious influences can be prevented and its healthy maturing favored?

One never knows exactly how a science will be used, constructively or destructively; but if there is any hope in science for the improvement of human relations and prevention of neurosis and the behavior disorders, including crime, tyranny, and war, then this hope might be expected to lie in what can be discovered about relieving the suffering of individuals. Hence we add the goals of contributing to the science of man and the utilization of this knowledge for the purpose not only of treatment, but also of prevention. Psychodynamics promises to become the basic science for psychotherapy in its efforts toward all of its major goals.

REFERENCES

Alexander, F. *The scope of psychoanalysis.* New York: Basic Books, 1961.
Bowlby, J. *Psychoanalysis and contemporary thought.* New York: Grove Press, 1959.
Erikson, E. Identity and the life cycle. *Psychological Issues,* 1, No. 1, New York: International Universities Press, 1959.

Freud, S. The ego and the id. London: The Hogarth Press, and the Institute of Psycho-Analysis, 1935.

Freud, S. *Collected Papers.* Vol. 5. London: The Hogarth Press and the Institute of Psycho-Analysis, 1950.

Freud, S. *An outline of psychoanalysis.* New York: Norton, 1949.

Freud, S. *Origins of psychoanalysis.* New York: Basic Books, 1954.

Freud, S., and Breuer, J. *Studies in hysteria.* New York: Nervous and Mental Disease Publishing Co., 1936.

Guntrip, H. *Personality structure and human interaction.* New York: International Universities Press, 1962.

Hess, E. H. Imprinting. *Science,* 1959, **130** (3368), 133–141.

Hess, E. "Imprinting" in animals. *Scientific American,* 1958, **198,** 81–90.

Harlow, H., and Zimmerman, R. R. Affectional response in the infant monkey. *Science,* 1959, **130,** 421–432.

Jones, E. *Life and work of Sigmund Freud.* New York: Basic Books, 1957.

Liddell, H. *Emotional hazards in animals and man.* Springfield, Ill.: Charles C Thomas, 1956.

Reik, W. *Ritual.* New York: Grove, 1962.

Saul, L. J. *Emotional maturity.* (2nd ed.) Philadelphia: Lippincott, 1960.

Saul, L. J. *Technic and practice of psychoanalysis.* Philadelphia: Lippincott, 1958.

Saul, L. J., and Pulver, S. The concept of emotional maturity. *Comprehen. Psychiat.,* 1965, **6,** 6–20.

Saul, L. J., and Watson, A. Milestones in psychology. In A. A. Roback (Ed.), *Present day psychology.* New York: Philosophical Library, 1955.

Saul, L. J., and Wenar, S. Early influences on development and disorders of personality. *Psychoanal. quart.,* 1965, **34,** 327–389.

Waelder, R. *Basic theory of psychoanalysis.* New York: International Universities Press, 1960. Pg. 212.

6

The Goals of Psychotherapy

John C. Whitehorn, M.D.

An Introduction to the Person

by Caroline A. Chandler, M.D.

John Whitehorn majored in philosophy at Doane College and entered Harvard Medical School in 1917. In 1932, he wrote a paper entitled "Instinct and Emotions" in which he formulated in original terms a theoretical concept of human behavior based on his observations of and "conversations" with mentally ill patients. With the publication of this paper, he won professional recognition as a clinical psychiatrist, and from that time on his rise to the heights of the psychiatric ladder was phenomenal. In 1938, he was appointed Professor of Psychiatry at the Washington University School of Medicine in St. Louis and Psychiatrist in Chief at Barnes Hospital, St. Louis.

During the three years he was at Washington University, Whitehorn fully developed and taught the basic theories of human behavior in illness and health which he had formed during his seventeen years of psychiatric research, treatment, and teaching at McLean Hospital and the Harvard Medical School. He believes that he reached the critical turning point in his career in St. Louis because by the time he was appointed the Henry Phipps Professor of Psychiatry and Director of the Department of Psychiatry at Johns Hopkins in 1941, he was fully committed to the idea that human behavior can be better understood in terms of "attitudes" rather than of instincts.

The corollary to this new approach of assessing people or patients in terms of their attitudes rather than instincts was that in order to find out how patients felt about something, one had *to ask them*. And so a new way of interviewing psychiatric patients by "seeing and treating them as human beings without catchwords, slogans or jargon" was introduced by John Whitehorn. This method represents his greatest contribution to American psychiatry.

If St. Louis was the turning point in Whitehorn's career, his nineteen years at Johns Hopkins were its culmination. It was during these years that he taught medical students and young doctors how to "see and treat patients as human beings," by example rather than precept.

In addition to his outstanding contributions in the areas of psychiatric research and training over a period of some thirty-five years, John Whitehorn devoted an enormous amount of his time and energy to the advancement of psychiatry as an organization. He was a member of the American Board of Psychiatry and Neurology from 1943 to 49 and during the years 1946, 1948, and 1949, he served as president of the Board. From 1954 to 1958, he was a member of the National Advisory Mental Health Council to the Surgeon General, United States Public Health Service. Between 1949 and 1951, he served successively as president-elect, president, and finally member of the Council of the American Psychiatric Association.

His contributions to the state of Maryland where he has lived ever since coming to Johns Hopkins in 1941 have been no less impressive than his efforts at the national level. From 1950 to 1960, he served as Chairman of the State Mental Hygiene Advisory Board and from 1953 to 1963 was a member of the Executive Committee of the Medical Care Committee of the State of Maryland. And although he retired as Professor and Director of the Department of Psychiatry at Johns Hopkins in 1960, he was appointed by the Governor to the Maryland Board of Health and Mental Hygiene in 1961, and he continues to serve as vice chairman of the Board at the present time.

Among the many honors conferred on Dr. Whitehorn, particularly noteworthy are his being named Honorary Associate Physician to Guy's Hospital, London, 1948 (to present) ; member of the War Department Commission on Combat Exhaustion, E.T.O., 1945; and recipient of the Emil Gutheil Medal by the American Association for the Advancement of Psychotherapy, 1961.

John Whitehorn's published papers, lectures, and other writings now number over one hundred twenty-five. He has also been a member of the editorial board of the *American Journal of Psychiatry* (1942–1962), the editorial board of *Medicine* (1956–1960), and the editorial council of the *International Journal of Social Psychiatry*.

THERAPEUTIC GOALS AND THEIR SIGNIFICANCE
FOR THERAPEUTIC STRATEGY

THE profession of medicine in general is dedicated to the care of the sick. This is an humbler aim, less glamorous than the conquest of disease. In psychiatry particularly, the care of the patient in a period of sickness is an important and basic purpose, for the psychiatric patient may be his own worst enemy. He needs care for the period of illness, in order to save him, so far as is feasible, from his own malign proclivities. Only patients who are kept alive can respond to therapy, and whatever serves to make life more endurable or to enlist the patient's interest or enthusiasm serves to some extent as part of therapy.

In psychiatry, as in all medicine, we rely heavily upon the healing power of nature and the biological potentialities for recovery and health, but with expectant optimism it is natural for us to try to offer an "assist" to nature. However, active intervention with the aim of assisting recovery cannot rationally be attempted without some idea, explicit or implicit, as to what is going on in the patient and what we are trying to do about it.

Medicine traditionally assumes that what is going on in the patient is a "disease," and the therapist's task is classically dramatized as a "fight" against the disease which has "attacked" the patient. This mode of medical thought has been firmly lodged in the professional mind by a long and honorable history, and the extraordinary effectiveness of this working concept in dealing with the infectious diseases has converted it almost into an axiom.

The concept of therapy as the cure of the disease, or victory over the germ, has found footing in the lay mind also, but perhaps not with the same domination, for patients are usually less concerned with the physician's over-zealous scientific interest in the disease than in their relief from distress. This patient-oriented way of thinking focuses upon the experience of suffering, upon the patient's role as the bearer of the pathos or suffering. To the patient, the doctor's concern about the disease is mainly justified because it leads to a potentially more effective and permanent way of relief from disease.

Let us put aside, momentarily however, the military metaphor of fighting the disease, as a useful instrumental abstraction but not the only way to think about therapy. Attempting a more general perspective, I think one can say that therapeutic interventions are aimed in general at one of three objectives (or maybe all three at once): (1) to save from death; (2) to relieve from distress; (3) to overcome disability. Concepts incorporating the first two aims have long ago been built into medical language—in the English term "disease" and the Latin synonym, "morbus." "Morbus" is not etymologically the exact equivalent of "disease," being derived rather from the word *morior*, to die, and representing therefore the threat of death as the antagonist against which therapy is to be directed.

For the third objective of therapy—to overcome disability—we have recently begun to think earnestly about rehabilitation or retraining or some other modality of intervention, but only on second thought do we think of these as medical functions or as therapy. Such professional thoughts are not new to the present decade, for surely, surgeons for centuries have aimed to assist nature in the restoration of optimal functional effectiveness, as in the setting of bones, the correction of deformities, and other operations. Nor do I mean to imply that the idea of overcoming disability is foreign to medicine, but, rather, that it has not occupied the focal spot in thinking about therapy so clearly as the other two aims—to save from death or to relieve from distress. To overcome disability has seemed a melioristic approach to the patient, offering some help toward doing better but not promising the complete contentment of a radical cure.

In the field of psychiatric therapy, at the present stage of progress, it appears to me that most psychiatrists face their therapeutic opportunities and responsibilities with such an essentially melioristic approach, aiming to help the patient overcome disabilities in some measure, and to do better. The widespreading idea of reaction-types, rather than disease entities, as the focus of differential diagnosis, has served to rationalize the melioristic approach.

We deal in psychiatry with many persons who are, in significant degree, *self-disabled:* seriously hindered in social functioning by inner personality conflicts; hampered in their grasp of so-called "reality" by self-constructed delusions, obsessions, and other reaction-formations; stiffened in personality structure and function by keloidlike scars; enslaved to the malign operations of unconscious dynamics by the miscarriage of the function of repression; or downgraded in their personal functioning by the force of bad habits. There is no promise of radical cure of *self-disablement* by any "silver bullet," or sulfa or antibiotic designed to knock out the offending organism, since the offending organism is the patient himself.

Nevertheless, there seems to have been some progress in therapeutic interventions aimed at wounding this noxious partner within the patient's skin—strategies of therapy which, by surgical procedures, electrical assaults, or drugs, selectively disable the patient from disabling himself so severely, and thereby yield a differential result algebraically favorable to the patient as a whole—or as a tolerably mutilated whole. With such methods of therapy, the balancing of potential gains against potential losses and against the possibilities and probabilities of other means of therapy has become an excruciatingly difficult and complex problem of therapeutic strategy.

We can set down, therefore, as one of the conscious strategic aims of some types of therapy, the therapeutically differential disablement of the patient, as an aid to his better overall functioning—a melioristic goal, but a drastic technique, sometimes miscalled "radical." One of the commonly used criteria of successful therapy of these types is *social improvement* or *social recovery*, meaning roughly the patient's level of ability to get along in a family setting, to hold a job, and to keep out of jail or the hospital. Such a minimal criterion of social recovery or improvement is not the optimal aim of therapy, but it is clearly a very pertinent consideration, particularly for patients who have been severely psychotic, because the outstanding practical disablement in severe psychoses consists in the severe impairment of one's social functioning.

There is a school of thought in psychiatry which views the disturbance of social functioning not just as a symptomatic expression of psychiatric illness, but rather as the reverse. The characteristic viewpoint for this group of psychiatrists may be formulated in the hypothesis that disturbances of interpersonal relationships (more precisely, maladaptive interpersonal attitudes and expectancies) constitute the *basic psychopathology* and that the ordinary, clinically recognizable symptoms of mental and emotional illness are the *manifestations* of these morbid interpersonal attitudes. From the viewpoint of this hypothesis, the morbid interpersonal attitudes may be viewed as the "disease," and the correction of such morbid attitudes, if accomplished completely, would be a radical cure. There would, however, be a logical place for melioristic, as well as radical, aims in the therapeutic strategy based upon this conception. It is my impression that this hypothesis, in one form or another, is widely utilized by American psychiatrists and that it plays a large role, explicitly or implicitly, in the planning of therapeutic strategy, even though tactics differ widely. There are also significant differences in theories as to the pathogenesis of morbid interpersonal attitudes.

Before turning to a consideration of these significant theoretical differences, which have a bearing on therapeutic aims and strategy, we should consider the way in which this general "interpersonal" view influences therapeutic strategy in trying to deal with anxiety. The naïvely sympathetic would-be therapist has a natural desire to relieve anxiety, in line with the general medical goal of relieving distress. The patient is also usually eager to be relieved of anxiety. Those therapists, however, who seek to lead the patient to correct his maladaptive interpersonal attitudes and to develop better attitudes, look upon the patient's anxiety as, in some measure, a necessary spur to effort and a necessary aspect to the learning process, without which there would be no modification of attitudes, and no progress; yet they recognize that anxiety may be a bar to progress or at least a hindrance when too great or when too tightly linked in phobic or depressive patterns of reaction. The attempt to control the intensity of anxiety within tolerable limits, and to utilize it, is, therefore, a large part of the tactics in those forms of therapy which aim at the modification of interpersonal attitudes.

There is some reason to think that the drastic types of physiological and pharmacological therapies may operate, in part at least, by moderating the anxieties of the patient, especially by interrupting fairly specific patterns of dread, and thereby freeing-up the patient in some measure, so that fresh relationships may be established and less malign patterns be formed.

Another basic strategic consideration in this context is that of immaturity of personality, the idea that there may be a deeply significant arrest of social and emotional development, leaving the patient seriously handicapped in interpersonal relationships by fixation at levels of infantile, childish, or adolescent attitudes and systems of value, thus seriously incapacitating one when faced with interpersonal situations of a later phase of life. For therapeutic strategy, the emotional relationship between patient and therapist may be viewed, in this context, as providing a fresh opportunity for the untying of knots and the acceptance and utilization of new and more mature emotional attitudes regarding authority relationships, affectionate relationships, and interpersonal responsibilities, whereby the fixated immature patterns can be loosened and modified.

From my own experience, I am inclined to view this opportunity for emotional relearning as the crucial point in those types of therapy attempting the improvement of interpersonal attitudes. For such purposes one can operate helpfully with the concept of the "meaning" of experience and behavior. In psychotherapy aimed at the modification of attitudes, it is of crucial strategic importance to recognize that the patient must experience during therapy some acute emotional disturbance, without which no significant change in attitude is likely to occur.

A third strategic consideration in the therapy which aims at the improvement of interpersonal attitudes may be roughly designated as habit. Here it is of specific importance to help the patient integrate his gains with the more constructive and adaptive habits and attitudes in his past life.

We may consider at this point the claim commonly expressed by psychoanalysts a couple of decades ago that psychoanalysis was the only real psychotherapy as it was based upon the only real psychopathology. The arrogant tone of such comments, characteristic of a vigorous movement of rebellion, has moderated somewhat with the years and with the broader validation and acceptance of some psychodynamic principles which have been enunciated as part of the psychoanalytic doctrines.

There is, however, a rather specific viewpoint which has sharply characterized psychoanalysis as a therapeutic method, and which delineates quite clearly the goal of such therapy. This is the view which looks exclusively into the dynamic operations of the *repressed unconscious* for the pathogenesis (and the cause) of psychopathological developments. In this conceptual framework, which we may call the classical psychoanalytic view of the early twentieth century, the strategic goal of psychotherapy, if proposed as radical therapy, should be the removal of the repression and the disclosure to consciousness of the hidden meanings and motivations, since their pathogenicity was considered to be uniquely related to the special dynamics of the repressed unconscious. It is a common reproach that the frequent ineffectiveness of abreaction therapy and of insight therapy disprove such claims. This reproach may not be altogether conclusive since it can be countered by the claim that in such instances "true insight" has not been achieved, or that a real abreaction has not occurred.

One is at the border here of the difficult metaphysical problem as to the nature of truth or reality. Keeping on the practical side of this metaphysical border, there still is a clearly discernible characteristic in the aim of strict classical psychoanalysis as therapy, and that characteristic lies in the crucial pathogenic importance assigned to those psychodynamic operations which go on beneath the barrier of repression and in the crucial psychotherapeutic significance of bringing them to consciousness. Hence the tactical importance which is attributed to free association and dream analysis by those holding such views. There is a correlative emphasis in tactics upon intense and intimate emotional relationships between patient and therapist, with high frequency of interviews and protracted duration.

My most sympathetic remarks have been concerned with therapy aimed at overcoming disability by the correction and improvement of the patient's interpersonal attitudes and expectancies. I see in this a reasonably specific basis for melioristic therapy and potentialities for occasional success in radical therapy, and I have attempted, around this general theme, to arrange sympathetically a conspectus of other views by which therapeutic aims and strategies are oriented.

GOALS OF PSYCHOTHERAPY

Scholarly minds are carefully elucidating the processes involved in psychotherapy, with much discriminating observation and experiment. For the rational study of any human activity, it is necessary to know or to postulate the purpose or goal of that activity. First, I can offer this formula: The goal of psychotherapy is health. This formula may appear self-evident; yet some discussion may be justified, if merely for clarification.

"Health" is a broad term with multiple meanings, and it needs definition and specification. To those in command of a task force of workers, the health of the workers means their ability to work effectively. To the person himself, it means something more—to "enjoy" health—not merely to function appropriately and effectively, in work, play, or in mere existence, but to do so with that inner sense of comfort, pride, and satisfaction which may be called the glow of health. Since human beings are unalterably forward-looking, it means also pleasurable expectations of continued competence and satisfaction in functioning. To work well, to feel well, to expect good—these might be called the primary dimension of health.

If one attempts, for study purposes, to construct a scale of health, these "good" and "well" terms seem, however, too vague. One seeks and finds more readily scalable positions in the negative directions of these dimensions—in degrees of disability, distress, or dread.

I have delineated thus very briefly a frame of reference and a statement of goals of psychotherapy which I feel has the practical value of penetrating to the basic issues in a manner which lends itself to actual research operations. This opinion seems validated by the investigations of Dr. Jerome Frank and his collaborators, who have made much use of practical scales for two of these three dimensions.

Let us, however, give another look at the statement that the goal of psychotherapy is *health*. By this choice of words I have brought this discussion into a region of possible controversy. The use of the word "health" has implied that the territory we discuss, namely psychotherapy, is a province of the healing, or medical, profession. This semantic gesture has not logically done any more than is done by the word "therapy"—which also allocates the activity to the healing profession—yet it is possible to pronounce the word "psychotherapy" with such emphasis upon the first part as to imply that it is the special province of the psychologist. Yet I wonder. We have also a term "pharmacotherapy" (meaning healing by drugs), yet we do not presume, no matter how we pronounce the word, that the pharmacist takes the responsibility for the patient's care. I believe that psychotherapy is primarily a responsibility of the medical profession and that the medical profession needs all the assistance it can get from psychologists and others in scientific investigation aimed at the understanding and the mastery of the processes and procedures involved in psychotherapy.

As a first approximation, I offered the formula that the goal of psychotherapy is health. Then I stated that practical specifications for working purposes are most conveniently located in the negative directions of the three dimensions of health, namely, in degrees of disability, distress, and dread. In evaluating progress toward the goals of therapy, this "3-D" system is contrived for easy remembering and is designed to take advantage of our mental habit of thinking in three dimensions.

Perhaps it is also merely a habit of the medical mind to think along the negative directions of these dimensions. Symptoms of illness are the regular medical stock-in-trade; we are accustomed to look for, recognize, and pigeonhole the symptoms of illness. We are not in the habit of thinking about the symptoms of health, and have not developed habitual pigeonholes for that purpose. The good physician does not really remain completely oblivious to the symptoms of health. He observes the brighter eye, the more erect posture, and the rising cadence of speech, but his system of notation or record-keeping is so strongly biased toward the pathological that he even writes down the word "negative" when he means healthy. Such is the power of jargon over thought.

The medical approach has also given us disease categories in the areas of our concern, for example, hysteria, schizophrenia, manic-depressive psychosis, and obsessive neurosis. In general medicine there have been magnificent gains achieved by this mode of guiding the search for therapy, whereby the disease is made the target, so to speak, of a specific therapy or of specific measures for control or prevention. Diabetes, syphilis, and tuberculosis may be cited as examples of fair degrees of success in target-oriented therapy; diphtheria and malaria as examples of even more brilliant success; leukemia and lupus erythematosus as examples which have so far defied the search for specific therapy, but offer some promise.

It is no trade secret that many psychiatrists are skeptical as to the validity of the disease-entity concept for conditions called hysteria, schizophrenia, manic-depressive psychosis, obsessive neurosis, and others, and as a corollary there is skepticism as to the likelihood of devising specific therapies. I would not favor abolishing these terms, for they have pragmatic value in facilitating communication, enabling workers to compare and collate observations with a moderate measure of probability that they are talking about the same types of patients. The usual skeptic's position is that these categorizing terms indicate, at the descriptive level, more or less distinguishable constellations of symptoms, with some likelihood, but no certainty, that distinctive pathological processes (either mental or nonmental) may be found to characterize or maybe even to determine the named categories. This is approximately the current position of psychiatrists as represented in the official system of classification, built around the concept of reaction patterns or reaction types. At this point, opinions begin to divide, some psychiatrists feeling much more convinced than others as to the existence and characteristics of specific pathogenic processes involved in specific reaction types. Some of the current hypotheses employ biochemical models of thought, some employ psychological models. It is from the latter— the psychological models—that one derives hypotheses for specifically disease-target-directed psychotherapeutic strategy.

If one postulates more or less specific intrapsychic conflicts as the pathogenic processes causing more or less specific morbid reaction types or mental diseases, then the goal of psychotherapy can be fairly definitely specified as being the reversal of the pathogenic process by the resolution of the intrapsychic conflict. It may be convenient in discussion to use the expression "the target of psychotherapy" rather than "the goal of psychotherapy" when the effort is directed against the disease process. Then, it may also be postulated that one of the crucial factors in the pathogenicity of an assumed intrapsychic conflict lies in the unconscious nature of the conflict, and on this assumption one of the goals or targets of psychotherapy would be to develop conscious awareness of the conflict, as a necessary step toward its resolution.

On such a two-factor theory of causation, it is conceivable that one or the other of the factors may be made the primary target of therapy, that is: (1) plans might be directed first to making the unconscious conscious, whereby the rational resources of the conscious mind might be enlisted with clear awareness in the effort to resolve the conflict; or (2) plans might be directed toward providing for some "corrective emotional experiences" for the patient, whereby some resolution or more tolerable modification of the conflict might first be gained without clearly spotlighting the issue in consciousness. If such a therapeutic aim as outlined under (2) proved attainable working essentially at nonrational or unconscious levels, the pathogenicity of the presumed conflict might be sufficiently modified or it might even conceivably be resolved to such an extent that relief or even recovery might be the result. A more complex strategy might be conceived of combining (1) and (2), whereby corrective emotional experiences at unconscious levels might modify the conflict enough to enable the patient to bring it more readily into consciousness.

For many who seek their guide lines for psychotherapy in the Freudian system of concepts, or are familiar with that system, these thoughts just presented make sense, I believe, despite the rather abstract language. In these more recent paragraphs, I have been presenting a target-directed concept of psychotherapy, a concept of an effort directed against a pathogenic process. This is in the classical medical model of the "remedy" for the disease. Yet medical tradition maintains that the doctor treats patients, not diseases, and despite the abstract terms used above, it should be clear that the patient was to be involved actively in the psychotherapeutic process.

At one time I said "whereby the rational resources of the conscious mind might be enlisted in the effort to resolve the conflict" and I also said that the patient might be enabled to bring the conflict into consciousness. Both instances referred to the activities and resources of the patient and clearly implied that the therapist would do well to evoke these resources and activities. I wish to make this point explicit, that even in discussing target-directed psychotherapy aimed against disease-processes, that is, efforts directed against the presumed cause, I have used language which clearly implies an evocative meaning in psychotherapy: therapeutic potential resides in the patient, and one of the aims of psychotherapy is to evoke this potential.

Here I wish to pursue another implication. To evoke effort from the patient is to exercise a leadership function, therefore, to choose a direction. We could use here the formula I offered first (the goal of psychotherapy is health) and say that the psychotherapist aims to evoke that in the patient which leads toward health.

For some purposes we could stop at this point; here, however, I feel impelled to press on and state more explicitly an impression which I have gained from the study of successful psychotherapists, namely that they do function as leaders, and that a psychotherapist does lead in a direction which, according to his values, means a good life for the patient. Values vary, as do conceptions of the good life; leadership toward the good life implies wisdom, as well as knowledge and skill. Here, I am entering territory where taste and preference prevail, and I wish to avoid misunderstanding. It is not my intention to say that this aspect of leadership should be so; rather, I merely record my impression that successful psychotherapy, when subjected to empirical scrutiny, is found to involve leadership toward preferred values, toward the therapist's conception of what constitutes value in life.

Specifically, some psychotherapists lead their patients toward freedom, others toward conformity. Neither goal is completely attainable. Interdependence is inherent in the institutions of domestication and socialization within which human life is lived and which require some degree of conformity; yet some measure of free play and spontaneity is necessary to make these institutions work. In the jargon of the sociologists, each must play some role or roles, and this means conforming in some measure to the expectations of others; yet the development of personal integrity, which is also a social necessity, requires that individuals have some feeling of inner freedom and self-fulfillment in enacting these roles.

Psychotherapists, as I have perceived them, have definite biases, placing high value upon one or the other of these goals—freedom or conformity—as expressions of their own personal orientation of life, and they manifest these value preferences in their therapeutic operations. Such manifestations of preference are ordinarily tacit or implied, rather than explicit. I am inclined to think, however, that these manifestations of preference constitute one of the major therapeutic forces, evoking like desires and efforts in susceptible patients and leading them toward the indicated goal, tempered by whatever wisdom for compromise can be brought to bear by both in the resolution of hindering conflicts where issues had been too sharply drawn and frozen.

As an example of those psychotherapists who place a high value on freedom, and who operate implicitly to evoke like aspiration and effort in their patients, I name Sigmund Freud. It is true that for a time he expounded a doctrine of complete determinism. Yet he showed himself capable of a noble inconsistency, for his mode of therapeutic operations seems well designed to activate and cultivate the patient's potentiality for freedom. Freud exemplified in his own life and work the ideal of scholarly detachment and independence of thought, and his therapeutic efforts can be interpreted, I think, as springing from a desire to assist others toward a similar freedom and detachment. The ideal human condition toward which Freud's therapy aimed appears to me to have been a state of freedom in which a person could, through understanding, hold himself inwardly free from the coercive prohibition of society and free also from the coerciveness of blind biological impulses.

Such an ideal state of inner freedom is more earnestly desired by some than by others. It is more likely to be an aspiration of intellectuals and upper-class persons than of lower-class persons. Many who think they aspire to freedom are only conforming to a fashion and shrink from the reality of it. Many patients who are unsuitably encouraged to seek emotional health by striving toward the freedom goal without wise consideration of other needs, fail in their quest or quickly drop out.

I have also known many patients who were helped by psychotherapy which was basically conformity-oriented. However, my own bias is in favor of freedom, and I suspect that others may share with me the feeling that conformity is a rather shameful term. Some seek a gentler word—adjustment—and, as if in embarrassment at so ignoble a profession of value, embellish their discussions with much talk about reduction of tensions, homeostasis, and sublimation. There seems to be an important positive implication of conformity, however.

When the policeman admonishes his client, "Now, come along quietly. Don't make any trouble, and everything will be all right," he is exemplifying in caricature what might be considered a pseudo-psychotherapy whose goal is a sort of universal gaol. It is not to this extremely negative type of conformity-oriented psychotherapy that I wish to direct attention now, but rather to a more positive implication of conformity from which I think it derives its real appeal and its genuine psychotherapeutic meaning.

In admitting to some feeling that there is something shameful in conformity, I think we manifest our unwise submission to one of the prejudices of our time and culture. I misdoubt the presumed ignobility of conformity. Woman conforms to man, and man to woman, with enthusiasm and pride; the suckling infant conforms to the mother, and mother to infant, with an eagerness which warrants one's thinking that conforming behavior may be infused with an inner glow of enthusiasm quite as genuine and noble as the aspiration for freedom. So, too, in the infinitude of human interactions, domestic and social, many transactions and relationships of sustenance and sharing may come to partake also of this inner eagerness for conforming. Yet it requires, for many of us in our time, something of an effort to perceive and maintain a view of the ennobling nature of conforming impulses. The conformity impulses are so conveniently exploitable that we have had much reason to become distrustful of them. Despite this uneasy distrust lest one be fooled into becoming a tool for the crafty or selfish purposes of others, there are highly respected professions, such as medicine and nursing, in which service to the needs of others, which is unmistakably a conforming type of behavior, has become an institutionalized ideal, as well as one of the natural human motivations. The manifestations of conforming impulses are sometimes labeled "unselfishness," an unfortunate word which makes an absurd mystery out of a quite natural impulse.

Some psychotherapists, as I have said, are so oriented to life that they are acquainted with the enthusiasm and eagerness of spirit which may be inherent in the conforming impulse; they manifest this type of action and its inherent enthusiasm, in their transactions with others, and thus may evoke in susceptible patients some like enthusiasm. Why does this phenomenon have special relevance for neurotic or psychotic illness? Why does it count in psychotherapy? I can offer a partial answer.

As I see it, one of the common sources of inner conflict and a fairly general foundation for ill-suppressed resentment lies in the fact that many persons, while enacting their roles in life (even aptly selected roles), become somewhat irked by the sense of constraint or coercion implied by the expectations of others. (One common verbal formulation of this complaint is the following: "I'm just taken for granted around here.") The vague uneasiness over being defined in one's role dampens one's enthusiasm and thereby enhances the vague sense of feeling cheated or belittled. Whatever helps one to recapture some sense of dignity and worth in the devoted enactment of one's role helps to mitigate this inner conflict.

In World War II I saw soldiers who had "blown their tops" after prolonged experience of combat, having lost their meaningful human orientations in a universe apparently gone mad with killing and being killed, who, in the medical station, recaptured some sense of meaningful devotion and rejoined their units with eagerness. It seemed to me that the medics accomplished this therapy in very significant part by their quiet enactment of a meaningful role of devoted service, as well as by their words or their drugs.

So, too, in civilian life it has frequently seemed to me that emotionally disturbed patients, irked by those no-longer-glamorized expectations of others which defined their roles, have found in nurses and doctors a manifestation of quiet dignity and pride in devoted service which gave these patients support and sustained them in meeting, with less sense of irksomeness, the expectations of their roles. Perhaps some of the neurotic habitués of out-patient departments seek, in a vague and groping way, for a comparable infection to lighten the burden of unrequited devotion in their role in life.

I have been discussing two special value systems, that of freedom and that of conforming to the expectation of others, which constitute, as I see it, goals toward which differing types of psychotherapists tend to lead their patients, goals going somewhat beyond a limited definition of health. Manifestations of behavior and attitude oriented toward these values appear to play a significant part in the processes of psychotherapy. These are phenomena deserving scientific study.

I have also indicated that patients differ in their aspirations and in their susceptibility to leadership in these directions. Some respond well to the type of psychotherapist oriented toward the value of freedom, others to the type oriented toward conformity. In very large measure we deal here with goals and operations not explicitly avowed, but inherent in the transactions between patient and therapist, expressions of personality rather than planned technique.

Coming back to the central issue of health as the goal of psychotherapy, I think that it still requires some amplification in the direction we usually call rehabilitation. This is an aspect of treatment sometimes lost from view when attention is focused sharply upon the disease-process as the target of therapy. In psychotherapy, however, the personal relationship tends to arouse in the therapist a concern for the patient's rehabilitation, either in the sense of his resuming a former functional role and capacity or in assuming new roles. In general psychiatric practice, institutional or private, there has been in recent years increasing practical attention to rehabilitation as part of medical responsibility, and I believe it is justifiable to state that this improvement in professional attitude has come about because of the more widespread interest in psychotherapy and the effects of this interest in inducing a greater dedication to the patient's welfare.

Increased interest in rehabilitation as a goal of therapy has been part of a change in attitude which I might succinctly describe as a reaffirmation of the melioristic approach. During the heyday of psychoanalytic presentations, its proponents viewed that method of therapy as the one and only instrument for getting at and really curing the cause of mental ills; but experience and comparisons have led to a more general recognition of the imperfections and limitations of psychoanalysis.

During this reevaluation, melioristic aims in psychotherapy have regained respectability. The melioristic approach may be characterized as that in which one views the patient as a person functioning not very well or happily and seeks to help him to a better mode of functioning, as contrasted with the perfectionistic view of seeking to achieve the complete elimination of his disease through the radical cure of its cause.

In simplest terms, it can be said that the goal of psychotherapy is health. For working purposes, three dimensions of health are specified: to work well, feel well, and expect well, most conveniently scalable in the negative directions of disability, distress, and dread. Along these dimensions, one can construct usable measures of success or failure in therapy.

If one chooses to focus sharply upon the pathological, the aims of psychotherapy can be formulated as target-directed efforts against pathogenic processes, as exemplified in such concepts as intrapsychic conflict and the unconscious. Even when committed to such specific target-directed psychotherapeutic efforts, one needs to recognize the evocative character of the process—that therapeutic potential resides in the patient and that part of the psychotherapeutic process is to evoke this potential.

Convictions that one has a correct understanding of pathogenesis incline one toward the perfectionistic formulation of goals; skepticism and humility incline one toward the melioristic formulation of goals. In the melioristic context rehabilitation seems logically a part of therapy.

Beyond the goal of health, as it may be defined strictly, lies a region of value-judgments, regarding preferences as to what life and health are for. High value placed upon freedom or upon conformity may implicitly determine the strategic aim of the therapist. Behavioral manifestations of these value-orientations are important factors in the processes of psychotherapy.

7

The Goals of Psychoanalysis

Reuben Fine, Ph.D.

An Introduction to the Person

by E. S. Shneidman, Ph.D.

Dr. Fine has reached a preeminent position in two areas of competence. He is known to many as one of the foremost psychologically trained psychoanalysts in New York and to critical readers of psychoanalytical theory for several contributions to *The Psychoanalytic Review*, for his psychoanalytical study of chess champions, and for his recent book on Freud. The scholarly, planned, thorough, and logical approach which distinguished his scientific writings is consonant with the fact that he is also internationally known as one of the great chess Grand Masters of the twentieth century, holds three world records for blindfold games in chess, and has written many books considered standard works on the subject.

That Dr. Fine can bring to his work with patients compassion and emphatic understanding, all who hear his reports at symposia and clinical presentations know full well. Along with his impressive, extraordinarily keen mind, one is also struck by his unusual ability to focus on and attend to the intellectual and affective issues at hand. In addition, he is helped along by what must be considered an unusual but realistic confidence in his own capacities.

Dr. Fine was born in New York City in 1914. He received a Bachelor of Science degree in mathematics, a Master of Education from City College of New York, and his Doctor of Philosophy degree from the University of Southern California. He has had a private practice in psychoanalysis for the past fifteen years, has been a Visiting Professor in Psychology at City College of New York from 1948 to 1958, and was Visiting

Professor in Psychology at the University of Amsterdam in 1961. Since 1960, he has been Attending Psychologist and Supervisor of Psychotherapy at the Elmhurst Hospital in Queens, New York. Students of psychodynamically-oriented psychology are well acquainted with his recent, succintly-titled book, *Freud.*

BROADLY speaking, two goals are pursued in psychotherapy: the reduction of anxiety and the promotion of growth. Psychoanalysis has shown that there is an intimate connection between these two, yet they are still different, both theoretically and practically. In this paper I shall limit myself to the second goal, and try to specify more clearly how the concept of the promotion of growth should best be approached. Naturally, this is not intended in any way to minimize the importance of the reduction of anxiety.

It has often been noted that our age of psychotherapy is one in which people feel the greatest uncertainty about major issues in living. Historically, this uncertainty is a sequel to the naïve certainty of previous centuries, which was based on faith in religion. It would be worthwhile to begin by comparing the religious and the psychotherapeutic[1] attitudes towards life.

In spite of their theoretical differences, the major religions of the modern world (Christianity, Judaism, Mohammedanism, Buddhism, and Confucianism) have similar attitudes toward fundamental problems of living. Four are particularly important:

1. Religion generally frowns upon bodily pleasures. In many cases the greater the ability of the individual to renounce these pleasures, the higher he stands in the scale of virtue. Asceticism and withdrawal from ordinary living may be glorified. As a result much of the effort of the religious leader goes towards urging his practitioners to forego pleasure.

2. Religion has an authoritarian structure and goes to great lengths to preserve this structure. One who "joins" a religion is willing to accept this structure and to try to fit into it. On the positive side, this hierarchical organization serves the function of promoting group feeling in the individual.

3. Religion prescribes roles for each individual within the community. Often, so many aspects of these roles are set in advance that little initiative is left. All religions have recognized that these roles will vary with age, and accordingly, full-scale religious adherence means that the person is guided in his path from birth to death, and beyond.

4. Religion generally denies the fact of death, and offers the believer a variety of palliatives to reduce the anxiety connected with this natural tragedy.

[1]The terms "psychotherapeutic" and "psychoanalytic" will be used synonymously throughout the present paper.

These palliatives are embodied in what the outsider regards as weird theological systems, the irrationality of which usually offers a first point of attack against the religion.

A first approach to the psychoanalytic way of life can be made by comparing its position with that of religion on the above issues. In spite of all the doctrinal differences, the following could be said:

1. Psychoanalysis generally approves of bodily pleasures. In many cases it finds that the repression of these pleasures leads to severe neurotic symptoms. Asceticism may be required by certain life circumstances, but is not in itself a virtue. On the other hand it is also recognized that excessive indulgence in bodily pleasures can be harmful, for either psychological or physiological reasons. The ideal of the psychoanalyst is a balance, and much of his effort goes towards helping the patient find such a balance.

2. Psychoanalysis has an antiauthoritarian structure. Most efforts on the part of the patient to get the analyst to "play God" will be rejected, and the need for such a God will be analyzed. The dependency accepted in psychotherapy is envisaged as a temporary measure; the eventual goal is to leave the individual on his own. This extreme emphasis on the individual is hard for many people to take.

3. Psychoanalysis seeks to clarify for each person what role or roles he would like to play in the community. It does not prescribe these roles, but helps the person decide which is most suitable to his character and life situation.

4. Psychoanalysis has nothing to say about death. It does not seek to palliate the anxiety associated with it, except in those cases where death is imminent. This enables it to dispense with the vast irrational systems of theology which haunt the religions.

A summary comparison of these two approaches shows that religion employs a variety of pleasure-denying and authority-submitting devices which serve to reduce anxiety, while psychoanalysis resorts to pleasure-affirming and authority-dissolving devices which make for greater growth but temporarily or at times even permanently expose the individual to more anxiety. The question then to be answered is, What kind of a growth pattern does the psychotherapist envisage for humanity at large and for his patients in particular? As put, the question makes clear that the psychotherapist should look upon himself as a secular philosopher whose major task is to teach people how to achieve more happiness in living.

The problem of the ideal growth pattern can be clarified by considering at length the main topics which ordinarily would be taken up in any intensive analysis. Anxiety as such will not be discussed, because we are emphasizing the ego structure that will permit the person to handle it; the analytic assumption is that if a satisfactory way of life is reached, anxiety is no longer a problem. The topics to be considered are: (1) age-specific needs; (2) the sense

of identity; (3) pleasure; (4) love; (5) sex; (6) hatred; (7) family structure; (8) creativity; (9) work; (10) family role; (11) the social order.

AGE-SPECIFIC NEEDS

The particular way of life that the person chooses (or that is chosen for
him) depends more than anything else on age. A vast mass of information has
now been accumulated about the needs of people at different ages; this information must play an essential part in every termination process in therapy.
While it is possible to summarize our knowledge in many different ways, I
find Erikson's epigenetic scheme the most illuminating. It is reproduced on
p. 77.

Erikson's scheme provides a useful framework into which many of the
questions to be raised later can be fitted. While it has its disadvantages, like
all schemes which tend to become too rigid for the living material, its advantages far outweigh this drawback.

A very important question concerning the developmental process relates
to the possibilities of and reactions to gratification and frustration. In general,
a curious paradox is encountered here. At earlier ages, gratification is easier,
while frustration is more traumatic; at later ages, by contrast, gratification is
harder, but frustration less traumatic.

There are all kinds of imbalances in human nature and in the relationship
of man to his fellowmen. Philosophers and social thinkers have been calling
attention to these imbalances for thousands of years. The psychotherapist can
at best reduce these imbalances; he can never eradicate them completely. In
other words, in attempting to help any individual create an optimal setup, we
strive for improvement, not for absolute perfection.

THE SENSE OF IDENTITY

Identity is a unifying concept which helps to make sense of the person's
life pattern. It is undoubtedly the most important single aspect of the personality structure. It is referred to in various ways—identity, self-image, and
ego structure or ego-ideal are the most common.

As Erikson's table suggests, the sense of identity is reached only after
long inner and outer struggles. It comes as a consequence of what he calls
psychosocial crises. At various stages in the individual's life, new developments, brought about by the maturational process, call for a new self-evalua-
tion and a new clarification of identity.

Up to puberty, the child is so preoccupied with the rapid changes through
which he is going that the sense of identity can only be inferred from various
aspects of his behavior. Once the physiological sexual changes have made their
appearance, however, it becomes apparent to the child that growth will not go
on forever. Furthermore, questions of marriage and career become topics of

Chronological Stage	Psychosexual Stages	Psychosocial Crises	Radius of Significant Relations	Related Elements of Social Order	Psychosocial Modalities
I. Infancy	Oral-respiratory Sensory kinesthetic (Incorporative modes)	Trust vs. Mistrust	Maternal person	Cosmic order	To get To give in return
II. Early childhood	Anal-urethral Muscular (Retentive-eliminative)	Autonomy vs. Shame, doubt	Parental persons	"Law and order"	To hold (on) To let (go)
III. Play age	Infantile-genital locomotor (Intrusive, inclusive)	Initiative vs. Guilt	Basic family	Ideal prototypes	To make (=going after) To "make like" (=playing)
IV. School age	"Latency"	Industry vs. Inferiority	"Neighborhood" school	Technological elements	To make things (=completing) To make things together
V. Adolescence	Puberty	Identity and repudiation vs. Identity diffusion	Peer groups and outgroups, Models of leadership	Ideological perspectives	To be oneself (or not to be) To share being oneself
VI. Young adult	Genitality	Intimacy and solidarity vs. Isolation	Partners in friendship, sex, competition, cooperation	Patterns of cooperation and competition	To lose and find oneself in another
VII. Adulthood		Generativity vs. Self-absorption	Divided labor and shared household	Currents of education and tradition	To make be To take care of
VIII. Mature age		Integrity vs. Despair	"Mankind" "My kind"	Wisdom	To be, through having been To face not being

SOURCE: E. Erikson (1959).

discussion in the family and peer groups. It is at this stage, around early adolescence, that the individual first acquires the capacity to verbalize a more enduring sense of identity. This sense may and usually does go through many vicissitudes in the course of life, but here it has attained its first clear-cut expression.

The clarification of the sense of identity in the psychotherapeutic process requires more than anything else a careful analysis of the sexual situation. For nothing is more basic to the self-image than how the person functions sexually, both specifically and in the broader meaning of the word. Much has been written about the identity conflicts of the individual in the modern world. Often it is maintained that the early psychoanalysts dealt with sexual problems, the contemporary with identity problems, and that these two are sharply different. That is not the case at all. The sexual conflicts of the modern adolescent are as turbulent as they ever were. Clearly there have been many changes in attitude towards sexual expression, but in terms of the total growth scheme, from oral to genital, and from material dependency to full intimacy and love, relatively little has been changed.

The psychological problem of finding one's sexual identity (What kind of a man am I? What kind of a woman am I?) is as acute as the physical. If the most fundamental physical expression is denied, the psychological does not fall far behind. Time and again we still see many cases of vocational or social disorganization, which stem quite directly from fear of sex. Homosexuality, which appears to be increasing, is at bottom an overpowering fear of the opposite sex.

Other aspects of the identity problem—familial, vocational, social—are quite familiar and little more need be said about them here. The main point is that it is a mistake to separate these out too sharply from the underlying sexual frustrations.

The discrepancy between the actual identity of the individual and the ego-ideal leads to all kinds of neurotic problems, including full-blown psychosis. From one point of view, it could be said that one criterion of normality is to recognize one's true identity, rather than spend one's life in a fruitless search for a new one.

The psychotherapist uses this knowledge to help the patient achieve a satisfactory sense of identity. Above all he is concerned with getting the patient to overcome the frustrations associated with his sexual background, and in tracing the relationship between feelings of inadequacy in the sexual role and in other roles.

However, we come back here to a dilemma touched upon in the previous section. What if social forces, despite our best efforts, prevent the individual from reaching real fulfillment in his or her sexual role? In that case the recognition of identity is apt to bring suffering rather than happiness, at least temporarily. Compensations may be sought in many different ways. We see here once more the interrelatedness of all aspects of the personality structure, and how impossible it is, except for purely theoretical purposes, to keep them sharply separate.

PLEASURE

The psychotherapist asserts unequivocally that pleasure is good. It is said that once when Freud was asked what is normal he replied: pleasure and achievement. And Menninger has urged that psychoanalysts come out quite frankly with their belief in a hedonistic way of life. Man is a pleasure-seeking animal and he should be encouraged to enjoy himself.

Several qualifications have to be made in the above. First of all, there are different pleasures appropriate to different stages of life. The person who maintains a pleasure characteristic of an earlier stage is fixated; such fixations prevent him from developing other parts of his personality and eventually lead to conflicts, just as the failure to use parts of the body leads to atrophy and illness.

Thus the course of development involves a constant shift from one source of pleasure to another. This development rarely proceeds ideally, so that each person has various holdovers from previous stages.

Second, analytic investigation has shown that not all pleasure is what it seems; it has its dynamics and unconscious motivations. As the therapeutic process goes on, and the unconscious becomes conscious, the sources of pleasure change. On the one hand old pleasures may be given up because they seem childish or petty. On the other hand new pleasures, formerly blocked by unconscious forces, may become available.

Third, excesses of pleasure frequently turn out to be harmful. Accordingly, the need with many people is to cut down the sources of pleasure, rather than to increase them. Analysis usually shows that overdoing any pleasure (e.g., smoking) has its unconscious roots.

Fourth, the factor of individual differences must be recognized. People have different levels at which they seek pleasure; we can postulate a *cathectic level* for each person, which is defined as the average level of intensity of the enjoyment that he prefers. Thus, the cathectic level would go through various ups and downs in the course of life. The cathectic level of the adolescent is much higher than that of his middle-aged parents, which often creates much friction in the family.

At any age each person has a certain cathectic level, which differs from those around him. This cathectic level is very hard to change; unless it is obviously pathological, as in a clinical mania or depression, psychotherapy does best to leave it alone.

These qualifications should not make one lose sight of the basic psychoanalytic hypothesis, that pleasure is good. Thou shalt enjoy life could be said to be the psychoanalytic commandment.

LOVE

Pleasure is the acme of self-gratification, love is the acme of gratification with another person. Nothing is more important than love in the growth process and in the resolution of neurotic conflicts.

In any discussion of love a difficulty very quickly makes itself felt in that the word has so many meanings. It is necessary to offer an analysis of the topic that will lead to some clear-cut definitions, not in order to be pedantic, but in order to be precise.

Most of what is described as love turns out to be a neurotic fixation when it is subjected to analytic scrutiny. Love may be a strong irrational transference, investing some shy frightened girl with all the marvellous qualities the little boy saw in his mother. Or love may represent a blind attachment, which does the person serious harm, yet which he cannot break. It was this kind of love that Somerset Maugham portrayed so beautifully in *Of Human Bondage*.

Love may be a reaction-formation against hatred. When it is, the hatred often breaks out as the love relationship collapses. If it has gone so far as marriage, the law courts are eloquent witnesses to the violent battles which this kind of love generated.

Love may be one form of masochism. This is found in the person who somehow manages to find one unrequited love relationship after another; in every one he suffers. Analysis frequently shows that if there is a chance of success in a love relationship with such people, it is quickly broken off.

The list of neurotic types of love relationships could be continued indefinitely. Suffice it to say that the characteristic element in the neurosis is the clinging to some earlier form of gratification.

For the person who is capable of normal or healthy love we can distinguish five stages in the growth towards such love. There are: attachment, admiration, physical enjoyment, total enjoyment, devotion.

1. *Attachment* is an attachment to the mother originally. It leads, in Erikson's terms, to a feeling of basic trust in other people, since the infant has had the experience of being well taken care of when he is helpless.

2. *Admiration* refers to the father. He is the major source of strength in the family in relation to the outside world, and children of both sexes look up to him; this admiration leads to autonomy and initiative, since the father under these circumstances will not keep the child dependent longer than is necessary.

3. *Physical enjoyment* refers to sex and begins at puberty. Granted, of course, that sexuality has a long history, the pubertal sex reaction still remains markedly different from anything ever experienced before. In the early stages of puberty, the desires are largely physical. It is no disparagement of love to think of it in this way; rather, the idea that love must be far removed from the body is an expression of the split between tender and sexual feelings which has characterized Western civilization for many centuries.

4. *Total enjoyment* refers to both sexual and emotional intimacy with a

person of the opposite sex. It comes in later adolescence and would normally lead to marriage.

5. *Devotion* is the basic parental feeling, maternal as well as paternal. The helplessness of the child calls for long periods of selfless devotion, even under the best of circumstances. At the same time the role of enjoyment in the parent's feelings about the child should not be forgotten. If it is, the result is a self-sacrificing kind of parent, who invariably creates deep guilts and neurotic conflicts in the children.

The psychotherapeutic process begins with an analysis of the neurotic love manifestations of the past and ends with a clarification of normal love. The discussion of love at the end of therapy should be specific and geared to the background of each individual patient. A French essayist has defined love as the absence of anxiety. This jibes with analytic experience, since the more the individual is able to love, the less anxious he becomes.

From both a theoretical and a practical point of view a very important question arises here: is normal love, of the kind sketched above, necessarily confined to one person? The answer depends on the stage. In the early periods, of attachment and admiration, there is only one mother and one father, and the child loves only one person of each sex. At puberty, however, where the primary characteristic of love is physical enjoyment, over-attachment to one person is hardly to be expected; the similarities are too great, the differences too small. In the next stage, that of total enjoyment, the choice becomes much narrower. Here one can ordinarily expect concentration on one person, but often for practical reasons, rather than as a compulsion. Finally, in the parental stage, devotion to one's own children could be expected to be the rule.

The above discussion raises many questions relating to love and the social order. In our culture the emphasis is on conformity rather than love. Indeed, there is reason to believe that psychoanalysis appeals to those who wish to love, rather than those who merely wish to conform, or those who seek power. Further, love is supposed to be confined to marriage, yet all experience indicates how difficult it is to achieve such a limitation. If love is a development within the individual, it eventually becomes a power of the subject, rather than an attraction exerted by the object, i.e., if John loves Mary, it is primarily because John has the capacity to love, and not because Mary is so unusual or so attractive.

But if love is the capacity of an individual to enjoy others, then an entirely new social climate is created. The psychotherapist deals with people who wish to love and be loved; he helps them to shift from a neurotic to a normal kind of love. Inevitably, such people will demand social conditions that gratify these increasing demands for love.

SEX

Normal sex is of course closely related to love, so that much of what was said in the previous section applies here. Nevertheless, there are certain specific questions with regard to sexuality which must be considered. By and large, as with love, psychotherapy helps the patient shift from neurotic to normal sex. Analysis reveals that the great majority of patients who come to treatment (and indeed, so far as can be seen, the great majority of people in our society) suffer from a variety of sexual complaints: premature ejaculation, fear of sex, frigidity, impotence, latent homosexuality, to mention only the most important. These disturbances for the most part yield rather readily to treatment. The patient's libido increases; he (or she) has more enjoyment in sex and a greater desire for it.

Concentration upon the details of the sexual experience usually reveals difficulties, the analysis of which leads to their disappearance and a consequence increase in pleasure. It is commonly found that even patients who come to treatment without any specific sexual complaints soon report that their sex lives are much more enjoyable than ever before.

By now it is widely accepted that for those who are not married, sex is a normal form of gratification, and little stigma is attached to it. Guilt feelings about such activities can be analyzed away with relatively little difficulty. At the same time the unmarried person who has a series of sexual affairs often finds himself dissatisfied with this state. After a certain point he derives less and less pleasure from this way of life, and begins to yearn for a more permanent relationship. This is part of the growth of love from physical to total enjoyment. Thus, a satisfactory marriage becomes a therapeutic goal for these patients, not because they need sex, but because it leads to a deeper sense of fulfillment.

For the majority of married couples, extramarital sex remains the great problem. They long for it and are afraid of it at the same time. Even analysts are divided on the subject, some feeling that it is a perfectly normal and harmless search for variety, others that it is a manifestation of a deep neurotic conflict. In some marriages the partners, especially the women, repress their wishes for extramarital contact and develop many sadomasochistic character traits as a result. In others, the partners act out their wishes without understanding their meaning or reflecting on the consequences of their actions.

A proper termination of analysis would not accept either of these solutions. As in other conflict situations there must be a strong ego which can make a conscious choice. By and large the main criterion by which to evaluate an extramarital relationship is whether it interferes with the marriage. If it does, then the person is seeking immediate gratification at the expense of future trouble. If it does not, there is no good reason why the person cannot be left free to pursue his own desires. In some groups (and in some other cultures) people prefer situations in which extramarital relations are permissible.

We see here one difference between a moralistic and a psychoanalytic approach. The moralist seeks to find a rule of conduct which will apply to all people and to impose this rule in an authoritarian manner. The psychoanalyst seeks to determine whether any particular course of action will have beneficial or harmful consequences, and allows the individual to make his choice accordingly.

HATRED

Hatred or hostility, apart from its intrinsic importance, becomes a problem for a number of reasons. First of all, it leads to unfavorable reactions from others, and forces the individual to live on a permanent war footing. Second, modern research has shown that internalization of hostility has the most serious consequences, including severe illness and, on occasion, even death. And third, hatred is not self-confining. It tends to expand to the classical triad of fear, guilt, and hate, and thereby to permanently cripple adequate functioning.

The therapeutic management of hatred depends, more than in other emotional reactions, on the therapist's theoretical views. The writer sees hatred as primarily the result of frustration, rather than as an instinctual drive on a par with sexuality. Once hatred becomes entrenched, it has, of course, tremendous force. The therapeutic task is therefore to get over the underlying causes of frustration or, if that is not possible, at least to handle them differently.

An important distinction must be drawn between assertiveness and aggression. Assertiveness is an aspect of every libidinal drive, while aggression is the wish to prevail over another person (or at least for purposes of conceptual clarity the two terms should be used in this way). In people who find themselves unable to act assertively, it is usually found that assertion in their minds is mixed up with the tabooed hatred and aggression. The therapeutic task thus becomes one of separating out these two and showing that it is possible to be assertive without doing harm to others.

But what if, as so often happens, a life situation has been reached where assertiveness in some vital area of living is not possible without doing harm to someone close? For example, we frequently see instances of self-sacrificing parents who bind their children to them by making them feel guilty about their assertiveness. In these cases the child is faced with a dilemma: if he leaves, the parents will feel hurt, or may even get sick or die; if he stays, his neurotic conflicts will get steadily worse. In these cases a philosophical problem is posed, in which the good to oneself has to be weighed against the hurt inflicted on others. It should be added, however, that in many such cases the hurt that would supposedly be done to others is exaggerated by childhood fantasies.

WORK

Work is part of the identity problem. It is of such fundamental importance, however, that it requires special treatment. Traditionally work has been looked upon as a burden to be discarded as soon as possible. "Gentlemen" did not work; that was left to the commoners, who were of a different breed. With the social upheavals beginning with the French and American revolutions, the entire attitude towards work and leisure began to undergo a radical reevaluation. Eventually, it has reached a point in the present world situation where in both democratic and communistic countries work is regarded as a positive good.

The kind of work adjustment that is made depends very heavily on social conditions. Thus the neurotic conflicts surrounding work could be expected to take markedly different forms at different times. Even in our own society the nature of the work problem varies considerably with the profession or occupation of the patient.

Furthermore, there is a sharp difference in the meaning of work to men and women. For the man it is, as a rule, far more crucial in his whole self-image and relatedness to the world; for the woman it is, as a rule, far more peripheral. This too could change with different social conditions, but we have to consider what exists today. Hence, the two sexes will be treated separately.

Under present social conditions a man has reasonable choice about the kind of work that he will engage in. This is even more true of that part of the population which finds its way into psychotherapy. In fact, the conscious or unconscious feeling that they should be achieving more is one of the most powerful inducements that leads men into psychoanalysis.

In this climate the most common problems encountered are working under the proper level, overambition, and not deriving enough satisfaction from work. Wherever it occurs, each of these must be "worked out" (the analytic phrase is quite appropriate here). At the end of analysis work should be a source of considerable positive satisfaction to the man.

For the woman the primary area of functioning is usually that of wife and mother. Work may enter into her life in one of two ways. She may have functioned satisfactorily as a housewife and mother, and now that the children are fairly well grown up she wishes to do more with her time. Work then becomes an adjunct to the rest of her life, though it may be pursued with considerable intensity. Or the woman may fail to find real satisfaction in the traditional feminine roles, and then seeks compensation in work. Here the neurotic conflicts as a rule go deeper, since even when she is successful, work still covers up other frustrations. The therapeutic task is of course in both cases to clarify the dynamics of what is going on. Considerable choice must always be left to the patient, since social conditions are changing so rapidly that the definition of the "feminine role" is a highly fluid one.

CREATIVITY

Creativity relates to the general attitude towards life. Change, creativity, artistry have been contrasted with repetition, stereotypy, and dullness. Psychoanalysis has emphasized and explored the creative aspects of living; some, like Jung, even wish to postulate a special creative urge.

In the analysis of creativity we run up against the two perennial problems of balance and the relationship to the social order. It has been pointed out that there is an inherent contradiction in psychoanalytic thinking, which still remains unresolved. On the one hand psychoanalysis emphasizes the meaningfulness of the id, and encourages the patient to find as much gratification as possible in life. On the other hand it stresses the ego, and its capacity to control the id and either hold it in check or steer it into reality-acceptable channels. Historically, this conflict is the same as the argument between romanticism and classicism, at an earlier period the Dionysian and the Apollonian ways of life. One philosophy urges the person to have every human experience, to live life to the hilt. The other stresses stability and peace of mind. Psychoanalysis has inherited both of these strains in Western thought and rather blindly attempted to satisfy the two, without considering all the consequences.

There are two types of problems surrounding creativity in the therapeutic process, depending on the background of the patient. The noncreative person who seeks treatment for fears or inadequacies or some other inner conflict eventually discovers in analysis that there is a certain emptiness about his way of living. This is more or less inevitable, since analysis raises the person's cathectic level above that of the surrounding milieu, and thereby leaves him dissatisfied with his previous pursuits. As one patient once put it, he could no longer put up with the life of the average American, sit home every night, watch television, and throw mental bricks at his wife.

In the course of therapy this kind of person frequently finds some creative outlet which gives him new and more meaningful experiences in life. Occasionally we see a patient who develops hitherto unrecognized artistic talent; on rare occasions some may even find a new profession. These are, however, the exceptions. More common are those who change their leisure-time activity and simply get more fun out of life.

The conflicts in which the professionally creative person becomes involved are vastly more complicated. Almost invariably the creative individual sees himself in a clash with society. Shall he pursue art for art's sake, or shall he compromise and make money? And if he makes a lot of money, how does he feel about himself and his artistic ideals? This conflict may be a "neurotic" one in the sense that it stems from unrecognized childhood fantasies, or may be a normal one, inevitable in the kind of society in which he lives. Only analysis can sift out the neurotic element from the reality.

Generally speaking, the artist in analysis does not exaggerate the reality difficulties that he is forced to contend with. What he does tend to underplay or ignore are the psychological tensions which are frequently found to underlie the choice of creative activity as a profession. For in order to acquire sufficient skill at any art form to pursue it professionally, he must at some time in his life have devoted a major portion of his energy to it. This intense absorption can come about only at the expense of ordinary living, as Otto Rank pointed out thirty years ago. In therapy the reasons for retreating from ordinary living must systematically be explored.

Furthermore, creative activity almost invariably brings the artist much closer to the id than noncreative activity. And the id is still not easily tamed. When Chagall says that an obsession comes into his mind, and he then paints it, few mortals can follow his example. The obsessions and images of the artist persist and plague him and are most resistant to any attempt to be curbed. The artist thus often lives in a state of constant tension, from which he can free himself only at the expense of giving up his art. Therapy must help the artist to distinguish between the creative transformation of the id and the neurotic submission to it.

A particularly common problem with the creative artist, one that often brings him into treatment, is the sudden failure to produce—the stage fright of the actor, or the block of the writer. This revolt against creative activity can be understood readily enough in terms of the breakthrough of repressed id impulses, and usually responds quite satisfactorily to therapy.

FAMILY ROLE

In its early revolutionary period (before 1930) analysis emphasized particularly the id—how its repression led to neurosis, while gratification led to happiness. This view led to attempts in many fields to encourage release. It soon became apparent that such indiscriminate release did not achieve the hoped-for results, and theory then began to emphasize control—where the id was, the ego shall be. Still later the stress on ego functioning led off in different directions, such as ego autonomy and the capacity to engage in neutralized activity.

More recently, especially in the past decade, the emphasis has shifted further to the role the person plays within the family. Both analytic experience and social research have shown that if a person has a consistent role to which he can adhere, he is apt to find much more happiness in life than by shifting his role all the time. The most important of these roles is that in relation to the family.

It is probable that family breakup leads to a schizoid or schizophrenic personality, withdrawn, isolated, with blunted affect, autistic. One of the most astounding research findings of recent years is Harlow's series of experiments with rhesus monkeys, in which it was shown that monkeys brought up without a real mother rarely managed to perform sexually and were markedly withdrawn in many other ways. It had long been hypothesized by analysts that children deprived of parental affection grow up seriously stunted in their interpersonal relations; now the same appears to be true of monkeys as well. As a result of all this, the therapeutic goal of analysis gradually has laid increasing stress on the need to conform to a suitable role within a stable family structure.

On the other hand it seems likely that an extremely cohesive family structure leads to a certain amount of depression. The Hutterites are one example. Such a finding is readily understandable, since the process of socialization ɪᵉqᵘᵉᵉˢ the gradual abandonment of many libidinal gratifications, and in nᵒᵉᵗ wᵃys it is easier to be too strict with a child than too lenient.

Thᵘˢ, studies of the family in the past two decades point to two consistent findˑᵘgs with regard to mental health. First, an unstable family produces a sense of isolation, withdrawal, affectlessness, and frequently overt schizophrenia. Second, a stable family produces an excessive libidinal repression which manifests itself as depression or even, at times, apathy.

In regard to the family, pychoanalysis has followed the path of many another revolution. At first the family, through the Oedipus complex, was seen as the *fons et origo* of all neurosis. The therapeutic task then was to get away from the family and find pleasure. Later, especially with the shift in emphasis to the mother-child relationship, the family has come to be seen as the greatest source of stability for the individual. Increasingly people come to analysis because they have no adequate family they fit into. A recent survey made the surprising discovery that more than half of the patients who come for help to one group of agencies did so because of intense conflict within the family. However, superficial counseling to restore the *status quo ante* overlooks the fact that the repression of libidinal gratification is one of the most potent factors in family discord.

As in so many other facets of termination, the therapeutic task is to strike a balance. Few people find real satisfaction in life unless they are content with their stable family role. But this family role must not deprive them of so much gratification that they live in a state of severe libidinal repression.

THE SOCIAL ORDER

Generally speaking, the patient comes into treatment with a strong feeling of inferiority to those around him. It does not take him long to discover that friends, relatives, and acquaintances all have a variety of problems, some worse than his, even though they are not in treatment.

Further, as he makes progress, he gets into another kind of clash with his environment. He develops new hopes and aspirations for love or creativity, and then finds that his old circle may not have the faintest idea of what he is talking about. This is especially common in, say, a child who comes from a culturally deprived family, but happens to many others as well. The result is that he becomes dissatisfied with his previous world and tries to locate a better one.

At the same time this is the world that the patient lives in. In therapy the analyst cannot create a new environment; he can only help the patient handle the one in which he finds himself. Thus the practical therapeutic task becomes one of picking out those aspects of the milieu which are worthwhile for him, and rejecting the rest.

Therapy, of course, brings up many other aspects of the social order. Inasmuch as the final section of this paper will be devoted to an extensive discussion of this topic, it will be deferred until then.

COMMUNICATION

Up to now, the topics discussed are familiar ones from the history of thought. With the idea of communication as a profound need in people, however, we come upon a wholly novel idea. For as the patient goes along, he learns that the process of making the unconscious conscious leads to a kind of experience the like of which he has never really had before. At times this is verbalized in a phrase such as: "There's no one else I can talk to the way I talk to you." At other times it is not put into words but is nonetheless sensed as something vitally significant by the patient.

What is so different about psychotherapeutic communication? Two things. First, the patient talks about matters which are customarily avoided or ignored, even in his most intimate relationships. He discusses dreams, fantasies, memories, sexual experiences, feelings of hatred, seemingly bizarre thoughts of all kinds which he never gets a chance to discuss in any situation in such detail. And second, the analyst listens in a nonjudgmental manner. This capacity on the part of the therapist to be nonjudgmental is likewise virtually unknown in the patient's experience.

The question may well be raised, Is it really necessary to confine such communication to the analytic situation? Even now the example of group analysis shows that it is not limited to the one-to-one relationship. Many analyzed people dislike the emotional distance which characterizes the average social situation, even though they have to learn to live with it. As society continues to change under the impact of the insights of psychoanalysis, eventually the psychotherapeutic situation will not remain so unique.

At the present time, the therapeutic task involved is usually phrased as teaching the patient to conduct self-analysis after the formal analysis is over. The capacity for self-analysis is developed in varying degrees by different people; it is not something that can be demanded indiscriminately of all. There is, however, no good reason why when both partners in any intimate relationship, e.g., parents and children, or marriage partners, have been adequately analyzed they cannot attempt to resolve difficulties that occur after the analysis by analytic means. In addition, as the grasp of dynamic psychology spreads, the use of communication and nonjudgmental understanding, which make up the heart of the psychotherapeutic process, will spread as well. Eventually, the psychoanalytic relationship, instead of being a hiding place for the "sick," could become a model for many other human relationships.

THE PSYCHOANALYTIC PHILOSOPHY

The psychoanalytic philosophy is that man can achieve a reasonable measure of happiness. In order to do this he must (summing up the previous sections) have his age-specific needs gratified, have an adequate sense of identity, search for pleasure, learn to love, enjoy sex, reduce hatred, find satisfactory work, be creative, have an adequate family role, see the social order realistically, and be able to communicate his inner feelings.

Something must be said here about the connection between this positive philosophy of life and the negative conflicts which are usually the immediate reason why a person seeks treatment. The actual therapeutic process, of course, does not proceed by inspirational exhortations to love or work, or the like; it proceeds by a minute analysis of the fantasy productions of the patient to show how he is fixated on childhood rather than living as an adult. Nevertheless, whenever anything is traced back to its infantile origins, there is some implication of a way out. If a man is over-dependent on his mother, the assumption is that this is no longer an age-specific need, that he can get over it and relate to other women.

Nor is there any assumption here that merely verbalizing a philosophy is going to shorten the analytic process. As a rule, quite the opposite is true: the patient who talks too much of the positive values often blocks the ways in which he is refusing to grow up. The writer agrees with Freud's (1964) conclusion in "Analysis Terminable and Interminable" that deep analysis is essentially an endless process and cannot be shortened without depriving it of all its potential. Nevertheless, the positive values serve as a goal towards which the analysis can strive. And without a goal the analysis can only too easily bog down and become a mechanical procedure.

The psychoanalytic philosophy can be summed up by stating that it is a search for inner and outer adjustment. The inner adjustment aims at a positive feeling about life and a balance between gratification and stability. The outer seeks to handle the social order realistically. This involves sifting out those aspects of the social order which conform to the ideals of good living from those which do not. As an individual, the person can do little more than prefer certain aspects of the social system and ignore others. As a member of a larger group of psychoanalyzed people he can, however, join with others in transforming the social order in accordance with his ideals. Some of these points must now be considered in more detail, especially communication, family structure, and the social order.

Communication

The inner changes brought about by psychoanalysis result from communication of fantasies to another person, who is specially trained to understand them. The suggestion has already been made above that the psychoanalytic relationship could serve as a model for other human relationships, rather than a peculiar sort of hiding place.

If such a suggestion were taken seriously, it would mean that people would be encouraged to relate their innermost thoughts and feelings far more freely than is the case. Such communication would take place under one of four conditions: to oneself, to another person, to the family, and to some other group.

Self-communication is self-analysis and is certainly readily realizable; for many analyzed people it is already taking place. The greatest obstacle is the fear that forbidden thoughts or feelings arouses.

Communication of analytic material to another person is scarcely possible unless the other person has been analyzed. In some cases this takes place now; usually it does not. An obstacle enters here in terms of the analyst's attitude towards such communications. Some would no doubt be in favor. Others, however, would see it as a dilution of the transference, and either be opposed or forbid it altogether. Here, as in so many other areas under consideration in this paper, considerable discussion among analysts is necessary, to clarify the philosophy which guides them.

Even more fundamental questions are raised by the communication of analytic material to other people in groups. As has been mentioned, the existence of group analysis shows that this is feasible. As a matter of fact, in the early days of analysis, before World War I, it was quite common for analysts to tell one another their associations and dreams; Brill, for example, reports the feeling of exhilaration that he experienced when he encountered such group analysis at Burgholzli. Since then much has happened, and today group analysis would be regarded as a controversial issue among analysts.

Yet, both theoretically and practically, group analysis as a means of increasing communication is both feasible and desirable. It would break down many of the barriers which customarily keep so many people stiff and tense in social situations. Ultimately it would have a revolutionary effect on social relationships, just as individual analysis has had such a revolutionary effect on two-person relationships.

Ours has been called the age of analysis; it has also been called the age of reanalysis. Increasingly, the observation has been made that people who have seemingly made a good adjustment as a result of one analysis nevertheless encounter conflicts at a later date and go back for more. Undoubtedly, one reason for this is the social milieu into which the individual is thrust at the termination of analysis. It differs so markedly from the world of fantasy and memory from which he has emerged that he may feel as isolated as before, though for a different reason. Furthermore, analysis has frequently been such a tremendous experience to him that he only naturally drifts towards people who have had similar experiences.

In this respect it could be said that there are two types of analytic patients. One is ashamed of his treatment, keeps it a secret, and wants to get out and forget about it as soon as possible. The other recognizes that he has been exposed to a novel and vital way of living, and wishes to share it with others. It is this latter kind of person who would be particularly attracted by group analytic experience.

Group analysis requires a professional leader and a professional setting.

However, it is not necessary to take such a step all at once. It would be more sensible to begin with group discussions of significant personal experiences, such as love, sex, creativity, marriage, and the like. From here some could go on to as deep an examination of life as they desire.

In the broadest sense psychoanalysis is a secular religion which seeks to show modern man how he can find happiness. There have been other secular religions in the history of the world, that is, Stoicism and Epicureanism in Hellenistic times, and Communism in ours. The supernatural element in Buddhism appears to be so scanty that it too could perhaps qualify in the category. All these movements have attracted millions of followers, which shows that the combination of ethics and theology which typifies traditional religions is not necessary to attract adherents.

What psychoanalysis has to offer that differentiates it from the approaches of secular religions is a profound grounding in psychology. Unlike the others, it spends most of its time on clearing away the many ways (fixations, to use the technical term) in which the individual holds on to his past.

As we know, Freud himself believed that in the long run the educational contribution of psychoanalysis would far outweigh its therapeutic value. At one time he even suggested that psychoanalysts should establish institutes to teach the art of love. The ideas proposed are but a natural extension of Freud's.

The innumerable professionals and nonprofessionals who expound the theories of modern psychology and psychiatry (i.e., essentially the theories of modern psychoanalysis) to the lay public are performing an educational function of this kind. Unfortunately, psychoanalysis itself teaches that didactic lectures are of no value. There must be a personal commitment and personal participation on the part of the listener.

Such commitment and participation are feasible in terms of group discussions of vital personal problems. Here and there one hears of groups of this kind which have gone on for years with a feeling of great benefit by the participants. There is no reason why such group activity could not be given professional leadership and steered in the most constructive directions. The organizations are available in which such group discussions can be initiated—social clubs, PTA associations, and the like. All are hungry for lectures and explanations about the new psychology.

Three dangers must be avoided in such public discussions. One is to have large groups which preclude individual participation; here group analytic experience can be called on to limit the number to a maximum of ten. Second, every precaution must be taken to see to it that the persons involved take it seriously. For this it is necessary to arrange for some continuity—a series of talks rather than a single one. Then some degree of anonymity must be provided the participants, otherwise they will not feel free to reveal significant material. And last, but in a sense most important, the discussions should concentrate on personal experiences, and should avoid general topics as much as possible. Eventually, as enough people become interested in such systematic psychoanalytic talks about life, they could form centers of their own and spread the idea. These could have some appropriate name, such as Centers for Creative Living.

A fourth area in which communication can be fostered is within the family. Insofar as can now be seen, all neurotic illnesses stem from failures in communication within the family. Some therapeutic experiments, such as Bell's family therapy, have shown that even in a relatively brief time, if family members start talking to one another, dramatic changes may ensue.

Parents have been particularly alert to the findings of the new psychology, and have tried to maintain a stable and meaningful family structure in line with what the experts have taught. Most of the time, however, the emphasis has been on what to do—allow the child freer expression of aggression, be consistent in your discipline, and so on. It is necessary to make clear that, apart from anything that is done, the freedom to communicate feelings and fantasies (including dreams) is a potent factor in mental health.

Family Structure

Psychoanalysis agrees that family stability is the most potent factor in mental health, but it has argued for extensive changes within the family, and urges more now. Thus, its position is that social change should take place through reform within the family, rather than by breaking up the present family structure and trying a totally different one.

Insensibly, Freud's early writings led to a number of changes within the family structure in existence at that time. These have resulted in the attitudes commonly seen today—an emphasis on love and sexual gratification as the ideal basis for marriage, much more permissiveness towards children, especially in the early years, and a general feeling that more effective changes come about from within than from without. Nevertheless, as the situation appears today, other changes seem indicated. To begin with, it should be remembered that all the members of the family are interrelated, so that what happens to one affects all. Each one must have an adequate and enduring sense of identity; otherwise all will suffer.

Marriage itself has come under heavy attack from many directions in the present century. Anarchists regarded it as a needless assertion of authority. Marxists saw it as a device of exploiting women. Early Freudians saw it as a defense against sexual pleasure. The numerous social upheavals of the past 50 years have made it physically impossible for large numbers of people to either be married or stay married. It is no wonder then that the meaning of marriage has been under constant scrutiny, and that the identifications within the family have been constantly changing.

Psychoanalysis has of course devoted considerable thought to the kinds of family environment that make for neurosis and those that make for mental health. By and large, all of the previous discussion is relevant. Perhaps most basic of all is the idea that the family should be based on love and harmony rather than hatred and discord. The meaning of these two different kinds of love and marriage is beautifully sketched by two poets. In one, Christopher Marlowe writes rhapsodically:

> Come live with me and be my love,
> And we will all the pleasures prove.
> That valleys, groves, hills and fields,
> Woods, or steepy mountain yields
> And we will sit upon the rocks
> Seeing the shepherds feed their flocks,
> By shallow rivers, to whose falls
> Melodious birds sing madrigals.
> And I will make thee beds of roses
> And a thousand fragrant posies,
> A cap of flowers, and a kirtle
> Embroidered all with leaves of myrtle.
>
> A gown made of the finest wool,
> Which from our pretty lambs we pull;
> Fair lined slippers for the cold,
> With buckles of the purest gold.
>
> A belt of straw and ivy-buds
> With coral clasps and amber studs;
> And if these pleasures may thee move,
> Come live with me and by me love.
>
> The Shepherd swains shall dance and sing
> For thy delight each May morning:
> If these delights thy mind may move
> Then live with me and be my love.

In sharp contrast to this is the bitter satire by C. Day Lewis:

> Come, live with me and be my love,
> And we will all the pleasures prove
> Of peace and plenty, bed and board,
> That chance employment may afford.
>
> I'll handle dainties on the docks
> And thou shalt read of summer frocks:
> At evening by the sour canals
> We'll hope to hear some madrigals.
>
> Care on thy maiden brow shall put
> A wreath of wrinkles, and thy foot
> Be shod with pain: not silken dress
> But toil shall tire thy loveliness.

Hunger shall make thy modest zone
And cheat fond death of all but love—
If these delights thy mind may move,
Then live with me and be my love.

The poets have put their fingers on one aspect of marriage too often neglected by the psychologists—the economic. What we have to say about reform within the family applies most to the affluent society. Where there is grinding poverty, either in society as a whole, or in certain classes, the psychological factor necessarily becomes secondary to the economic. Unfortunately, the psychologist is limited in any further comment about the economic situation, since it is not within his professional competence.

Within the average middle-class family seen in our society, certain problems persistently recur. The dominant picture is that of the domineering mother, the weak father, and the insecure children. It could be said that psychoanalysis is trying to change this pattern somewhat along the following lines:

1. The mother is often self-sacrificing and bossy. She has no life of her own. To some extent the analytic doctrine of tender love and care has brought her to this state. Mainly, however, it derives from a denial of pleasure, especially sexual frigidity. She rejects the husband in favor of the children because she anticipates too little gratification from him.

2. The father, rejected by the mother, turns to other gratifications. (It is noteworthy how often the "golf widow" appears in jokes.) He may turn to the children, and try to give them the love and care he has missed in his own life. He may turn to work, and try to make up in money what he lacks in love. Often he turns to other women, who reassure him without giving permanent gratification. To the outsider he looks weak and ineffectual, unable to assert himself in his own house.

3. The children are made to feel guilty by the constant sacrifices of their parents. Furthermore, quite often one parent or the other demands love from them to make up what is not forthcoming from the spouse. They may become much too demanding, fearful that independence will leave them deprived of love.

The reform within the family involves shifts all around. Basically, the parents must learn to retain their affection for one another, and not drift apart. When they assert themselves as individuals, the children respect them more and have better identification figures. The cycle of sacrifice (mother)—withdrawal (father)—guilt (child) can be changed to enjoyment (mother)—desire (father)—pride (child).

The Social Order

In various passages above, a number of references have been made to the social order. It is time now to subject the question of the relationship of psychoanalysis to society to a more systematic inquiry.

By now, the interrelationship of personality and culture is well established.

In terms of our immediate concern—the goals of psychoanalysis—it is most important to recognize here that "neurosis" is a vague and virtually meaningless concept. It is a truism that what is neurotic in one culture is normal in another.

If contemporary society is compared with the analytic ideal sketched above, many discrepancies are found. Age-specific needs are ignored. Millions have no clear sense of identity. Pleasure is looked upon as wicked in large circles. Love is either a childhood fixation or conspicuous by its absence. Hatred is widespread. Sexual frustration is rampant. A considerable number of people regard work as drudgery. The creative experience is foreign to millions. Many see no clear-cut role for themselves in the family. A larger sense of kinship, in terms of a feeling about the social order, is more often absent than present. The inability to communicate is so pronounced that the schizoid personality has become the rule rather than the exception.

In short, there is a wide gap between the reality and the analytic ideal. The phenomenal growth of psychotherapy is due to the increasing recognition of this gap, not to any epidemic outbreak of mental illness. Recent studies have even turned up the surprising result that a phenomenally high percentage of the population manifests the most serious kind of disturbance. Investigators find 50, 60, even 80 percent of the population grossly maladjusted. Again, it must be assumed that this has always been the case, and that the finding is due to improved instruments rather than any increase in illness.

Neurosis is defined in the analytic sense as distance from the ideal; then it can be said to affect 99 percent of the population. Thus, the essential thesis of this paper emerges: *The ultimate goal of psychoanalysis is the reform of society.*

In comparison with other attempts at social reform, the psychoanalytic is gradual, evolutionary rather than revolutionary. The many years we are compelled to spend with one person to produce an effective change in itself would create a feeling of caution about any sudden transformation. Unconscious psychological attitudes cannot disappear overnight, and the psychoanalyst can readily understand the frequency with which revolutions have eaten their own children.

The analytic reform of society operates through the individual, though the relationship of the individual to the institution has to be evaluated in each instance. Even if only one person changes, society has been altered to that extent, though of course it is usually meaningless in the larger scheme of things. But once enough individuals have changed, a real reorganization of the social order begins to take shape.

Naturally the psychoanalyst recognizes that social forces can swamp any individual or small group. What this means, however, is that on many issues the majority view tends to prevail. To this two exceptions must be made. First, a minority can frequently continue to press its position until it has become a majority. And second, very often the major concessions may be made to the minority opinion, or it may eventually even be incorporated by the majority in the course of time.

In order to approach social problems with any prospect of success, it is necessary to have a large amount of factual information. As a rule, this information is not available to the analyst. Accordingly, when he offers ex cathedra opinions, he often exposes himself to justifiable derision. For example, the notion that anti-Semitism is due to the Christian's fear of circumcision, which unconsciously means castration, is an obvious absurdity, yet it has been seriously put forth.

Nevertheless, the situation is entirely different if the psychoanalyst or psychoanalytically trained psychologist is able to marshal the relevant facts. Then he is as expert as anyone else in the particular problem, and has the additional—and weighty—advantage of being able to appraise what role the psychological factor plays. Gradually, the social sciences are being brought around to such a point of view, and the psychological element is being given increasing weight in the evaluation of social situations.

The idea that psychoanalysis ultimately is a vehicle of social reform meets with unexpected support and unexpected opposition. Support of course comes from those elements in our society which derive from the liberal-humanistic tradition of western civilization. For psychoanalysis is but another facet of the scientific revolution which has had such a major influence in making modern man what he is. The values of psychoanalysis are the values of humanism: pleasure, creativity, work, even communication in one sense. What is foreign to the humanist are the startling psychological discoveries of psychoanalysis —the unconscious, psychosexual development, transference, the ubiquity of neurosis, and so on. Once he is exposed to the evidence for the propositions of psychoanalysis, however, and considers them with an open mind, he gradually tends to accept them, though often enough in watered-down form. This slowly growing acceptance by scholars from other disciplines has been part of the whole evolution of psychoanalysis. It can be anticipated that this process will continue.

Unexpected opposition comes from within the ranks of psychoanalysis itself. It is argued that psychotherapy has learned how to help individuals; it should not presume further. It is maintained that our society is not as bad as some extremists would have us believe, and that the best that the patient can hope for is a reasonable adjustment to it. These arguments cannot be answered in a paper such as the present, which is after all essentially the statement of one man's position. Nonetheless, it seems likely that most psychoanalysts prefer to remain aloof from social-philosophical issues because they do not know where such involvement will get them, rather than because of any basic disagreement with what has been described here as the analytic ideal. And in addition many are so immersed in the numerous pressing tasks that face them, that they have little leisure or inclination to grope with the larger philosophical problems.

Finally, though it may seem quite Utopian in the present precarious state of the world, the question may be raised as to what role the psychoanalyst would play if society could be transformed in accordance with the analytic ideal. Certainly, it could be anticipated that the extensive need for treatment existing today would diminish considerably. Hopefully such a reform within the family would eliminate a large number of neurotic conflicts. Still, the world is never ideal, and some would surely remain. Some need for therapy would, therefore, always exist.

But far more important would be the analyst's role as a teacher and supervisor of the normal growth process. His function would be primarily prophylactic—he would guide the whole process of development, from birth to maturity, at home and in the schools. Whenever anything went wrong, it would be his job to detect the first warning signals and to take appropriate action.

On matters of importance, Freud once said, your heart, not your head must be trusted. The psychotherapist should hold on to his fervent conviction that it is within the power of his profession to bring mental health to mankind.

SUMMARY

1. This paper attempts to clarify the concept of growth which is inherent in psychoanalysis. Such a clarification leads to a formulation of the psychoanalytic way of life, or what is referred to as the analytic ideal.

2. A comparison is drawn between the religious approach to living and the psychoanalytic. By and large religion employs a variety of pleasure-denying and authority-submitting devices, which serve to reduce anxiety. Psychoanalysis resorts to pleasure-affirming and authority-dissolving devices which make for greater growth but temporarily, or at times even permanently, expose the individual to more anxiety.

3. The analytic ideal is discussed via eleven topics that are central to the philosophy of living. These are age-specific needs, identity, pleasure, love, sex, hatred, work, creativity, family role, the social order, and communication.

4. For the best summary description of accumulated knowledge about age-specific needs reference is made to Erikson's epigenetic scheme.

5. The sense of identity is undoubtedly the most important single aspect of the personality structure. It is intimately related to the degree of gratification experienced in the sexual (including love) role.

6. The psychotherapist asserts unequivocally that pleasure is good.

7. Love is the acme of gratification with another person. A scheme of development of love feelings is sketched. Five stages are distinguished: attachment, admiration, physical enjoyment, total enjoyment, and devotion. Much of what is called love is not love in the analytic sense, but a neurotic fixation appropriate to some earlier age level.

8. As with love, psychotherapy helps the patient shift from neurotic to normal sex. The liberation seen in many people turns out to be apparent rather than real, and the need for real sexual growth remains as great as ever.

9. Hatred is the result of frustration and has highly undesirable conse-

quences. A distinction must be drawn between assertiveness, a normal component of any drive, and aggression, defined as the wish to hurt others—assertiveness without aggression is possible.

10. Work is part of the identity problem. It is viewed as a positive good. The role of work varies in the psychic economy of the two sexes.

11. Creativity is a positive good in living. In our society it poses fewer problems for the person who does not work in a creative field than for one who does.

12. A secure role within the family makes a vital contribution to mental health.

13. The psychoanalyzed person inevitably finds himself at odds with many aspects of the social order. He learns to handle society realistically, avoiding both senseless conformity and blind rebellion.

14. The communication experience in the psychoanalytic process opens a wholly new world to the patient. It is the most original contribution of psychoanalysis to the ideal way of living.

15. In sum, the psychoanalytic philosophy believes that man can achieve a reasonable measure of happiness. In order to do this, he must have his age-specific needs gratified, have an adequate sense of identity, search for pleasure, learn to love, enjoy sex, reduce hatred, find satisfactory work, be creative, have an adequate family role, see the social order realistically, and be able to communicate his inner feelings.

16. The psychoanalytic relationship could serve as a model for other human relationships, rather than a peculiar sort of hiding place.

17. The family structure is the most potent factor for mental health, but extensive changes are needed in it.

18. When compared with the analytic ideal, contemporary society is found to be sadly deficient. Even in terms of gross symptomatology, pathology is extraordinarily high.

19. In the light of everything said before, the central thesis of this paper emerges: the ultimate goal of psychoanalysis is the reform of society.

REFERENCES

Day-Lewis, C. *A time to dance.* Reprinted by permission of Harold Matson Co., Inc.
Erikson, E. Identity and the life cycle. In *Psychological Issues.* Vol. 1, No. 1. New York: International Universities Press, 1959.
Freud, S. Analysis terminable and interminable. In *S. Freud, Standard edition of the complete psychological works of.* . . . Vol. 23. London: The Hogarth Press and the Institute of Psycho-Analysis, 1964. Pp. 209–253.

8

The Therapeutic Aims of
Direct Psychoanalysis

John N. Rosen, M.D.

An Introduction to the Person

by Charles T. Sullivan

The name of John N. Rosen is associated with "direct psychoanalysis," which he developed for the treatment of psychotics (Brooklyn State Hospital, 1943–1944; New York State Psychiatric Institute and Hospital, 1944–1945). Rosen demonstrated that many so-called "deteriorated" or "hopeless" cases could be treated effectively with new techniques based upon the discoveries of Freud, Abraham, Federn (who suggested the term "direct psychoanalysis"), and others. His early publications, brought together in *Direct Analysis: Selected Papers,* described some of his technical innovations and indicated some of the theoretic and prognostic implications of his work.

Initially, Rosen's contributions were doubted or derided. The preceding generation of psychiatrists had tried the psychoanalytic approach (e.g., Burgholzli Mental Hospital, Zurich, 1902–1910; Manhattan State Hospital, 1908–1913) and had concluded that relatively few institutionalized patients were amenable to psychoanalysis. Rosen's contemporaries were infatuated with the "somatic" approach, particularly with lobotomy, insulin shock, and electroshock treatment. Consequently, Rosen got little encouragement either from Freudians or from anti-Freudians as he persisted in the development of direct psychoanalysis. It was not until 1956, with the establishment of the Institute for Direct Analysis (Temple University Medical Center, Philadelphia), that his work was given any prolonged and serious study. The research activities of the

Institute and the publications resulting from them have clarified many aspects of direct psychoanalysis.

The actual John Rosen is remarkably different from the legendary figure which often bears his name. He is an effective teacher and counsellor, a discreet confidant, and a diplomat in delicate situations. Rosen belongs, with Freud, in the company of those who have made psychiatry more truly *psychiatric*. To quote Hippocrates: "Physicians are many in title but very few in reality.... First of all, a natural talent is required; for, when Nature opposes, everything else is in vain. ...." This continues to be a troublesome fact of psychiatric life, for the demands upon the talented are great, the resentment of them is bitter, and the substitutes for them—the emotional "medicines" we seek—are not yet operational.

THE purpose of this chapter is to discuss the therapeutic aims of direct psychoanalysis. In the course of this discussion, certain other aspects of direct psychoanalysis will also be mentioned; but the chapter presupposes that the reader will already have some familiarity with our theory and our techniques. For additional information about these other aspects of direct psychoanalysis, the reader may wish to consult such works as those by Brody (1959), English and associates (1961), Scheflen (1961), and Rosen (1962b).

In essence, direct psychoanalysis is a Freudian method of psychiatry. It was developed originally (Rosen, 1946) for the understanding and treatment of psychotic individuals. More recently (Rosen, 1962a) its development has extended to the understanding and treatment of neurotic individuals as well. As direct psychoanalysis has been extended and refined over the last two decades, its therapeutic aims have changed somewhat. The first part of this chapter will indicate what these changes have been. The second part of the chapter will present and discuss our current formulation of therapeutic aims. The third part will contrast the therapeutic aims of direct psychoanalysis with those of other procedures, e.g., conventional psychoanalysis and pharmacotherapy. In conclusion, the fourth part of this chapter will discuss the achievement of our therapeutic aims and the ways in which we attempt to measure this achievement.

HISTORICAL BACKGROUND

An early reference to the therapeutic aims of direct psychoanalysis was made in my paper on the resolution of catatonic excitement. I introduced the description of several cases (1946, p. 29) with the following statement:

The author has applied certain basic psychoanalytic concepts to penetrate the psychotic systems of individuals in acute catatonic excitement in an attempt to aid them to re-establish contact with reality through the medium of their contact with him. In order to establish such contact, the author deliberately assumed the identity, or identities, of the figures which appeared to be threatening the patient, and reassured the latter that, far from threatening him, they would love and protect him.

Shortly thereafter, I came to understand the psychotic's receptivity to this kind of treatment in terms of *transference*, and so, in spite of Freud's conviction that the psychotic individual is incapable of transference, I found it necessary to revise my formulation of therapeutic aims. "The task is not completed with the resolution of the psychosis," I said (1947, p. 44), "and can only be considered concluded when the transference is as completely worked out as we aim to do in ordinary analytic procedures." I viewed the direct psychoanalytic treatment of the psychotic as having two parts, the first part aiming to resolve the regressive, dream-like, or *nightmarish* aspects of the psychosis— as I had originally learned to do with individuals in acute catatonic excitement. "The second part," I said (1947, p. 71), "is a more orthodox form of psychoanalysis, where the aim is to construct a stable personality and a mature character." I was able to demonstrate the effectiveness of this two-part treatment not only with "catatonic" individuals, but also with individuals who might be diagnosed as "hebephrenics" and as "paranoid schizophrenics." My report (1947, pp. 44–96) on the results obtained in 37 cases was published in *The Psychiatric Quarterly* together with an illuminating discussion by Paul Federn, Jule Eisenbud, Paul Hoch, and other psychiatrists and psychoanalysts.

At that time, I had been observing many individuals whose brains had been "numbed" by electroshock treatment, so that, temporarily, they appeared to be "recovered" from psychosis. Since electroshock treatment was much in vogue during the 1940's, many individuals were discharged from institutions in this quiescent state, only to appear to be fully psychotic again, as soon as the physical effects of the treatment had worn off. To distinguish results of this kind from the results of direct psychoanalytic treatment, I defined the "recovery" of the psychotic individual in the following terms (1947, p. 46):

It does not mean merely that the patient is able to live comfortably outside an institution, but rather that such a degree of integrity is achieved that the emotional stability of the patient and his personality and character-structures are so well organized as to withstand at least as much environmental assault as is expected of a normal person, that is, of a person who never experienced a psychotic episode.

This definition was based largely upon my experience in the 37 cases mentioned earlier. With direct psychoanalytic treatment, all of these individuals recovered from psychosis—the first part of the treatment lasting, on the average, about four months—and most of them remained free of psychosis for at least five years thereafter, according to information which I obtained in 1952.

This experience led me to conclude that direct psychoanalytic treatment could confer upon the psychotic individual something analogous to the "immunization" which medicine can confer in dealing with certain kinds of physical disease, such as smallpox. I first used this analogy (Rosen, 1951) in 1950, when addressing the New York Psychoanalytic Society on the *optimum conditions* for direct psychoanalytic treatment of psychotic individuals. By these optimum conditions, I meant: (1) no exposure to shock therapy; (2) no institutional incarceration; (3) no substantial loss of the capacity to verbalize, however bizarre the verbalizations might seem to be. Granted these optimum conditions, it was my experience that the psychotic individual would in most cases recover to a very comfortable level of maturity. There would be a continuing relationship with the psychiatrist, perhaps, but this relationship would ordinarily be limited to occasional professional visits and infrequent visits of a social nature, and to the friendly exchange of good news or holiday greetings in telephone calls, cards, or letters.

The concept of optimum conditions and the analogy with immunization were discussed (Whitaker, 1958) at the Sea Island Conference of 1955, where my fellow-participants included Gregory Bateson, Thomas P. Malone, and Carl A. Whitaker. Malone (Whitaker, 1958, pp. 190–191) commented: "Our experience in Atlanta is exactly like yours and confirms it totally. If the patients have not had abusive treatment, they get well fast and they stay well." In retrospect, I would say that the therapeutic aims of direct psychoanalysis were, at that time, conceived mainly in terms of rapid recovery of psychotic individuals from the more regressed phases of psychosis, followed by more conventional psychoanalytic work to educate and strengthen the individual against a possible recurrence of psychosis. I emphasized the rapidity of treatment, and I aimed toward the psychiatric equivalent of vaccination or immunization. At the Sea Island Conference (Whitaker, 1958, p. 195), I said:

The recoverable patients are really surprisingly easy to reach—that is why I, for the first time in fifteen years, envision a hope. If there could be set up all over the United States psychiatric first-aid stations manned by personnel capable of reaching and reversing the early psychotic trend, perhaps there need be no hopeless cases.

Similar views have been expressed, more recently, in the final report (1961) of the Joint Commission on Mental Illness and Health, *Action for Mental Health,* and elsewhere (Kubie, 1961; Robinson, 1963).

I had these therapeutic aims in mind when the Institute for Direct Analysis was established, in 1956, at Temple University Medical Center. The Institute was a research facility for the multidisciplinary study of various aspects of direct psychoanalysis, for instance, the "techniques" used in treating psychotics, the therapeutic results of treatment, and the possibilities of teaching direct psychoanalysis to psychiatric residents and other young or mid-career psychiatrists. At the same time, the Institute provided a kind of laboratory for formulating and testing various concepts and hypotheses, for instance, the concept of optimum conditions, or the hypothesis that direct psychoanalysis can, in some sense, "immunize" the recovered individual against the recurrence of psychosis. Although the therapeutic aims of direct psychoanalysis did not constitute a focal area of research at the Institute, they were discussed to some extent by many of the research personnel. While I was functioning primarily as a kind of guinea pig in this research, I took the opportunity to reconsider my formulation of many aspects of direct psychoanalysis, in particular its therapeutic aims and the unique "parent-child" relationship—between the psychiatrist and the neoinfantile psychotic—in which these aims are best pursued.

From my point of view, it appears that the conception of the direct psychoanalytic treatment unit as a kind of psychiatric first-aid station can be supported by the results obtained in treatment at the Institute. Since the treatment sessions were always conducted in the presence of assistants, researchers, and students, ranging in numbers from a minimum of three or four to dozens, scores, or even hundreds on occasion, it might be inferred that even better results would be obtained with a more relaxed and more personal atmosphere.

However, in the course of this experience at the Institute for Direct Analysis, it became apparent to me that my therapeutic aims had been somewhat overoptimistic in regard to the psychotic individual's capacity for absolute strengthening or improvement. As I have stated elsewhere (1962b, p. 62), "We do not maintain that we attempt or succeed in producing a splendid personality through psychotherapy. To put it bluntly, we cannot make a silk purse out of a sow's ear." In other words, we work with the material at hand. Psychotic individuals, like nonpsychotic ones, can be different from one another with infinite variety. They vary in their capacity to withstand emotional stress, for instance, and in their capacity to acquire conscious "insight" into their difficulties; they vary in education, in appearance, in "charm," in job skills and aptitudes, and in many other ways. Most of these differences, whether they originate in hereditary endowment or in environmental circumstances, are simply beyond the reach of psychiatric intervention as we know it. We cannot, indeed, make a silk purse out of a sow's ear, nor could we do the opposite. Psychosis, the common denominator of these individuals, does not make them equal to one another, or equally accessible and responsive to our treatment.

With these considerations before us, let us now discuss a current formulation of the therapeutic aims of direct psychoanalysis. This discussion will include not only our aims with respect to individuals who are psychotic, but also our aims with respect to those who are "neo-neurotic" (no longer psychotic) and those who are neurotic without ever having been psychotic.

A CURRENT FORMULATION OF THE THERAPEUTIC AIMS OF DIRECT PSYCHOANALYSIS

In the most general sense, direct psychoanalysis aims at restoring to manifest "normality" the individual who is manifestly "abnormal." As I stated in *Direct Psychoanalytic Psychiatry* (1962b, p. 6):

We define being "normal" as getting along in society, and being "abnormal" as failing to get along. The "normal" individual is one who conforms at least within the limits of social tolerance. This definition includes both the individual who conforms tolerably without thinking much about it, and the individual who manages to conform outwardly, despite his nonconformist tendencies.

We find this social-behavioral definition of "normality" and of our therapeutic aims to be adequate for our regular usage. It has several advantages over more elaborate or more sophisticated definitions. First, it is readily understandable to the individuals whom we treat, as they approach recovery, and it is readily understandable to their families and friends. Second, it is readily understandable to psychiatrists of different persuasions, even if they do not agree with it. Third, it is readily understandable to representatives of disciplines other than psychiatry, whether they be anthropologists, philosophers, or policemen.

In a more specific sense, and more in keeping with its Freudian orientation toward psychosis and neurosis, direct psychoanalysis aims at restoring to psychical cohesion, or integrity, the individual whose psyche is evidently nonintegrated or disintegrated. We view this disintegration of the psyche as a continuous process. In the psychotic individual, this process of disintegration seems to correspond with the series of "phases" of psychosis which I have described elsewhere (1962b, pp. 53–57). Before he became psychotic, this individual was neurotic; and neurosis, too, seems to include various phases which would correspond with various degrees of disintegration of the psyche. As he ceases to be psychotic, under the influence of our treatment, this individual becomes "neo-neurotic." He experiences a neurosis comparable to his prepsychotic neurosis. His further recovery can be described in terms of a gradual reintegration of the psyche.

Wherever we find the individual as treatment commences—in whatever "phase" of neurosis or psychosis he seems to be located—we try to estimate the extent to which his psyche is disintegrated. Our plan of treatment always takes this consideration into account.

What do we mean by "nonintegration" or "disintegration" of the psyche? We view the psyche, as Freud described it, as consisting of ego, superego, and id. These three components are capable of such close integration that they can be virtually indistinguishable from one another. As Anna Freud (1936, p. 6) has remarked "The super-ego, like the id, becomes perceptible in the state which it produces within the ego: for instance, when its criticism evokes a sense of guilt." In other words, nonintegration or disintegration is experienced by the ego, as a distancing from itself of the superego or, as the case may be, of the id. It is probably an unconscious portion of the ego which experiences this distancing per se; the conscious experience of the individual would be something like the "sense of guilt" which Anna Freud gives as her example. An outsider, even if he is psychoanalytically sophisticated, cannot perceive the actual state of the psyche's integrity; he can only estimate it on the basis of the individual's observable behavior, which is susceptible to understanding and interpretation on many occasions.

In the present discussion of therapeutic aims, I will only indicate briefly our understanding of why this psychical disintegration occurs in some individuals, and our understanding of the appropriate steps to be taken in direct psychoanalytic treatment. Briefly, then, we understand that certain individuals are poorly integrated, psychically, because their superegos are virtually unassimilable by their egos. In our theory, unlike Freud's, the superego is acquired from the individual's "early maternal environment," and it functions primarily as a representative of the mother and the mothering he knew. Inadequate mothering—which can be deficient in some respects and excessive in other respects—gives rise to an inadequate, unassimilable superego. As the individual struggles to reach maturity, he is crippled by his ego's inability to integrate with his superego. Direct psychoanalysis, in a word, attempts to improve the individual's chances for psychical integrity by reducing the malevolent influence of the existing superego. At the same time, it seeks to introduce a more benevolent influence by encouraging the individual to identify with a "good foster mother," i.e., with the direct psychoanalyst himself. For a more complete discussion of these points, the reader is referred to my other publications (1962b; 1963b).

Our psychodynamic formulation of therapeutic aims, in terms of the reintegration of a disintegrated psyche, is compatible with the social-behavioral formulation which we presented earlier. The psychotic individual, whose psyche is extensively disintegrated, cannot consistently conduct himself within the limits of social tolerance. This would hold true even in a society composed entirely of psychotics, no matter what the local standards of normality and abnormality might be; for psychosis is, among other things, an *asocial* condition or orientation. The psychotic individual is *inwardly* oriented, for the most part. He is correspondingly indifferent, for the most part, to *outward* circumstances. He may not hesitate to walk through a stranger's living room or some other socially off-limits place. Sooner or later, he is going to walk into trouble.

The "neo-neurotic" individual, whose psyche is not yet integrated or reintegrated, may get into trouble with his family, his friends and neighbors, or his employer and fellow employees, if he is sent back among them too soon. In direct psychoanalysis, we try to minimize the risks by sending the individual on a series of trial visits, at first with the company of one or more of our assistant therapists, and with the close surveillance of the psychiatrist in charge. Even with such precautions, there still may be unpleasant incidents, or worse; our best hope is to use every therapeutic device that may keep these unfortunate developments to a minimum. Incidentally, we reserve the term "neo-neurotic" for individuals who have been treated by direct psychoanalysis. These individuals are not to be confused with the prematurely-discharged men and women who may commit murder or mayhem within hours after leaving the grounds of their hospital.

The neurotic individual who has never been psychotic is somewhat comparable to the "neo-neurotic," with regard to the relatively moderate disintegration of his psyche. But unlike the "neo-neurotic" individual, the ordinary neurotic has not undergone the double experience of being psychotic and being treated by direct psychoanalysis in that condition; the ordinary neurotic may be receiving some other kind of psychotherapy, or he may not be receiving treatment of any kind. As a rule, this individual may be able to conform within the limits of social tolerance, as long as these limits do not conflict with his particular neurotic manifestations. Conflict arises when, for example, an individual with claustrophobia is forced to ride in a small and crowded elevator in order to reach his office, or when, for another example, a drug addict lacks the money to support his addiction. Then, in a sense, the individual is forced to choose between intolerable anxiety and inconvenient social mores or restrictions. In most instances, the ego will elect to avoid anxiety by breaking the rules. Even if this choice results in a new experience of anxiety, chances are that it will be relatively less severe than the anxiety which a breach of the neurosis would arouse.

Before concluding this part of the discussion, I will take note of some other comments which have been made concerning the therapeutic aims of direct psychoanalysis. I will confine my attention to a few of the more recent ones; others have been discussed elsewhere (Rosen, 1962b, pp. 62–63; 237–240) and need not be reiterated here.

J. H. Pathman (1960, p. 344) seems to regard direct psychoanalysis as "juggernaut therapy." His supporting remarks are worthy of being quoted at some length, since they illustrate the emotional bias of the commentator who has taken no opportunity to observe direct psychoanalysis for himself.

Direct analysis utilizes a primitiveness of transactions between the patient and therapist. . . . In reading the verbatim interaction between the patient and therapist, one may recoil in dismay and view the treatment as brutal and sadistic or bizarre and shocking. . . . Of importance are the reactions of the supporting personnel who are present at the sessions and who like a Greek chorus chant (symbolically) in the background. . . . Dispassionate and objective procedures are strangers in this arena.

M. Wexler (1962, pp. 171–173) takes an altogether different tack; he denies "that there really exists some organized theory and technique to be subsumed under the title 'direct analysis'," yet he warns against its "difficulties, weaknesses, and dangers," and he suggests "that the clinical effectiveness of direct analysis is on a par with the therapeutic impact of a good state hospital." He implies that direct psychoanalysis aims at the "remission of psychotic symptoms," and he refers to "a paternalistic, authoritarian demand for improvement," but he gives no suggestions as to how the psychotic individual is able to remit his psychosis or his symptoms on demand. A more deliberate study, by E. J. Murray (1962), discusses direct psychoanalysis from the viewpoint of learning theory, in terms of rewards (for more mature behavior) and punishments (for more psychotic behavior). Having made this distinction,

Murray indicates his preference for the use of rewards, rather than punishments, in the reeducation of the psychotic individual. His views are perhaps typical of the learning-theory approach (Parsons, 1963, p. 613), where "much of the literature, in both the animal and human areas, indicates that reward is more effective in changing behavior than punishment." They are not in harmony with the psychoanalytic approach, where much of the literature indicates that the superego relies primarily or exclusively upon punishment in changing the behavior of the ego. It should be understood, of course, that direct psychoanalysis utilizes primarily *verbal* rewards and punishments in its reeducation of the psychotic.

A COMPARISON OF THE THERAPEUTIC AIMS OF DIRECT PSYCHOANALYSIS WITH THOSE OF OTHER PROCEDURES

It may help to illuminate the therapeutic aims of direct psychoanalysis if we compare them with the therapeutic aims of other procedures, e.g., conventional psychoanalysis and pharmacotherapy.

Conventional psychoanalysis, in the treatment of neurotics, emphasizes the exploration of the individual's psyche. Its therapeutic aims are described usually in psychodynamic terms, rather than in social-behavioral terms. Thus, according to C. P. Oberndorf (1953, pp. 242–243): "Psychoanalysis differs from other forms of therapy in that it attempts a reconstruction of the personality rather than a limited goal of symptom relief."

The details of this "reconstruction" have been specified by Freud, in somewhat different ways at different times in his career. His paper on "Psycho-Analysis" (1923, p. 251) includes the following statement:

It may be laid down that the aim of the treatment is to remove the patient's resistances and to pass his repressions in review and thus to bring about the most far-reaching unification and strengthening of his ego, to enable him to save the mental energy which he is expending upon internal conflicts, to make the best of him that his inherited capacities will allow and so to make him as efficient and as capable of enjoyment as possible. The removal of the symptoms of the illness is not specifically aimed at, but is achieved, as it were, as a by-product if the analysis is properly carried through.

In certain respects, this is not unlike the statement of the therapeutic aims of direct psychoanalysis which was made earlier in the present paper. For instance, it refers to "unification and strengthening" of the individual's ego, as our statement refers to the reintegration of his psyche; and it refers to the limitations imposed by the individual's "inherited capacities," as our statement does also. But Freud puts great emphasis upon the individual's conscious recollection of past traumata, as if this recollecting were in itself therapeutic. Franz Alexander (1959, p. 322) said that "Freud never changed his view that remembering of repressed traumatic situations is the ultimate goal."

We deny that such remembering or recollecting is the essence of effective psychotherapy, either for the neurotic individual or for the psychotic. Accordingly, we view conventional psychoanalysis as a method of psychological exploration which is not essentially therapeutic, in spite of its therapeutic intentions. Conventional psychoanalysis insists that the individual will recover from his neurosis as he acquires *insight* into the etiology of his problems; but we have observed many individuals who, after years of conventional psychoanalysis, could accurately be described (Salter, 1963, p. 147) as being "perceptively neurotic." They have been extensively and expensively educated in Freudian theory and terminology, but they are still as neurotically disabled as they were at the beginning of their explorations.

A few psychoanalysts have experimented with variations of the conventional or classical procedure; for instance, Ferenczi (1920) advocated more "activity" on the analyst's part, in order to overcome an occasional "stagnation" of the analysis. Initially, in Ferenczi's (1925, pp. 223–224) words, "it was never intended that the activity of the physician should go beyond that of interpretation and the occasional setting of tasks." Ultimately, however, Ferenczi's activity seems to have become irrational and uncontrolled; Jones (1957, p. 163) comments, "as Freud put it later [1933], the analytic situation was being reduced to a playful game between mother and child, with interchangeable roles." For a variety of reasons, Ferenczi's earlier and more moderate "deviations" in technique were never subjected to a detached empirical evaluation. Rank's "deviations" have been ignored in the same way; Jones (1957, p. 147) refers to them flatly as "errors in technique." In recent years, something of a debate (Oberndorf, 1953, p. 221) on "the controversial question of pervading passivity or activity" has arisen. The extreme of "passivity" is discussed by Kubie (1952, pp. 58–63) who asks rhetorically, "Why does there have to be an analyst at all?" The various degrees of "activity" have been discussed by many writers; and the present situation seems to be one of confusion. The American Psychoanalytic Association's Committee on Evaluation [1947–1951] reported (Oberndorf, 1953, p. 234) that it was "impossible to find a definition of psychoanalysis that is acceptable to even a large group of members [of the Association]." Accordingly, when we are describing or assessing the procedures of "conventional" psychoanalysis, we are referring mainly to Freud's own statements about it.

Essentially, as we see it, conventional psychoanalysis is a method of psychological investigation. The analyst has the role of *unintrusive* observer. He is supposed (Freud, 1912, p. 118) to be "opaque to his patients and, like a mirror, should show them nothing but what is shown to him." Correspondingly, the patient is supposed to be an *unobtrusive* student of his own psyche. The analyst, still maintaining his mirror-like attitude, tries (Freud, 1920, p. 19) to "force as much as possible into the channel of memory and to allow as little as possible to emerge as repetition," i.e., as *acting-out* (cf. Rosen, 1963a). The analyst (Freud, 1920, p. 19) must get the patient "to reexperience some portion of his forgotten life, but must see to it, on the other hand, that the patient retains some degree of aloofness." Freud (1920, p. 19) goes on to say: "If this can be successfully achieved, the patient's sense of conviction is won, together with the therapeutic success that is dependent on it." In short, Freud is opposed to *activity* on the part of the psychoanalyst and to *acting-out* on the part of the individual being analyzed. Freud prefers "some degree of aloofness" on both sides. He emphasizes the intellectual, *analytic* aspects of psychoanalysis.

With this emphasis upon intellectual achievement, it would follow that the more intelligent individual is the more promising "analysand;" and Freud (1923, p. 250) actually discriminated against "weaker intelligences." He said emphatically that "it would be uneconomical to squander such expenditure upon completely worthless persons who happen to be neurotic." At this time, I will not comment on the social or ethical implications of his views, but will point out a more technical implication of them: When psychoanalysis is conceived in terms of the individual's intellectual achievement, with the analyst functioning (Freud, 1940, p. 181) as "teacher and educator," then the course of "treatment" cannot help but be protracted and complicated. We would have a similar situation in physical medicine if we insisted that the surgical patient become educated in the science of pathology and the history of surgery, or if we insisted that the individual with ulcerative colitis become educated in the histology and biochemistry of the gastrointestinal tract. In physical medicine, as we now understand it, such education of the patient would appear to be gratuitous and irrelevant—or even deleterious, since it might conceivably interfere with the progress of treatment and recovery. In psychotherapy, as we now understand it through the development of direct psychoanalysis, the individual should not be educated in the science of psychology, Freudian or otherwise. His "education" should be confined to the vital area of his own environmental relationships: primarily those of the present, secondarily those of the past.

Turning now to the therapeutic aims of pharmacotherapy, we find that several different formulations are available. These can be enumerated briefly:

1. *Social aims* such as preserving the individual's job "by avoiding the amnesia and emotional trauma that EST [electro-shock therapy] causes," saving the individual expense by accelerating treatment, and so on (Robie, 1959, p. 285);
2. *Institutional aims* such as making the individual easier to manage, or making him more accessible to psychotherapy, "suggestion therapy," "work therapy," and the like (Kalinowsky and Hoch, 1961; Ostow, 1962; Robie, 1959);
3. *"Symptom removal" aims* such as the inhibition of "hypermotility," or the alleviation of "states of apathy and fatigue" (Freyhan, 1959, p. 323);

4. *Psychodynamic aims* such as altering the level or distribution of libido in the ego (Ostow, 1962), or inducing "a relative shift from internal object to external object cathexis" (Azima *et al.*, 1959, p. 248) ;

5. *Biochemical aims* such as the regulation of the neurohormone *serotonin* or the neurohormone *norepinephrine* in the brain (Kalinowsky and Hoch, 1961).

These and other therapeutic aims are being pursued, singly or in various combinations, by an ever-increasing number of psychiatrists who feel that pharmacotherapy may be the "break-through" in the treatment of both psychotic and neurotic individuals. Before commenting on these aims, we wish to point out that they have been conceived *ex post facto*, for the most part. As Kalinowsky and Hoch (1961, p. 331) have stated: "All psychiatric treatments [i.e., somatic methods] were found empirically, and only later theories were developed to explain their action. . . . No theoretical concepts led to the introduction of any of the new drugs into psychiatry." Typically, a behavioral or biochemical *effect* of a drug has been discovered by accident, and has then been reformulated, following further refinements, as a therapeutic *aim*. Such a procedure does not necessarily invalidate the original empirical findings or the subsequent therapeutic intent, but it does suggest (Rosen, 1961) that any insistence upon a biochemical etiology of psychosis is somewhat premature.

The diversity of therapeutic aims in pharmacotherapy seems to arise from the diversity of interests among those who are engaged in its development and use. Of the ones which I have enumerated here, social aims would seem to reflect the interests of the conscientious physician in any medical specialty; institutional aims reflect the interests of the administrator or the public health official; symptom removal aims reflect the attitude of those who understand psychosis or neurosis in terms of immediate, manifest behavior; psychodynamic aims reflect a Freudian or "depth-psychology" interest; and biochemical aims reflect the interests of the laboratory scientist.

Some of these special interests are explicitly opposed to one another; for instance, we find here a psychiatric version of the traditional *mind-body* debate. One side (Kubie, 1952, p. 100) holds that "in human life the biochemical function of any biogenetic act is almost incidental to its psychological function." The opposing side (Bailey, cited in Jackson, 1960, p. 92) holds that "the demonstration of a chemical factor in the causation of schizophrenia would not help us to understand the contents of schizophrenic delusions. . . . it would merely make them superfluous."

From the direct psychoanalytic point of view, there is no necessity to choose between the psychical and the somatic aspects of the individual, even if these aspects could always be distinguished from one another and studied separately. The individual consists of psyche *and* soma, not psyche *or* soma.

From our point of view, consequently, we can agree with some of the

therapeutic aims of pharmacotherapy. Our therapeutic aims are comparable
to the ones which we have referred to above as social and psychodynamic,
although we might disagree on certain of the more specific details. Regarding
institutional aims, we sympathize with those administrators and public health
officials for whom the problems of management and of sheer numbers in the
input and output of hospitals must be primary concerns. From their point of
view, the development of "tranquilizers" and other drugs must seem to be a
blessing and a miracle.

Regarding so-called symptom removal, we must protest the equating of
"symptoms" with the underlying disturbances of the psyche or—in the case
of so-called organic psychoses—with disturbances of the soma. While some
psychiatrists (Freyhan, 1959) speak of "target symptoms," with the implication that these constitute the essence of the psychotic or neurotic disturbance,
we prefer to speak of the individual's "manifest content." We regard psychotic
or neurotic manifestations as *clues* to the underlying disturbance of the psyche,
and as *cues* to guide the direct psychoanalyst in his understanding and treatment. We agree with Freud's statement, cited earlier, that the disappearance
of these manifestations is a by-product of treatment, rather than an end in
itself.

And finally, regarding the biochemical aims of pharmacotherapy, our
position is that biochemical changes undoubtedly accompany any psychical
change, whether it is brought about by psychotherapy, by the experience of
falling in love, or by the experience of being in a crowded theater when somebody yells "Fire!" and the audience breaks into a panic. The reverse procedure—effecting changes in the psyche with biochemical agents—has been known
to drug addicts, alcoholics, and other consumers of "magical" substances for
many centuries. Even the ordinary consumption of food and drink may be
said to bring about psychical as well as somatic changes. And we suspect that
the extraordinary consumption of drugs or alcohol by some individuals is, in
a symbolic sense, an attempt to experience the bliss and security of the infant
nursing at its mother's breast. We might even speculate that some of the favorable results attributed to pharmacotherapy are attributable, instead, to the
maternal symbolism of yet another "magical" substance which seems to promise security and bliss.

THE ACHIEVEMENT OF OUR THERAPEUTIC AIMS

No matter what the therapeutic aims of a particular psychiatrist may be,
it is not easy for him to see whether or not they have been achieved. Nor is it
easy for him to be sure that any given results are really due to the specific
effects of his treatment. As Karl Menninger (1962, p. 3) has observed: "The
patient comes to be *treated* and everything that is done for him, so far as he
is concerned, is treatment, whatever the doctor may call it." In recent years,

psychiatrists have become more and more concerned with the "placebo effect," not only in pharmacotherapy (Kalinowsky and Hoch, 1961, pp. 11–13) but also in connection with psychotherapy.

Despite this cautious attitude on the part of some psychiatrists, however, the discussion of therapeutic results has become chaotic. Criteria of "success" or "failure" are rarely made explicit, so that statistics must be taken on faith. But statistics vary widely from one report to another, particularly in studies of pharmacotherapy. Kalinowsky and Hoch (1961, p. 13) have stated:

There is something seriously amiss with methodology when wide discrepancies varying from "no improvement" to "complete remission in a large proportion of patients" are reported by different observers using the same drug in similar dosages in patients put into the same diagnostic category.

In this state of affairs, it is difficult to guess whether the fault lies with the drug, the patients, the observers, the criteria of evaluation, or the "diagnostic categories" themselves.

Conventional psychoanalysis avoids this kind of difficulty by avoiding the statistical evaluation of results. According to Jones (1957, p. 68) Freud felt that statistics were "irrelevant or inapplicable." One report (cited in Hendrick, 1958, pp. 243–245) from the Berlin Psychoanalytic Institute [1930] indicated that "cure" was achieved in 111 out of 604 cases (including 3 "cures" among 34 cases with a diagnosis of "psychosis" and a "complete analysis"). Commenting on a study (Knight, 1941) which included these reported results, K. E. Appel (1944, p. 1107) said: "The statistical results of psychoanalytic treatment . . . differ little from those of other methods of therapy."

More recently, the American Psychoanalytic Association (cited in Oberndorf, 1953, p. 234) conducted a study [1947–1951] in which it was found "that a very strong resistance exists among the members . . . to any investigation on the problem of evaluating results, even on the basis of their own definition" of psychoanalysis. Despite this "resistance," Hendrick (1958, p. 247) says that data were assembled on 9,000 cases including 2,500 completed analyses, "but in 1958 the project was discontinued because of difficulties in statistical evaluation."

Coincidentally, 1958 was the year in which four psychiatrists (Horwitz et al., 1958) published an uninvited "study" of the therapeutic results of direct psychoanalysis. I have commented elsewhere (1962a) on the scientific quality of this "study," and on my own follow-up of the cases with which it purported to be concerned; I have also called attention to the independent evaluation of psychotic individuals treated at the Institute for Direct Analysis. In the present chapter, I wish to focus attention upon some of the nonstatistical aspects of these results. As clinical psychiatrists, how do we determine if and when our therapeutic aims have been achieved?

In answering this question, I must refer back to the distinction I made earlier between two different kinds of therapeutic aims, those which I have called "social-behavioral" and those which I have called "psychodynamic." Obviously, the attentive psychiatrist is guided by the manifest behavior of the individual whom he is treating, from the first encounter to the last. The psychiatrist formulates his psychodynamic understanding of the individual on the basis of these manifest, behavioral clues. In the direct psychoanalysis of the psychotic, as treatment progresses, we estimate the progress by means of these behavioral indicators.

Eventually, when the individual appears to be ready for a trial-visit to his home environment, we send him in the company of one or more of the assistant therapists. They provide a measure of control which the individual himself may not yet be ready to provide; and they observe and report on his conduct during the visit. Even before we reach this point in the treatment, I might add, the assistant therapists are with the individual continuously in the treatment unit, where their responsibilities include the necessary control and observation of behavior. The assistants report their observations to the direct psychoanalyst at the beginning of each day's treatment session. In addition, they keep a file of written reports for each day.

This supply of information on the social-behavioral status of the individual being treated is an important supplement to the psychiatrist's own observations. It provides him with a relatively more objective and more accurate account of what the individual has been doing than he could get from the individual himself. This is true not only when the individual is in the deeper phases of psychosis, but also when he has progressed to the point of making trial-visits to his home, and when he has begun to renew the associations with his friends, neighbors, and fellow employees on the job. On many occasions, during treatment sessions, the direct psychoanalyst will ask, "What have you been doing today?" or "How was your visit with the family?" He pays close attention to the individual's response, or lack of response; for this, too, is a part of the individual's "manifest content." But he can verify or amplify the individual's response with the information which the assistant therapists will report to him.

In short, the direct psychoanalyst depends largely upon social-behavioral indicators in his determination of the extent to which his therapeutic aims have been achieved, at any given time during the course of treatment. He does not guess about the individual's capacity to get along in society, and he does not rely upon the individual's assurances of feeling "fine" and being "perfectly happy" with the family and others.

Since this chapter has made several comparisons of direct psychoanalysis with conventional psychoanalysis and with pharmacotherapy, it will conclude by making one further comparison. Our procedures for controlling and observing the social-behavioral aspects of the individual have been described briefly. Conventional psychoanalysis does not include any comparable procedures. As we noted earlier, conventional analysis emphasizes the intellectual and psychodynamic aspects of the individual's recovery. It prohibits the kind of activity which is called "acting-out," and it lacks the means of obtaining objective information on other kinds of activity. The individual is expected to report his dreams, as a matter of course, but the analyst cannot verify these reports. In the same sense, the analyst cannot verify what the individual tells him about his life during the other 23 hours of the day.

Pharmacotherapy, usually administered in an institutional setting, may or may not be related to the details of the individual's behavior inside or outside the institution. But even if the particular psychiatrist who uses pharmacotherapy does happen to be concerned with the individual's behavior, he must rely upon his own fragmentary observations and upon the fragmentary observations of ward personnel who have many other patients in their charge. One has only to visit such a ward, or to visit an "after-care" facility, and see the kind of behavior which "tranquilized" or "energized" individuals exhibit, to wonder what meaning may be given to the evaluative labels such as "social recovery" which are customarily attached to these individuals. We would not attach a label of "social recovery" to an individual simply because he could sit in a recreation room for a few hours with a magazine in his hands and a dreamy expression on his face, instead of assaulting ward personnel or fellow-patients. "Social recovery" and other degrees of recovery must be defined in more positive terms, even if we are resigned to the fact that our realistic hopes for many individuals must be relatively limited.

In conclusion, I believe that psychotherapy which is truly *healing* to the disintegrated psyche of the neurotic or psychotic individual will be the ultimate result of Freud's discoveries. Half a century ago, Bleuler (1911, p. 389) said: "We still owe it only to Freud that it has become possible to explain the special symptomatology of schizophrenia." As I have indicated here and elsewhere, it is my belief that understanding and explanation are not in themselves therapeutic. But it seems to me that many of Freud's discoveries are capable of being adapted for therapeutic purposes. This possibility is substantiated by our continuing experience in psychotherapy, and it is basic to our hopes for the future.

REFERENCES

Alexander, F. Current problems in dynamic psychotherapy in its relationship to psychoanalysis. *Amer. J. Psychiat.*, 1959, **116,** 322–325.

Appel, K. E. Psychiatric therapy. In J. McV. Hunt (Ed.), *Personality and the behavior disorders.* Vol. 1. New York: Ronald Press, 1944. Pp. 1107–1163.

Azima, H., Durost, H., and Azima, Fern J. Alterations of schizophrenic psychodynamic structure concomitant with reserpine administration. In J. H. Masserman (Ed.), *Biological psychiatry.* Vol. 1. New York: Grune & Stratton, 1959. Pp. 244–258.

Bleuler, E. *Dementia praecox or the group of schizophrenias* [1911]. New York: International Universities Press, 1950.

Brody, M. W. *Observations on "direct analysis."* New York: Vantage Press, 1959.

English, O. S., Hampe, W. W., Jr., Bacon, Catherine L., and Settlage, C. F. *Direct analysis and schizophrenia.* New York: Grune & Stratton, 1961.

Ferenczi, S. The further development of an active therapy in psycho-analysis [1920]. In S. Ferenczi, *Further contributions to the theory and technique of psycho-analysis.* London: The Hogarth Press and the Institute of Psycho-Analysis, 1926. Pp. 198–217.

Ferenczi, S. Contra-indications to the 'active' psycho-analytical technique [1925]. In S. Ferenczi, *Further contributions to the theory and technique of psycho-analysis.* London: The Hogarth Press and the Institute of Psycho-Analysis, 1926. Pp. 217–230.

Freud, Anna. *The ego and the mechanisms of defense* [1936]. New York: International Universities Press, 1946.

Freud, S. Recommendations to physicians practising psycho-analysis [1912]. In S. Freud, *Standard edition of the complete psychological works of. . . .* Vol. 12. London: The Hogarth Press and the Institute of Psycho-Analysis, 1958. Pp. 109–120.

Freud, S. *Beyond the pleasure principle* [1920]. In S. Freud, *Standard edition of the complete psychological works of. . . .* Vol. 18. London: The Hogarth Press and the Institute of Psycho-Analysis, 1958. Pp. 1–64.

Freud, S. Psycho-analysis [1923]. In S. Freud, *Standard edition of the complete psychological works of. . . .* Vol. 18. London: The Hogarth Press and the Institute of Psycho-Analysis, 1958. Pp. 235–254.

Freud, S. *An outline of psycho-analysis* [1940]. In S. Freud, *Standard edition of the complete psychological works of. . . .* Vol. 23. London: The Hogarth Press and the Institute of Psycho-Analysis, 1958. Pp. 139–207.

Freyhan, F. A. Psychopharmacology: A review. In J. H. Masserman (Ed.), *Biological psychiatry.* Vol. 1. New York: Grune & Stratton, 1959. Pp. 323–325.

Hendrick, I. *Facts and theories of psychoanalysis.* (3rd ed.) New York: Knopf, 1958.

Horwitz, W. A., Polatin, P., Kolb, L. C., and Hoch, P. H. A study of cases of schizophrenia treated by "direct analysis." *Amer. J. Psychiat.*, 1958, **114**, 780–783.

Jackson, D. D. (Ed.) *The etiology of schizophrenia.* New York: Basic Books, 1960.

Joint Commission on Mental Illness and Health. *Action for mental health.* New York: Basic Books, 1961.

Jones, E. *The life and work of Sigmund Freud.* Vol. 3. New York: Basic Books, 1957.

Kalinowsky, L. B., and Hoch, P. H. *Somatic treatments in psychiatry.* New York: Grune & Stratton, 1961.

Knight, R. P. Evaluation of the results of psychoanalytic therapy. *Amer. J. Psychiat.*, 1941, **98**, 434–446.

Kubie, L. S. Problems and techniques of psychoanalytic validation and progress. In E. R. Hilgard, L. S. Kubie, and E. Pumpian-Mindlin, *Psychoanalysis as science.* New York: Basic Books, 1952. Pp. 46–124.

Kubie, L. S. Preface. In A. E. Scheflen, *A psychotherapy of schizophrenia: direct analysis.* Springfield, Ill.: Charles C Thomas, 1961. Pp. ix–xiv.

Menninger, K. A. *A manual for psychiatric case study.* (2nd ed.) New York: Grune & Stratton, 1962.

Murray, E. J. Direct analysis from the viewpoint of learning theory. *J. consult. Psychol.*, 1962, **26**, 226–231.

Oberndorf, C. P. *A history of psychoanalysis in America.* New York: Grune & Stratton, 1953.

Ostow, M. *Drugs in psychoanalysis and psychotherapy.* New York: Basic Books, 1962.

Parsons, O. A. Clinical psychology. *Amer. J. Psychiat.,* 1963, **119,** 611–615.

Pathman, J. H. Juggernaut therapy: Book review of M. W. Brody, *Observations on "direct analysis." Contemp. Psychol.,* 1960, **5,** 344.

Robie, T. R. Iproniazid chemotherapy in melancholia. In J. H. Masserman (Ed.), *Biological psychiatry.* Vol. 1. New York: Grune & Stratton, 1959. Pp. 285–291.

Robinson, R. L. Abstract of the President's message to Congress on mental illness and retardation. *Am. J. Psychiat.,* 1963, **119,** i.

Rosen, J. N. A method of resolving acute catatonic excitement [1946]. In J. N. Rosen, *Direct analysis: Selected papers.* New York: Grune & Stratton, 1953. Pp. 28–43.

Rosen, J. N. The treatment of schizophrenic psychosis by direct analytic therapy [1947]. In J. N. Rosen, *Direct analysis: Selected papers.* New York: Grune & Stratton, 1953. Pp. 44–96.

Rosen, J. N. The optimum conditions for the treatment of schizophrenic psychosis by direct analytic therapy. *Psychoanal. Quart.,* 1951, **20,** 161–162. (Abstract)

Rosen, J. N. Book review of D. D. Jackson (Ed.), *The etiology of schizophrenia. Psychoanal. Quart.,* 1961, **30,** 276–283.

Rosen, J. N. Direct psychoanalysis. *Trans. N. Y. Acad. Sci.,* Ser. 2, 1962, **25,** 201–221. (a)

Rosen, J. N. *Direct psychoanalytic psychiatry.* New York: Grune & Stratton, 1962. (b)

Rosen, J. N. "Acting-out" and "acting-in." *Amer. J. Psychother.,* 1963, **17,** 390–403. (a)

Rosen, J. N. *The concept of early maternal environment in direct psychoanalysis.* Doylestown, Pa.: Doylestown Foundation, 1963. (b)

Salter, A. *The case against psychoanalysis.* (2nd ed.) New York: Citadel Press, 1963.

Scheflen, A. E. *A psychotherapy of schizophrenia: direct analysis.* Springfield, Ill.: Charles C Thomas, 1961.

Wexler, M. A temple for Rosen? Book review of A. E. Scheflen, *A psychotherapy of schizophrenia: direct analysis. Contemp. Psychol.,* 1962, **7,** 171–173.

Whitaker, C. A. (Ed.) *Psychotherapy of chronic schizophrenic patients.* Boston: Little, Brown, 1958.

9

*Phrenophobia and Disabling Anxiety**

Victor Raimy, Ph.D.

An Introduction to the Person

by Fred H. Herring, Ph.D.

Dr. Raimy did his graduate work at Ohio State University, where Horace B. English and Carl R. Rogers encouraged him in the fields of personality theory and psychotherapy. However, his initial papers on the self-concept were, except for the Stogdills, and a summer visitor, Kurt Koffka, little noticed.

His interest in the self-concept began about 1939, with a simple hypothesis—people behave in terms of how they perceive themselves. This interest stemmed from work on hypnosis originally intended for a master's degree. Raimy was puzzled by noting that age-regressed hypnotic subjects seemed to organize their behavior around a simple imperative sentence, "You are now 6 years old." Writings on such phenomena were silent, but Carolyn Zachary had, in some of her work, written casually of a child's "self-concept." Raimy's dissertation on the self-concept and personality organization showed essentially that if therapy was successful, persons thinking poorly of themselves before therapy thought much better of themselves after treatment. Although World War II prevented its publication, the dissertation appeared frequently in reference lists from 1945 to 1955, and is still occasionally listed.

In the immediate post-war period, while Raimy was searching for some way to map the self-concept, which he regards as the most useful

*Paper read at symposium on Goals of Psychotherapy held at the American Association for the Advancement of Science Meeting, Denver, Colorado, December 29, 1961. This study was partially supported by a small grant from the Council on Research and Creative Work of the University of Colorado. Appreciation is also expressed to the V.A. Hospital, Denver, Colorado, for its cooperation and the many facilities provided.

117

approach to tapping its mysteries, clinical psychology began its explosive development. As Executive Officer and later compiler and editor of the proceedings from the 1949 Boulder Conference on Graduate Training in Clinical Psychology, Raimy was for a decade continually concerned with training clinical psychologists at the national level as well as being Director of Clinical Psychology Training at the University of Colorado.

He served as the first Executive Officer of the Education and Training Board of the American Psychological Association, later on other boards of the A.P.A., including the Policy and Planning Board, the Board of Professional Affairs, and for two terms on the Association's Board of Directors. He was a consultant to the Veterans Administration, nationally, regionally, and locally, to various hospitals, and to the Office of Vocational Rehabilitation, along with other such appointments. In addition, he chaired the Department at the University of Colorado over an eight-year period.

Finally, in the early 1960's, Raimy had his second idea. He had felt unable to accept Freud because he thought that Freud's highly complex and subtle thought processes were projected into Freud's conception of man, and—as Raimy avers—man is really a fairly inefficient organizer of vast masses of data into simple, and often vague, patterns of objects and events. He sees man as a lawyer who, while constantly mindful of the evidence, is constantly pleading his case to himself and to others, constantly dealing with the data as he sees them, constantly fooling himself and others, yet constantly dealing with rather simple changes on mostly similar themes. So his second idea is that a person's behavior is guided essentially by his beliefs and convictions about himself and his world. If a person's convictions about himself can be mapped, it is then possible to map the basic dimensions of his self-concept.

Returning to psychotherapy in the 1960's, he is now trying to look more systematically at college students, neurotics, and hospitalized psychotics to see not only if they truly have convictions about themselves, but also whether these convictions have a major influence on their behavior. The following is his first paper on such a conviction and was a clinical investigation of the limits of a conviction.

My task here is to describe a very concrete psychotherapy goal on which I have been working with Dr. Fred H. Herring, Chief, Clinical and Counseling Psychology, the Denver V.A. Hospital, while engaged in psychotherapy mostly with hospitalized veterans and some college students. My single apology is that we have not as yet managed to obtain other than clinical impressions in support of our contentions.

REDUCTION OF DISABLING ANXIETY AS A GOAL

Readers will not be shocked or stimulated to hear that disabling anxiety is one of the hallmarks of many mental patients, or that the reduction of such anxiety is a limited but legitimate goal of psychotherapy. There may well be two kinds of psychotherapy, even though the operations may be similar. One kind would aim at anxiety reduction to enable the patient to carry on a relatively normal life; the second kind of therapy would aim at changing long-term trends in the personality which theoretically produce frustrations and maladjustments, and perhaps culminate from time to time in mental breakdowns.

Once anxiety has been markedly reduced, then it seems to me that the patient is a much different person than he was when suffering from lack of concentration, depression, irritability, hostility, insomnia, inability to carry on his job, inability to engage in normal social relationships, and all the other disabilities which face the mentally disturbed person. One can assert that if methods can be found to reduce disabling anxiety, much of the problem of mental disturbance has been dealt with, as the patient without excess anxiety can often resume normal life activities; if he has been hospitalized, he can often be discharged which is, in itself, a major benefit.

Parenthetically, two items of explanation must be introduced at this point. First, we are in no position to present a complete psychopathology of acute anxiety, as our work on this topic has taken place largely over the last 15 months. One cannot see many patients while doing psychotherapy with them even on a short-term basis. Only a few of the hospitalized patients have been psychotics. The college students would probably be diagnosed as mild anxiety attacks in a variety of personality patterns. When, therefore, the reduction of disabling anxiety is referred to, I hope that the reference is to serious situational disturbances, neurotic breakdowns with anxiety and depression, and possibly acute psychosis.

My second explanation has to do with the tranquilizing and energizing drugs which have been administered to almost all of the hospitalized patients I have seen as part of their routine hospital treatment. These drugs, as is now generally agreed, do reduce anxiety in many disturbed patients. I can hazard no guess as to the relative effectiveness of the ataractics versus psychotherapy, but shall return later to the drugs and their psychological effects.

ANXIETY AS A CONVICTION ABOUT SELF

At this point I should like to sketch a psychological approach to mental disturbance which may have implications for the psychotherapy of persons with acute anxiety. Data will not be presented to support its validity as I am only too well aware that acute anxieties, particularly when drugs have also been administered, can be relieved more easily than almost any other form of disturbance. At the present time, our investigations have been limited to an exploration clinically of some of the manifestations of acute anxiety.

Before World War II, I was much interested in the proposition that behavior is *partially* determined by the person's self-concept. The word "partially" in that assertion is still necessary as it is hard to conceive of behavior which is determined entirely by the self-concept or entirely by the external situation as perceived by the person. Reduction in self-esteem also appeared at that time as an indicator of mental disturbance but not necessarily as a basic source. In searching for a better approach to thinking about the role of the self-concept in relation to mental disturbance, one always encounters the problem of finding essential structural components of the self-concept which are also meaningful.

Attitudes toward the self have served as convenient terms to refer to such components, but I have never had much faith in attitudes per se, because to me the self-concept exists in some fashion in the phenomenological realm, and attitudes for most psychologists exist in the objective realm, even when immediate report is used as a method by which attitudes are inferred. By means of what may be more than verbal legerdemain, I am now beginning to think that the essential structural components of the self-concept may be referred to as *convictions* about the self. Similarly, one's conception of the world outside of one's skin may be organized around components which are convictions about the world. One may, if he wishes, substitute George Kelly's term "constructs" for the word "convictions," but in the first place, I prefer for the time being to avoid getting involved with Kelly's specialized definition of construct, and in the second place, I am trying to emphasize the primacy of convictions about the self in order to see what such exploitation may lead to.

I should try to define "conviction" at this point, but I must leave you as well as myself dissatisfied by simply saying that a conviction about the self is a strong belief about the self upon which one acts. The source of the conviction lies in empirical evidence which the person has obtained from either internal or external observations. He learns his convictions. Functionally, I am suggesting that if you change some of a person's convictions about himself you will have changed some of his self-concept and you can therefore expect to change his behavior. As you can see, the theory thus far is highly simplified and possesses only plausibility for me, which is not, where theory is concerned, an extraordinarily significant virtue.

What do convictions have to do with mental disturbance? While seeing both college students and hospitalized adult male veterans, I was struck by one thing they all seemed to have in common: all of them expressed in one way or another a conviction that they might be losing their minds. A 20-year-old sophomore from Indiana, whose presenting problem was his failure to obtain grades which satisfied his father, admitted with elaborate casualness that since he had had great difficulty in high school in social relations with girls, he had wondered from time to time whether he did not have a streak of insanity inherited from an uncle. A 29-year-old veteran with an admission diagnosis of pre-psychosis had been told by his mother since he was 12 that "you are crazy." When I first saw him in the hospital several days after admission, he was shakily pessimistic about his chances of avoiding insanity and half hoped that it would happen soon, as it would be a great relief. More recently, a 28-year-old housewife whom I had been seeing supposedly for marital counseling, almost precipitated her admission to a hospital with a nervous breakdown the day after she saw the movie *Splendor in the Grass,* in which a frustrated girl is sent to a Kansas mental hospital and emerges two years later with her marital problems solved.

PHRENOPHOBIA AS A CONVICTION

If behavior is organized, at least in part, in terms of convictions which one has about oneself, what happens if one has a conviction that he is in danger of losing his mind? For this state of affairs I have been using the term "phrenophobia" to mean, more generally, a dread of loss of control or dread of approaching insanity or dread of disintegration of the self. Can one have a conviction about the future? All of common sense seems to answer in the affirmative, although except for highly predictable events like the rising of the sun or the collecting of taxes, future-oriented convictions are probably always conditional. For this reason, a conviction that one might be about to break mentally carries an additional degree of dread, for a conditional conviction contains a large amount of uncertainty which is more difficult to live with.

How does phrenophobia develop? The simplest answer seems to be that over a period of time a person can collect such evidence about himself that he may be forced to conclude that he very well may be "cracking up." The evidence can be obtained from internal observations as well as from his interpretations of what he thinks others think of him. The motive behind his examination of his mental status may be a defense or it may simply be the need to make some sense out of a confused situation, or it may be both. The intensity of the conviction may vary from zero to certainty, but at the point where it produces his preoccupation with himself, severe anxiety probably occurs, thus, by feedback, creating additional symptoms.

Just how far phrenophobia in and of itself may force the person along the road to psychosis is for me a moot question. We certainly have many instances from medicine in which fear of an imaginary illness such as cancer or heart disease may produce appalling anxieties and appalling restriction of activity. If psychosis occurs after exacerbated anxiety, however, the suspicion is always present that anxiety was disturbance-producing up to a point, but the breakdown was due to an intervening, predisposing, psychotic weakness.

What is the incidence of phrenophobia in mental patients? Such a question would appear to be answerable fairly readily simply by using questionnaires or brief interviews. For reasons which I shall discuss later, the answer is not obtained so easily. I have, however, asked psychotherapists and others how often they have encountered phrenophobia. One organically-minded psychiatrist answered thoughtfully that he could recall one patient who was fearful of becoming psychotic. At the other extreme, a psychoanalytically-oriented psychiatrist answered immediately that *all* of his patients have such a fear, but it is only a displaced castration fear. Other replies have rung all the changes between the extremes. One tolerant friend who first estimated that he had encountered such a fear in about 20 percent of his patients in psychotherapy, later told me that he had asked his current patients and found that all had such a fear.

In Frederick Thorne's recent book, *Personality: A Clinical Eclectic Viewpoint* (1961), Dr. Thorne reports that 78 percent of "100 consecutive office practice cases accepted for psychotherapy" reported symptoms to him of "feelings of imminent mental breakdown." Another 22 percent reported "feelings of actual disintegration occurring." In discussing these data, Thorne also comments, "Many of the clients stated that their worst fear was 'losing my mind,' and they indicated that they would rather have any other kind of physical illness because that would not involve loss of feelings of selfhood." There is an old slogan which probably applies here: "Better the grave than the asylum."

DENIAL OF PHRENOPHOBIA

Although all the patients I have seen have mentioned such a fear, we have encountered major difficulties in directly obtaining information from them about the details of their phrenophobias. Vocabulary appears to be very important, as the old-fashioned, forthright, "Have you ever thought you might be losing your mind?" almost invariably results in a firm denial. If one asks, "Have you ever thought you might crack up?" the chances are very good that the patient will answer in the affirmative, but very rarely will he supply any but the most meager details, and ordinarily he will not elaborate spontaneously unless he is at the moment gripped by acute anxiety. More innocuous terms such as "fear of losing control," or "fear of losing a marble," (note that "*a* marble" works but "losing *your* marbles" does not) are much more acceptable than "fear of losing one's mind" or fear of "going crazy."

Related to the patient's sensitivity to the semantics of the problem is the astonishing denial reaction which is almost invariably to be expected. Here is a typical denial gambit.

Patient: I don't know how much more of this I can stand. If I keep on like this, I'm likely to go crazy.
Therapist: With much more strain, you are fearful of going crazy.
Patient: Who, me? I never said anything like that. Maybe the thought crossed my mind, but I never really did.

There is a retrospective variant of that sample exchange which also occurs frequently.

Patient: I guess I've run out of ideas and it's only 10:15.

Therapist: (Hopefully.) Well, last week when you were feeling pretty rocky, Joe, you said that you had been afraid at one time of having a nervous breakdown.

Patient: I said that? Gee, I don't remember a thing about it. That's never even occurred to me that I can remember.

Rarely have I found a patient who does not immediately turn into a Philadelphia lawyer if I ask him to discuss his fear of "cracking up." Exasperation used to mount in me when men who had openly expressed fear of insanity during an early interview, and had even discussed the fear when under pressure, later blandly denied both the fear and the conversation, and often ended the interview with solicitous inquiries about the state of *my* mental health. The outright denials and self-contradictions are even more interesting when one realizes that all of the patients with whom I have attempted to discuss this topic were hospitalized on mental wards, and all knew they were mental patients with uncertain diagnoses and prognoses.

We suspect that the denial of phrenophobia where it obviously exists is significant of the extent to which it is dreaded, but it may have less importance than I had originally surmised. Dr. Fred Herring, my collaborator, participated in a study at V.A. Hospital McKinney, where it was found that *medical* patients contradicted themselves frequently in regard to the reporting of symptoms.

There is little likelihood that anyone familiar with mental patients will argue about the appearance of phrenophobia in such persons, although there may well be a difference of opinion about its high incidence. There will, I am sure, be a much greater difference of opinion about the significance of phrenophobia in the mental economy of the patient. The literature on this topic is surprisingly sparse, although there are very frequent incidental reports of phrenophobia as a symptom. I suspect that most writers and most clinicians in this field have simply accepted phrenophobia as a symptom which is to be expected from *anyone* who is experiencing mental disturbance. Why, one asks, should anyone be surprised to learn that an upset college student or, more particularly, a hospitalized mental patient expresses a fear that he might be losing his mind?

Still other sensible questions are asked: Don't you think you are simply recognizing that mental patients have anxiety? Don't you recognize a defense and a wishful expression by the patient? As you might gather, these question are usually rhetorical and often end with further solicitous inquiries about my mental health.

Surprisingly enough, I do agree that one should expect mental patients to be fearful of their mental stability, I do agree that phrenophobia is intimately linked with anxiety, and I do suspect that phrenophobia is frequently, if not always, a defensive symptom. Nonetheless, I am dissatisfied with the cavalier dismissal of phrenophobia as an epiphenomenon which disappears only when *real* problems have been solved by or for the patient.

FREE-FLOATING ANXIETY AND PHRENOPHOBIA

Phrenophobia may well explain at least some instances of free-floating anxiety. Without necessarily disputing the analytic notion of free-floating anxiety as being due to unconscious impulses of anger and sex which threaten to break through, there is another conception of such anxiety which sees it as a conviction, loosely held, of impending personal disintegration. Although classically free-floating anxiety is defined as anxiety without an object, the self *can* be an object and one *can* be fearful of one's loss of control over the self.

Patients themselves frequently state directly that they are afraid of loss of self in some fashion, even when they deny that they know of what they are afraid. Here are several examples of such statements:

"I don't know what I am afraid of; I just feel like I may fall apart."
"It's just this awful feeling of anxiety as though I won't be able to keep going."
"It's this feeling of doom—as though something awful will happen to me."

Why do patients deny that their fears have an object when they so clearly are afraid of something happening to the self? The obvious answer seems to be that fear of loss of self or of personal disintegration is not a publicly acceptable category for explaining fear in our culture any more than is an explanation based upon fear of being bewitched. In many primitive cultures, fear of bewitchment *is* a socially acceptable explanation. Fear of loss of self is not even a privately acceptable explanation for fear in our culture, since most of us accept as adequate explanations only those categories which are acceptable to the culture in which we live.

Patients believe that they must display their sanity in their explanations, otherwise they are illogical and their sanity is, therefore, open to question. Some of the acceptable categories for explaining exacerbated fear in our culture are (1) actual insanity; (2) some physiological sickness probably connected with the nerves; (3) impending loss of significant persons in one's life or loss of physical possessions; (4) impending loss of status; (5) impending physical harm from an external source; and possibly (6) unconscious factors over which the patient has no control. There probably are other categories which are culturally and privately acceptable, but the six above constitute an illustrative list. If none of these can be invoked as an explanation of fear, then the fear is regarded as objectless.

Nonetheless, at least for persons who have some interest in the self-concept or the similar notion of self-identity, fear of loss of or drastic change in the self does make sense psychologically, just as the patient has expressed it. Free-floating anxiety does often have an object which can usually, if not always, be detected in the spontaneous descriptions of the patient which indicate that he fears personal disintegration. Such a fear is also a future-oriented conviction.

PHRENOPHOBIA AND ANXIETY

The reader should not be too shocked at this point to hear that in many respects we are suggesting that at least some acute anxieties are precipitated by fear of loss of mental stability which, phenomenologically, is equivalent to loss of self. Does such loss of self square with the man in the street's conception of what can happen to his mind?

Although I have made no systematic study of this question, I have talked to many persons on this topic. In their thinking, the mind is usually equated with the brain; the brain is thought of as one of the two organs of the body which are fragile, glass-like organs which are highly vulnerable to injury. The brain and the heart are thought of as organs which, if shattered, may never heal or regenerate. They are both viewed as essential for maintenance of normal existence. Everyone knows, of course, how much mental deficiency and psychosis have been caused by mother dropping baby on his head. The very terms in common use, "He cracked up and lost his mind," are themselves symbolic of the fragile, brittle conception of the mind.

As has been described above, there is reason to believe that fear of loss of sanity is likely to be found in many patients with acute anxiety, and when one is reduced in intensity so is the other. Obviously, I am suggesting that phrenophobia has a causal relation to the development as well as to the reduction in anxiety. Yet the dilemma is also obvious: correlation does not prove causation. Although I am not without concern in regard to this major dilemma, there is little which can be done at the moment to resolve it. The dilemma constitutes one of the major weaknesses of the system being presented from both a logical and an empirical standpoint.

If I may soberly dismiss the dilemma for the time being, I believe that there is a way of defining subjective anxiety which can make it consonant with phrenophobia and which can point to a close identity between the two. So far, I have spoken of phrenophobia only loosely as a fear of insanity or a fear of loss of self. A better definition might be *the dread of uncontrollable, irreversible, and undesirable change in the self* (by which I mean the self-concept).

I have found it of interest to compare this definition with Freud's conception of the origins of anxiety. As Rollo May points out (1950), there is a developmental hierarchy starting with "the fear of loss of the mother at birth, loss of the penis in the phallic period, loss of approval of the superego in the latency period, and finally, loss of life, all of which go back to the prototype, the separation from the mother."

A two-finger exercise suggests that loss of the penis would probably represent an undesirable and irreversible change in the self-concept. (Only consider what the classic discovery, "I have been castrated!" has accomplished for the female self-concept.) Similarly, loss of self-esteem certainly implies undesirable change in the self-concept, while fear of loss of life needs no elaboration.

What about separation from the mother as a fear of drastic change in the self? Although identification supposedly develops after early infancy, object cathexes in the Freudian system would nicely account for the child's regarding himself as being dependent upon and "tied to" the mother. Fear of separation from the mother would then represent fear of drastic change in the self. With such reinterpretations as these, it is not too difficult to maintain a phenomenological view of phrenophobia as a major source of acute anxiety.

I must introduce a caution here. I should like to deny that phrenophobia ordinarily engulfs a person and minutes later catapults him into a nervous breakdown. Such precipitous development of mental disturbance can probably occur in the traumatic neuroses where a sudden loss of one's conviction of relative invulnerability seems to be a cardinal factor. Ordinarily, however, phrenophobia has a history in the person's past as well as in his immediate, real-life situation.

Historically, the roots of phrenophobia are probably to be found in the usual sources of insecurity and preoccupation with one's self. The precipitating events which may lead to phrenophobia I have termed the "disturbance glissade." To save time, I shall briefly outline what are seen as a coherent series of events:

1. The person becomes ego-involved with an insoluble problem which he can neither solve nor ignore.
2. Tension develops which distorts both his internal and external perceptual fields.
3. The distortion produces confusion in the self-concept and in his perception of his world.
4. The confusion produces disorganized behavior which the person views as symptoms, since it represents perceived change in his behavior.
5. He regards the symptoms as "uncontrollable" and threatening.
6. He must seek an explanation for his symptoms. If he can find a satisfactory explanation by means of culturally accepted categories for explaining symptoms, his disturbance may be halted and reduced. If, however, he cannot find such a satisfactory explanation, he may be forced to conclude that he may be in danger of insanity, loss of control, and so forth.
7. If he becomes convinced that he may "lose his mind," there is increased anxiety because of feedback from the conviction. There is an intensified search for additional symptoms of what he fears, and intensification of the confusion and tension.

In such a fashion, one can conceive of phrenophobia as a major source of anxiety which is also linked with one's personal history and one's real-life problems.

Before returning to psychotherapy, I should like to recapitulate our thinking about the background for at least some cases of acute and disabling anxiety. In this phenomenological conception, anxiety is viewed as a dread of un-controllable, irreversible, and undesirable change in the self. The dread is seen as a future-oriented conviction about the self which patients find difficult to discuss but which is present in a large number of them. A dilemma exists as to whether the dread is cause or effect where clinical anxiety is concerned, although it may well be both. Free-floating anxiety is regarded as having a phenomenological object—fear of personal disintegration. It has also been suggested that Freud's notions about the origins of anxiety may be special cases of the more general dread of impending change in the self. Finally, phrenophobia is regarded as having both a personal history as well as immediate roots in the real-life situation of the highly anxious patient.

PHRENOPHOBIA AND PSYCHOTHERAPY

What implications does such a conception of disabling anxiety have for its psychotherapy? The central core of this approach is based, of course, upon the notion that such patients have a central conviction about the probability of their losing their sanity or their control of themselves. Psychotherapy, it would seem, should then be directed toward changing that conviction.

If one attempts to change a conviction, how might one approach such a task? The approach we have been using for at least the last six months is to attempt to present the patient with counterevidence in the interviews. The attempt is simple in conception and not too difficult in execution, although, like all other skills, one can make considerable improvement in technique with practice.

The major technique is an attempt to explain exhaustively to the patient how his symptoms can be produced by anxiety, fear, tension, or whatever synonym appears meaningful to this particular patient. Direct reassurance about insanity is also provided when it can be done without misleading the patient or going beyond the prognostic probabilities. Since problems arise with direct reassurance, I am more cautious in its use than I may sound.

A separate paper could be written on the problem of explaining to the patient how his hostility may arise from anxiety; such an explanation seems to appear plausible to the patients, although less so to my colleagues. Linking current anxiety symptoms with the patient's real-life problems is not difficult in short-term psychotherapy, although exploring longer-term personality trends (or convictions about the self) is more difficult. Finally, I still believe that it is very helpful for the therapist to establish a very free, accepting relationship with the patient in order to motivate him to return for further interviews as well as to hold his attention.

If the presentation of counterevidence to the patient sounds like an intellectual approach, I am afraid I must plead guilty. I don't feel guilty, however, since, if we were to examine the raw data of most psychotherapeutic interviews, I suspect we would find that the therapist is frequently engaged in presenting the patient with evidence running counter to the supposed convictions which the patient has about himself. Most interpretations and many reflections are almost by definition counterevidence. Confrontations of the patient with his own contradictions can also be viewed as counterevidence. The more implicit presentations of counterevidence by the therapist are more difficult to describe, but from the patient's standpoint the therapist's refusal to criticize, his reassuring discussion of symptoms, and his attitude of accepting the patient as capable of discussing himself logically are all cues which offset the patient's conviction of his impending crack-up.

At the beginning of this discussion I suggested that the effects of the tranquilizing drugs are consonant with this conceptual approach. Although there are frequent side effects which may deepen the patient's apprehensions about himself, it seems to me that more frequently such drugs do provide the patient with very definite, internal evidence that he is not as close to the verge of cracking up as he thought he was. Quite apart from any direct pharmacological effect which the drugs may have upon whatever "disease process," if any, underlies the patient's disturbance, the drugs do appear to provide the patient with evidence about himself which a psychotherapist would be hard put to duplicate by means of any verbal or nonverbal weapons in his therapeutic armamentarium.

CONCLUSION

I have been describing a conception of acute anxiety and a therapeutic approach based upon the notion that some acute disturbances may be due to the patient's fear of impending insanity or any of its synonyms. Although straying far from the topic of this symposium, I suspect that we need more specific goals in psychotherapy in addition to the broad ones of reorganizing personality, relieving symptoms, or making the unconscious conscious. The reduction of acute anxiety appears to be a legitimate goal, as acute anxiety is frequently disabling. I have suggested that there may be at least two kinds of psychotherapy, and I have attempted to present a conception of one which aims at the reduction of acute anxiety.

The reader may wish to know how effective is the approach I have been describing. As everyone knows that therapeutic outcome is probably an obscene topic in the first place, and that its assessment is beset by unmentionable pitfalls in the second place, all we can say on the basis of limited experience is that the approach via phrenophobia seems to me to work no worse than any of the other methods I have tried.

REFERENCES

May, R. *The meaning of anxiety*. New York: Ronald, 1950.
Thorne, F. C. *Personality: a clinical eclectic viewpiont*. Brandon, Vt.: Journal of Clinical Psychology Press, 1961.

10

Behavior Therapy and Psychotherapeutic Goals

Joseph Wolpe, M.D.

An Introduction to the Person

by Arnold A. Lazarus, Ph.D.

Joseph Wolpe was born in Johannesburg, South Africa in 1915. He grew up in Johannesburg and then studied medicine at the University of the Witwatersrand, where, even as a student, he displayed a keen interest in research and contributed papers to scientific journals. After obtaining his M.B., B.Ch., degrees he entered general medical practice for several years before enlisting in 1942 as a military medical officer. Then, in 1948, he obtained his doctorate in psychiatry.

Dr. Wolpe is widely respected as a brilliant, compassionate, and tolerant human being whose cultivated esthetic appreciation is combined with personal simplicity and warmth. His most obvious attribute, however, is a penetrating clarity of thought. Underlying his impressive academic record, and the mainstay of his system of psychology and his psychotherapeutic emphasis, is an uncanny ability to refute confused or obscure reasoning with astonishing rapidity and accuracy.

In his typically thorough fashion Dr. Wolpe delved deeply into the neurophysiology of learning and added original thought to this subject. He turned away from nebulous psychoanalytic theorising towards the controlled experimental data emanating from the laboratories of Pavlov, Thorndike, Watson, Tolman, Skinner, and, above all, Clark L. Hull. His own ingenious laboratory studies on the acquisition and elimination of experimental neurosis in cats formed the main basis of his M.D. thesis.

While in private psychiatric practice in Johannesburg he also lectured in the Department of Psychiatry at the University of the Witwatersrand. His writings enriched the literature on learning theory and
objective pyschotherapy. He was awarded a Fellowship at the Center for
Advanced Study in the Behavioral Sciences, Stanford, California, 1956–
57, where he wrote his book *Psychotherapy by Reciprocal Inhibition.*
This book formed an impressive link between the laboratory and the
clinic and synthesised the implications and applications of his basic
hypothesis: "If a response inhibitory to anxiety can be made to occur in
the presence of anxiety-evoking stimuli, it will weaken the connection
between these stimuli and the anxiety responses."

As Research Professor of Psychiatry at the University of Virginia
School of Medicine since 1960 he has published extensively and lectured
in numerous centers of the U.S.A., Canada, and the United Kingdom and
in Prague. In 1965 he moved to Temple University School of Medicine in
Philadelphia.

To have pioneered a psychotherapeutic system so utterly at odds with
orthodox opinion requires brilliant originality of thought coupled with
a rare degree of courage and integrity. As the doyen of behavior therapy,
Dr. Wolpe is eager to implement extensive controlled studies which will
test the value of his methods beyond scientific doubt. It is never easy to
challenge orthodox tradition, especially when that tradition can be
neither verified nor disproved. But one fact is obvious: in psychotherapy
Dr. Wolpe has offered a new framework of thought.

DEFINITIONS

Therapy is any procedure designed to remove or ameliorate disease or
malfunction within the human organism. Therapeutic effort is justified to the
extent that the disease or malfunction shortens life or impairs human happiness whether by interfering with the fulfillment of needs or desires, or by
causing pain or other suffering. To illustrate, a rodent ulcer would usually be
judged worthy of therapeutic effort because it may ultimately cause death,
while a small, unobtrusive, and stationary fibroma of the skin might well be
left alone. Similarly, in a city dweller, a phobia for heights would justify
treatment, but a phobia confined to snakes probably would not (Lang and
Lazovik, 1963).

A *patient* is a person who requires therapy and receives it. Usually it is
the patient who takes the initiative that leads to therapy, for he is likely to be
the first to be aware of his own disorder.

In all fields, therapy may be either fundamental or palliative. *Fundamental* therapy aims to remove in final fashion the organic state of affairs that

is the basis of the disorder. *Palliative* therapy aims at alleviating the ill effects of the organic state of affairs and not at removing or diminishing it.

Like other branches of medicine, psychiatry employs both fundamental and palliative methods. Some psychiatric disorders, for example general paresis and, it now appears probable, schizophrenia, are primarily due to *organic lesions or abnormal biochemical states*, and in these the only therapy that can be fundamental is that which reverses the abnormal physical state. The same applies to those disorders due to *faults in the organic process of growth* e.g., mongolism.

All remaining psychiatric illness is a function of *learning or of failure of learning*.[1] *Neurotic* illness is due to the acquisition of habits that are both unadaptive and persistent—most characteristically, anxiety-response habits (see below). Psychopathic illness appears to be based upon a failure to learn habits that are socially important. This kind of failure—a "learning deficit"— is also the evident basis of a variety of minor maladjustments, such as enuresis (Jones, 1960; Lovibond, 1963).

Psychotherapy is any procedure that brings about the unlearning of unadaptive habits or the acquisition of adaptive habits that have been lacking. Though the two processes—learning and unlearning—may, obviously, be intertwined in a number of ways, in a therapeutic setting one or the other is primary as a rule. It may, for example, become possible to establish effective social habits in an individual only after the elimination of particular interpersonal anxieties.

The general goal of psychotherapy is, through learning, to remove suffering or improve functioning. This goal finds more explicit expression in the criteria put forward some years ago by Knight (1941) in an endeavor to increase the rigorousness of psychoanalytic research. They are criteria to assess the effectiveness of psychotherapy: (1) symptomatic improvement; (2) increased productiveness at work; (3) improved adjustment and pleasure in sex; (4) improved interpersonal relationships; and (5) enhanced ability to handle ordinary psychological conflicts and reasonable reality stresses. Not all of these criteria are relevant goals in every case, but there is probably no patient who is a suitable subject for psychotherapy to whom one or more of them would not apply. They reflect the usual reasons that motivate patients to seek therapy, and their successful attainment is unequivocally manifest to the patient.

Knight's criteria have been explicitly adopted by most behavior therapists as a therapeutic yardstick. It is worthy of remark that psychoanalysts have not adopted them, or, at best, only in part, perhaps because their therapeutic experience does not lead them to expect these kinds of success. This may well be the reason why they usually estimate their results on other criteria that, one may suppose, they believe to be commoner products of their thera-

[1]Learning is of course based upon organic changes in neuronal systems (see, for example, Wolpe, 1952b; Briggs and Kitto, 1962).

peutic efforts. Thus, they refer to such criteria as maturity, insight, acceptance of heterosexuality, solution of the internal conflict, receding of childhood transference, and working through of the Oedipus constellation (Wilder, 1945). A psychotherapist is of course free to adopt any criteria that he wishes, but he should bear in mind that even when behavioral change can be shown it cannot be regarded as *therapeutic* change (see definition above) unless there is also diminution of suffering or improvement of function such as defined by Knight's criteria.

THE RATIONALE OF BEHAVIOR THERAPY IN NEUROSES

Behavior therapy comprises those psychotherapeutic practices that make *deliberate* use of principles of learning derived from experimental psychology. Since all psychotherapeutic effects involve the making and breaking of habits through learning, it is plain that when change occurs without the learning process having been employed deliberately, that process must nevertheless have been in action. It is only to be expected that such inadvertent effects will quite often also occur when deliberate conditioning procedures are being used.

A *neurosis* is formally defined as a persistent habit of unadaptive behavior acquired by learning in an anxiety-generating situation. Autonomic responses experienced as anxiety or anxiety-equivalents are the central feature of most neurotic habits.

The above definition was derived from observations made in experimental neuroses in cats (Wolpe, 1952; 1958). Experimental neuroses had been produced in many laboratories following Pavlov's pioneer work (1928), but for a long time there was general acquiescence in Pavlov's view that the neuroses were based upon a pathological neural state brought about by a "clash" between excitation and inhibition. Modifying a technique of neurosis induction that had been extensively used by Masserman (1943), I demonstrated (1952a; 1958) that the behavior of experimental neuroses is learned, and, like other learned behavior, stimulus-bound. The neuroses were produced by shocking cats in a small cage. After a number of shocks it was found that merely placing the animal in the experimental cage on a later occasion would bring forth reactions that could be deemed *learned* because they were similar to those observed at the time of the shock—muscle tension, agitation, dilatation of the pupils, and other manifestations of anxiety. This habit of response *persisted* indefinitely and was not ameliorated either by repeated exposure to the experimental cage (without further shocks) or prolonged absence from it. *Unadaptiveness* was strikingly revealed in the refusal of the animals to accept food in the experimental cage after 24 to 72 hours of starvation. The behavior of the animals thus complied with the essential features of the definition of neurosis given above—acquisition by learning, persistence, and unadaptiveness.

It is necessary to ask whether this definition also fits human neuroses. There are several reasons for thinking that it does. The first is that it is a clinical fact that, like the experimental animals, the great majority of patients diagnosed as neurotic suffer from obstinate habits of responding with anxiety to situations in which most people are at ease, such as aloneness, crowds, reasonable criticism, or space restriction. As in the animal cases these habits are remarkable for their obduracy. Another reason is the following: that human neuroses are due to learning is often clearly evident from the history of their onset, which may feature either a particular event that once aroused great anxiety or a chronic or recurrent situation that evoked anxiety perhaps less severe but over a longer time. Whatever the details of the precipitating circumstances, some of the stimuli prominent at the time of causation are among those subsequently found capable of evoking the neurotic anxiety responses.

A third reason is that human neurotic reactions resemble those experimentally produced in displaying the phenomena of stimulus generalization. The experimental animal responds with anxiety to rooms similar to that in which he was shocked, and with an intensity that depends directly upon the degree of their resemblance to that room; and the human subject too shows a maximal response to a zenithal stimulus, and a weakening response as resemblance to this declines. To take an actual example, a patient maximally anxious when exposed to the scrutiny of 50 or more people had diminishing anxiety as a direct function of decreasing numbers (see below).

Cognisant of these parallel features of experimental and clinical neuroses, one is not surprised to find that there is also a similarity of effective therapeutic procedures. The successful therapy in animal cases followed a course so clear that it soon became completely predictable, and yielded a general principle that led to a considerable number of clinical techniques. The fact that a hungry animal was inhibited from eating while highly anxious in the experimental cage encouraged the idea of experimenting with offerings of food in conditions where less anxiety was evoked. Lower intensities of anxiety were observed in the experimental laboratory outside the cage, and still lower in other rooms. Meat pellets were eaten in these places in ascending order while signs of anxiety waned, finally disappearing. Eventually eating became possible in the experimental cage itself, where also, after repeated portions of food, all signs of anxiety abated.

These and related experiments indicated a reciprocal antagonism between the anxiety responses and the feeding responses. In any situation where the anxiety was strong enough to inhibit feeding, it would persist, and could, if desired, be made to spread to new stimuli. But where the feeding tendency was relatively stronger so that feeding occurred in the face of some anxiety, the anxiety-response habit was weakened.

PSYCHOTHERAPEUTIC METHODS

From the above experiments emerged the reciprocal inhibition principle of psychotherapy: *if a response inhibitory of anxiety can be made to occur in the presence of anxiety-evoking stimuli it will weaken the bond between these stimuli and the anxiety.* Experience with human neuroses indicates that the principle has general validity, and the following responses, each of which, empirically, appears to inhibit anxiety, have been successfully used to weaken neurotic *anxiety-response* habits. They have been described in practical detail by Wolpe and Lazarus (1966).

1). Assertive responses (Salter, 1949; Wolpe, 1954; 1958). See Cases 1 and 3 below.
2). Sexual responses (Wolpe, 1958). See Case 2 below.
3). Relaxation responses (Jacobson, 1938; Wolpe, 1954; 1958; 1961b; Bond and Hutchison, 1960; Lazarus and Rachman, 1960; Clark, 1963; Ashem, 1963). See Case 3 below.
4). Respiratory responses (carbon dioxide oxygen mixtures) (Wolpe, 1958).
5). Conditioned motor responses (Wolpe, 1958).
6). "Anxiety-relief" responses (Wolpe, 1958; Lazarus, 1963).
7). Feeding responses (Jones, 1924; Lazarus, 1960).
8). Emotive imagery (Lazarus and Abramovitz; 1962).

In addition to the responses *deliberately* used against anxiety there are, of course, the emotional responses induced in many patients by the interpersonal aspects of the therapeutic situation itself (Wolpe, 1958). These responses are presumably the basis of most of the therapeutic effects (i.e., breaking of neurotic habits) in all forms of psychotherapy other than behavior therapy but inevitably play an important part in behavior therapy too (see below).

Another application of the reciprocal inhibition is in counterconditioning by aversive stimulation of fetishes (Raymond, 1956; Glynn and Harper, 1961), some cases of obsessional neurosis (Wolpe, 1958), and homosexuality (Freund, 1960). Besides this, the reactive inhibition mechanism has been used to treat tics (Yates, 1958).

Among methods of applying the reciprocal inhibition principle there is one, utilizing deep muscle relaxation, that particularly clearly parallels the animal therapy described above. It is called *systematic desensitization,* and its use will be briefly described. The patient is given an abbreviated course of training in progressive relaxation (Jacobson, 1938). This is done in the course of about six interviews, during which *anxiety hierarchies* are also constructed. An anxiety hierarchy is a list of stimulus situations to which a patient reacts with neurotic anxiety. Any of innumerable themes can form the subject matter of hierarchies. They range from classical phobias to situations involving social disapproval or other complex stimulus constellations.

In the desensitization procedure itself the patient is made to close his eyes and relax as deeply as possible and then asked to imagine scenes, beginning with the weakest scene from one of the hierarchical series. With presentations separated by pauses of several seconds the same scene is repeated until it ceases to arouse any anxiety at all; whereupon the therapist starts on the next scene in the hierarchy. In step with his progress in the sessions the patient reports a progressive decrease of sensitivity to the corresponding real situations encountered in life. Simple though it may seem, behavior therapy requires a high level of training. In every case *a skilled stimulus-response analysis is indispensable* if misdirection of effort is to be avoided.

CHARACTERISTICS OF THE ACHIEVEMENT OF PSYCHOTHERAPEUTIC GOALS BY BEHAVIOR THERAPY

In keeping with the assertion at the beginning of this paper that the foremost goal of psychotherapy is the conquest of suffering and disability, it is usual for behavior therapists to give their most immediate attention to whatever reactions are central to the patient's complaints. Since the treatment focuses on changing unadaptive emotional habits (and not merely quelling symptoms which are the consequence of these habits), when success is obtained it is both fundamental and usually lasting. New conditioning alone can restore extinct neurotic habits.

The treatment, however, frequently has repercussions that go a long way beyond the goals for which the therapist has directly striven; for, rid of the neurotic reactions that have harried his waking hours, the patient feels more free and potent. He responds anew to the world around him, so that even commonplace experiences may yield unaccustomed pleasures. He becomes progressively more effective in all his activities. Very often the changes are relevant to Knight's second, third, fourth, and fifth criteria—which may be achieved as by-products of eradicating the autonomic habits that have underlain the symptoms that brought the patient to treatment.

Improved function is of course to be expected in activities implicated with the neurotic fears, but other areas can benefit in a variety of indirect ways. The removal of interpersonal fears may change the sexual object of choice even to the extent of a transformation from homosexuality to heterosexuality; and the deconditioning of fears to particular stimuli may bring with it a disappearance of psychosomatic conditions like asthma, migraine, or neurodermatitis.

The following examples illustrate what may be implicated in the achievement of psychotherapeutic goals by behavior therapy.

Case 1

Deconditioning of interpersonal anxieties with recovery from homosexuality as a by-product. A 32-year-old completely homosexual hairdresser, always timid and unsure, had become increasingly anxious and unhappy in the previous 7 years. Various types of conventional psychotherapy, including a few months of psychoanalysis, had not arrested his "journey downward."

Behavioristic analysis revealed inappropriate fearfulness and extreme submissiveness in many interpersonal situations, both at work and socially. For example, he would be bowled over emotionally by any adverse criticism from a customer, no matter how unjust. The primary goal of psychotherapy was to eliminate the neurotic habits of anxiety-response in interpersonal situations, and the strategy to this end consisted of encouraging assertive behavior in all these situations. After 21 sessions over 3 months his neurotic anxiety responses had almost entirely ceased and he had become entirely at ease with customers, friends and casual contacts.

No direct attempt was made to influence his homosexuality, and at the end of treatment he was instructed to do just what pleased him sexually. Four months later he formed an association with a very pleasant homosexual partner, but within a few weeks found he could no longer respond to his friend sexually. Attempts at relations with other men also subsequently failed. He then began to take out a "platonic" girl friend of several months' standing. One night about three months later, he kissed her while slightly drunk, and found it very pleasant. Thereafter his sexual responses to her grew stronger and stronger, and then he consulted me to inquire whether he dared marry her. I encouraged this, but he handled her ineptly and was rejected. A year later he had a hectic and very satisfying affair with a divorcee, which launched him on a regular heterosexual sex life. Eighteen months after this he wrote that he had married and his wife was pregnant. For the previous 4 years he had not had the slightest homosexual inclinations.

The final attainment of sexual normality had, in its turn, important effects on the patient's view of himself in relation to society. He felt he could hold his head high and all vestiges of the feeling of being a "second-class citizen" disappeared. (Other details of this case have been reported elsewhere (Stevenson & Wolpe, 1960).

Case 2

Behavior therapy of impotence with secondary social consequences. This case was the reverse of Case 1, in that beneficial change in social responses was secondary to the overcoming of sexual anxieties.

A 36-year-old realtor had suffered from premature ejaculation from the beginning of his coital life 20 years previously. Ejaculation had always occurred within a few seconds of intromission. He had been married for 12 years, and his wife, although receiving some satisfaction from digital orgasms, had become increasingly resentful and dissatisfied and had been showing interest in other men. Two years of psychoanalytically-oriented therapy had not improved the situation in any way.

It is an essay in the obvious to say that the most clear-cut goal of psychotherapy was the cure of the premature ejaculation. Study of the case made it plain that the impairment of sexual function was due to anxiety responses to stimuli within the sexual situation.

There was also some neurotic anxiety in a variety of interpersonal contexts, and to overcome this was seen as a secondary goal. The means of dealing with the sexual dysfunction consisted of deconditioning the interfering anxiety-response habits, mainly by using sexual feeling-responses to inhibit small magnitudes of anxiety. These magnitudes were kept within prescribed bounds by controlling the closeness of the sexual approach. The method of general approach (Wolpe, 1958) was combined with Semans's technique (1956) for increasing pre-ejaculatory latency. The patient was also trained in progressive relaxation and at 3 of the sessions systematic desensitization was employed for critical phases of the sexual approach. Some general assertive training was also given to decondition the anxiety underlying minor inadequacies in dealing with people.

The sexual anxieties, and in consequence the premature ejaculation were overcome in 14 interviews during the course of 6 weeks. At that time the patient was regularly able to maintain an erection for more than 15 minutes during intercourse. His wife was having coital orgasms for the first time, and on one occasion had four of them during one intromission. Both partners were experiencing deep emotional satisfaction.

The patient had meanwhile become much more confident in a large variety of situations, and was getting more enjoyment from communion with other people than ever before. His Willoughby score had fallen from 30 to 13. This case is more fully described by Wolpe and Lazarus (1966).

Case 3

Treatment of a fear of aloneness and elimination of gall bladder syndrome. A 41-year-old housewife was referred for psychiatric treatment by a physician who had been unable to find an organic basis for her belching, abdominal distension, and other symptoms suggestive of gallbladder disease. She complained of a great deal of emotional tension much of which was occasioned by recurring "threats" of being left alone. Any prospect of being alone in her apartment for more than an hour was very disturbing, and so was a solo journey by car in excess of 10 miles. Prolonged solitude brought about increasing anxiety and ultimately panic. She was also easily upset by the disapproval of other people and very poor at handling differences with them. In addition, she had neurotic anxiety reactions at witnessing people being injected, and scenes related to death, blood, and fighting. She had recently been seeing a "dynamic" psychiatrist weekly for a year, and as no improvement had eventuated he had told her that there was nothing to do but "live with her phobias".

The goal of psychotherapy was to overcome the whole gamut of neurotic reactions. It was expected that their removal would automatically make her first a happier and then a more effective human being. A decision had to be made regarding the order in which the fears should be attacked; and it was decided to begin with the fears of other people that impeded her handling of them and soon afterwards to institute, in parallel with this, deconditioning of the fear of aloneness. The other anxieties could be dealt with later. The subsidence of her gallbladder symptoms was seen as an incidental goal that would be achieved by overcoming her neurotic anxieties.

The interpersonal fears were treated by the instigation of appropriate assertive behavior. Within a few weeks she made important advances, and the diminution of anxiety from this source led to a material decrease of gall-bladder symptoms, but no change in the fear of aloneness. This was treated by the technique of systematic desensitization (see above) causing her to imagine, while in the deeply relaxed state, circumstances of separation from her husband that, as her tolerance grew, was progressively extended in time and distance. There was complete transfer from the imaginary to the real, and eventually she could endure with complete calm being alone for 24 hours with her husband 70 miles away, and became able to drive a car alone any distance without anxiety.

The other phobic reactions were similarly handled with equal success, and, as expected, there was a complete subsidence of the gallbladder syndrome except for some resurgence during premenstrual phases. Treatment had required 33 sessions over 13 months, and all the goals that had been set were accomplished. At a follow-up three years later the patient stated that she had been free from anxiety in all the previously phobic areas and had not suffered from recurrence of the gallbladder syndrome or any new symptoms.

WITH WHAT SUCCESS DOES BEHAVIOR THERAPY ACHIEVE PSYCHOTHERAPEUTIC GOALS?

Outcome Studies

It was stated earlier in this paper that the goals of behavior therapy are generally set in accordance with Knight's criteria. In addition to a large number of reports on individual cases or small groups, the results of treatment in several series of cases large enough to be statistically meaningful have been published in recent years. In 1958 I reported that 89 percent of 210 patients comprising three series were either apparently recovered or at least four-fifths improved on Knight's criteria. In the final series of 88 patients[2], in 78 of whom therapy was successful, the median number of interviews was 23 and the mean 45. In a group of 18 phobic children, Lazarus (1960) obtained 100 percent recoveries in a mean of 9.5 sessions. He later published his results with re-

[2]Two patients, one in the "much-improved" group and the other a failure, later turned out to be schizophrenic. A patient who did well in general but who had been regarded as only moderately improved because his "writer's cramp" persisted was reassessed as "much improved" when it was found that the disability of his hand was due to a neurological lesion.

spect to 408 cases who consulted him in the course of 4 years (including those whom he saw only once). Of these 321 (78 percent) "appeared to derive definite and constructive benefit." Of the 126 most severely neurotic of these patients 61.9 percent were rated completely recovered or markedly improved in a mean of 14.07 sessions. There were 18 such successful results among 44 patients who had been under treatment with other therapists for 10 years or more. Hussain (1964) has claimed that 100 out of 105 patients whom he has treated by conditioning methods have been either apparently cured or much improved on Knight's criteria, after treatment that generally took less than 3 months. A comparative evaluation of the results of behavior therapy and those of psychoanalysis has been presented elsewhere (Wolpe, 1964a). In this comparison behavior therapy shows up very favorably, but the data are uncontrolled. Recent controlled studies, e.g., Paul (1966), are equally favorable.

Relapse and Symptom Substitution

A critical question is, of course, the permanence of results obtained by conditioning methods. They practically always appear to be lasting. In 1958 I reported that among 45 patients followed up for periods ranging from 2 to 7 years there had been only 1 relapse. Lazarus (1963) has followed up 20 of his patients for an average of 2.15 years with no relapse, unless one regards as such an individual who became morbidly depressed after he had been involved in an accident in which a child was killed. It has so far been the experience of all competent behavior therapists that relapse is very unusual. When it does occur it is related to *reconditioning* and not to an eruption from still-contained repressed forces.

An instance of such reconditioning was afforded some years ago by a patient who had been treated for very severe and widespread neurotic conditionings one of which was of marked anxiety to manifestations of illness in others as well as her own. She responded well to behavior therapy which included extensive desensitization to illness of others, so that she could witness great physical distress without feeling anxiety. About 6 months later she became markedly disturbed when she herself was admitted to hospital for uterine bleeding. This caused a partial resensitization in the whole stimulus area connected with illness. This had happened because I had not considered that her own hospitalization might be more anxiety-evoking than that of other people, and while I had also desensitized her to a series of "hypochondriacal" reactions, i.e., anxiety reactions to pains and other nonsignificant somatic symptoms, I had omitted to take into account serious illness.

Symptom-substitution in the psychoanalytic sense has not been encountered after behavior therapy. When occasionally recession of a symptom has been followed by exacerbation of another it has usually been due to misguided therapeutic tactics resulting from an inadequate conception of the case. For example, a certain therapist found that as a woman's compulsive eating was being successfully overcome by the conditioning of an aversive reaction to food, she became increasingly anxious and depressed. More thorough scrutiny of the case revealed that the eating was an anxiety relieving response. The first goal of therapy should have been to decondition the neurotic anxiety responses to which the compulsive eating was secondary (being reinforced by its anxiety-reducing effect).

Quite often, reactions regarded as relatively unimportant are brought to the fore upon recovery from more important ones. In some unusual cases a new symptom may make its appearance upon the removal of more severe reactions that have overridden it, and then this new reaction can in its turn be subjected to deconditioning. An interesting example is reported by Lazarus and Rachman (1960). A woman of 29 who had always been tense and anxious had developed a phobia for dogs following a traumatic incident at the age of 24. She underwent 3 years of psychoanalysis during which her dog phobia disappeared *but was replaced by a state of chronic anxiety* so severe that she "felt that suicide was her only release." It seemed that the psychoanalysis "had merely blanketed her specific phobia with general anxiety." After six weeks of conditioning therapy (28 sessions) she was much improved, but her dog phobia had returned. A further 28 sessions were devoted mainly to overcoming this phobia. A year later she was still well and the dog phobia remained extinct. This history illustrates both symptom substitution following psychoanalysis and the handling of symptom substitution by conditioning.

In the great majority of cases no adverse sequelae of any kind are observed to follow the deconditioning of neurotic habits. On the contrary very often the disappearance of one constellation of reactions creates an optimism that facilitates recovery from others.

It seems that, in accordance with the expectations of learning theory, all recoveries from neurosis tend to be lasting—and it does not matter in the course of what kind of therapy they may have been procured. A survey of follow-up studies (Wolpe, 1961) by various authors on neurotic patients who had either recovered or improved markedly after different kinds of treatment other than psychoanalysis, showed that out of 249 patients followed up from 2 to 15 years only 4 (1.6 percent) had relapsed.

The demonstration that without psychoanalysis recovery has an endurance that can hardly be bettered shakes to its foundations the psychoanalytic theory of neuroses. The stability of the results of behavior therapy is particularly significant, because behavior therapists make no interpretations and conduct therapy as if the "mechanisms" assumed by psychoanalysts do not exist. The results of behavior therapy would not be so consistently lasting if the psychoanalytic mechanisms were truly the basis of neurosis.

When "dynamic" therapists are confronted with these results they frequently state that *their* cases would not lend themselves to behavior therapy, being more "complex." This claim is not justified by facts. Many of the successes of behavior therapy have been psychoanalytic failures; behavior therapists accept for treatment *all* neurotic cases that come their way; and, as has been pointed out in detail elsewhere (Wolpe, 1964), even the most complex cases, when subjected to a stimulus-response analysis, tend to acquire a phobia-like "look", precisely because the disturbed reactions are seen to have clearly defined antecedents. The outlines of almost any neurosis appear much more clear-cut when analyzed behavioristically than when seen through psycho-analytically-tinted spectacles.

Personality Change

There are some who look askance at behavior therapy on the alleged ground that it attacks mere symptoms, and does not concern itself with the "more basic" goal of producing personality change.

It has already been stressed in this paper that behavior therapy is directed against *habits*, not symptoms, and that in fact any therapy that effects change can only do so by procuring the unlearning of habits. If personality is defined as the totality of a person's habits of response, every change of habit implies change of personality. If a person acquires or loses an anxiety response habit, his personality is to some extent changed.

But behavior therapy very frequently leads to personality changes beyond those implicit in the overcoming of the specific neurotic conditionings. The liberating effects of removal of a troublesome neurosis are almost universal, and typically illustrated in the three cases described in this paper. The elimination even of so limited a reaction as acrophobia may have profound consequences. Because the patient comes to be at ease in a range of situations previously forbidding, behavior that was previously impossible can be performed and new and more adaptive habits developed. And a sense of new-found freedom permeates personal relations, for the inferiority that used to accompany the old disability is automatically dispelled. Ashem (1963), reports a common experience when he recounts how three months after the desensitization of a 5-year-old disaster phobia the patient's wife stated that he was "better than he had been since she had known him", and remained in excellent spirits in the face of adverse life circumstances.

Furthermore behavior therapy takes account also of preconditioned sensitivities that may have predisposed to the neurotic reactions. Sometimes the recovery of the preconditioned emotional habit is included in the treatment of a major presenting neurosis, because the latter is essentially an intensification of the former. In other cases, the preconditioned habit requires attention in its own right. When there are multiple preconditionings their removal may proceed in different ways, as in the following example: An attorney of 45 came for treatment of severe claustrophobia. He had originally had a very mild claustrophobia ever since a childhood experience in an elevator. Ten years previously, while presenting a brief in a small court on a very hot day, he had felt slightly faint and short of breath. Suddenly the magistrate had said to him,

"Do you feel well, Mr. H.?" Mr. H. was panic-stricken, and from that day his claustrophobia became severe and he also acquired a fear of courts. As might be expected, treatment of the long-standing mild claustrophobia was implicated in densensitization of the claustrophobic reaction as a whole. But the patient also obviously had strong anxiety response habits to criticism and disapproval especially from authority figures, and measures against these neurotic habits were an indispensable part of the treatment.

It is integral to properly conducted behavior therapy to make the fullest possible survey of the patient's functioning in all the major areas of his life, and to try to pinpoint *all* stimulus sources of neurotic reactions. To this end, the therapist takes a detailed history of the patient's development, and the status of his performance at work and play, and in social and sexual relations; questions him closely about all sources of disturbance and augments the information so obtained by the Willoughby (1934) and Bernreuter (1933) Self-Sufficiency Questionnaires and a Fear Survey Schedule (Wolpe and Lang, 1964).[3] The patient is not regarded as recovered as long as he has more than a negligible degree of anxious responding to any stimulus to which anxiety is unadaptive.

The question remains whether behavior therapy achieves the kind of personality change claimed to be achieved by psychoanalysis. Before attempting an answer it must again be said that behavior therapy does not need to have recourse to such goals as a means of side-stepping the *therapeutic* goals—the conquest of suffering and disability. In the sense that the deconditioning of anxiety and the building of effective new habits carry with them the development of happier human beings with improved interpersonal relations, behavior therapy can certainly be said to achieve the broad psychoanalytic goal of "a better integrated personality." It does not claim to work through the Oedipus constellation or bring about a recession of childhood transference or the like, nor is it likely to aim to do so until it is shown that there is a correlation between such achievements per se and changes of practical importance to the economy of the individual.

[3]This is a list of 72 stimulus items to which a fear reaction is unadaptive. The patient checks each item on a 5-point scale in answer to the question "How much fear do you have?" The five responses are: 1) None. 2) A little. 3) A fair amount. 4) Much. 5) Very much. Some of the items are: being alone; reciting in public; thunder; one person bullying another; being teased; cemeteries; failure; flying insects; blood; journeys; people in authority; nude men or women.

REFERENCES

Ashem, B. The treatment of a disaster phobia by systematic desensitization. *Behav. Res. Ther.*, 1963, **1**, 81–84.

Bernreuter, R. G. The measurement of self sufficiency. *J. abnorm. soc. Psychol.*, 1933, **28**, 291–296.

Bond, I. K., and Hutchison, H. C. Application of reciprocal inhibition therapy to exhibitionism. *Canad. med. Assoc. J.*, 1960, **83**; 23–25.

Briggs, M. H., and Kitto, G. B. The molecular basis of memory and learning. *Psychol. Rev.*, 1962, **69,** 537–541.

Brody, N. W. Prognosis and results of psycholanalysis, In J. H. Nodine and J. H. Moyer (Eds.), *Psychosomatic medicine.* Philadelphia: Lea and Febiger, 1962.

Clark, D. F. The treatment of monosymptomatic phobia by systematic desensitization. *Behav. Res. Ther.,* 1963, **1,** 63–68.

Freund, K. Some problems in the treatment of homosexuality. In H. J. Eysenck (Ed.), *Behavior therapy and the neuroses.* New York; Pergamon Press, 1960.

Glynn, J. D., and Harper, P. Behavior therapy in transvestism. *Lancet,* 1961, **1,** 619.

Hussain, A. Behavior therapy in 105 cases. In J. Wolpe, A. Salter, and L. J. Reyna (Eds.), *Conditioning therapies.* New York: Holt, Rinehart and Winston, 1964.

Jacobson, E. *Progressive relaxation.* Chicago: University of Chicago Press, 1938.

Jones, H. G. The behavorial treatment of enuresis nocturna. In H. J. Eysenck (Ed.), *Behavior therapy and the neuroses.* New York: Pergamon Press, 1960.

Knight, R. P. Evaluation of the results of psychotherapy. *Amer. J. Psychiat.,* 1941, **98,** 434–446.

Lang, P. J., and Lazovik, A. D. The experimental desensitization of a phobia. *J. abnorm. soc. Psychol.,* 1963, **66,** 519–525.

Lazarus, A. A. The elimination of children's phobias by deconditioning. In H. J. Eysenck (Ed.), *Behavior therapy and the neuroses.* New York: Pergamon Press, 1960.

Lazarus, A. A. The results of behavior therapy in 126 cases of severe neurosis. *Behav. Res. Ther.,* 1963, **1,** 69–79.

Lazarus, A. A., and Abramovitz, A. The use of "emotive imagery" in the treatment of children's phobias. *J. Ment. Sci.,* 1962, **108,** 191–195.

Lazarus, A. A., and Rachman, S. The use of systematic desensitization psychotherapy. In H. J. Eysenck (Ed.), *Behavior therapy and the neuroses.* New York: Pergamon Press, 1960.

Lovibond, S. H. The mechanism of conditioning treatment of enuresis. *Behav. Res. Ther.,* 1963, **1,** 17–22.

Masserman, J. H. *Behavior and neurosis.* Chicago: University of Chicago Press, 1943.

Paul, G. L. *Insight versus desensitization in psychotherapy.* Stanford: Stanford University Press, 1958.

Pavlov, I. P. *Conditioned reflexes.* G. V. Anrep (Ed.). London: Oxford University Press, 1927.

Raymond, M. J. Case of fetishism treated by aversion therapy. *Brit. Med. J.,* 1956, **2,** 854–856.

Salter, A. *Conditioned reflex therapy.* New York: Creative Age Press, 1949.

Semans, J. H. Premature ejaculation: a new approach. *S. Med. J.,* 1956, **49,** 353–358.

Stevenson, I., and Wolpe, J. Recovery from sexual deviations through overcoming nonsexual neurotic responses. *Amer. J. Psychiat.,* 1960, **116,** 737–742.

Wilder, J. Facts and figures on psychotherapy. *J. clin. Psychopath.,* 1945, **7,** 311–347.

Willoughby, R. R. Norms for the Clark-Thurstone Inventory. *J. soc. Psychol.,* 1934, **5,** 91–96.

Wolpe, J. Experimental neuroses as learned behavior. *Brit. J. Psychol.,* 1952, **43,** 243–268. (a)

Wolpe, J. The neurophysiology of learning and delayed reward learning. *Psychol. Rev.,* 1952, **59,** 192–199. (b)

Wolpe, J. *Psychotherapy by reciprocal inhibition.* Stanford: Stanford University Press, 1958.

Wolpe, J. The prognosis in unpsychoanalysed recovery from neuroses. *Amer. J. Psychiat.*, 1961, **117**, 35–39. (a)

Wolpe, J. The systematic desensitization treatment of neuroses. *J. nerv. ment. Dis.*, 1961, **132**, 189–203. (b)

Wolpe, J. Behavior therapy in complex neurotic states. *Brit. J. Psychiat.*, 1964, **110**, 28–34. (a)

Wolpe, J. The comparative clinical status of conditioning therapies and psycho-analysis. In J. Wolpe, A. Salter, and L. J. Reyna (Eds.), *The conditioning therapies.* New York: Holt, Rinehart and Winston, 1964. (b)

Wolpe, J., and Lang, P. J. A Fear Survey Schedule for use in behavior therapy. *Behav. Res. Ther.*, 1964, **2**, 27–30.

Wolpe, J., and Lazarus, A. A. *Behavior therapy techniques.* New York: Pergamon Press, 1966.

Yates, A. J. The application of learning theory to the treatment of tics. *J. abnorm. soc. Psychol.*, 1958, **56**, 175–182.

11

The Goals of Psychotherapy from the Existential Point of View

Adrian van Kaam, Ph.D.

An Introduction to the Person

by Susan Annette Muto, B.A.

Dr. van Kaam was born in The Hague, Holland, in 1920. A consultant in the so-called life schools for young adults in offices, mills, and companies in Holland, he aimed at integrating the dynamic principles of religion and psychology into a series of courses on various subjects preparing girls between 17 and 25 for vocational and marital life. He delineated his findings on the psychological and religious background of these girls in his Dutch M.O. dissertation for a Degree in Educational Psychology. During this time he was also a counselor in the Dutch Governmental Psychological Observation Center for Juvenile Delinquents, "Kamp Overberg," at Veenendaal, Holland, and was influential in opening the first school of life for boys in Gemert, Holland.

Upon arrival in the United States in 1954, Dr. van Kaam began studying psychology at Western Reserve University. While working on his doctorate, he trained in psychotherapy under Carl Rogers at the University of Chicago and under Dr. Rudolph Dreikurs at the Alfred Adler Institute in Chicago. During the summer of 1957, he participated in special studies in personality theory at Brandeis University under Dr. Abraham Maslow, Dr. Kurt Goldstein, and Dr. Angyall. After receiving his Ph.D. from Western Reserve in 1958, he taught at Brandeis for a year and has since lectured at Boston College, Harvard University, Penn State, and various clinics and mental hospitals.

Now a professor of psychology at Duquesne University, he is the founder and director of the Institute of Man, a center of study and research in which experts in various fields collaborate to deepen understanding of man in his manifold aspects and relations. He is also editor of *Humanitas,* journal of the Institute of Man; *Envoy,* published monthly by the Center of Religious Anthropology of the Institute; and *The Review of Existential Psychology and Psychiatry.* In addition to directing Duquesne's academic program in Religion and Personality, Dr. van Kaam teaches both graduate and undergraduate courses in psychology and personality theory. From May to September, 1966, he was visiting professor at the University of Heidelberg, Germany.

Besides his *Religion and Personality,* Dr. van Kaam has recently published three new books: *Personality Fulfillment in the Spiritual Life, Existential Foundations of Psychology,* and *The Art of Existential Counseling: A New Perspective in Psychotherapy.* His articles appear in *Envoy, Insight, The Journal of Individual Psychology, Humanitas, Journal of Humanistic Psychology, Review of Existential Psychology and Psychiatry,* and many more professional and scholarly publications both in Europe and America.

Author, teacher, lecturer, and for many, good friend, a man whose spontaneity and keen sense of humor are evident in all he does, Dr. van Kaam has truly taken to heart his personal commitment to reality. He says that within every person is a unique potential structure of existence. Once committed to actualizing this structure, the person is set on the path of becoming what he is to be. While discovery, commitment, and realization may be the ideal goals of psychotherapy, Dr. van Kaam also sees them as beacons showing us how life can be most fully lived.

I SHOULD like to discuss not the immediate aims of psychotherapy but rather its long-distance goals. I shall concentrate, therefore, not on the direct liberating effect of therapy itself, but on the possibilities for openness and growth which emerge from this liberation.

What is man like when he has been set free by psychotherapy? To clarify my view of this new man, I must first make clear my view of psychotherapy. As a psychotherapist I address myself to a fellow human being. I see and experience him as a person called to actualize himself within his unique life situation. He came to me because he felt vaguely that something was wrong; he was dissatisfied with his life, his existence seemed dreary, meaningless, and without value; he was in trouble with people around him, in his daily work, and within himself; he suffered from disturbing symptoms which diminished his efficiency. I can briefly summarize his feelings and symptoms by saying that my client had lost the ability to understand and to realize the unique meaning of his existence within his unique life situation. Therefore, as a good therapist I must foster an atmosphere which will enable him to understand himself within his situation, to face his personal responsibility.

OPENNESS TO AUTHENTIC GUILT

My client must recognize and work through his own authentic guilt instead of becoming fixated on his neurotic guilt. During this process of growth I should be careful not to burden him with my personal feelings of guilt, with my own expectations, or with norms which dominate the cultural structures to which I personally have committed myself. Authentic guilt, responsibility, and commitment must grow out of his own true experiences. They must be truly his and not mine. He must find his own personal response to his reality independent of my response to my reality. He cannot become "whole" if he does not discover his own decisive answer to his own life but blindly incorporates my personal answers which may be alien to his very individuality. If he blindly adopts my personal style of existence, he will foster a harmful split between his own unclarified self and my superimposed self. My client can reach wholeness only if he discovers his own authentic guilt which is covered over by layers of neurotic guilt. He has a right to his own guilt; psychotherapy should enable him to discover this personal guilt which is linked with a personal experience of responsibility for his own becoming.

ACCEPTANCE OF A DYNAMIC EXISTENCE

Psychotherapy will enable my client not only to discover his true guilt and responsibility, but also to experience that life is growth, development, and actualization. This growth may take the form of freeing himself from the paralyzing influence of a one-sided mode of existence, or it may mean the development of new authentic modes. Growth also implies the integration of old and new modes of existence into a wholesome style of life. The liberation from inauthentic modes is characteristic of the initial phase of psychotherapy. The discovery of hidden repressed modes of being and the development of new authentic ones are prevalent in the second period of therapy. The integration of newly-emerged with past authentic modes of existence into a new style of life appears more clearly at the end of the therapeutic process. Of course, these three movements of growth are not mutually exclusive. On the contrary, they coincide. We can say only that one or the other is more dominant at a certain stage of the therapeutic process.

My client's therapeutic experience that his life is growth and becoming implies his acceptance of the fact that his personality will never be "finished" or "totally understood" or ever "without mystery or problem," that he will always be on the road, always a traveller, an adventurer, a pioneer who never reaches the far West of his full existence. The final aim of psychotherapy is thus not a static well-being on the part of my client but his full acceptance of a dynamic existence opening up to continually new horizons.

Such therapy will enable my client to adapt himself continually to his own emerging possibilities of being and to realize these possibilities in his life. For the human self reveals itself in constantly new aspects to be actualized. Neither therapist nor client can predict the appeals of tomorrow. But therapy can create a readiness to listen to the challenges which will announce themselves. I think, therefore, that it is crucial for my client to grow to the insight that his actual personality is not unchangeable.

FAITHFULNESS TO THE INFRA-STRUCTURE AND FLEXIBILITY TOWARD THE SUPER-STRUCTURES OF EXISTENCE

When I say actual personality I mean the structural totality and specificity of the modes of existence which my client has developed up to this moment of crisis in his life. He may believe that his personality is fixed forever. He may perceive himself as a thing molded once and for all. He may use his belief in his unchangeability as an escape from the burden of becoming. Therapy should enable my client to become aware of what is authentic and inauthentic in this view of himself. There are various authentic structures of personality which can emerge from the deepest core of his being when he is in dialogue with his various life situations. For every individual has deep within himself a unique potential structure of existence which can be realized in a variety of superstructures.

This fundamental structure, or infra-structure, cannot be changed without violating him as an individual. What can change, however, is the concrete realization of this hidden structure. My client came to me because of his failure to actualize this unique structure which he fundamentally is. In other words, the constellation of his actual modes of existence is inauthentic because of his anxious introjection of foreign elements which are at odds with what he basically is. This situation makes it impossible for him to be what he should be in his concrete daily existence. This constellation of adopted actual modes of existence may cover up the unique style of being which is truly his. No therapy, to be sure, can give the client an exhaustive understanding of all that he is. Good therapy, however, will enable him to discover and realize himself increasingly in the infinite plurality of encounters in his daily life during, and especially after, the time that he is in therapy.

One of the bases of the unique style of each human existence is that each individual has his own typical constellation of those drives, impulses, and basic motives which are characteristic of our species. These fundamental forces are present in every human being at least potentially. But their relative strength and actual intensity, their mutual relationships, and their fundamental configuration differ from individual to individual. I do not speak here about differences due to environment, education, and personal life situation, but about those more basic differences which are given from the outset as the raw material of human personalities. It is true that every one of my clients will eventually decide on the fundamental orientation of his existence—his existential project—in the light of his life situation. Yet the specific style of his existence or the concrete embodiment of his project will emerge from his uniquely given constellation of forces which we call drives, inclinations, impulses, and motives. Openness to both his life situation and the unique power configuration of his dynamic forces will lead gradually to his authentic and unique style of existence. For this reason, every theoretical simplification or reduction of the complexity of human existence by the therapist is potentially harmful. This does not mean that psychological theories are useless. On the contrary, each scientifically acceptable hypothesis enriches the therapist with a new possibility for understanding certain realms of experience in his clients. The existential attitude in psychotherapy, however, implies the use of these acquired sensitivities within a wide openness for the infinite variety of possibilities of human existence.

For example, my client's preoccupation with study can be an expression of sexual curiosity, a compensation for a feeling of inferiority, an escape from social life, sheer pleasure in the intellectual, dedication to a cause, or a form of obedience to parents, school, or other institution. But this involvement in study may also be a result of an irreducible unique predisposition. In the latter case it is a natural expression of the unique personality structure of my client and not a reactive phenomenon. Of course, many reactive motivations may be present together in my client. In this case, they may influence one another. But this does not mean that I can *a priori* consider one motivation and its contribution to a subsequent mode of existence as merely a derivation of another motive which co-constitutes a certain mode of existence. For example, sexual curiosity may lead to a more generalized intellectual curiosity and influence its development. But this does not mean that intellectual curiosity can be reduced to mere sexual curiosity.

LIBERATION FROM PSYCHOLOGISM, PUBLIC IMAGE, AND SCIENTISM

The person who comes for psychotherapy today is frequently influenced by certain reducing concepts of psychology and psychiatry which are popularized by the mass media of communication. He may not realize that each one of these various theories reveals only certain possible aspects of human existence and by no means all possible aspects. As a result he may begin to see himself almost solely in the light of one or the other psychological theory. Such a narrowed consideration of his personality will lead necessarily to a blindness for those possibilities of selfhood which are not emphasized by the particular theory in question. Many people are crippled in their personality development by the influence of popularized psychology and psychiatry. Therefore, one of the long-range aims of contemporary therapy is to liberate people from the tyranny of popular concepts which, like a thick fog, render real personal self-experience impossible.

Another purpose of psychotherapy today is to enable the client to free himself from another tyranny, the despotism of the public image. Contemporary civilization makes people strongly aware of their public image. Government and industry, schools and social organizations, and the worlds of entertainment and even of religion are unhealthily conscious of how they appear in the eyes of others. The promotion of an attractive image is an ongoing concern, an anxious preoccupation. An individual who is deeply influenced by such concern ceases to be a real person. He cares more about how he looks to others than about what he is. He is more sensitive to the preferences of others than to his own feelings. He is inspired by the ideals of the majority rather than those ideals which are in harmony with his own deepest being.

If the demon of the public image takes firm possession of him, be becomes unable to distinguish between his own feelings and the impersonal urges of the crowd. My client may have risen to the heights of administrative, academic, political, or ecclesiastical success by his clever catering to the crowd or to his superiors. He may not be consciously aware that he has paid the highest price for this popularity, his own priceless individuality. The more intelligent, creative, and idealistic the client basically is, the deeper he will be disturbed by his selling out, by the prostitution of his talents. His most profound self may be compared to a call girl available to the best-paying patron and obligingly conforming to his every wish.

Preoccupation with the public image has become a cultural disease which has led many potentially creative individuals to an apathetic, impoverished life of quiet desperation. Many such men, suffering from a meaningless existence, present themselves for therapy. In this case, one of the aims of therapy is to help them to discover their own individuality under the mask of their public image.

I consider another aim of contemporary therapy to be the gradual growth of an attitude which I would call "patient self presence." Many people come into therapy with the fantasy that they will enjoy flashes of insight which will lead to sudden changes in their lives. This expectancy of swift improvement as a result of therapeutic manipulation is due not only to "magic" thinking but also to the "scientistic" attitude fostered in our civilization. Physical science, the exploration and manipulation of physical objects, is desirable in its own realm. But scientism, or the expansion of the methods of physical science to nonphysical subjects such as human existence, the free project of life, and the growth of the self, is most undesirable. It is not a clearly formulated doctrine but an all-pervasive mode of being which is assumed especially by those who know little about science itself. This attitude of scientism leads its victims to manipulate their lives as if they were physical objects, algebraic equations, or experiments in chemistry. Such people may come into therapy convinced that their main problem is that they have not yet found the efficient method or technique for successful self-manipulation. Their scientistic mode of existence leads them to expect a fast diagnosis and an effective "recipe" for a swift metamorphosis of their personality. One of the chief things they learn in psychotherapy is that one cannot deal with a false mode of existence as with a diseased leg or liver, that an attempted equation of psychological with physical healing is misleading.

In the long, sometimes tedious process of psychotherapy, these clients experience that an unwholesome mode of existence is usually formed by an accumulation of experiences over a long period of time. They realize gradually and slowly that the manifold experiences which built this unsavory mode of being were not worked through at the moment that they were introjected; they were not freely and wisely appropriated. The clients now see, in the process of therapy itself, that not only the insight into the complex structure of a mode of existence but also the slow and painful growth beyond this mode requires an arduous and patient dialogue with the myriad manifestations of this mode in innumerable concrete life situations. Therapy is the development of the ability for persevering dialogue with the disclosures of one's existence in daily life. One of the long-range aims of psychotherapy, therefore, is to prepare the client to be patiently present to himself as manifested in his life situation. For this art often remains unlearned in our technological society.

ACCEPTANCE OF AUTHENTIC CONFLICT

I do not believe that it is the aim of psychotherapy to solve all conflicts and problems of the client. Psychotherapy helps man to uncover the unique fundamental structure of his personality and to commit himself to the actualization of this structure. Therapy helps him to transcend the spurious and inauthentic structures which superseded his authentic being. It strengthens him against both the demon of the public image and his scientistic inclination to self manipulation. He develops from a mechanic of life into a living person, but this does not mean that he will not be faced with contradictions and conflicts within his personality. Contradiction and conflict are potentially present in his basic given structure of existence. The various modes of being in the world which he can develop on the basis of his true self must be balanced and integrated with one another. The aim of psychotherapy is not to solve his conflicts but to enable him to see and experience these opposed inclinations more clearly within himself. Psychotherapy brings to light what the person is and sets him on the path of becoming what he is to be. It changes neither the unique and fundamental structure of his existence nor its inherent conflicts and contradictions.

The end of therapy is the beginning of conflict. Once man has come to himself through psychotherapy he is able to discover, maintain, and restore the balance between the opposing forces which are characteristic of his unique personality. A client may discover, for example, an inclination to dependency which may not be reducible to any other "cause" in his past or in his environment but which is truly inherent in the very structure of his existence. In this case he himself must take his stand toward this inclination and learn how to live wisely with this particular expression of himself in his life situation. In this sense we may say that it is an aim of psychotherapy to initiate authentic conflict which replaces the inauthentic conflicts of the client's past.

Having stated these general aims, I may now become somewhat more specific in anlyzing the main attitudes which I expect to develop in my client after successful therapy.

EXISTENTIAL HONESTY

I consider it one of the long-range aims of psychotherapy that my client will be able to be true to himself and to others. One of the outcomes of therapy should be that the client is able to recognize his own identity, that he knows what he himself thinks and feels about the various aspects of his life situation. This does not mean, of course, that he takes into account only his own perceptions. It means that ultimately only he himself must make the final decisions in his life according to his own personal insight, which is enriched, deepened, and tempered by a personal evaluation of the insights of others.

This basic honesty implies that my client has learned in psychotherapy to abdicate all attitudes, actions, customs, words, and expressions which he experiences as untrue. This striving to diminish in his existence the strength of the defensive systems which he has developed in anxious self-protection must continue after therapy. This task is never finished, for the defensive and neurotic systems of existence always remain available in the personality and reemerge immediately when the person feels threatened. So long as he does not develop this fundamental and courageous honesty, he will not be able to achieve an authentic human existence.

Why is it so difficult for my client to abdicate all that is not authentically himself? I think that a deep existential anxiety makes my client hold on so desperately and tenaciously to his defensive attitudes. Deep down, he is aware that up to now his real potential self-structure could not actualize itself, smothered as it was by the powerful defensive structures of his existence. He realizes, therefore, that the loss of his "borrowed feathers" would reveal him in the ugly nudity of a not yet actualized personality. On a deep level, this perception gives him the anxious feeling that he is entering an emptiness in which he will lose all his moorings and certitudes. Thus his resistance to honesty is not so much a matter of bad will as of anxiety at seeing and revealing himself as small, limited, weak, and insufficient. Everyone wants to be somebody, a person who really counts. Man is perhaps most afraid of the possible discovery that he is really unimportant. It would be easier, perhaps, for my client to accept himself as bad than as insignificant. Frequently his inclination to attract the attention of others arises from a defense against his anxiety that he may discover his own insignificance rather than from a real belief in his own importance. My client may feel unconsciously so unimportant and meaningless that he is overwhelmed by the constant fear that others may see him in the same way if he surrenders his make-believe attitudes and behavior. His secret perception of himself as small and worthless opens up for him a world in which people are constantly on the verge of discovering him. It is understandable that this fear leads to a forced and spasmodic concentration on his own behavior, words, and expressions.

Therefore, when the client begins to give up his defensiveness, his behavior becomes immediately freer, more relaxed and natural, less tense and guarded. This breakdown of the old defensive structure is already in and by itself an expression of the new man. It is true that at first the client may appear less forceful and certain than before. However, the strength which he shows now, no matter how little, is truly the force of his own being and, therefore, far stronger than his forced, artificial, self-conscious attitude of the past which may indeed have seemed very impressive to weak people in his environment. This new authentic strength, when he maintains it after therapy, will gain in depth; it will be free from the anxiety which invested so much energy in former defensive structures. Sooner or later this authentic strength, which the person really has, will influence others far more deeply than the former show of force or cleverness and the past pretense of power and unshakeable self-reliance. At the moment that my client dares to be small, worthless, and unimportant he is no longer the insignificant man which he was, because the very courage to be what he is endows him with the radiance of a significant, unalienable existence.

This basic honesty gained in psychotherapy also enables my client to admit his own mistakes easily and swiftly. In the past he was afraid that any mistake he made would jeopardize his very existence or destroy the esteem which he had in the eyes of others. He was inclined to identify his whole personality with his duty in society. If anyone attacked his work or devaluated his contribution, he experienced it as an attack on his very personality. He felt threatened in the core of his existence. It is one of the long-range aims of psychotherapy to make it possible for the client in his future life to understand his mistakes as signposts of improvement and growth. He must be able to risk himself in the life situation. He must dare to make mistakes and to accept the consequences of these mistakes without anxiety, bitterness, and resentment. One direct result of this newly acquired attitude will be a gain in his creativity and productivity. For creativity and effective presence to the life situation are frequently blocked by anxiety about making mistakes. Creativity can flourish only when a person feels free to be found imperfect and prone to failure. Many people lead ineffective lives because they feel compelled to retire as soon as they make mistakes and are blamed for them.

Of course, it will take a lifetime to make concrete in daily endeavor this basic honesty which the client has found in psychotherapy. In the realization of his honest self-insight, he will time and time again discover resistances in himself. Therapy should establish a readiness to cope with these resistances, a willingness not to be more nor less than he really is, but to be faithful to the task which is imposed by his life situation.

EXISTENTIAL COMMITMENT

The readiness to listen to the appeal of the life situation implies commitment. Existential commitment means that my client has given up his self-centered, autarchic existence and put himself at the disposal of the demands of life. This does not mean that he surrenders himself blindly to another person or institution, but that he is willing to live a project of life that, according to his own insight, is in tune with the realistic demands of his existence. Instead of saying, "I decide what I like to do," he now says, "I personally decide what is asked of me in my life situation." What he gives up is not his own judgment, insight, freedom, and responsibility, but his ego-centrism. He refuses to make his egoistic concern the last and only criterion of his life project. Rather he responds freely to the life situation in which he finds himself, and he does so in harmony with his own being. This implies that my client experiences that there is something higher than himself. In other words, there is a supra-personal element in his surrender. This surrender liberates him from his ego-centric prison and integrates him within reality, life, and history.

The commitment at which therapy aims does not find its source in a greater confidence in one's isolated self. On the contrary, authentic self-confidence is more the outcome than the source of existential commitment. Free and relaxed self-confidence is rooted in the experience of one's integration in life, in culture and society, in nature, in the world of supra-personal values, and in being and its mysterious ground. If my client is religious, he may experience self-confidence because of his rootedness in the mystery of the divine. Existential commitment diminishes existential anxiety. Authentic freedom is not based on belief in one's own strength, but on joyful surrender to life with all the risks which it implies.

The client who leaves therapy with this attitude is less clear and certain about the concrete details of his future, but he is filled with trust that life will suggest to him the right solutions at the right time if he lives in a relaxed openness for all the messages which life may give him. Before therapy, anxiety about the unknown and the untried severely hindered his self-realization. Now, however, he feels ready for whatever may happen to him. His faith in existence, his surrender to being convinces him that he will find light to take the next step at every winding of the road of his life. He no longer feels that it is necessary for him to see the whole road clearly before he feels free to move.

Existential commitment implies the acceptance of existence in all its aspects, whether they give rise to joy or pain. After successful psychotherapy, my client will be able to bear the suffering which is unavoidable in life. Before therapy, his growth was impaired by his attempts to avoid painful experiences.

Now, however, he dares to expose himself to the reality of life. Doing so, he actualizes his possibility for a fuller and deeper understanding of human existence. Many aspects of life are revealed only in suffering that is faced and worked through. My client will be increasingly able to accept without fatalism or apathy, resistance or resentment, escape or avoidance the suffering which life brings to him. In other words, suffering is still present, is still painful; yet it does not disturb his inner freedom.

This ability to face suffering paradoxically enables my client to enjoy freely the gifts of his life. When one is afraid of suffering, he cannot enjoy the blessings of life in and for themselves. He uses them frantically in order to escape the burden of existence. While attempting to forget the painful aspects of existence in a wild enjoyment of life's pleasures, he is continually haunted by anxiety about the burdensome aspect of life that may reveal itself again when enjoyment ceases. He who cannot suffer fully is also unable to enjoy fully. People who are haunted by anxiety about pain are hesitant when the possibility of deep and intense joy reveals itself at certain moments of their existence. They prefer ephemeral pleasures to existential joy which touches the very core of their being. They are afraid that such a joy may create a possibility for overwhelming pain. Fundamentally they are right. For example, the overwhelming joy of a deep and unique love always implies the risk of overwhelming pain in case the beloved dies, disappears, or betrays one. Happiness entails a threat which may evoke anxiety.

Therefore, many clients are not able to enjoy with a full and relaxed presence the great gifts of life which have come their way. One manifestation of their anxiety is a lack of inner freedom in regard to what has been given to them. Their attitude is characterized by an anxious, possessive holding on to these gifts. This fearful preoccupation makes it impossible for them to enjoy really and fully. For authentic enjoyment is only possible if one accepts without after-thought the good gifts of life and is ready to let them go when they fade away. In other words, existential commitment is just as necessary for true enjoyment as for true suffering. Both are possible only when one surrenders in freedom to the mystery of existence. I do not mean that after psychotherapy my client should throw himself into joy or pain in blind surrender. Good therapy establishes a quiet openness for all the aspects of life, which does not mean that the person lets himself be passively overwhelmed by happiness or suffering. Life is a gift and a task. Everyone has to decide in his concrete life situation how far a joy or a pain is a gift or a demand for action. The realistic openness acquired in psychotherapy will enable the client to determine to what degree pain and joy are to be experienced without activity or resistance and to what degree they invite him to action.

Before psychotherapy the client is inclined to avoid the appeal of the present by living in the past or the future. But he discovers in therapy that surrender to the mystery of existence always means a full presence to the situation here and now. He learns to accept every existential moment with all the risks and possibilities which it implies. For he has realized in the long process of psychotherapy that real life can be lived only today, not yesterday or tomorrow.

Thus it is an aim of psychotherapy to prepare the client for a gradual transcendence of his self-centeredness in commitment to reality. He should experience that commitment to life, to his duty, to the demands of the present, to others which is the condition for an enhanced, unique, and personal existence. The real self grows only in self-commitment and realizes itself only in a transcendence of the inauthentic, defensive, anxious self. This commitment is an expression of man's total readiness to make himself available to life as honestly understood in the light of his own unique possibilities. This free and total commitment leads to unity and integration in the personality of my client. He becomes at one with himself. This unity leads to new force and strength in his personality and in the execution of his daily assignments.

For example, a client who was a college teacher experienced great difficulties in the preparation of his lectures and in the composition of scholarly papers for presentation at conventions. One of the reasons why he experienced inner resistance and division during the performance of his duties was the fact that he was not wholly and freely committed to his study. He prepared his lectures and wrote his articles because he was concerned about the esteem of his students, colleagues, and superiors. He was not motivated by a real inner commitment to his writing and his teaching. As a result, his preparation was a chore that increasingly burdened and bored him. It became almost impossible for him to concentrate on the literature which he had to analyze in preparation for his classes. Just as soon as he sat down behind his desk with a stack of books and articles before him, he felt tired, exhausted, and disgusted. His mind wandered off in all directions except that of his study. What exhausted him was not the task itself but an inner conflict between what he himself desired to do and the demands imposed on him by his position as a teacher. He wanted and did not want to study. In fact, a considerable amount of his energy was invested in the struggle against his inner resistance to the task at hand. After therapy, however, he was a renewed man who was able to prepare his lectures effectively without the overwhelming fatigue which he formerly experienced. He had learned in therapy to commit himself to his task freely, to give up his inner resistance, and to conquer the split in his existence. All his energy was now available for the task at hand. This does not imply that his work no longer had unpleasant aspects, or that it lost its own intrinsic difficulties and problems. But the client's existential commitment made it possible for him to accept his task fully with all its pleasant and unpleasant angles. He became a relaxed, energetic, well-prepared teacher.

Existential commitment determines whether or not a person will freely actualize his existence or will be stunted in his growth by inhibition, fixation, or perversion. Of course, such a commitment is not an act which is performed once and for all. After psychotherapy, my client must renew his commitment many times during his life. He must continually regain the attitude of commitment and inner freedom. For his defensive, ego-centric, and infantile structures never disappear totally. Consequently good therapy cannot aim at a once-and-for-all commitment. It aims at an attitude of self-commitment and a readiness to restore free commitment every time that it is lost through external pressures and inner anxiety which lead to the reemergence of defensive structures.

It is difficult for many clients to understand that commitment leads to authentic self-confidence. Many clients are successful businessmen, scholars, scientists, or leaders who have achieved powerful political or ecclesiastical positions. They come into therapy because of neurotic symptoms which make them uneasy and less efficient than they would like to be. The idea of commitment and surrender does not appeal to them. Their outlook is precisely opposed to commitment. They feel that they were able to gain power by looking out for themselves, by clever manipulation of their environment, by the art of forming friendships and relationships which fostered their rise in society. They declared that people in their environment admire them for their ruthless strength and harsh self-confidence. They do not realize that concentration on their own success has isolated them from the fullness of existence, that manipulation of life and preoccupation with power, possessions, and status lead to existential impoverishment and emptiness, and that such material success is accompanied by loss of rich humanity. This is also true of those clients who demand love, friendship, and protection from others instead of giving to others. They do not understand that every time they demand something from life they isolate themselves from life. My client should learn not to ask what he can demand from life but what life demands from him.

Sometimes during therapy a client may even be inclined to use commitment as a means of manipulation of his life. In this case he has not yet achieved authentic commitment because the latter, while being in tune with the uniqueness of the self, is not directed toward the self or its actualization as an ultimate aim. The person who attempts inauthentic commitment is still self-directed. All that happens to him is the expansion of his self-prison and the addition of a new weapon to his arsenal of manipulating devices. Only a commitment which is not self-centered but conscious and free has a liberating effect on human existence. Only such commitment makes man a full participant in the mystery of being and offers him a center from which he can live an integral life, undivided by ego-centric tendencies.

THE ACCEPTANCE OF ONESELF

Commitment to reality implies that my client accepts himself with respect. He assumes a responsibility for the gift which he himself is. He must realize his own unique potentialities and defend himself when necessary. Commitment to existence sometimes means that the client must learn to place himself in the

foreground when he would prefer to retire because of anxiety, defensive mod-
esty, or ego-centric, false humility. He must accept himself with both his gifts
and his limitations as a life assignment. Some clients do injustice to their own
existence by dedicating themselves to others to such a degree that they neglect
to care for themselves. As a result, healthy and wholesome care for their
own existence is often replaced by hidden pity and by complaint about themselves. Instead of boldly seeking their rights, they express unconscious dissatisfaction in small idiosyncrasies and in stubborn insistence on insignificant
privileges.

Commitment to himself implies my client's will to become independent
in his inner life. Too strong an attachment to his parents and his milieu will
render it very difficult for him to commit himself to his own independent
growth. Moreover, if my client did not receive from his parents the care and
guidance which he needed for his development, he feels a deep lack in his
personality. He seeks restlessly for the fulfillment of need which was not offered
by his parents. As a result he becomes fixated on the search for parental love,
tenderness, and protection. It is true that the psychotherapist can to some
degree fulfill this need. Nevertheless, he can never really make up for all that
the client missed in his childhood. The client must realize that something was
really missing in his early life, a painful lack that cannot be completely filled
at this later stage of his existence. Commitment here and now to reality means
that he must be ready to accept consciously and freely the painful reality of
his past, to assume responsibility for himself, and to renounce his unconscious
search for fulfillment of infantile wishes which should have been satisfied when
he was a child, but which unfortunately cannot be fulfilled now that he is an
adult. Only when he is able to commit himself unconditionally to life, even at
the cost of this personal fulfillment, will he be able to grow and to overcome
this handicap. Only when the client consciously gives up his need for wish
fulfillment can he discover in himself the existential value which he expected
to receive from outside himself.

The deed of commitment helps the client to develop modes of existence
which were unjustly withheld from him as a child. This does not mean that he
will not need others for his full development. It means, however, that he cannot expect others to orient themselves toward him spontaneously as if he were
a young child. He must realize that he will receive the love and the dedication
of others only by going out toward others. The more he goes out toward others,
the more he will receive the love that he missed so much as a child. Of course,
it is initially impossible for the client to understand this possibility of receiving love for love. The therapist, therefore, must ease the way by showing
unconditional care and interest in the client. On the other hand, he does not
treat the client as a mother treats her baby, for thus he would confirm the
client in his infantile needs. Successful therapy, however, will prepare the
client for commitment to life and others in spite of infantile needs. This com-

mitment in turn will help the person to experience increasingly the love of others whom he will meet in his many encounters during and after psychotherapy.

Sometimes a client cannot reach independence and full commitment to his own life because of a constantly negative relationship to his parents and to other figures who later replace his parents. In this case, the person tries to free himself by attacking the ideas, feelings, and life style of parents and parent figures. He complains about their old-fashioned ideas; he tries to subject and to conquer them so that they will think, feel, and act in the same way as he himself does. This attempt leads to a new kind of dependency in the client, that is, his need to direct the thought and the life style of others, and to force them to agree with him renders him most dependent upon them in his inner life. He is continually distressed by the different way in which older people or superiors live and act. His emotional life is very much bound by this negativity, which makes him unhappy, tense, and frustrated. Therapy aims at the liberation of the person from these negative, as well as positive, bindings. Only after this liberation can the client freely grow in his relationship to parents and to parent figures whom he meets in the course of his life.

SUMMARY

In this paper I have discussed some of the long-range aims of psychotherapy. I have considered it the ultimate purpose of psychotherapy to awaken those possibilities for openness and growth which emerge from a true therapeutic liberation. In order to clarify my view of these new possibilities, I explained first of all my view of psychotherapy itself. Psychotherapy is a process in which a person is set free so that he may actualize his unique self in his unique life situation in accordance with the demands of reality.

After explaining my view of therapy, I described the many attitudes and characteristics which are typical of a person set free by psychotherapy and living the fuller life at which psychotherapy aims. Ideally, this person has gained an openness to his true and personal guilt which helps him to become aware of the moments in which he is unfaithful to his real self. Instead of a static life, he lives a dynamic existence opening up to continually new horizons, which implies his readiness to adapt himself continually to his newly emerging possibilities of being. He is open and faithful to his own fundamental potential structure of existence while remaining flexible in regard to the concrete structures in which this potential structure may express itself. He constantly purifies his self-awareness from the distorting influences of reductionistic psychologism, of the tyranny of the public image, and of scientism. He courageously accepts and faces the challenges of authentic inner conflict. He develops the attitude of existential honesty, which implies both an awareness of his defensive inauthentic structures and a readiness to weaken their impact on his daily life. This existential honesty also makes him willing to admit his limitations and mistakes and to accept, without panic, their consequences.

Psychotherapy, moreover, aims at the development of existential commitment in the client. Commitment implies his willingness to live a project of life which, according to his own insight, is in tune with the demands of reality. He now places the source of his self-confidence, not in himself, but in reality and its ground. Existential commitment also means the full acceptance of both the joyful and the painful aspects of reality. This commitment, moreover, leads to an undivided presence to the task of here and now. Finally, therapy aims at the client's acceptance of himself, which implies self-respect and a healthy standing up for his own rights. This respectful self-acceptance also means his willingness to grow in inner independence from parents, parent figures, and his environment.

These are the attitudes and characteristics which I see as some of the long-range aims of psychotherapy. I realize, of course, that these are ideal aims which will probably never be realized totally in a client. Many clients are living under such handicaps that we cannot hope for their total liberation and the resulting fullness of existence at which therapy ultimately aims. The ideal aims of psychotherapy are a guide, an orientation, a beacon pointing the way. They tell us what we should strive for even if a client can realize the ideal only to a modest degree.

BIBLIOGRAPHY

Combs, A. W. Phenomenological concepts in non-directive therapy. *J. consult. Psychol.*, 1948, **12**, 197–208.
Combs, A. W. A phenomenological approach to adjustment theory. *J. abnorm. soc. Psychol.*, 1949, **44**, 29–39.
Combs, A. W. Counseling as a learning process. *J. couns. Psychol.*, 1954, **1**, 31–36.
Combs, A. W., and Snygg, D. Implications of the phenomenological approach for the evaluation of psychotherapy. *Psychol. Serv. Center J.*, 1950, **2**, 96–102.
Combs, A. W., and Snygg, D. *Individual behavior: a perceptual approach to behavior.* (Rev. ed.) New York: Harper & Row, 1959.
Frankl, V. E. *From death-camp to existentialism: a psychiatrist's path to a new therapy.* Boston: Beacon Press, 1959.
Gurwitsch, A. *Field of consciousness.* Pittsburgh, Pa.: Duquesne University Press, 1964.
Hora, T. Epistemological aspects of existence and psychotherapy. *J. Indiv. Psychol.*, 1959, **15**, 166–173.
Jourard, S. I-Thou relationship versus manipulation. *J. Indiv. Psychol.*, 1959, **15**, 174–179.
Kwant, R. C. *Encounter.* Pittsburgh, Pa.: Duquesne University Press, 1960.
Kwant, R. C. *The phenomenological philosophy of Merleau-Ponty.* Pittsburgh, Pa.: Duquesne University Press, 1963.
Luijpen, W. A. *Existential phenomenology.* Pittsburgh, Pa.: Duquesne University Press, 1960.
May, R. *Man's search for himself.* New York: Norton, 1953.

May, R., Angel, E., and Ellenberger, H. *Existence, a new dimension in psychiatry.* New York: Basic Books, 1958.

May, R., and van Kaam, A. L. Existential theory and therapy. In *Current psychiatric therapies.* Vol. III. New York: Grune & Stratton, 1963.

Rogers, C. R. The loneliness of contemporary man. *Rev. Existential Psychol. Psychiat.,* 1961, **1,** 94–101.

Rogers, C. R. *On becoming a person.* Boston: Houghton Mifflin, 1961.

Sechehaye, Marguerite. *A new psychotherapy in schizophrenia.* New York: Grune & Stratton, 1951.

Strasser, S. *Phenomenology and the human sciences.* Pittsburgh, Pa.: Duquesne University Press, 1963.

van den Berg, J. H. *The phenomenological approach to psychiatry.* Springfield, Ill.: Charles C Thomas, 1955.

van Kaam, A. L. Commentary on "Freedom and responsibility examined." In Esther Lloyd-Jones and Esther M. Westervelt (Eds.), *Behavioral science and guidance, proposals and perspectives.* New York: Teachers College, Columbia University Press, 1963.

van Kaam, A. L. Freud and anthropological psychology. *The Justice.* (Newspaper of Brandeis University), May, 1959.

van Kaam, A. L. *The third force in European psychology.* Greenville, Delaware: Psychosynthesis Research Foundation, 1960.

van Kaam, A. L. Assumptions in psychology. *J. Indiv. Psychol.,* 1958, **14,** 22–28.

van Kaam, A. L. Phenomenal analysis: exemplified by a study of the experience of "really feeling understood." *J. Indiv. Psychol.,* 1959, **15,** 66–72.

van Kaam, A. L. The fantasy of romantic love. In *Modern myths and popular fancies.* Pittsburgh, Pa.: Duquesne University Press, 1961.

van Kaam, A. L. The impact of existential phenomenology on the psychological literature of Western Europe. *Rev. Existential Psychol. Psychiat.,* 1961, **1,** 63–92.

van Kaam, A. L. Humanistic psychology and culture. *J. Humanistic Psychol.,* 1961, **1,** 94–100.

van Kaam, A. L. Clinical implications of Heidegger's concepts of will decision and responsibility. *Rev. Existential Psychol. Psychiat.,* 1961, **1,** 205–216.

van Kaam, A. L. Review of *The divided self* by R. D. Laing. *Rev. Existential Psychol. Psychiat.,* 1962, **2,** 85–88.

van Kaam, A. L. Counseling and existential psychology. *Harvard Educ. Rev.,* Fall, 1962.

van Kaam, A. L. Existential psychology as a theory of personality. *Rev. Existential Psychol. Psychiat.,* 1963, **3,** 11–26.

van Kaam, A. L. Sex and existence. *Rev. Existential Psychol. Psychiat.,* 1963, **3,** 163–182.

van Kaam, A. L. *Religion and personality.* Englewood Cliffs, New Jersey: Prentice-Hall, 1965.

van Kaam, A. L. *Existential foundations of psychology.* Pittsburgh, Pa.: Duquesne University Press, 1966. (a)

van Kaam, A. L. *Personality fulfillment in the spiritual life.* Denville, New Jersey: Dimension Books, 1966. (b)

van Kaam, A. L. *The art of existential counseling: a new perspective in psychotherapy.* Denville, New Jersey: Dimension Books, 1966. (c)

12

The Goals of Intensive Psychotherapy

Alvin R. Mahrer, Ph.D.

THERE are at least four aspects to the goals of psychotherapy. The first derives from an explicit concept of the structure of personality and human psychology. Given a particular structural model of personality, certain goals should follow systematically. The second and third aspects derive respectively, from concepts of optimal functioning and disturbances of that functioning. The goal of the second aspect is to achieve a state of optimal functioning. To assuage suffering and repair the difficulties arising from disturbances of the optimal state is the goal of the third. The final aspect refers to the actual, technical therapeutic processes of helping the person toward optimal functioning; its goal is to use these means to bring about desirable changes.

THE STRUCTURE OF PERSONALITY

Primitive Personality

The development of personality begins with those figures to whom the infant is a meaningful object. There are significant interactions between these early figures and the infant and among these figures themselves. The infant himself is just one figure in this larger field of interacting personalities, a field which constitutes an entity open to study and description in terms of the psychological nature of each of these figures and their psychological interrelationships. From this picture we must make the first conceptual leap toward a description of the beginnings of personality: *This total primitive field of meaningfully interacting figures is, in addition, a working model of, i.e., constitutes, the basic personality of the child.* From such a point of view, the infant's physical existence is but one element in this field; his basic personality is not limited to this physical organism.

Accepting this concept as a point of departure, we are confronting the infant's *primitive personality*, a stage of personality development which exists prior to his becoming a more or less intact, organized unit which interacts with a separate outside world. Thus, the rudiments of personality lie within the nature of this total psychological field rather than in the interactions between the physical infant and his external environment or in biological drives, neurophysiological processes, or constitutional forces (Mahrer, 1962a).

Several implications arise from this conceptual leap. Within the field of the primitive personality, there are already existing psychological foci of interactions among the significant figures, foci which, by means of our conceptual leap, are also the rudiments of the child's own psychological pushes and pulls. For example, the mother's needs to be nurturant and maternal are already in the child's developing personality by virtue of their having been in the field of interacting personalities from the very beginning. Our problem lies in understanding how the pushes and pulls of already existing needs in the infant's primitive personality become his own basic needs. The first implication, then, is that the needs which lie behind the psychological interactions of the figures in the field of which the physical infant is a part are the rudiments of the infant's basic needs.

The nature of the relationships in the original field of interacting personalities is an enormously powerful factor in what goes on in that field. Thus, *the nature of the relationships among basic needs* is one powerful determinant of what happens in the personality. The importance of the relationships among the elements rather than the elements themselves has already been established in approach-avoidance models (Dollard and Miller, 1950) and earlier in a topological field theory of personality (Lewin, 1935).

But relationships among basic needs are not the only powerful factor. To the basic needs themselves may be attributed a property which is referred to in words such as *drives, impulses, urges,* and *libido,* all implying an *outward thrust.*

In terms of psychotherapeutic goals, we have so far ascertained that our patient is made up of a primitive personality containing basic needs with one property of relating to one another and a second property of thrusting outward. Knowing that the primitive personality includes the physical organism and the field of interacting personalities, perhaps we may draw further implications, not only for the rudiments of the infant's basic needs, but also for the understanding of early actions, behaviors, and experiences. Early behavior, it should be remembered, is carried out by the physical organism, whereas basic needs reside in the larger field of interacting personalities, i.e., the primitive personality. Thus, a child's affectionate behavior may be related to needs for affection which are simultaneously a part of the child's primitive personality and the mother's own personality. A father's needs to be dominant may be expressed in the physical child's manifest dominant or submissive behavior. A child's primitive personality may contain basic needs for sexuality in the form of a mother's hidden and unexpressed sexual needs, and these basic needs may lie behind the child's overt sexual behavior. Understanding the behavior of the child as related to the larger field of interacting personalities is quite consonant with the classic symbiosis hypothesis (Fingarette, 1962, p. 151) in which the child's behavior is described as emanating from the total family network (Jackson, 1957).

Present Functioning Personality

Let us consider that an early experience, instead of fading away, extinguishing, or even being in the past, simply exists after its occurrence, as if it had a property of ongoingness, of perseverence (Whorf, 1956). We have now given the primitive personality very important added stature: Its ongoingness means that the basic needs are still thrusting outward into, and relationships among the basic needs are maintained in, the present. Without any special mechanisms of maintenance (cf. Ellis, 1959, p. 339), the past is forever with us.

Mediating Needs

Because the primitive personality thus harnesses the present to its services, the patient's personality structure thus becomes more complex in two major ways. First, the basic need may lead to the development of other needs to serve as a pathway for its outward thrust. Shrewd business behavior, for example, might well be related to a need for intellectual capability, itself a pathway for needs to be a controlling leader, and this need in turn facilitating the outward thrust of a basic need for power.

Second, its nature and ongoingness established, the primitive personality, by implication, will tend to impose itself upon the person's entire world and to find contemporary ways to maintain old relationships among basic needs. Thus good relations among basic needs for dependency and basic needs for maternalness may be mediated into the present in the form of a highly dependent person who forms harmonious relations with maternal individuals, or in the form of a highly maternal person who forms harmonious relations with dependent individuals. The nature of the relations among basic needs is maintained in the present.

The outward thrusting nature of the basic needs and the strong tendency of the primitive personality to maintain itself and the nature of the relations among its basic needs combine to produce a complex but organized human being in a complex but personally organized and meaningful world. Actual behavior, because these two factors combine in its production, is a bifurcated phenomenon which facilitates the outward thrust of, and preserves the state of relations among, the basic needs.

The contours of personality structure briefly sketched above (cf. Mahrer, 1966) thus imply these goals: (1) *to bring about optimal relations among basic needs*; (2) *to free those needs of undesirable relationships*; and (3) *to facilitate the outward thrust of such needs.* Our next task is to define optimal and undesirable modes of functioning.

THE OPTIMAL STATE

Our picture of personality suggests certain notions about the optimal state of psychological functioning. As a start, it would seem that proper functioning revolves about two core notions. The first concerns optimal relations among the basic needs, and the second pertains to the maximizing of the outward thrusting nature of these needs.

Optimal Relations Among Basic Needs

The first type of desirable state involves some kind of good, i.e., harmonious, integrated need relations. Since the focus here is on the relationships themselves, this optimal state would be relatively independent of the nature or content of the basic needs: whether the needs concern sexuality, aggression, or dependency is irrelevant. Integration among the basic needs should yield a certain kind of person as an automatic consequence rather than as a direct goal per se (Goldstein, 1947), for aiming directly at achieving this kind of person without a state of basic need integration will probably be more or less fruitless. Also, our model of the structure of personality tells us that persons with integrated basic needs are relatively similar to one another, since we are dealing with need relations independent of the nature or content of the needs.

One pervasive consequence of integrated basic needs, regardless of their content, is a feeling of inner peace and harmony. This deep, pervasive sense of unity, of being at one with oneself, is one meaning of achieving a rare state of inner peace, one of the two highest goals of psychotherapy. Such a feeling may be localized within the patient himself, but, like the difference between the physical child and the larger primitive personality, it includes the total personality. The patient feels it, but as a totality with his whole meaningful world, not as a calm pool in a strange and removed outside environment.

This state is the major consequence, and it shows itself in many ways. For one, inner peace and comfort allow the freedom of inner contemplation. The patient can turn to his inner world, can be alone with himself. This condition is not unlike the Rogerian conception of self-acceptance or the existential notion of knowing oneself (Van Dusen, 1957, p. 320).

Second, when basic needs are integrated, rather than drying up the wellsprings of creativity, creative drive should be enhanced by reducing internal turmoil and distress.

In a third way, integration of the basic needs releases the person from the iron mantle of the primitive personality into the state of freedom heralded by existentialist writers. According to these writers, man tends to avoid responsibility for his own actions by inventing an array of deterministic forces, drives, instincts, psychoses, genetic determinants, and other means (perhaps including the primitive personality) of separating himself from the terrifying state of freedom. Nevertheless, once the patient is freed from the terrible restrictions of the primitive personality, he is able to experience the tranquil aspects of this sense of freedom.

Along with this freedom comes the opportunity to establish new kinds of relationships with figures who initially participated in the primitive personality. If distance and separation characterized the father-son relations in the primitive personality, the integration of basic needs now frees the son to establish new kinds of relations with father figures and also frees him from being overly susceptible to the pulls and pushes of the old primitive bonds as if he were interlocked with the psychological nervous system of the contemporary father.

Fifth, negative feelings of loss, abandonment, aloneness, and separation often accompany the person's fruitless efforts to turn the present world into a duplication of the old primitive personality. Such quests are dropped with the achievement of integration and inner peace, with its consequent feelings of oneness and communality with one's world.

Sixth, tension and unsettledness in the patient's external world, whatever their source, are significantly reduced when relations among basic needs become more integrated. Conflicts remain, but the crucial consideration is that the integrated person does not use external conflict as an externalization of his own internal unintegrative sufferings. An internal peaceful unity can now reflect itself on the external world.

Finally, when basic needs are integrated, there is likewise integration between the person himself and his external world, which evidences itself in the following ways. First, there should occur a rather widespread disappearance of what Sullivan calls (1956) parataxic distortions, as well as whole tendencies to misinterpret meanings, distort cues, or read inaccurate motives into the actions of others. Second, instead of using mechanisms of avoidance and defense against the outside world, the person is inevitably more attuned and responsive to others in a way which allows the feelings of others to reach him. In Rogers' words (1963, p. 18–20), this person is "open to his experiences." When the external world has such a clear avenue to the responsive and open person, he would seem to be much closer to reality and to the kind of relative truth espoused by Kirkegaard (May, Angel, and Ellenberger, 1958). Finally, integration will bring with it a sense of identity and oneness with the external world, as if the boundaries of the person were stretched beyond himself to encompass his outside world.

This description of a person whose basic needs are integrated has one basic theme associated with this goal of integration. This theme is the manifestation of integration in optimal feelings of inner peace and wholeness, a state which encompasses the patient's larger total personality (and includes, of course, his relationship with his broader psychological world).

The Outward Thrust of Basic Needs

Optimal functioning includes a maximizing of the outward thrusting nature of these same basic needs. The focus for the second of the two highest psychotherapeutic goals is not on the relationships among the needs, but rather on lifting each need into the world of real experience.

Once again, our task will be to describe a person who has achieved this state. Actualizing basic needs should result in certain characteristic ways of being which cannot be achieved by other means such as exhortation or perhaps even insight (Hobbs, 1962). A few such general characteristics do exist, despite the fact that since the consequences of releasing basic needs depend on the nature or content of the needs, a condition of optimal functioning should tend to enhance differences among individuals (the opposite of the universalizing effect of integrating these needs).

Whereas integration among basic needs yields a sense of tranquility and harmony, the releasing of basic needs into maximized experiencing should bring a feeling of pleasure and satisfaction and a vital sense of being. Defensive behavior and indirect means of expressing basic needs now give way in this direct opening up; for example, relatively basic needs for sexual expression will be allowed more direct experiencing, together with accompanying satisfaction. The person himself becomes characterized by new sincerity and openness, genuineness and honesty.

Basic needs differ in the nature of the experiences they offer rather than in their "value" on the basis of some value system which considers some needs desirable (or healthy) and others less desirable (or unhealthy). Proper functioning calls for the elimination of friction among and experiencing of those needs, whatever their nature; for example, capacities for being solitary and withdrawn are given the freedom of experience once they are freed from causing pain and are helped to become integrated with other needs. With a wider range of potential experiencings, an optimally functioning person can be both independent and dependent, dominant and submissive, if these fall within his sphere of needs, and will have the satisfaction of experiencing each accordingly.

The nature of this satisfaction which suffuses the patient's personality is determined by the nature of the need. The sheer experiencing itself of love and profound affection and even abject loss, helplessness, envy, hatred, and rage is satisfying, once these needs are fully integrated with other needs. The feelings with which these needs are accompanied are qualitatively different, depending on how they get along with other needs. Anger as a basic integrated need is accompanied with a meaningful, satisfying feeling, whereas anger as an unintegrated basic need is accompanied with terrible strains and fears.

The releasing of basic needs will almost inevitably mean a burgeoning capacity for the experiencing of what would previously have been considered undesirable feelings. A person may experience the profoundness of psychological pain, but there is an enormous qualitative difference between the pain and suffering which results from the release of basic needs in an integrated personality and that which spills out of terrible internal unintegration.

On the other hand, the fully experiencing person is open to his own good feelings of happiness accompanying achievement, warmth at being with another person, aliveness together with a humorous situation, pleasure in the freshness of new experiences, and generally the feeling of experiencing all the qualities represented within his basic need-system.

Perhaps now the goals of psychotherapy may become a little clearer if we accept the model of human personality and the concept of optimal functioning. Essentially, *optimal functioning implies two major goals of psychotherapy:* (1) *The person would be characterized by a profound sense of inner peace and harmony, which characterizes his total optimal functioning i.e. a state of integration of basic needs.* (2) *He would be characterized by satisfaction and a vital sense of feeling and experiencing, i.e., a state of experiential actualization of basic needs.*

Retaining our structural model of personality, our next task is to investigate how difficulties can interfere with optimal functioning and to describe how things may go wrong and what "bad" feelings are like. The goal of psychotherapy would then be to help the person toward the optimal state.

PSYCHOPATHOLOGY

Optimal functioning depends on two fundamental factors: the relationships among basic needs in the primitive personality and the characteristic nature of these basic needs to thrust out into experience. These two factors also play the major roles in psychopathology. We shall begin with difficulties arising from relationships among basic needs.

Unintegrated Relations Among Basic Needs

In our original conceptual leap, we allowed the early field of interacting significant figures to be treated as if it were also a model of the infant's (primitive) personality, with the physical infant as just one element in this field. Based on this working model, the child's personality is then hampered from the beginning to the extent that difficult or unsmooth relations exist among needs in this field of interacting personalities. The friction which exists between a father's overt sexual behavior and a mother's frigidity may well become important in the child's basic personality, just as that personality may incorporate the disharmony between the mother's outgoing, warm responsiveness to others and the father's tendencies toward social withdrawal. When the field of interacting personalities is characterized by thinly veiled hostility existing between a father's fears of failure and a mother's efforts at dominating males, the child's primitive personality already has the beginnings of basic discord and unintegration. A similarly foreboding state of affairs occurs when the primitive field of interaction is filled with difficult relations between needs within a single individual, as, for example, between the mother's aggressive demandingness and her willingness to give and nurture; or between her needs to be an adult and her own infantile tendencies.

Regardless of the nature of the needs involved, the more the primitive personality is characterized by friction and unintegration, the greater is the potential for psychopathological difficulties. This personality model may be contrasted with one in which psychic conflicts emerge from instincts being opposed by an external-world-developed ego (Fenichel, 1954b, p. 25). *Our* primitive personality is described in terms of the amount of unintegration among the basic needs, rather than in terms of the strength of any given need or the presence of troublesome or difficult needs, drives, instincts, or endowments.

The unintegration which originates when an unintegrated field emerges as the individual's primitive personality contains a formidable potential for psychological pain, pain not from any given need, but from the unintegrated nature of relationships among the basic needs. Earlier, we suggested that the primitive personality operates as if it had the property of ongoingness, and furthermore, that it tends to impose itself upon the person's entire world so that the nature of the relationships among the basic needs is a powerful determinant of how his life is structured. The stage is thus set for psychological pain and behavioral psychopathology. For example, a child whose basic needs to be dominant conflict with strong submissive cravings may be psychologically destined to become the neighborhood baby, his need relations accompanied by unhappiness and other signs of unintegration. Again, a primitive personality with considerable friction between warm responsiveness to others and tendencies toward social isolation may fashion a child who is terribly unhappy, frustrated, and uneasy in his lonely, withdrawn life as he yearns, decade after decade, for someone with whom he might be truly close and warmly affectionate. Unintegrated need relationships have emerged into unintegrated experiences.

The poor relationships among the basic needs not only dictate and give structural meaning to the nature of the person's life experiences. They also emerge in the form of a fantasy lurking behind the person's moment-to-moment clinical functioning. If a father's hostile tendencies were the center of sufficient unintegration, the child may recoil from hostile gestures of his own or from others, as if in terror of some homicidal scene which in actuality had never occurred. Primitive relationships may give rise to inner scenes of rape, sadism, violence, rejection, brutality, all surrounded with fear, pain, and other nonintegrative signs. These frightening fantasies and the ability of the primitive personality to determine the nature of early life relationships and experiences may help to account in part for the onset of pathological behavior (Mahrer and Young, 1962).

As the person moves along through life, other needs develop which mediate between the basic needs and the actual experiences of life. These additional needs avoid and contain the basic pain of unintegration, so that when that pain suffuses these needs and finally emerges, its intensity is somewhat reduced and its form modified. The neighborhood baby whose dependency needs were surrounded by nonintegration, and whose peers bossed and mistreated him, may come to avoid, modify, and reduce this pain by developing mediating needs for group belonging and even leadership. Behind his uncertainties, friction, and frustrations in his capacities for leadership and his actual acceptance in a group still lies, however, the somewhat more intense original pain, although the manifested difficulties both reduce and modify the basic distress. Beneath his live clinical experiences of leadership and group acceptance is a vivid fantasy which manifests the fear of being unsuited for leadership and being unaccepted in the group. Thus, in a somewhat new, contemporary form the old, unintegrated, primitive personality's relations still hold. These mediating needs are ". . . involved in the continuous job of repressing mental content from awareness" (Bullard, 1959, p. 49) to the extent that they inhibit the raw pain associated with the unintegrated basic needs.

Probably the major way in which the primitive personality does damage is through the painfully unintegrated relations among the basic needs. This pain lies one short step behind the patient's daily relationships. As a directing factor behind his total world of meaningful relationships, the old primitive personality acts as if it possessed a will of iron, for it utilizes the mediating needs to establish a contemporary version of the old primitive relationships, no matter how much the nonintegration hurts. As if this were not enough, there are additional ways in which the primitive personality's unintegrated need relations prevent optimal functioning.

If the primitive personality includes nonintegration between wishes to be nurtured and protected, and a punitive frigidity, the person may well lead a life aimed at wresting maternal love and affection from nongiving females. This kind of lifelong quest is not only often doomed to failure and frustration, but also, because it is an outgrowth of the unintegrated relations among the basic needs, it is therefore likely to be accompanied by a continual sense of unhappiness and lack of satisfaction. In a similar way, the sense of hollowness and futility which underlies many apparently important life goals may be traced to unintegrated need relations. Unintegration surrounding a basic need for sharing and being with others may propel a person into an adult life of repeated marriages, liaisons, and companionships, all characterized by a sense of hollowness, frustration, and lack of satisfaction. Severe primitive unintegration connected with sexual needs may well dictate that the culminating adult sexual involvements inevitably fail to satisfy, and that a feeling of hollowness and frustration regularly accompany sexual relationships. Because primitive unintegration may deposit a sense of hollowness, frustration, and a lack of satisfaction behind basic needs, mediating needs which are developed later will then find specific, personally-contoured ways in which experiences will occur with ironic hollowness, frustration, and lack of satisfaction.

Another contemporary manifestation of primitive unintegration is the feeling of helplessness and the sense of being unable to cope with overwhelming life forces (Fromm, 1947; May, Angel, and Ellenberger, 1958). Existentialists have provided insightful descriptions of both the nature and clinically pervasive manifestations of this condition. A current sense of helplessness would therefore be an experienced manifestation of one's lifelong helplessness to escape from the primitive relationships.

The primitive personality offers other obstacles, for while it tends to persevere and persist, paradoxically, life experiences tend to pull the person away from the primitive world. Whereas the child's basic personality included the early world of interacting figures, life experiences form an awareness that those figures are not really a part of one's own personality. Such a condition frequently takes the form of a feeling of separation, loss, aloneness, abandonment, and distance, a condition which perhaps underlies the female's sensing that the male part of her is really no longer there, and the male's inner knowing that he has lost his father figure. This condition may help in part to underscore Freud's (1937, p. 356) empirical observation of the difficulty or even impossibility of psychoanalytically resolving the above problems in the female and male respectively.

The Outward Thrust of Basic Needs

We have been witnessing the damage which can be accomplished by unintegrated relations among basic needs, but unfortunately this is only one of two factors in the unfolding of psychopathology. The outward thrust of basic needs plays the other important role. Our model of personality sketched earlier contains, between the basic need and the patient's actual behaviors, a series of intermediate needs, each one serving as a pathway toward the next underlying need until the basic need itself is reached; it is within this context that the balance of psychopathology may be understood as possessing a goal-directed component aimed toward the subsequent need.

Psychological pain and misery often take over insidiously the role of mediating the expression of basic needs. As Szasz (1961) rather forcefully insists, we should acknowledge how effectively psychological distress is able to motivate others to action. Even when psychopathology is pitiably ineffective in its goal-directed function, it may nevertheless be understood as being pointed toward the subsequent need, its posture alone showing its attempt.

An underlying need to withdraw punitively from others may be served admirably by a profound and miserable mediating depression, i.e., being depressed may serve as a means of punishing others. The condition of being depressed may be accompanied by the outward thrusting expression of punitive withdrawal, or may merely be aimed at the expression of the deeper need without any significant release of the need for punitive withdrawal. In either case the depression is a means of expressing the deeper need.

Basic needs for love and affection may be reached by means of a state of abject helplessness which is in turn attainable through repeated demonstrations of inability and failure. The misery of being incapable and inadequate may be painfully genuine, even though the unfortunate individual spends an entire lifetime in this state, which is pointed in the direction of gaining love and affection.

From this point of view, the entire realm of clinical problems and "symptomatology" may lend itself to understanding in terms of its goal-directed component (Mahrer, 1962b). All of these behaviors share the property of one need unfolding into a subsequent (deeper) one as a kind of pathway for the ultimate expression of the basic need.

Under better circumstances, when the person is operating at least in the direction of optimal functioning, one need tends to serve as a pathway for the more or less direct expression of the basic need. Needs for close and affectionate interpersonal relations may be accompanied with good feelings of gratifying aliveness as these needs serve as a pathway, for example, toward the expression of more basic sexual needs. When things are not going so well, however, the mediating needs are surrounded by pain. These may include needs to torment into submission, to engage in secret masturbatory fantasies, to become a powerful masculinized individual, to gain care and protection, to be paternally understanding, to be helplessly ineffectual, and others, all of which may share both some degree of pain and also a directionality toward the release of underlying sexual needs.

Our goals in psychopathology, then, are *to bring a degree of integration to an unintegrated set of basic needs and to allow the experiencing of basic needs without intermediate pain.* Our first goal is to reduce or eliminate unintegration among the basic needs, a state characterized by pervasive inner disharmony and accompanied by an experiential psychological world which is also characterized by disharmony. Our second goal is to reduce or eliminate a broad array of mediating needs representing the repertoire of psychological pains which are locked in the service of underlying needs.

We now turn to the bolder outlines and more working goals of psychotherapy in reducing psychopathological functioning and moving the personality toward optimal functioning.

REDUCTION OF PSYCHOPATHOLOGY AND ACHIEVEMENT OF OPTIMAL FUNCTIONING

With some ideas of the structure of personality, of what optimal functioning is, and of how things might go wrong, we now confront the problem of what to do. Our model of personality gives some guidelines for the "process" goals of psychotherapy. There seem to be two major therapeutic processes. The first aims at the reduction of unintegration and the achievement of integrated relations among needs. The second aims at the facilitation and accommodation of the outward thrusting nature of needs. Thus the therapeutic movement is one of penetration, with disengagement of the penetrated layers of needs and a releasing of progressively deeper needs and integrated systems of needs. Each of the two major therapeutic processes will be discussed in turn.

Reduction of Unintegration and Achievement of Integration

In mediating needs. The reduction of unintegration and the achievement of integration call for an intense and complete experiencing of the pain-surrounded unintegrated relations among the ongoing mediating needs. At the behavioral level the patient is clinically demonstrating, feeling, and experiencing needs which are accompanied with a certain amount and kind of distress. The therapist helps the patient to focus upon and to experience to completion the full suffering and anxiety which mark the posture of one ongoing need to another. While this process does not alter the nature of the current needs, their relationships move toward acceptance, harmony, and a significant measure of inner peace within the system of mediating needs.

Since each mediating need is functionally tied to a deeper need, the therapeutic process is not only one of experiencing fully the relationships among the network of needs, but is also an uncovering process, disengaging one layer of needs and moving downward into a deeper layer of mediating needs, continuing the therapeutic concern with the relationships among the needs at that level. The integrating process thus works on needs at progressively deeper levels of personality. Regardless of the level, the experiencing process brings one need into full exposure to other needs, with the patient undergoing the full brunt of the unintegrated relationship. He may run the gamut from tension to fear to stark terror in experiencing the impact of the unintegration surrounding his own homosexuality and the homosexuality which he imposes upon the external world. The experiential process uncovers his own personal homosexual scenes and lets him go through them in gripping detail until they are released and completed. Then, former nonintegration is replaced by a new acceptance and tranquility between the homosexuality and the related needs.

While he is coming to experience the full weight of whatever unintegrated, pain-filled need is motivating him at this point in therapy, the patient also disengages himself from the continual creation of painful unintegrative situations in his daily life. The feelings are experienced with full intensity in the therapy hour, but the daily life is relieved of the self-inflicted unintegrative hurt.

Since the pain of unintegrated relations among basic needs is mediated by needs superimposed over the basic needs, the process of penetrating and exposing hurt meets resistances which become increasingly intense as the uncovering process continues (cf. Freud, 1950a, p. 288) and as the deeper, earlier hurts are found in childhood experiences which often must themselves be unfolded (Bergman, 1949; Freud, 1950b, p. 367). For example, as a female patient is helped to dislodge the manifest unintegrative pain contained in her criticisms of her husband, the process of penetration may uncover a deeper depression which, when it in turn is experientially penetrated, exposes an agonizing feeling of being useless and unwanted. Uncovering this underlying feeling reveals the basic needs, with enormously unintegrated relations centering on primitive sexual needs.

This process of experientially uncovering and exposing has two goals, one of which is the very straightforward aim of reaching the level of basic needs where the primitive unintegrations are occurring. The therapist can begin correcting the basic unintegrations only when he can work directly with the primitive unintegrative friction itself. The second goal may seem a little paradoxical in that the process of arriving at the bedrock of personality not only exposes the source of greatest pain but also frees the patient of the layers of unintegrative pain which were superimposed on the primitive personality. Together with a much more direct experiencing of the unintegrative pain centering on her primitive sexual needs, the patient is freed of the agony of feeling useless and unwanted, of the depression, and of her clinically manifested pain contained in criticisms of her husband. Removal of the unintegration contained in the mediating need systems and its replacement by integration still leaves the unintegration in the primitive personality, but the therapeutic impact upon the patient is a new sense of inner peace and a rather pervasive sense of being at one with oneself.

In the Primitive Personality. Having penetrated to the level of the basic needs and their unintegrated relationships, the therapist and the patient are now at the same point we were when we made our first conceptual leap, i.e., significant personalities interacting with each other and with the physical child, the total field constituting the patient's primitive personality. If the rudiments of the patient's basic personality lie in this early field, then bringing about integration in the field should also bring about integration in the patient's basic personality.

A primitive personality may incur enormous unintegration emanating from homicidal rages which, in the early field of interacting personalities, stem from the father's hidden homicidal feelings toward females. The integrating of this basic unrest in the patient's primitive personality will come about as the patient undergoes the totally full experience of the released homicidal rage, both as it relates to the father's own efforts to contain the rage and to the friction between the father and females. The homicidal rage that the father defended against in himself and that lay behind the unintegrative relations between the father and mother, the patient must experience directly, as if it were his own (as indeed it is, for he has suffered indirectly from it all his life).

Behind another patient's tense, rigid efforts to establish a life barricaded against any possible insecurity lies a primitive field of interacting personalities characterized by fears of rejection and withdrawal. The parents each feared rejection by the other, and the mother's relationship to the child was filled with an overprotection which masked her tendencies to flee from a binding, close maternal relationship with her child. This kind of primitive unintegrative relationship bred fantasies of violent rejections and catastrophic breakdowns in the early field. As the patient was enabled to enter into and complete these violent and catastrophic rejections, the unintegration in the early field was replaced by integration. Similarly, integration also comes when psychological forces which lie behind unintegration are experienced to completion. In the early field of interaction of the former patient, homosexual urges may lie behind the father's unintegrative rages against females. The primitive fears of rejection in the case of the latter patient may stem from the mother's totally intolerable sexual desires. The patient himself must experience these urges and desires to completion before achieving integration.

The therapeutic goal is to remove the unintegrated relations among the basic needs rather than to bottle up these strong drives, to divert them, to learn to adjust to them, or to erect firmer defenses or controls over them in an effort ". . . to cure neurosis by assuring control over instinct" (Freud, 1937). Our goal may also be contrasted with a program of enhancing or facilitating so-called "good, healthy" needs such as affection, concern for others, or mature adult responsibility while effecting a limitation or reduction of "bad, unhealthy" needs such as aggression, self-concern, or social withdrawal. Indeed, needs avoid altogether classification in categories of sick and healthy, adjustive and maladjustive (Szasz, 1961, p. 279).

Reduction of Painful Mediating Needs; Maximizing the Outward Thrust of Needs

Our second goal is to accommodate the outward thrusting nature of the basic needs by opening up to actual experiencing the successive mediating needs. In line with Freud's dictum, "Everything is harmful that hinders the fulfillment of gratification" (Freud, 1950a, p. 238), this goal may be restated as the facilitation of the maximal gratification of experiencing basic needs (cf. Gendlin, 1961; Gendlin, 1962). Guidelines for the accomplishment of this goal ought to be consonant with and drawn from our structural personality model.

To open up the basic needs to actual experience, each need is going to have to be released into experience, one at a time, until the basic need itself is brought up to the behavioral surface. While the patient's clinical behavior is pointed in the direction of the subsequent need, unfortunately it is most often unsuccessful in actually reaching or releasing this next underlying need. It is the therapist's function to know the next underlying need which is pressing for release into experience and to create "the necessary and sufficient conditions for therapeutic personality change" (Rogers, 1957) in order to aid the patient in his attempts to release each successive experience of feeling. Such a goal of psychotherapy calls for a deep understanding of what the patient's movements seem to be directed toward, and great attention to the series of feelings ready to be experienced. This goal of experientially releasing the series of succeeding needs is in the same general family of ideas as the psychoanalytic notion of bringing the repressed into consciousness (e.g., Breuer and Freud, 1936; Bergman, 1949) and the Jungian conception of pushing out and expanding the limits of consciousness (Wheelwright, 1956, p. 129).

If a patient's behavior is geared toward a feeling of acceptance and unequivocal regard, this feeling is to be allowed its full measure of experiential release through whatever mode of experiencing seems appropriate, whether in the therapeutic relationship, in the realm of the inner dream-fantasy life, or in the ongoing external world. Such release of this feeling (need) not only provides for increased satisfaction, but also opens the pathway toward the subsequent feeling (need) which contains still greater potentials for pleasureful satisfaction. The therapist should not be surprised by the content of the next need or feeling to be experientially released. Often the need is surrounded with pain and turmoil, but the need is arched in the direction of some subsequent need filled with potential pleasure and gratification. The process of treatment calls for these kinds of feelings or needs to be treated similarly to the more obviously pleasureful ones, i.e., to allow the experiencing of the need or feeling toward which they are directed. Similarly, the therapist should not be surprised by the opening up of new horizons of pleasure and satisfaction as pleasureful, satisfying needs are unfolded.

As progressively deeper needs or feelings emerge, there is a kind of sloughing off of the mediating ones, including those which carry with them a measure of goal-directed hurt and pain; their psychological *raison d'etre* no longer holds and they are therefore displaced finally by the deeper needs or feelings and by the gratifying experiencing of these more basic needs. For example, painful feelings of being sexually inadequate may be directed toward the gaining of dependency gratifications so that full access to the experiencing of the dependency no longer makes it necessary to reach out toward this state by means of the painful sexual inadequacy.

How is any need or feeling released into the vital actuality of sheer experience? The patient is helped to undergo a detailed living-through of the real world of inner feelings so that it is completely felt and intimately experienced. This may occur in the live relationship between patient and therapist; in the world of inner feelings stimulated by events in the patient's daily life; or in the vital world of real inner experiences aroused in relation to events which took place throughout the totality of the patient's history of past experiences. In all this, the twin guides are the patient's ongoing clinical behaviors, feelings, and moment-to-moment experiencings and the world of still deeper needs or feelings as disclosed in a full and thorough exposure of, for example, dreams. These two realms provide the essential data for the careful understanding of the patient's individual personality structure and reveal to the therapist what needs or feelings are pressing for positive experiential release.

The therapeutic process has been one of progressive release of mediating needs or feelings beginning with whatever clinical feelings or needs the patient brings to therapy initially and proceeding from need to need, feeling to feeling, down to the basic needs. Therapy thus progresses far beyond the morbid, the problematical, the psychopathological. It focuses also on the pleasureful, the exciting, the satisfying, in its effort to expand and release the still greater underlying potentials. It begins, in large part, with "good" mediating needs, with exciting and intensely satisfying functionings. In experiencing the open delight of good feelings, the patient comes ever more alive.

Ideally, the process of replacing unintegration among basic needs with integrated relationships has dovetailed with the progressive emergence into experience of the mediating needs so that when the basic needs themselves are ready for experiencing they are free of unintegrative pain. The process of freeing and releasing ends with these basic needs regardless of their content: we have now reached the primitive personality. Our purpose now is to establish a direct contact between the basic needs and experience, to turn the outward thrusting nature of the basic needs toward the world of actual experience rather than their being turned upon each other in an ominous state of unintegrated tension.

How may this be accomplished? For the most part, the work has already been done in the process of releasing the mediating needs. This brings the integrated basic needs and the entire harmonious primitive personality face to face with the actual world of experience. The therapist can further aid the maximal amount of contact between these two realms by helping to provide the basic needs with behavioral outlets and by helping the external world of experience to fit nicely with the contours of the basic needs.

In providing mediating or basic needs with outlets, behaviors must bridge the gap between needs and experience. Whether these be behaviors of responding, attending, opening up oneself, or active behaviors of doing and manipulating, the patient must often be aided in the development or utilization of behavioral means of touching experiences. The process of extracting positive behaviors becomes critical during this stage of therapy. At this point the external world has its own obligation to offer the maximal experiential fit with the patient's basic needs. At this stage in treatment truly significant and perhaps sweeping changes are called for in the external world. The nature of the basic needs can now stand as determinants of the contours of the patient's external world. The formerly frigid woman with integrated, released basic needs to be feminine and maternal now makes significant changes in her life in order to offer maximally gratifying experiences for her basic needs. The man who now possesses freed, integrated basic needs for warmth, affection, and meaningful involvements gives up a life designed to keep him safely distant from others, and effects the necessary and appropriate changes in his life to maximize the experiencing of these basic needs. During these final stages of treatment the patient is helped to effect further significant positive behavioral changes and to effect further appropriate changes in his life situation.

This final goal has been one of instrumentation, i.e., it is a means of reaching the more ultimate goals described earlier. *The goal of psychotherapy, then, is to provide working therapeutic methods of achieving optimal functioning and reducing psychological pain.* Complete experiencing of the relationships between needs allows painful unintegrated relationships among progressively deeper needs to be replaced with harmonious, integrated relations. Experiential releasing and the emerging of each successive need or feeling assures that the basic needs may be given expression and experiential actuality.

When our proposed four sets of goals are considered as a package, they seem to constitute a relatively organized functional unit, but perhaps we might take a longer view toward still another goal whose presence is both exciting and ominously disconcerting to psychotherapists. Perhaps the ultimate goal of psychotherapy is to make understandable the wealth of enormously valuable material presented to us in the course of intensive treatment, so as to aid in the development of continuously improving, useful, meaningful, systematic theories of personality. This in turn will add guidelines toward ways of facilitating optimal personality development and ways of enabling society to develop along optimal lines. This final goal of psychotherapy is to provide more and more knowledge so that there will be less and less of a need for psychotherapy as we know it today.

REFERENCES

Bergman, P. The germinal cell of Freud's psychoanalytic psychology and therapy. *Psychiatry*, 1949, **12,** 265–278.

Bullard, D. M. (Ed.) *Psychoanalysis and psychotherapy: selected papers of Frieda Fromm-Reichmann.* Chicago: University of Chicago Press, 1959.

Breuer, J., and Freud, S. *Studies in hysteria.* Washington, D.C.: Nerv. and ment. Dis., Publ. 1936.

Dollard, J., and Miller, N. D. *Personality and psychotherapy.* New York: McGraw-Hill, 1950.

Dreikurs, R. Adlerian psychotherapy. In Frieda Fromm-Reichmann and J. L. Moreno (Eds.), *Progress in psychotherapy.* New York: Grune & Stratton, 1956. Pp. 111–118.

Ellis, A. A homosexual treated with rational psychotherapy. *J. clin. Psychol.*, 1959, **15,** 338-343.

Fenichel, O. Symposium on the therapeutic results of psychoanalysis. In Hanna Fenichel and D. Rapaport (Eds.), *The collected papers of Otto Fenichel.* Second series. New York: Norton, 1954. Pp. 19–24. (a)

Fenichel, O. Early stages of ego development. In Hanna Fenichel and D. Rapaport (Eds.), *The collected papers of Otto Fenichel.* Second series. New York: Norton, 1954. Pp. 25–48. (b)

Fingarette, H. Real guilt and neurotic guilt. *J. exist. Psychiat.*, 1962, **3,** 145–158.

Freud, S. *The problem of anxiety.* New York: Psychoanalytic Quarterly Press and W. W. Norton, 1936.

Freud, S. Analysis terminable and interminable. *Internat. J. Psychoanal.*, 1937, **18,** 373–405.

Freud, S. Sexuality in the aetiology of the neuroses. *Collected papers.* Vol. 1. London: Hogarth Press, 1950. Pp. 220–248. (a)

Freud, S. The future prospects of psycho-analytic therapy. *Collected papers.* Vol 2. London: Hogarth Press, 1950. Pp. 285–296. (b)

Freud, S. Further recommendations in the technique of psycho-analysis. *Collected papers.* Vol. 2. London: Hogarth Press, 1950. Pp. 342–391. (c)

Freud, S. Fragment of an analysis of a case of hysteria. *Collected papers.* Vol. 3. London: Hogarth Press, 1950. Pp. 13–146. (d)

Fromm, E. *Escape from freedom.* New York and Toronto: Holt, Rinehart and Winston, 1947.

Gendlin, E. T. Experiencing: a variable in the process of therapeutic change. *Amer. J. Psychother.*, 1961, **15**, 233–245.

Gendlin, E. T. *Experiencing and the creation of meaning.* New York: Free Press, 1962.

Goldstein, K. The idea of disease and therapy. *Rev. Relig.*, 1947, **13**, 229–240.

Hobbs, N. Sources of gain in psychotherapy. *Amer. Psychol.*, 1962, **17**, 741–747.

Jackson, D. D. The question of family homeostasis. *Psychoanal. quart.*, 1957, **31**, 79–90.

Lewin, K. *A dynamic theory of personality.* New York: McGraw-Hill, 1935.

Mahrer, A. R. A preface to the mind-body problem. *Psychol. Rec.*, 1962, **12**, 53–60. (a)

Mahrer, A. R. The psychodynamics of psychiatric hospitalization. *J. nerv. ment. Dis.*, 1962, **135**, 354–360. (b)

Mahrer, A. R. *Therapeutic experiencing: a theory and technique of intensive psychotherapy.* Denver, Colorado: Veterans Administration Hospital (mimeo.), 1966.

Mahrer, A. R., and Young, H. H. The onset of stuttering. *J. gen. Psychol.*, 1962, **67**, 241–250.

May, R., Angel, E., and Ellenberger, H. F. (Eds.) *Existence: a new dimension in psychiatry and psychology.* New York: Basic Books, 1958.

Rogers, C. The necessary and sufficient conditions for therapeutic personality change. *J. consult. Psychol.*, 1957, **21**, 95–101.

Rogers, C. The concept of the fully functioning person. *Psychother.: Theory, Res. and Pract.*, 1963, **1**, 17–26.

Saul, L. *Technic and practice of psychoanalysis.* New York and Montreal: Lippincott, 1958.

Sullivan, H. S. *Clinical studies in psychiatry.* New York: Norton, 1956.

Szasz, T. S. *The myth of mental illness.* New York: Hoeber-Harper, 1961.

Van Dusen, W. The theory and practice of existential analysis. *Amer. J. Psychother.*, 1957, **11**, 310–322.

Wheelwright, J. Jung's psychological concepts. In Frieda Fromm-Reichmann and J. L. Moreno (Eds.), *Progress in psychotherapy.* New York: Grune & Stratton, 1956.

Whorf, B. L. *Language, thought, and reality.* Cambridge, Mass.: Technology Press, 1956.

13

Values and the Process of Experiencing

Eugene T. Gendlin, Ph.D.

An Introduction to the Person

by Sidney M. Jourard, Ph.D.

The late Franklin J. Shaw was fond of saying that it was through wresting with large contradictions that people grew. One such growing, complex person is Eugene Gendlin. He is a sensitive psychotherapist, with a great gift for unarmoring himself in the presence of a patient, the better to experience the impact of the other on him, though this talent also makes him vulnerable to great hurt. Side by side with this facet of the man is the drive to get things done—to develop an organization of psychotherapists, to edit a journal, and to be effective in the world of men.

This already powerful set of contradictions includes another which is almost orthogonal: the philosopher-theorist versus the empirical scientist. Eugene Gendlin has wrestled with a perennial problem in our discipline, that of developing concepts that deal with process rather than with fixed entities; he has then gone beyond this, to seek ways of measuring variables and dimensions that have grown out of his definitional work. He has made, and will continue to make, substantive contributions.

Dr. Gendlin came to psychology from an initial interest in philosophy. He took his Master's degree in the latter discipline at the University of Chicago in 1950. Eight years later, he completed his doctorate, having been associated during this time with Dr. Carl Rogers. From 1958 until 1963, he was the research coordinator for the Psychotherapy Research Group at the University of Wisconsin, an association which he terminated to take his present position at the University of Chicago again.

    I am indebted to Philippa Mathieu for her extremely instructive seminar on Values in Psychotherapy, held at the Wisconsin Psychiatric Institute, 1963.

Dr. Gendlin was born in Vienna, a city which has given the fields of psychology and psychiatry other men of stature. Freud compelled us to look at neglected aspects of man's experiencing, but he saw it in a pessimistic light. Gendlin is showing us that we have the freedom to create the meanings that our experiencing offers us.

I. VALUE CONCLUSIONS AND VALUE PROCESS

PEOPLE usually tell us their value-conclusions (their choices, preferences, and goals) but they tell us little of the *experiential process* they engaged in to arrive at these conclusions. In this paper I will attempt to formulate some of the characteristics of an experiential process whose outcomes we usually respect as compared with a process of valuing we generally do not respect. I will try to show that the problem of values can be seen quite differently and more usefully if we consider not only value-conclusions, but also the characteristics of the process.

1. For example, if a young man in psychotherapy decides to apply to medical school, the value problem is not really the value he or we put on medical school, prestige, or on helping people through medicine. Rather, the question is, What kind of process, what kind of "working through," led to his decision? If he has worked through only a very few of his feelings; if, for example, he has yielded to his family's wishes without resolving a sense of resentment, we are likely to consider the therapeutic process in this respect a failure, no matter how strongly we share his value-conclusion about a medical career. Conversely, if he has referred to many of his personal feelings concerning his life and family, if he has in many instances found these feelings becoming more differentiated and yielding up meanings he previously did not differentiate, and if this process has led with experiential clarity to this choice, we feel the therapy was successful even if we ourselves do not fully share all the value-conclusions of the patient's choice. Another example is the following: If a student in therapy decides to quit school, again our own values about higher education do not determine the probable rightness or wrongness. Rather, it will depend upon whether the decision arises directly from an increased ability to make free choices, from differentiations of feelings and meanings, or whether he is fleeing from unexamined difficulties and giving in to a sense of failure which he has not worked out.

These examples attempt to show that what counts is *the manner of the process leading to value-conclusions*, not the abstract conclusions alone. What we usually term "values" are only conclusions. In the above examples I held the conclusion constant. I tried to show that a positive or negative manner of process can lead to a given conclusion. I will argue that the whole value question is clarified if we consider this differing manner of process.

The differences in process are not merely private: we can observe the process differences in how an individual speaks. Major observable differences in later behavior are predictable from different manners of this process. For example, many industries select people for positions according to the kind of process they have gone through in deciding to apply. This is called a consideration of the applicant's "motivation," but more specifically, we mean the *experiential process* whereby he has become so "motivated." The value-conclusion (his decision to apply) does not tell us enough. For, from differences in the motivational process, the process by which applicants came to the decision to apply, we predict different kinds of behavior.

Two individuals may arrive at the "same" verbal value-conclusion and may hold it with equal firmness, yet the experiential meaning each has for this value-conclusion may be very different. One young man leaves school and applies for the position; his leaving school, however, remains an unresolved failure that haunts him through life. For the other young man, it is a move of freedom and ownership of his life; for the first time he acts on his own from genuine interests.

In our considerations of value problems, we must look not only at the value-conclusion, but also at the experiential process through which the conclusion is arrived at. Otherwise, utterly different concrete conditions will be incorrectly classified as the "same" value-conclusions.

2. Here is a second aspect of this question of values in psychotherapy: The client's movement toward this or that value-conclusion is temporary. (Of course he may commit himself to permanence through external ties, and this *is* a danger.) A student may decide to leave school and, through this freeing process, he may discover his ownership of life, and his own felt interest in things. Thereby he may, a little later, decide in a new way to go to school. This new decision may come even before he has had a chance to drop out of school, or it may come some time later. The experiential process often seems at a given moment to be leading to one value-conclusion. A little later it may head toward quite a different or opposite value-conclusion. Quite often several such shifts of seeming direction can occur within a few minutes, as the therapeutic process moves from one differentiation of feeling to another.

The therapist ceases to be helpful if he balks at moving along with his client just because, for the moment, the experiential process *seems* to be moving toward a value-conclusion he finds difficult to bear. In the experiential process (the process of differentiating one's felt meanings) the seeming value-direction shifts very often. Actually, what we term its seeming value-direction is not the direction of the process itself.

3. The process clearly has its own direction, given by the present, immediately confronted, felt meaning. Attention to and differentiation of this felt meaning is *forward* for the experiential process. Anything else is *backward* or *sideways*. The value-conclusion we interpolate only seems implied in a given moment of the process. We interpolate a straight line forward from just this

one felt meaning. We fear that a student will quit school if he differentiates and confronts this strong feeling of inability, failure, hatred, lack of motivation. and of being forced to study. We fear that a man who comes more and more to see the meanings in his desire to get a divorce will actually do so. If we let a client confront and differentiate his felt desire to die, to give up, to avoid coping with anything more, we fear that he will actually commit suicide.

Nor am I saying that we should not fear, or that we can help fearing. What I do assert is that if a given felt meaning offers itself as "next" to be differentiated, then for the present experiential process the differentiation of this felt meaning is "forward." This felt meaning, however, tells us nothing about the value-conclusion at which the individual will eventually arrive. When a given felt meaning is differentiated and felt through, the process will move on. The patient will inwardly confront another different felt meaning. That one will then be "next." Differentiating that felt meaning will then be forward for the experiential process. What value-direction will then seem to be implied by that next felt meaning is not forseeable. It may seem to be in the same direction, or in the opposite direction, or it may shift the scene to altogether different issues.

When we travel in a car on a road that leads west we may frequently travel north or south for a stretch, for the road takes all sorts of curves, and its direction is by no means always west. Especially in mountainous country serpentine curves seemingly lead backwards and forwards; yet it is always clear where the road is. On the map it may be marked as a straight line going west, but on the actual ground we must follow the road, not going off into the bush just because for the moment the road has turned.

The third characteristic of the experiential process I am discussing is that it has its own determinants of what is forward for itself. The next felt *direct referent* which the client inwardly finds arising is forward. Or, if he confronts no such felt meaning, then his own inward *scanning* is next. Soon, there will be a felt meaning to be differentiated. The client can talk about anything else, can examine other things, can argue with himself in various directions, can explain or rationalize anything he wishes, yet nothing changes until he does confront this "next" felt meaning which has remained unchanged by all the previous talk. As he attends to it, this one felt meaning *unfolds* into very many different aspects and meanings. As it "unfolds," he can feel it "give" or change (in a bodily, physical way, like a feeling of hunger or pain). There is a physically felt relief when one grasps inwardly what a felt meaning really is. Sometimes the exactly right words have this effect. At other times the client may say, "Oh . . . !" and he knows (in a feeling way) what "it" is, quite some seconds before he finds words that fit.

Elsewhere (Gendlin, 1964), I have termed the phases of this process "direct reference," "unfolding," and "referent movement." After such referent movement, the inward *scene* has changed. Different felt meanings now wait to be differentiated. The interpolated value-direction may now seem quite different. What is important for our discussion is that the process is *not determined by any value-conclusions* that are *aimed at,* but by its own experiential, felt data to which the individual inwardly refers.

4. It is true that often the client does hold certain value-conclusions and strongly wishes to remain loyal to them. As value-conclusions, these are quite helpless to affect the experiential process. They do not determine where the process leads. On the other hand, the client usually has many feelings concerning these value-conclusions. Such concrete feelings become differentiated, and they are a part of the experiential process. Most often he holds to such value-conclusions for reasons relevant to his sense of self and his way of being alive.

In an experiential process, such value-conclusions become related to very specific experiential meanings, in comparison to which the old value-conclusions now seem much too general. Yet he can often keep them in this changed, experientially connected form. A client who has, for example, developed an ability and love for study may find in psychotherapy that this has been an avoidance of coping with the world—but he need not thereby lose his ability to study nor his love of it. Likewise, a biting, bitter sense of humor may lose its hurting manner but none of its sharpness. A client may have a conflicted mixture of authority problems in his religion together with a deep personal sense of some sort of spirituality; the latter is maximized when the former dissolves. If the client is outwardly a well-functioning, go-getting doer, he does not lose this ability or the joy of it, when he temporarily shelves his active adult self for a psychotherapy hour in which he lives the feelings of a small helpless child, wanting not to cope with anything, only to be cared for.

Notice that the above examples could be taken to imply value-conclusions and value-choices. I say "could be" because as I have phrased them, they concern concrete aspects of experiencing. I think the descriptive language I am employing gives a faithful account. It is *not* a choice between value-conclusions, or between value systems, value concepts, or values of any sort. We differentiate and symbolize the felt meanings which emerge. We do not apply concepts of values (value-conclusions) to choose what fits our values. The order of events is quite the reverse. First we differentiate the concretely felt meanings of experiencing. The feel of these new meanings determines much more specific value choices. Thus, I may first find that a certain way I feel about my religion puzzles and dismays me, and turns out to be, at a first differentiation, my hatred of what the religious people around me did to me. This feeling seems quite opposed to the broad value-conclusions I hold. Later, it may turn out to have more specific aspects, for instance, the inward cry that I *can* be good and valuable, despite the worthlessness and guilt that those people made me feel. Still later it may become further differentiated. There may, for example, arise a felt sense of being at peace and deeply whole.

This series of examples is meant to illustrate that *the concrete differentiation of highly specific aspects of experiencing comes first.* We do not use concepts or value-conclusions to evaluate various aspects of our religion, calling

some "authority aspects" and others "genuinely spiritual." Such a sorting
would be a conceptual one, and would lead to the old question: What value
system decides which is which? But we do not even *have* concepts for these
specific experiential differentiations. Indeed, the reverse is the case. During
psychotherapy the client must invent concepts and define them for his personal
momentary use precisely by making them refer to the highly specific, new
aspects of felt meaning which he must first concretely differentiate.

The choices are made on the basis of these concrete experiential differentiations. Such choices have an experientially felt specificity, clarity, and sureness. What is the source of such experiential "sureness"? It lies in the concrete
feel of the specific experienced meanings themselves, once differentiated.

In another example, an individual feels a desire to be free of artificial expectations, and the very feel of this desire to be free is positive. It is not a matter
of "valuing freedom." The individual may conceptually deplore this feeling. He
may view it as going against every positive value he conceptually holds for
himself. But, there it is, and it feels good. He wants to be free of artificial
expectations.

He is stuck now, however, because he also feels that he wants to achieve
this and that kind of success. The question, "Why does he feel that?" can be
answered with all kinds of conceptual and dynamic explanations that are useless for him. Such a question can obtain an effective answer only as he again
focuses on the felt meaning of his desire to achieve. He is afraid, he now finds,
afraid of getting utterly lost in the world if he doesn't achieve. In fact, among
other aspects, he now finds that he is afraid in many ways, very afraid. The
idea that he will not achieve, but rather just merely live, makes him afraid. It
seems awful, too frightening, to "merely live"—to be "just another person
among people." Here is his fear of life, his motivation to avoid life and the
world! He need not phrase it that way. He need not evaluate it as bad. It feels
bad!

The order in which experiential valuing occurs is the reverse of how it is
so often portrayed. We do not first adopt value-conclusions from some system
and then apply them to choose between different possibilities. First we must
confront and differentiate experienced meanings (felt meanings). Then we find
that these now differentiated felt meanings have a significant feel of good or
bad, resolved or conflicted. If the latter, we resolve them by differentiating still
further and further. For any meaningful problem many steps are required,
many instances of "direct reference," "unfolding," and "referent movement."
The seeming interpolated value-direction may shift many times. The process
has its own direction, its own concrete referent which is "next" for it, and the
felt meanings have their own inward feel of resolution or conflict, constriction
or relief, resentment or freeing, fresh realness or stuffy, isolated autism, and
just plain good or bad.

Not only in regard to values, but in regard to any symbolization of felt
meanings, there is a two-sided problem: When is the correct and releasing

process complete? Symbolizations may, in the very change they bring through being accurate, lead to the emergence of further felt meanings which are unresolved and require further symbolization. Or they may not. A given step may fully resolve it. One checks the symbolization against many explicit concerns and many directly felt concerns, and one finds that the matter is "resolved." One feels "whole" or "clear" or whatever poetic words one wishes to use for this condition. However, there is an additional side to this question. Any new events or situations, questions or circumstances can, again, require further steps of process. Such further steps do not mean that the earlier steps were "wrong" in the sense that one must backtrack. But changing circumstances and new questions can require further steps which can lead to verbally opposite conclusions (thus making the earlier verbal conclusions now seem "wrong"). This two-sidedness, this fact that an aspect of the process can be "complete," and yet is also open to further interaction involving further needs for resolution, is an aspect of the basic relationship between experiencing and symbols (Gendlin, 1962).

Value-conclusions do not determine the directions or outcomes of the process of differentiating experiencing. Nor does felt rightness indicate value rightness. With the felt relief of some differentiation the individual knows directly in a felt way what "this feeling" is. The differentiation may involve great felt relief even when what emerges is an even worse situation and more troublesome conflict than he had supposed. Although the direction may seem deplorable to him, he feels unquestionable relief as he differentiates. (It is as if he is so glad to know, at last, what the feeling is. However it isn't really a gladness at *knowing*, since, if he had been told this piece of knowledge without the *concrete* differentiation's having occurred, he would not have felt at all glad.) "*Now* I really have no idea what to do about that," he may say, referring to the newly revealed state of affairs. "That's really much worse than I thought, and I really *am* baffled now." Yet he feels physically good, having taken the resolving, differentiating step.

Value-conclusions are always general and broad. On the other hand, the experiential aspects of felt meaning which one differentiates are extremely specific (they may be hard to state in words, but they are "this, here"—quite a specific concrete aspect I feel now and refer to). The value-conclusion question is, "Will he stay in school, and are scholarly aspirations good?" The experientially concrete aspects of felt meaning are "this sense of being trapped," and "that feeling of doing something freshly because its fascinates me." The value-conclusions are assumptions, premises, themselves needing the support of an even broader value system, which in turn leads us to questions of just what supports a value system. The experientially differentiated aspects of felt meaning need no conceptual value system at all for their felt sense of life-enhancing, experiencing-maximizing, interpersonal-vivifying quality, or their constricting, fear- and conflict-producing, isolating, and life-minimizing quality.

For all these reasons, we should not cease to participate in the process even when we do not like the value judgments implied in any one moment's experiential process. Much less could we possibly direct the process by first choosing conclusion-values.

In summary, we have: (1) distinguished between value-conclusions and the experiential process which can lead to them; (2) we have said that the seeming value-conclusion implied in a moment's differentiating is temporary and may shift with each step of differentiation; (3) that the experiential process has its own direction, given by the sequence of concrete felt meanings which arise as one focuses on, differentiates, and unfolds a felt meaning, resulting in a referent movement or felt change through which new and different felt meanings now arise; (4) therefore, value-conclusions cannot possibly determine the experiential process. On the contrary, the newly differentiated aspects of felt meaning themselves indicate the need for further differentiation as they feel constricted, conflicted, and bad; or, they mean resolution as they feel whole, sound, and deeply resolved. Value-conclusions are always much too general and therefore cannot be employed to differentiate and sort out specific aspects of experiencing. On the contrary, these aspects must be concretely differentiated first.

II. ARE THERE UNIVERSAL VALUES?

So far, we have concentrated on characterizing this experiential process. If it can be adequately described, then it can be recognized and its results can be empirically studied and compared with behavior resulting from other modes of arriving at value conclusions. A number of studies (Gendlin, 1960; 1961; 1962; 1966; Holloway, 1961; Kirtner and Cartwright, 1958; Mathieu, 1961; Rogers, 1951; 1959; 1960; Tomlinson and Hart, 1962; and Walker, Rablen, and Rogers, 1960) indicate that one can reliably recognize verbal behaviors indicative of this process, and that one can predict differential behavioral consequences from high and low levels of it. If it is possible to study what the outcomes of this kind of process really are, then we need not arbitrarily assert its "goodness." We can formulate its outcomes empirically. We can also empirically investigate whether, as I think, men always choose (i.e., engage in) this process when they can.

But characteristic behavior outcomes are not the only regular feature of this process. It also seems that only certain kinds of value-conclusions can result from it! As yet we have no genuine research confirmation of this assertion, but it is an empirical question: Is it the case that a great many kinds of value-conclusions are never the result of this experiential process? Is it the case that only certain kinds of value-conclusions can result from it? Just what common characteristics do these "universal" kinds of value-conclusions which do result from this experiential process share?

In the main discussion so far we asserted only that there is a recognizable *process* of differentiating one's experiencing. We did not say anything about the kind of conclusions that result. We spoke as if we cared only that the process be genuine, as if any and all varieties of conclusions could result (and would have to be "respected," as we phrased it). Indeed, we have presented no other criterion by which anything could be right or wrong! However, this view does not imply that anything whatsoever may be good or right.

If it is the case that only certain value-conclusions can arise from the experiential process I am describing, then there is a value system implicit in the human organism. This would be neither a system of *concepts* applied to man nor a system based on conceptual *premises*. Rather, the "system" would be the organismic nature of human experiencing.

Experiencing as we feel it inwardly and symbolize it in words is a bodily sentience, an aspect of body life. Body life is an interaction process with the environment. When we find "meaning" in what we bodily "feel" (for example, when I say that this feeling I have now is "hunger"), we symbolize meanings that are physically given in the body's life process. Of course, we give shape and form to meanings with language and symbols; in the body, however, meanings are not given as conceptual or linguistic entities. Yet we can feel and differentiate experiential meanings *about* others and about things around us, because body life is an interaction process with the people and things around us. Personality is a "being-in-the-world" or a "living-toward" people and things. Hence it is not mysterious why we always find *meanings* when we focus our attention on the bodily *feel* we have. Bodily felt experiencing has meanings, that is to say, we can put symbols into connection with it. Whereas, at a given moment, most words and phrases do not affect our feeling at all, the "right" phrase is experienced with an unmistakable, physically felt relief (which we express as "Yes, that's it, that's just what I mean!"). This "connection" between our felt meaning and *just these words* tells us that the words are referring to, acting upon, and carrying forward our felt meaning.

It will therefore not be surprising if there are definable general values at which any human body and person will arrive when an experiential process of differentiation as outlined above occurs. It would mean that all human bodies and persons are organized in certain ways. Certainly, there are also respects in which we vary greatly from each other, but it may well be a variety within a certain invariant organization. This organization makes possible the manner of experiential process we have been discussing, the way in which it can be differentiated, how its felt meanings evolve and move and, hence, perhaps also some respects in which all possible value-conclusions will be found to be similar if they have been arrived at by such a process.

Most of what has been said and written against "systems" has been directed against systems of *concepts*. One would not want to deny that the human organism is a "system." In fact, it is the most complex and highly organized system we know of. A good many invariant parameters must obtain for such a system to keep itself alive (and it does tend to keep itself alive—a system which tends to disintegrate or die would soon *be* disintegrated or dead).

I am therefore sure that only certain kinds of value-conclusions can occur as outcomes of this experiential process. However, this is an empirical question. What kind of outcomes does this process produce and what kind does it not produce?

The manner of this process of differentiating and carrying forward experiencing is, of course, itself a "value," since I am in favor of making this process happen. I can say broadly how one should respond to make it, rather than something else, happen. I would like eventually to base my preference for this process on the empirical findings of just what kind of conclusions emerge. I would like to think that any of us would choose these conclusions, and hence this process. We need no moral or value system that says, "You *should* choose this process," if we empirically find that we all *do* choose this process and its conclusions when we are able to choose it (when it is made to happen).

III. EXPERIENCING AND INTERPERSONAL INTERACTION

Does the value theory we presented mean that the other person (the therapist or the person we are close to and interact with) affects us not at all? Is the experiential process we discussed only a "differentiating" of felt meanings that are already there? Not at all. The therapist or any other person close to us vitally affects how we feel, who we are, and the manner in which at that moment we find ourselves being alive with him (Binswanger, 1947; Buber, 1948; Gendlin, 1964; Heidegger, 1960; Kirtner and Cartwright, 1958; Mead, 1938; Merleau-Ponty, 1962; Sullivan, 1953).

When we differentiate and symbolize a felt meaning by using words (just those words which, at the moment, feel exactly right), a physically felt *change* or "referent movement" occurs, indicating that one alters the felt meaning by accurately symbolizing it. Similarly, when another person responds accurately to my felt meanings, just by his so doing I feel an increased aliveness and bodily sensed release which, of course, constitutes a change. Language symbols are similar to interpersonal responses in human interaction: both are modes in which felt meanings become "symbolized" and thereby carried forward.

We generally talk as if meanings must be either represented accurately just as they are, or changed. Indeed, in the case of logically defined meanings that is so: when a concept is logically defined, it must *either* be rendered just as defined, *or* we change it. However, the bodily concretely felt meanings of experiencing are not "meanings" in this sense of logically defined concepts. Felt meanings share the special characteristics of body organization: The body is organized as interaction. When it exhales CO_2 it is ready to inhale oxygen. When it is hungry, it is ready to ingest food materials. When it reaches a certain condition, it is ready for sexual interaction with another organism. The most accurate response to these body organizations is oxygen or food, or another sexual organism. The point I wish to emphasize is that precisely these most "accurate responses" also *change* the organismic and concretely felt condition to which they respond.

Life process is always interaction with the environment. When the proper environmental objects occur (and note, not just any object is a fitting one for respiration, digestion, or reproduction—only certain objects fit the body interaction), then interaction is carried forward, and the momentary condition (which we called the "felt meaning") is thereby changed.

Words have meaning for us only through their felt meanings. Without that meaning, a word would only be a noise (like a word in a foreign language we do not know). Language is learned in infancy only in the context of interpersonally meaningful interaction. Thereby, words come to have organismic meaning and are small steps which carry the organismic interaction process forward. Between bodily hunger and food, for example, human society has interposed many steps, such as going home, washing one's hands, saying, "I am hungry" to someone, etc. Therefore, words have the power of accurately symbolizing a felt meaning and thereby changing it (carrying it forward).

Hunger does not say exactly what we will eat, but it does broadly prefigure the carrying forward of the digestive process. Only certain objects will "fit" as food for the organism; only a particular kind of change is meant by "eating and digesting." This kind of change is what I call "carrying forward." For a thousand other changes are possible, e.g., poisoning or destruction of the stomach. "Carrying forward" is clearly a special kind of change, namely the further ongoing of the body's life process. A response is called "accurate" just because it fits the interactive pattern of the body and therefore makes the further interaction process happen.

When another person responds to me, both his words and his personal reactions to me can be "accurate" in the sense that they not only correctly represent the felt meaning I now have, but also thereby carry it forward. For example, after some struggle to find words, I may tell you that I am afraid of people, that I don't trust you, that I am worthless, that I am sick and disgusted with putting up with myself, that I do not want to cope with anything more, and that I want to commit suicide. These verbal symbols may somewhat "move" the felt meaning I have, and may give me the physically sensed relief of their "rightness." I may feel as if, at last, I were more directly facing and knowing my situation. But equally, these correct words will carry forward and change my feeling.

An experiencing organism—a human body—is an interactive system. Concretely, it lives as an interaction with oxygen, food, and other humans. To be "afraid of people" is not just a fact, a datum to be correctly described. As a felt meaning it is the present condition of an interactive organism. Hence, when I tell another person (who responds deeply) of this felt fear of people, the nature of that very meaning is changed as I relate it. For to be "afraid of people" is a stopped version of personal interaction (just as hunger is a stopped version of digesting food). Thus the words and the personal response not only say what the individual feels, but they carry forward what he feels. They not only state the implicit meaning of the experiencing; they *make the further experiencing process happen*.

Carrying forward can occur through various verbal symbols and personal responses. However, this variety is still quite small compared to the great variety of words and responses which will not "fit" and will not "carry forward." To "make the further experiencing process happen" is thus a quite specific change, despite the variety of ways in which it can occur. In our example, above, the feeling of "not wanting to cope with anything more" may soon become differentiated further. The therapist's responses make happen this further concrete interaction process, some of which can be differentiated as wanting to be held and cared for, rather than coping with anything more.

When responses or words are exactly accurate they thereby carry forward the experiencing process, and this is the change we "respect" and "value," not because it accords with already accepted value-conclusions, but because of the kind of process it is. Hence the experiential process I have been describing is not a matter only of differentiating the felt meanings that are already there, but rather of carrying forward and "making happen" the *further* experiencing process which then has even further felt meanings leading still further.

IV. THE REVERSAL OF WHAT DETERMINES AND WHAT IS DETERMINED

1. The psychotherapy process determines values. The present theory does not base the psychotherapy process on values, but rather bases values on the nature of the psychotherapy process. The nature and direction of experiencing (its verbal or personal symbolizing and responding) is not based on, or directed by, values, but the reverse. If there is a universally human value system, then it is the human organism's life process which we feel concretely, and whose being carried forward we feel when symbols and responses fit.

Let me now briefly discuss our reversal of the order in which these things are usually thought to determine each other. On what values is our choice of our kind of psychotherapy process based? On none at all! Psychotherapy *is* a certain kind of process (though much which is called by that name effects no useful results at all, or is a different kind of process—for example, a resignation process, or an inquiry process, or a practical teaching process). The value theory here presented rests on the fact that there is an experiential process of a certain kind. This experiential process has its own nature and cannot be conducted in different directions or as determined by prechosen conclusions.

2. The psychotherapy process determines therapeutic outcomes. Therapeutic outcomes currently are discussed as if they were arbitrary choices. Do you aim at adjusting the client to his society, or do you aim at creativity and nonconformance? Does a therapeutic outcome involve a more open awareness of anxiety or a decrease in anxiety? From our theory it follows, however, that the "therapeutic" outcomes are those which arise *from* this process. As therapist I do not prechoose them, nor can the client. If by differentiating and resolving, a client arrives at a certain surprising choice, my reaction is not, "It can't have been successful therapy, since that was the outcome." Of course, if I have not lived a fully resolving process with the client, then I might say that. But if I have participated in the experiential clarity with which the surprising outcome emerged, then I have just learned and now know that a human being *can* resolve such a matter in this surprising way. I say, "How interesting—I never would have thought that such a way existed, but now I see that there is such a way."

Thus we do not (and cannot) with value-conclusions choose the outcomes we call therapeutic. Rather, the order is reversed: What outcomes are "therapeutic" we learn empirically from the process.

3. *The psychotherapy process determines therapeutic responses.* Another version of the reversal is this: What should the therapist do to bring about therapeutic change? Is it not a "value-question" to decide how, as a therapist, I ought to respond? Does it not hinge on "value-choices" or implicitly held values, of, say, freedom, self-determination, openness to experience, and others? From the value theory here presented the opposite follows: Such "value choices" really hinge on the nature of the process. I prefer the client to arrive at his own felt meanings and their resolution, not because I value democracy and self-determination, but because the nature of the process is such that intellectual insight and pressure rarely help much. Without the client's own direct reference to his concrete felt meanings, psychotherapy does not occur. I am willing to argue with the client—if only we soon return from this arguing to again referring directly to his felt meanings. I am willing to impose upon him in many ways, if only we soon again return to his necessarily free inward sensing of his own meanings. I am willing to urge him strongly to do what I think best, but I do not want to stop him from discovering the reverse, if it happens to be the next step of his experiential process. In short, it is not my values that determine what therapy process we get. Rather, the nature of a therapy process (if it is to occur at all) determines certain basic aspects of what it is to be a therapist.

The great variety of current therapeutic approaches, all with approximately equal percentages of success, shows that the differences in orientation which we have so long argued about are not essential aspects of therapeutic responding. It may be that my formulation of what is essential will also miss. Yet I think that reference to the individual's felt meanings, and "making the further process happen" are essentials, and, in one form or another, characterize what all effective psychotherapists attempt. These characteristics of the therapist's function are determined by the kind of process psychotherapy is and by how a therapist can maximize that process and make it happen.

Many people have spoken as if the psychotherapy process as such had no character of its own, and needed its character determined by the therapist's values. But the experiential process I have described has its own nature and direction, and this determines (it is not determined by) the therapist's choices.

4. The psychotherapy process determines what health is. One wants to "get the patient well," but who decides what "well" means? If something can be called health, for the human person, then it is not a matter of someone's choice, but resides in the nature of the human being. Personality is an aspect of the living organism, that is to say, of an interactive process. This process can occur fully in a great variety of forms, but many more varieties of narrowing and stoppage also exist. In general, we can say that any mode in which the organism can fully live—can fully go on—is health, while its stoppage or narrowing is not health. To enable the experiential interaction process to move on is "getting well," "psychotherapy," "experiencing more fully," etc.

For example, is voyeurism as healthy as intercourse? Is an orgasm through voyeurism the same as an orgasm in intercourse? Is our negative evaluation of voyeurism just a cultural or personal "value"? In voyeurism, the individual's sexual process is stopped at the mere seeing of the sexual object—he cannot proceed to personal interaction and body to body contact. His orgasm is physically and personally different from that of intercourse, and no matter how frequently he has such orgasms he can get prostate troubles that do not occur with satisfying intercourse. On the other hand, if the last statement and similar empirical differences should not be confirmed by research, then I should be mistaken in this instance. I would then know that my negative evaluation of voyeurism was, after all, a mere bias.

My assertion, however, concerns not this specific example, but the general difference between ongoing and stopped processes. If continuance of the process is health, and if that is what we maximize and make happen in psychotherapy, then it becomes clear why every step of differentiation feels so good and physically releasing, even when what is found at a given step seems worse than expected.

The concrete process of personality and body life is universal; however, its specific forms and varieties are not. To live as a human person, a great many details of civilization and individuation are necessary, yet all these vary. Concepts —cultural and individual forms—are always just one way of selecting, completing, and shaping aspects of the concrete process. All felt meanings can be shaped and finished conceptually in many different ways which "fit" and "carry forward" the experiencing process. (Yet this is not an arbitrary matter: only some forms will fit and carry forward. All others will not.) Despite this partial relativity, we need conceptualization; we must shape this way or that, else we cannot carry experiencing forward at all.

Personality requires *some* cultural and individual form and shape, yet these forms vary greatly. Therefore, if there are universal human values, if there is such a thing as "health" for the human person, then it will not be statable as any one of the variety of finished and conceptualized concepts of health which we find or formulate. Rather, what is universal is the concrete process (not my particular conceptual formation of it), which I have called experiencing and which you feel and at which all my words in this paper point. We cannot always distinguish *conceptually* between forms which enable the concrete process to go on, and forms which stop it. What tells us most about this division is the moving forward of the experiential process itself. If, when permitted and responded to so as to be able, the individual always (empirical question) differentiates and strives to change and resolve a certain condition, that condition is a stoppage. Only because there is such a process of experiencing can we speak of "therapeutic," "health," and "psychotherapy." For this reason most of what we know about personality, health, and illness came from observations of psychotherapy (Fine, 1962; Freud, 1920; Freud, 1940; Rogers, 1951; 1958; 1959; 1960; 1961a; 1961b; 1961c; 1962; Sullivan, 1953). The concrete experiential process determines what personality health is.

V. KINDS OF INFLUENCE

We have now sufficiently discussed how definitions of psychotherapy, health, and therapeutic response are determined by the nature of the process, rather than the process being determined by value choices. We must deal with one more question, that of influence. The therapist influences his patient. Should he or not? Does he or not? Can he help influencing? Is not all therapy a kind of "conditioning," and if so, isn't it better that we choose the values we implant (Skinner, 1948)? Why let them be accidents of our unreflected bias?

We have already answered this in saying that the very nature of the psychotherapy process precludes a kind of "influence" based on values we choose to implant. One cannot know in advance the specific turns of differentiation which a genuine experiencing process must take. Without these turns, one will not really get the result one wants, though one may get verbal assent to the conclusion he wishes. The direction of the concrete process is given in the progression of felt meanings, though neither client nor therapist may like a particular step of differentiation which, nevertheless, is clearly "next." Thus, the nature of the process is such that implanting our own values is not a type of influence possible in genuine psychotherapy.

We do not mean that the therapist does not influence. However, we must discuss the kind of influence it is. "Making the therapy process happen" as it has been described is itself, of course, a powerful influence. Nor is "conditioning" or implanting values ineffective. It is a kind of influence which can have many consequences, but psychotherapy is not one of them. Let us examine more closely different kinds of influence and their results.

First of all, it is a facile and incorrect assumption that if I influence you it must be in a direction that makes you more similar to me. The therapist's values do not simply transfer to the client, or the parent's values to the child. In fact, the influence is quite often the reverse.

The therapist (or anyone else) has no means by which to reach into another person and transfer values to him. Let us look instead at what we actually do. We respond more positively at some times than others. We reward and punish. Does this always bring on the values we reinforce with the reward? Not at all. We may effect resentment and reactiveness, get emotional blockage, difficulty, fear, anxiety, confusion, attempts to please or to hide confusion, and others. In short, we can get all kinds of results other than the simple transfer of values from one person to the other. How many sons of strong fathers are engaged in changing the world in the opposite direction from their parental values? Such a reaction *is* a result of influence, but not the one discussed or aimed at.

More importantly, the discussion always looks to the verbal or formal conclusion rather than the concrete process. In reaction to a parent one does not have a value in the same sense as when the value stems from one's own experiential process. We recognize this when we do not take seriously, for example, the reformist values of a young person who is "really rebelling against his father," rather than having genuine experiential values. But, similarly, if the individual happens, by some pressure, fear, or confusion, to assert that he now holds just those values which some authority figure imposed on him, then, too, we do not consider such values genuine in him. We predict different and much less effective behaviors from such a man than when his values are genuinely differentiated in relevant experiencing.

Brainwashing was for a time thought to be that magic (which we do not possess) of reaching into another person and making him over according to our wishes. Closer study (Hoh, 1964) of Chinese methods reveals that the brainwashing of Americans was only a consistent process of personality disintegration. It most certainly had effects. Fear, self-hatred, groveling, and inaction are concrete and definable results, but they are not the transmission of values. Similarly, if the therapist chooses to "strengthen the patient's defenses," he certainly behaves in ways that can have effects, but these will be confusion, emotional blockage, fear, and avoidance, which will be clearly different from anything we would want to call psychotherapy. Emotional blockage and stoppage of experiencing is usually recognizable and different from experiencing being carried forward, *whatever may be the verbal similarities of stated conclusions.* And many predictable behaviors arising later are also empirically differentiable.

But, this kind of "conditioning" can also be viewed in another way. We may "reward" the individual with our closeness and personal interaction, and this may be called the "reinforcement." We may be said to "condition" people to express their feelings, and to differentiate their experiencing and then say that the process of experiencing is "self-reinforcing." Even when the verbal

content at the moment may be such as none would value, the forward movement of the process and its felt relief is "reinforcing," as is the accompanying
personally close and welcoming interaction.

However, for the process to occur, the interaction must happen regardless of just what happens to be the content at a given moment. When a therapist's "negative reinforcement" is some form of withdrawing or pushing the
client away, the process then stops. (Therapists are not always equally glad
to move with the process. Negative reinforcement happens. But it does not
guide therapy, it stops it, and much effort from both the client and therapist
may be required to let the process resume and move its "next" step.)

Such a translation of our value theory into the language of reinforcement must not blind us to two important differences: (1) The process, not the
content, is "reinforced" by the therapist; (2) Differential reinforcement is
basically different from "reinforcement of process." Differentially reinforcing
either does not (thankfully) succeed at all, or the consequences are stoppage,
blockage, fear, avoidance, and trouble.

We must emphasize the concepts necessary to make these distinctions, for
without terms that refer to the experiencing process, we cannot talk meaningfully about "reinforcing" this process. To clarify this problem we need to differentiate between several kinds of influence, all of which can occur and have
predictably different behavioral consequences. To test and measure these behavioral consequences we must be able to define these different kinds of influence. For this we must have terms and distinctions referring to the manner
of experiential process. The two basic kinds of "influence" are: (1) value-
conclusions adopted without an experiential process from which they could
arise; and (2) value-conclusions adopted from an experiential process leading
to them.

Under the first type above, a further distinction must be made: (1a)
Value-conclusions without an experiential process leading to them can be
adopted in a sense which inclines one to readiness to experience what the conclusions imply. In this trouble-free form of 1, the individual expects to experience some day what the value-conclusions involve. This expectation makes
him more able to perceive the relevant, rather than other, equally valid, meanings in such experiencing, should it arise. The expectation also makes him
more willing to give time, patience, and repeated trials to opportunities for
such relevant experiences. In all these ways, influence type 1a succeeds in
making it more likely that the individual will, at some time, arrive at the
experiential concreteness of the values he has verbally adopted.

Predictable behaviors for 1a will be those showing inability to do what
an individual who has the experiential process could do (adapt, creatively
employ, explain, show in detail, respond well to certain situations requiring
these values, etc.). On the other hand, influence type 1a does not lead to those
further behavior differences to be cited in 1b.

(1b) Value-conclusions can be adopted without the experiential process leading to them, but accompanied by experiences of confusion, denial, conflict, and surrender of certain areas of enterprise. Such an adoption usually makes it less likely that the individual will ever obtain the experiential process leading to these values, than that he will arrive experientially at other values. It has a thousand side effects, including the predictable behavior differences involved in attempting to act as though he really had the given values, along with failure consequences, conflicts or inferiority, abasement, and resentment. Brainwashing is an example of influence type 1b, but nearly everyone has experienced less drastic instances.

The confusion which besets value theory is that types 1a, 1b, and 2 can all occur. When one speaks only of getting a certain kind of value-conclusion in the subject or patient, one ignores the differences. Also, if one puts the emphasis on one statement by the subject (what he says he now holds as a value) or on one specific behavior choice, then the differences are temporarily obscured. We can get the individual to apply for medical school in modes 1a, 1b, or 2. A man may be religious or an atheist in modes 1a, 1b, or 2. Most value-conclusions can be induced by influence types 1a, 1b, or 2. But we need terms to define and observe these process differences. Then the predictable behavior differences could be tested. Study of this kind exists under the term "motivation," though it does not yet get at the experiential process differences involved.

It is also important for our theory to note that living must involve influence types 1a and 2. Not all values and meanings are discovered through our own independent creativity—most of what we know and experience we were helped to have. As interactive organisms, we developed into persons because parents and others "made happen" and "carried forward" our experiencing processes. We must take conclusions and principles from those we trust, long before we find them in our own experience; we cannot always wait to behave honestly or sensibly, until we have experientially traced out each conclusion.

My assertions in no way oppose loyalty to principles or conclusions obtained on trust, in the form of 1a. In fact, often when one acts on 1a, the experiential process *then* appears: situational opportunities for it then arise. But the differences between 1a, 1b, and 2 are crucial, both for an empirical predictive science of man, and for psychotherapy and living. These differences are equally crucial for value theory, since we can now define as type 2 the kind of "influence" involved in psychotherapy.

Once we make these differences, other clarifications follow. For example, it is possible to merge 1a and 2 in the same operation. A teaching machine which drops candy for the right answers does 1a and 2. The candy gives the 1a type of "reinforcement" for right answers. It promises, "This direction is right." It says, without explaining why, "You have taken the right step, given a right answer." You may have guessed the answer, or figured it out. On the other hand, the teaching machine does not really determine the direction or rights and wrongs of the case through dropping candy. The field of study, be it mathematics or aesthetics, determines the steps of learning. No amount of candy will produce anything except type 1*b* confusion if the machine attempts to teach steps that don't make sense, i.e., that cannot be *experienced* as meaningfully following from each other. As I have said throughout this paper, in some respects great variety is humanly possible, but that does not mean that any and all steps are possible. One can teach old-fashioned art or abstract art, but one could not go very far teaching bad art. What is "bad art," considering the wide disagreements in aesthetics? "Bad art" is the sort in which one cannot take very many steps of differentiating enjoyable aspects. Some steps will be possible if the "bad art" is art at all, but not many. Similarly, one could not teach very much false mathematics with mere "reinforcement."

Psychotherapy involves influence type 2. It also involves some of 1*a*, but the steps of the process we described are not such as a therapist can usually outline beforehand, as a mathematics teacher can do. There are a few such steps—there are times in psychotherapy when the therapist sees the next step first. But that happens only moments, or at most, weeks, in advance. It does not happen at the start of therapy, and what is most important, such foreknowledge does not involve a choice by the therapist, any more than the mathematics teacher fashions the teaching machine according to his own personal values. The process of making sense (in psychotherapy the process of making sense of one's personal felt meanings) determines what steps can be differentiated and taken, as against mere jumps that carry no personality change with them and involve no carrying forward of the felt experiencing process. Specific conclusions may be verbally similar, but the patient's concrete condition and the resulting behaviors are totally different.

VI. PROCESS VALUES

Our value theory arrives at "process values" and this word can be used in six related senses, each of which can be taken as the values this paper presents:

1. The experiential *process, not the value-conclusions alone,* tells us what a value really is in an individual. The same verbal value-conclusion can mean very different concrete process conditions and very different resulting behaviors. By process values we may mean that we value the experiential process (a certain manner of it), not the value-conclusions alone.

2. The experiential process we have described seems regularly to arrive at certain values. While these are phrased and represented in many different ways, they are universal process values founded in the basically common biological and interpersonal organization of human organisms. They can be called process values because we can study empirically whether it is true that *the experiential process regularly arrives at them.*

3. Universal values in any concrete instances have the form and involve the distinctions and objective embodiments of specific individuals trained in

specific cultures. Hence process values do not rest on any purely individualistic or merely instinctual base as though the individual could omit his culture, his training, his intellectual insights, and perceptual differentiations. Rather, process values are largely those aspects in which his culture has trained and predisposed him, as well as those which he may creatively discover. Process values in this sense are those which a human individual *can* differentiate in his felt meanings, and *can* experientially resolve as we have described, in contrast with aspects that are also culturally taught but which no human being can experientially resolve or differentiate in his directly felt meanings. Every culture includes values and trainings of both sorts.

The felt meanings of experiencing implicitly include what we have learned, our cultural training, a great many perceptual and intellectual distinctions, and much more which we do not verbalize, but by which we are implicitly guided. We behave and respond in situations on the basis of felt meanings. In any one second we guide ourselves by thousands of considerations simultaneously. That is possible only because we respond on the basis of our felt meanings, and these implicitly contain thousands of preconceptual meanings. Therefore, culture and intellect are not omitted when we say that felt meanings are the criterion of the process we are discussing.

The role of culture and intellect has long been a theoretical problem in the theories of those (for example, Rogers) who point to the crucial role of the organism in personality growth and the realization of values. The values and meanings at which the client arrives are not all original creations. Only relatively few really new meanings and creative modifications occur, compared to the mass of culturally handed down and learned meanings which have become part of our organismic and conditioned organizations, and which we therefore can again differentiate in our felt meanings. If this point is not fully made clear, it may seem as though the experiential process we are discussing either glorifies a brutish instinct over intellect, or imputes to each single individual the original creation of all the meanings and values of the race. Experiencing (feeling, felt meanings) implicitly contains very many preconceptual meanings, organismically patterned and conditioned. It is in a felt preconceptual way that we have the thousands of common meanings we employ when we act and when we elaborate our ideas, and make intellectual and perceptual distinctions.

In this third sense, then, process values are the individual's discovery and interpretation of his culture and training as he can find these in his felt meanings. In this sense process values can be opposed to introjection or conformity. Training and culturally inherited meanings (when they can be genuine) can be found implicitly in our felt meanings. When so found, they are always aspects of a somewhat creative and individualized mode of felt resolution, and their validity rests not on the culture which predisposes one to the discovery, but on the fact that these values and meanings *can* be experienced and resolved. Only some values of any culture have this kind of universality. Other culturally taught values are always rejected when felt meanings are differentiated and carried forward.

4. But if these "universal" human values are always shaped and formed through cultural and individualized specifics, can we say anything at all about just what the universal process values *are?* So far, we have said that they are the experiential process (not the verbal value-conclusions), that they can be called "universal" because the described experiential process always arrives at them, and that they include that portion of one's specific cultural, intellectual, and individual training which can be experientially felt, differentiated, and resolved. We can now add, as another sense of process values, what "universal" values are: instances of the process of experiencing being fully ongoing rather than stopped or narrowed. Of course, many different phrasings and cultural and individual forms of such universal preferences are possible.

Whatever its specific form, the universal aspect of a value is its implicit preference for the process of experiencing to be fully ongoing, rather than forced, constricted, or stopped. When free to differentiate felt meanings, the human individual (this is a testable hypothesis) prefers ongoingness, depth, inward resolvedness, and interactive fullness to fear, confusion, blockage, and resignation from certain vital dimensions of being human. Even when he has formally avowed such resignation and holds value-conclusions supporting the resignation, he will later, when it becomes possible, opt *for* the differentiated aspects of experiencing which he thought were closed to him earlier. Thus, while conceptual, cultural, and individual formulations will differ, universal process values are the sense in which a given value or preference is an instance of more fully ongoing experiencing itself (see Gendlin, 1962, ch. 5).

While we cannot verbally separate the universal from the different ways of phrasing and objectifying it, we can say that the fully ongoing experiencing process is valued and constitutes health for the individual. As Aristotle asserted, the process of human living (when it goes on fully) is the basis of human values. Thus, the universal parameters of value-conclusions are those which move the experiencing process forward, as compared with those that imply stoppage.

Examples of such values were stated beautifully by Rogers (1961): (Here we have a version of the ancient values of sincerity, independence, worth, realism, consideration for others, and love.)

Clients in psychotherapy tend to move away from facades. Pretense, defensiveness, putting up a front, tend to be negatively valued.

They tend to move away from meeting the expectations of others. Pleasing others, as a goal in itself, is negatively valued.

Being real is positively valued. The client tends to move toward being himself, being his real feelings, being what he is. This seems to be a very deep preference.

Self-direction is positively valued. The client discovers an increasing pride and confidence in making his own choices, guiding his own life.

One's self, one's own feelings come to be positively valued. From a point where he looks upon himself with contempt and despair, the client comes to value himself and his reactions as being of worth.

. . . To be open to and sensitive to his own *inner* reactions and feelings, the reactions and feelings of others, and the realities of the objective world—this is a direction which he clearly prefers. The openness becomes the client's most valued resource.

Sensitivity to others and acceptance of others is positively valued.

Finally, deep relationships are positively valued. To achieve a close, intimate, real, fully communicative relationship with another person seems to meet a deep need in every individual, and is very highly valued.

These values are another phrasing of what has traditionally been called the virtues. But which aspects of the variety of the virtues do we find here? Only those which are conceptualizations of the very ongoing of the process of human experiencing and interaction. Hence, we may call these process values, instances of preferring the process itself.

5. Another sense of holding process values is our choice of this experiential process for ourselves and those we care for. We take a value stand in so choosing. The other assertions in the theory here presented involve no such choice. They are empirically testable hypotheses concerning the conclusions and resulting behavior differences which the described experiential process is said to produce.

6. Finally, if we do choose that process, what kinds of operational moment to moment value choices do we make when attempting to engender this experiential process and carry it forward in ourselves or another person? In this last sense, process values are operational and specific. They must be formulated in terms of the momentary circumstances of different situations and contexts. Only a random list of examples such as that found at the end of this chapter could be given, and every psychotherapist could write his own such list. Such operational process values are determined by the nature of the experiential process they aim to engender; they are behaviors and choices which are preferred because they engender the experiential process we have been discussing.

Here is a random list of examples of operational values of the therapist. These values come from the process described earlier.

1. Ulcers are not, in themselves, a good thing.
2. Everyone deserves positive responses and closeness from some other human.
3. We never *deserve* anything; we are really given it before we even could deserve it.
4. I am a separate person. I am not the client nor is he me.
5. Now that we know each other deeply, we are connected in that we can never unknow each other, nor undo having lived closely with each other.
6. It is all right to be angry at me, though I may react angrily or defensively, too.
7. Every kind of feeling you actually have is all right to feel, though the action which seems to you to be indicated by the feeling may not be all right at all.

8. Looking *toward* your feeling will get us further than looking away from it.

9. The best explanation isn't as good as a moment's attention to your felt meaning.

10. What *I* think is very important, but it doesn't replace your looking at your felt meanings, and the steps you then see.

11. You can cry.

12. I will walk and do things while you cry, to be sure that I don't fade out just because you feel something strongly. I want to make sure you know I'm here.

13. When we're stuck, it's because of something involving both of us.

14. When I've done a stupid thing it's best to say so, plus the feelings I *now* have about it.

15. Society has a great many policemen and social protection functionaries, but few whose role is to stick to someone while he sees how he feels. Therefore, I need not be a policeman if there is a chance that as a therapist I might be of help.

16. It is a good thing to give the inward self, the felt meanings which you are, room to breathe and speak.

17. Even the worst thing you might find in yourself can change if we allow it to be felt.

18. If everything seems meaningless because you have ground it all up by endless hurting inner slosh, then it is all right to put it on a shelf for a while, if that feels right to you.

19. We can be together intensely even without words or analyses or content.

20. We need not fill the time with words.

21. I may look at you into your eyes, or touch you with my hand, if I feel that we need contact and that words or silence divide us.

22. Feelings differ from action. Our relationship is totally trusting and open to the flow of every kind of feeling because I know I won't let them become action. I know I will not make love to you in action, whatever sexual feelings we may have. I know it so fully that I can let either of us have whatever feelings and urges may come up. I will not betray this safety.

23. Needs are all right to feel and have. Trouble results when we fight the fact that we have a need (when we fight *any* fact before we let it be a fact).

24. You may need me; you may feel endless and unfair demands with regard to me. It is all right to feel like a small child (it is easy to love a small child). Small children are nice things. We are precious inside ourselves.

25. When something I think could conceivably have a chance of helping you, I say what I think plus my awareness that it might be bunk, or that it might be true but not fit you.

26. You can feel two logically opposite ways about the same thing. It is quite human to do so.

27. You can hate your mother or father and still not condemn them.

28. You can feel wild fury and still that doesn't make you a dangerous person—nor are you more dangerous than if you avoid letting that anger be felt in you.

29. The side of you is always wrong which, for whatever reason, impatiently condemns you before you get a moment to even look and see how you feel.

30. You may be right in your worst self-criticism, but never right in making your inner self a shut-off or cowering, silent, hardly alive, dull ache. You may be that bad, but it is right to like yourself enough to listen to yourself kindly.

31. When it seems to me that you are not telling me the truth of your experience, I tell you what I think you experience, though I know that it can't be exactly as I guess. But I ask: What *do* you have there, which is something like what I am thinking of?

32. It makes no difference to me what we *call* something you directly refer to and feel. Whatever words get it right for you, are right. (The difference between your words and mine does tell me something more than I knew before, about exactly how it is in you.)

33. External situations can be perceived in very contrary ways from one minute to the next. That is all right. You need not be consistent about that.

34. When I strongly feel that you ought to behave differently, or that something you do is morally wrong, or will have bad results, I tell you so flatly and strongly. After I feel you perceive what I think, then your experiential meanings, not mine, are the basic criteria.

35. I will not let you (or me) make me dishonest, insincere, emotionally tied up or constricted, or artificially nice or social, if I can help it at all.

36. It is all right to behave toward me in ways that are objectively bad (that I would ordinarily resent) if we can get to the experiential meanings you are behaving from. Usually, these really need a positive and desirable response you never get, except from me, because of the trouble your behavior usually arouses in others. But you can't change till after you get the positive carrying-forward for this positive drive that is trapped in this undesirable mode of behaving.

37. I will never try to prevent you from getting something clearly explicit, even when I am afraid of, or disgusted with, what it is.

38. If you get cut off or feel you must no longer relate to me, then I still have the right to relate to you, and I'll go after you.

39. It is never good to be psychotic.

40. It is never the best alternative for anyone to remain sick or resigned, although to feel this may be necessary for the next step to occur.

41. Dependency is best resolved through a still fuller relationship in which the part of you that now can live only with me, lives often and deeply enough with me so that it can *later* live without me.

42. It is better that I look like a fool (that my having been stupid is revealed), than that we get stuck.

43. If you *feel* it, then it makes some kind of sense. Only by letting it be, and finding its sense, can you really use the better judgment which you also have.

44. A therapeutic feeling-change is different from merely "controlling" a feeling.

45. When you let go (which doesn't happen till you can) of your artificial and stiff controls, you will not be out of control. A more natural control is inherent in experiencing, and it takes over.

46. A feeling is not altered merely by seeing that it is logically or objectively nonsense.

47. Your good adult self will not get lost if you let go of it for a moment.

48. Something may be perfectly true, yet it may not fit. The next step of felt process may be different from this perfectly true thing.

49. When you reach out to me in that way which pushes most people off, I can let your reaching for me succeed, and it will not confirm you in your bad behavior.

On the contrary, it will relieve whatever has been making you do your reaching for others in this negative way.
50. When I feel something strongly, I can find some words you'll understand that will let me express it.

REFERENCES

Binswanger, L. Uber die daseinsanalytische Forschungsrichtung in der Psychiatrie. *Ausgewählte Vorträge und Aufsätze*. Bern: I. A. Francke, A. G. Verlag, 1947.

Buber, M. *Between man and man*. New York: Macmillan, 1948.

Dunn, H. *High level wellness*. Arlington, Virginia: R. W. Beatty, 1961.

Fine, R. *Freud: a critical re-evaluation of his theories*. New York: McKay, 1962.

Freud, S. *Jenseits des Lustprinzips*. In *Gesammelte Werke*, Vol. 13. London: Imago Publishers, 1942. (Vienna, 1920)

Freud, S. *An outline of psychoanalysis*. New York: Norton, 1949. (Abriss der Psychoanalyse. In *Gesammelte Werke*, Vol. 16, London: Imago Publishers, 1940.)

Gendlin, E. T. Experiencing: a variable in the process of therapeutic change. *Amer. J. Psychother.*, 1961, **15**, 233–245.

Gendlin, E. T. *Experiencing and the creation of meaning*. New York: Free Press, 1962. (a)

Gendlin, E. T. Need for a new type of concept: current trends and needs in psychotherapy research on schizophrenics. *Rev. exist. Psychol. & Psychiat.*, 1962, **2**, 37–46. (b)

Gendlin, E. T. A theory of personality change. In P. Worchel and D. Byrne (Eds.), *Personality change*. New York: Wiley, 1964.

Gendlin, E. T. Expressive meanings. In J. Edie (Ed.), *Invitation to phenomenology*. Chicago: Quadrangle Books, 1965.

Gendlin, E. T. Experiential explication and the problem of truth. *J. Existentialism*, 1966, **6**, 131–146. (a)

Gendlin, E. T. Research in psychotherapy with schizophrenic patients and the nature of that "illness." *Amer. J. Psychother.*, 1966, **20**, 4–16. (b)

Gendlin, E. T., Beebe, J., Cassens, J., and Oberlander, M. Focusing ability in psychotherapy, personality, and creativity. Paper for the Third Amer. Psychol. Ass. Conference on Research in Psychotherapy, Chicago, 1966.

Gendlin, E. T., Jenney, R. H., and Shlien, J. M. Counselor ratings of process and outcome in client-centered therapy. *J. Clin. Psychol.*, 1960, **16**, 210–213.

Gendlin, E. T., and Tomlinson, T. M. Experiencing Scale, Mimeographed. Wisconsin Psychiatric Institute, University of Wisconsin, 1962.

Haydu, G. *The architecture of sanity*. New York: Julian Press, 1958.

Heidegger, M. *Sein und Zeit*. Tubingen: Niemeyer, 1960.

Holloway, A. Interview profiles of level of experiencing and success in psychotherapy. Unpublished doctoral dissertation, University of Chicago, 1961.

Holt, R. R. Indoctrination and personality change. In P. Worchel and D. Byrne (Eds.), *Personality change*. New York: Wiley, 1964.

Jourard, S. M. *Personal adjustment*. New York: Macmillan, 1963.

Kirtner, W., and Cartwright, D. Success and failure in client-centered therapy as a function of initial in-therapy behavior. *J. consult. Psychol.*, 1958, **22**, 329–333.

Maslow, A. H. *Toward a psychology of being.* Princeton: Van Nostrand, 1962.

Mathieu, Philippa. Client-therapist interaction variables. Paper read at Amer. Psychol. Ass. Convention, September, 1961.

Mead, G. H. *The philosophy of the act.* Chicago: University of Chicago Press, 1938.

Merleau-Ponty, M. *Phenomenology of perception.* New York: Humanities Press, 1962.

Rogers, C. R. *Client-centered therapy: its current practice, implications and theory.* Boston: Houghton Mifflin, 1951.

Rogers, C. R. A process conception of psychotherapy. *American Psychologist*, 1958, **13.** Also in *On becoming a person.* Houghton Mifflin, 1961.

Rogers, C. R. A tentative scale for the measurement of process in psychotherapy. In E. Rubinstein (Ed.), *Research in psychotherapy.* Washington, D.C.: American Psychological Association, 1959.

Rogers, C. R. Significant trends in the client-centered orientation. In D. Brower and L. E. Abt (Eds.), *Progress in clinical psychology.* Vol. 4. New York: Grune & Stratton, 1960.

Rogers, C. R. *On becoming a person.* Boston: Houghton Mifflin, 1961. (a)

Rogers, C. R. The process equation of psychotherapy. *Amer. J. Psychother.*, 1961, **15.** (b)

Rogers, C. R. Toward a modern approach to values: the valuing process in the mature person. Talk given at conference on the theoretical bases of counseling, Univ. of Florida, Gainesville, Fla., January, 1961. Revised, November, 1962. (c)

Shlien, J. Toward what level of abstraction in criteria. In H. Strupp and L. Luborsky (Eds.), *Research in psychotherapy.* Vol. 2. Washington, D.C.: American Psychological Association, 1962.

Sullivan, H. S. *The interpersonal theory of psychiatry.* New York: Norton, 1953.

Skinner, B. F. *Walden two.* New York: Macmillan, 1948.

Tomlinson, T., and Hart, J. A validation of the process scale. *J. consult. Psychol.*, 1962, **26,** 74–78.

Walker, A. M., Rablen, R. A., and Rogers, C. R. Development of a scale to measure process changes in psychotherapy. *J. clin. Psychol.*, 1960, **16,** 79–85.

14

Goals of Psychotherapy

Albert Ellis, Ph.D.

An Introduction to the Person

by Robert A. Harper, Ph.D.

Dr. Albert Ellis was born in Pittsburgh, grew up in New York City, did his undergraduate work at City University of New York, and completed his graduate work in clinical psychology at Columbia University. Early in life, Ellis had strong literary interests and talents (including poetic ones), but veered, as an adult, increasingly in the direction of analyzing and modifying human behavior.

For several postdoctoral years Ellis was an almost-orthodox Horneyian psychoanalyst. He began to realize increasingly, however, that the much-touted psychoanalytic procedures might go on for hundreds of hours and leave the patient's disturbed behavior unaltered. As his experience increased, so also did his use of directive techniques and so, too, evolved RT, i.e., rational therapy (more formally, rational-emotive psychotherapy).

RT has an experimental as well as a clinical root, for Ellis is one of the very few psychotherapists in private practice who has done some basic research. His studies explore various areas of neurosis, psychosis, sexual behavior (normal and pathological), courtship and marriage, and the therapeutic process itself. He has published well over 200 papers in professional journals and anthologies, has written a large number of popular magazine articles, and has authored or edited over 20 books and monographs. His devotion to his work is like that of Bertrand Russell and Albert Schweitzer; he considers it more interesting and enjoyable than much defined by others as recreation.

Besides his writing and psychotherapy practice, Ellis has heavy public lecture, professional discussion, radio, and television schedules. He conducts many training workshops in RT for various professional conferences and institutions as well as for the Institute for Rational Living, Inc., of which he is Executive Director. Besides what is possibly the heaviest private practice of any psychologist in the United States, Ellis is a Consultant in Clinical Psychology for the Veterans Administration and is or has been a high ranking officer or Board member of the following organizations (among others): American Psychological Association's Division on Consulting Psychology, American Academy of Psychotherapists, Society for the Scientific Study of Sex, New York Society of Clinical Psychologists, American Association of Marriage Counselors, Psychologists in Private Practice, National Council on Family Relations, and Psychologists Interested in the Advancement of Psychotherapy.

RT is a form of psychotherapy, but it is also a way of life. Through the Institute for Rational Living, Dr. Ellis hopes to train and educate large numbers of persons of various ages and occupations to live and to help him promulgate a way of life that he considers a realistic road to human happiness.

My main goals in treating any of my psychotherapy patients are simple and concrete: to leave the patient, at the end of the psychotherapeutic process, with a minimum of anxiety (or self-blame) and of hostility (or blame of others and the world around him); and, just as importantly, to give him a method of self-observation and self-assessment that will ensure that, for the rest of his life, he continues to be minimally anxious and hostile. Does this mean that I think human anxiety and hostility are invariably self-defeating and that there is no good reason why a presumably well-adjusted person *need* experience these emotions in an intense and sustained manner? It definitely does.

Let me, to avoid confusion and make my case clear, operationally define anxiety and hostility. Human beings, in order to preserve themselves in a difficult and alien world, must to some extent be fearful, cautious, or vigilant. If they did not have inborn tendencies to learn easily to look before they leap, they would quickly kill themselves. Operationally defined, therefore, fear consists of the following idea or attitude or internalized sentence: "It would be unfortunate if I hurt myself or got killed; therefore I'd better watch my step, e.g., look before I leap, see whether other people are going to attack me, mind my *p*'s and *q*'s when I am being observed by my teacher or boss, etc." Fear, in other words, is prophylactic, and includes the notions: (1) something or someone is dangerous to me; (2) therefore I'd better *do something* to protect myself against this dangerous thing or person.

Anxiety is quite different from fear in that it invariably includes a third idea, namely, "Since I am inherently an inadequate, incompetent, and worthless individual, and since such an individual can*not* satisfactorily meet any real danger that threatens him, I therefore cannot possibly cope with this dangerous person or thing with which I am confronted, there is consequently nothing I can do to save myself, and I *must* be destroyed." Anxiety, in other words, to the ideas of danger and action against this danger, adds the superfluous, and essentially metaphysical (that is, unprovable) ideas that the threatened individual is intrinsically or innately unable to cope with the potential or existing danger; that he will probably *never* be able to do so; that his cause is consequently *hopeless;* and that by demonstrating that he cannot cope adequately with a *present* danger (or possibility of danger) he indisputably proves that he can *never* properly handle a similar kind of threat.

Stated still differently—since it is most important that we understand what anxiety truly is before we try to eliminate it—anxiety includes not only the person's estimation of the real danger involved in the *situation* which he is in, his objective appraisal of his probable *ability* to cope with this situation, and his guesses as to which *solutions* might be best to get him out of this presumably dangerous situation. Going further, and, alas, much further, than this, anxiety includes the individual's moralistic, negativistic, highly pessimistic evaluations of *himself,* and his implied or stated conclusion that *he* will never be able to handle this or any other similar dangerous situation. Anxiety, moreover, invariably includes an unprovable over-generalization: namely, that because the individual *has* not as yet figured out a good solution to the danger that he thinks is threatening him, and perhaps because he *has* not been able to cope satisfactorily with similar dangers in the past, he positively *will* not be able to solve the problem, now or ever.

Because anxiety—unlike fear, which is situation-appraising and action-inducing—is self-appraising and action-inhibiting, it practically always leads to unfortunate results. Instead of observing his presumably dangerous circumstances and trying to meet them today or prevent their occurring tomorrow, as an appropriately fearful person would do, the anxious individual mainly observes his own hopeless ineptness to meet the assumed danger. He consequently meets it badly or runs away from meeting it; he usually creates an even more dangerous (or presumably dangerous) situation; he then blames himself even more for being a hopeless incompetent; and he winds up, of course, by becoming more and more anxious. His self-blame impedes performance; he once again wrongly concludes that he *cannot* cope (instead of *has* not coped) with danger; and he becomes increasingly self-blaming, and increasingly unable to cope with danger. Anxiety, therefore, is dysfunctional and impedes performance, whereas fear may be functional and enable the individual to deal properly with a dangerous situation.

Hostility, like anxiety, also has two parts, a sane and an insane part, when it is operationally defined. The first, or sane, part of hostility consists of what may be called discomfort, displeasure, annoyance, or irritation with an unpleasant situation or a difficult person. Thus, when it rains when you want to go on a picnic or when someone unjustly censures you, you irritatedly may say to yourself: "I definitely don't like this annoying situation (or person); now let me see how I can go about changing it (or dealing with him) so that it (or he) is no longer annoying." This sentence, like that which accompanies fear, has two main ideas: (1) something or someone is unpleasant or irritating to me and (2) therefore I'd better *do* something to change this thing or person and thus minimize my irritation.

Hostility, like anxiety, is radically different from displeasure or annoyance in that it invariably includes a third idea, namely, "Since this thing or person that is bothering me is noxious, and since the thing theoretically *could* not exist, or the person theoretically *could* not be the way he is, it is logical for me to conclude that this thing *should* not exist and this person *should* not be the way he is." Or, another way of stating this idea is to say that the angry person grandiosely and falsely concludes that "Because I don't *like* this thing or person it or he *shouldn't* exist." This anger-creating idea, of course, is a metaphysical or unprovable assumption: because there is simply no provable reason why a thing that I dislike *shouldn't* exist just *because* I don't like it and because it *could* be different.

Anger, like anxiety, is dysfunctional in that, where the annoyed or irritated individual frequently does something effective to remove the source of his irritation, an angry or hostile person mainly stews in his own juices, spends most of his time and energy cursing the source of irritation rather than doing anything to change it, usually encourages the people at whom he is angry to turn against him and to become even more irritating, and finally ends up in the center of a vicious circle of self-created and self-perpetuated hostility. Moreover, since anger (like anxiety) is generally an unpleasant feeling, he needlessly stirs up his own guts by bringing it on. Unlike anxiety, anger does have some advantages, since the hostile individual can despise others and feel "superior" to them, thereby giving himself some amount of satisfaction. But the real gains to be derived from hostility are rarely worth the enormous costs it generally entails; and it is therefore (unlike irritation and annoyance) an emotion that is to be sanely fought and conquered.

Both anxiety and anger frequently, though not always, include another metaphysical notion that connects them with each other, and tends to make the anxious person angry and the hostile person anxious. Thus, the anxious individual, after convincing himself that he *himself* is a worthless slob who cannot possibly cope adequately with the dangerous situations that arise in his life, also often tells himself: "Because I am so helpless and hopeless in the face of danger, it is *unfair* that situations and people should threaten me instead of helping me. These situations and people *should* be different from the way they are, because I *need* them to be." He thereby makes himself hostile as well as anxious.

Similarly, the hostile individual, after convincing himself that people *shouldn't* be the way they are, frequently also tells himself: "I can't *stand* things and people the way they are; I just can't *cope* with their being this awful way." He thereby makes himself anxious or self-hating.

Moreover, since blaming oneself, and thus becoming anxious, will normally lead to the kind of confused thinking that will also, quite easily, induce one to blame others; and since blaming others for being the way they are will frequently irradiate to similarly irrational, self-blaming thoughts, anxiety and hostility will more often than not tend to go together. The essence of both these negative emotions is blaming, moralizing, or denigrating a person's worth when he is behaving in a typically fallible, human manner.

My therapeutic goals, therefore, invariably consist of trying to help my patients become minimally anxious and hostile, without, at the same time, trying to help them become rash and uncautious or pollyannaish and unirritated. Although I do not believe that it is possible for human beings to become *totally* unanxious or unhostile, since they have in my estimation distinct inborn, biological tendencies to think unclearly about their own and others' behavior, and hence to confuse anxiety and fear, hostility and annoyance (Ellis, 1962a; 1966), I do believe that they can laboriously learn, or train themselves over a considerable period of time, to be anxious or hostile only intermittently and moderately instead of (as they normally do in our society) to be persistently and intensely angry at themselves and others.

Let me emphasize, in this connection, that I am not primarily interested, as many other therapists seem to be today, in getting my patients to *express* or *abreact* or *act out* their anxiety and hostility. I try to get them to admit that they are self-blaming or angry; and then, as quickly as they are able to do so, to *work against, change,* and *eradicate* their anxious and hostile feelings. If, in the process, they express previously suppressed or repressed negative attitudes toward themselves or others, fine. I use the material they express, and work with it—or get *them* to work with it. But the expression of their feelings per se is of little interest to me, and I am convinced, in fact, that therapists who encourage such expression frequently help their patients either to adjust to their anxiety and hostility (that is, to feel more comfortable with it) or to enhance it—both of which results I consider to be undesirable.

Virtually all anger and anxiety, I insist, can be and should be eliminated from human affairs. Not, let me say again, reality-based annoyance and fear; but needless hostility and self-blame that invariably exist over and above, and are unwittingly or consciously *added* to, normal irritation and vigilance. And these senseless additions can be subtracted again, I hold, if the patient is clearly and concretely shown exactly *how* he is unconsciously creating aggression out of frustration, panic out of alertness. This is precisely what I aim to do with my patients: unmistakeably show them exactly how they *are* adding idiotic and unprovable assumptions to their sensible observations and premises, and how by removing these irrational assumptions they can translate their anger back into annoyance, their anxiety back into appropriate fear.

More specifically, I try to show my patients what specific irrational hypotheses and illogical deductions they are making to create their needless anxiety. The main irrational ideas that all humans seem to subscribe to in order to manufacture their own states of panic, self-blame, and self-doubt are, as I have shown in several previous publications (Ellis, 1962a; Ellis and Harper, 1961a; 1961b), these:

1. The idea that it is a dire necessity for an adult to be loved or approved by virtually every significant person in his community.
2. The idea that one should be throughly competent, adequate, and achieving in all possible respects if one is to consider oneself worthwhile.
3. The idea that human unhappiness is externally caused and that people have little or no ability to control their sorrows and disturbances.
4. The idea that one's past history is an all-important determiner of one's present behavior and that because something once strongly affected one's life, it should indefinitely have a similar effect.
5. The idea that there is invariably a right, precise, and perfect solution to human problems and that it is catastrophic if this perfect solution is not found.
6. The idea that if something is or may be dangerous or fearsome one should be terribly concerned about it and should keep dwelling on the possibility of its occurring.

The main irrational ideas that men and women seem to endorse in order to create their own states of anger, moralizing, and low frustration tolerance are these:

1. The idea that certain people are bad, wicked, or villainous and that they should be severely blamed and punished for their villainy.
2. The idea that it is awful and catastrophic when things are not the way one would very much like them to be.
3. The idea that it is easier to avoid than to face certain life difficulties and self-responsibilities.
4. The idea that one should become quite upset over other people's problems and disturbances.

It is these fundamentally irrational, unprovable premises that I continually show my patients that they (consciously or unconsciously) believe; that literally cause them to feel and behave badly; that they keep endlessly reiterating to themselves without effectively challenging; and that they must persistently, in theory and in practice, work, and work, and work still harder against to disbelieve if they are ever to overcome their basic anxiety and hostility. Exactly how do I induce my patients to look their own irrational assumptions straight in the eye and to question and challenge these self-defeating philosophic premises? In several main ways, including the following:

1. I literally force my patients to look at the simple exclamatory sentences that they are telling themselves to create their emotions of anger and hostility. Whenever a patient tells me, for example, "My wife accused me of being unfaithful to her, and that got me terribly angry, because it was so untrue and so unfair of her to accuse me of it," I stop him immediately and ask: "What

do you mean *that* got you angry? How could her false accusation do anything whatever to you? You mean, don't you, that your wife accused you unjustly and then *you* got yourself angry by idiotically telling yourself: (1) 'I don't like her false accusation,' and (2) 'And because I don't like it, she shouldn't make it.' Isn't *that* what got you upset, your own irrational premise, rather than *her* accusation?"

I keep showing my patients, in other words, that it is never the external stimulus, at point *A*, which makes them angry or anxious at point *C*. Rather, it is the nonsense they *tell themselves*, at point *B*, about what occurred at point *A*. Thus, it is never their wives or bosses or mothers-in-law who upset them at point *C* by doing something they don't like at point *A*, but it is only what they *tell themselves* about this disliked deed and its perpetrator at point *B* that truly disturbs them. If I keep teaching them—yes, literally teaching them—this *A-B-C* principle of how they always—yes, always—keep upsetting themselves at point *C* by telling themselves some drivel at point *B* about what happened at point *A*, they almost invariably, in time, see that they have the power to disturb or not disturb themselves, and eventually most of them use this power to keep themselves calm and happy rather than anxious and angry.

2. I am exceptionally active-directive with most of my patients, since the system of rational-emotive psychotherapy that I employ—as I note in a recent paper (Ellis, 1962b)—"insists that patients must not only gain insight into what nonsense they are consciously and unconsciously telling themselves, but that they must both think and *act* in counterpropagandizing ways. In RET, therefore, actual homework assignments are frequently given to individual and group therapy patients: assignments such as dating a girl whom the patient is afraid to ask for a date; looking for a new job; experimentally returning to live with a husband with whom one has previously continually quarreled; etc. The therapist quite actively tries to persuade, cajole, and, at times, even command the patient to undertake such assignments as an integral part of the therapeutic process."

Let me say, in this connection, that recently I very firmly gave a 30-year-old male, who had never really dated any girls, an assignment to the effect that he make at least two dates a week, whether he wished to do so or not, and come back and report to me on what happened. To my surprise, he immediately started dating, within two weeks had lost his virginity, and quickly began to overcome some of his most deep-seated feelings of inadequacy. When I used to practice classical psychoanalytic and then psychoanalytically-oriented psychotherapy, I would have taken many months, and perhaps years, to help this boy to the degree that I was able to help him by a few weeks of highly active-directive rational therapy.

3. I am exceptionally verbally active with my patients, especially during the first few sessions of therapy. I do a great deal of talking rather than passively listening to what the patient has to say. I do not hesitate, even during the first session, directly to confront the patient with evidences of his irrational

thinking and behaving. I most actively interpret many of the things the patient says and does, without being too concerned about possible resistances and defenses on his part. I consistently try to persuade and argue the patient out of his firmly held irrational and inconsistent beliefs. And I unhesitatingly *attack* his neurosis-creating ideas and attitudes after first demonstrating how and why they exist. As I note in my manual of rational-emotive psychotherapy, *Reason and Emotion in Psychotherapy* (Ellis, 1962a), "to the usual psychotherapeutic techniques of exploration, ventilation, excavation, and interpretation, the rational therapist adds the more direct techniques of confrontation, confutation, deindoctrination, and reeducation. He thereby frankly faces and resolutely tackles the most deep-seated and recalcitrant patterns of emotional disturbance."

4. My therapeutic approach is unusually didactic. I continually explain to my patients what the *general* mechanisms of emotional disturbance are, how these usually arise, how they become ingrained, and what must be done to combat them. I freely assign reading material, including my own and other authors' writings on personality and psychotherapy, and discuss any questions the patient may have about the material he reads. I firmly believe that people with emotional disturbances do not understand how and why they got disturbed, any more than physics students at first understand how and why the universe got the way it is. I therefore enlighten my patients, as soon as possible, and teach them many things a good psychology professor would teach them— except that the teaching is usually of an individual nature, and is specifically designed to utilize the facts of the patient's current life.

Although I used to believe that I was unusually didactic about my therapeutic approach, I have recently discovered that some other rational-emotive psychotherapists, such as Dr. Maxim F. Young of Philadelphia, are even more so than am I; and that they spend much of the first few sessions teaching the patient psychological principles, and getting him to report back on his reading assignments. This technique, I am told, works surprisingly well, especially with schizophrenic and borderline psychotic patients, who are benefited by a highly structured therapeutic situation.

5. I make surprisingly little use of the transference and counter-transference relationship in my work with patients. I am deliberately not very warm or personal with most of my patients, even those who crave and ask for such warmth, since, as I quickly explain to them, their main problem is usually that they think they need to be loved, when they actually do not; and I am there to teach them that they can get along very well in this world *without* necessarily being approved or loved by others. I therefore refuse to cater particularly to their sick love demands.

Transference phenomena are also minimized in my form of rational-emotive psychotherapy because I usually see my patients once a week or less; speak directly to them in a face-to-face situation; directly answer any personal questions that they may ask about me; and do not go out of my way to interpret transference manifestations that do arise unless I think that they are pertinent and helpful. Moreover, I insist that the patients work out their problems with the significant people in their own lives, rather than with me.

At the same time, one highly important aspect of relationship does enter into my form of therapeutic activity, and that is that I serve as a much different kind of model for my patients than do the other significant figures in their lives. Thus, if they become angry at me, as they frequently do, I do *not* return their feelings with anger of my own; and if they indicate that they do not love or approve of me, I do *not* indicate that that is awful, and that I cannot live successfully without their approval. In many ways, I tend to show them, in the course of the therapy sessions, that it *is* possible for a human being to act sanely and appropriately, with a minimum of anxiety and hostility; and by serving as a more rational model than they normally encounter in the rest of their lives, I help them see that it is possible for *them* to behave in a less self-defeating manner.

6. The approach I take to therapy is unusually philosophic rather than merely psychological. Rather than merely showing my patients the psychodynamics of their disordered behavior, I continually demonstrate to them what might be called the philosodynamics of this behavior. That is to say, I insist that the real reasons why they act in a certain self-defeating way do not lie in their early experiences or their past history but in the philosophic attitudes and assumptions they have been making, and still *are* making, about these experiences and history.

If, for example, I find that one of my patients has a full-blown Oedipus complex—which I do not often find these days, but which does occasionally turn up—I do not merely show him the details of how he lusted after his mother and was afraid that his father would castrate him. Instead, I try to get him to focus on the philosophic underpinnings of his complex, namely, the *beliefs* that if he engaged in a wicked act like desiring his mother, he would be no damned good as a person, and that, if his father jealously disapproved of him for his incestuous feelings, it would be terrible for him to bear this disapproval. Then, as noted above, when I clarify to the patient what his philosophic, disturbance-creating assumptions are, I make no bones about making mincemeat of these assumptions, that is, demonstrating that they could not possibly be valid, and that as long as the patient falsely maintains them, he *must* get the neurotic or psychotic behavioral results that he is now getting.

Quite didactically, moreover, I present to the patient what is usually, for him, a quite new, existentialist-oriented philosophy of life. I teach him that it is most possible for him to accept himself as a worthwhile human being *just because he exists*, because he is alive, and because as a living person he has some possibility of enjoying himself and some likelihood of combatting his own unhappiness. I vigorously attack the notion that his intrinsic value to himself depends on the usual socially-promulgated criteria of success, achievement, popularity, service to others, devotion to God, and others. Instead, I show him that he must, if he is really to get over his deep-seated emotional disturbances, come to accept himself *whether or not* he is competent or achieving and *whether or not* he has a high extrinsic value to others.

7. I endeavor, with all my patients who are capable of working hard at overcoming their underlying disturbances, to give them three kinds of insight, rather than the limited "insight" that is usually given them in psychoanalytic therapies. Insight number 1 is the patient's seeing that his present neurotic behavior has antecedent causes. This is the kind of insight or understanding that is stressed by most psychoanalytic and other schools of therapy. I endeavor to give the patient some degree of this brand of self-understanding, but do not particularly harp on his seeing that all his present behavior is rooted in his past experiences or that he is behaving poorly today because he similarly behaved when he was a child.

I much more importantly stress Insight number 2—the patient's seeing that the reason why the original causes of his disturbance still upset and disorganize him is because he himself still *believes in,* and endlessly keeps repeating to himself, the irrational beliefs that he previously acquired. More precisely, I take a patient who, let us say, presently hates his parents, and may first show him that this hatred originally arose from (let us assume) his jealousy over his mother's paying too much attention to his father and too little attention to him when he was a child. This would be helping him acquire Insight number 1.

At the same time, however, I would show this patient that the real cause of his disturbance, even during his childhood, was not his mother's relative neglect of him for his father but his early belief that *it was horrible* for her to neglect him in this way and that she and his father *shouldn't* have been the kind of people that they were. Without this value system or philosophy of life, the patient never would have become upset in the first place, no matter how much his parents tended to neglect him; and it is therefore not their neglect but his beliefs *about* it that originally led him to hate.

More importantly, if he still hates his parents and is upset about them, this proves that he is still endlessly repeating to himself the original philosophy that he had about their behavior toward him: that is to say he still continually tells himself that it *is* horrible for parents to be neglectful and that they *shouldn't* be the way they are. If I enable this patient to see, very clearly and precisely, that *he* has continued to upset himself by continuing, most actively and vociferously, to subscribe to his childish philosophies about the horror of being neglected, and that his *own* internalized sentences about parental neglect, rather than that neglect itself, is *now* bothering him, I have thereby helped him to acquire Insight number 2.

Still more to the therapeutic point, I then go on to help the patient attain Insight number 3: his fully acknowledging that there is no other way for him to overcome his emotional disturbance but by *his* continually observing, questioning, and challenging his own belief-systems, and *his* working and practicing to change his own irrational philosophic assumptions by verbal and by motor counterpropagandizing activity. Thus, I would show the patient who hates his parents that if he is to overcome this irrational hatred (and a host of psychosomatic and other symptoms that may well accompany it), *he* must keep looking at his *own* idiotic assumptions about the horror of being neglected by them when he was a child and must work and work and work against these superstitions until he rids himself of them. Unless he acquires this kind of Insight number 3, all possible degrees of Insights number 1 and 2 are not likely to help him overcome his neurosis.

These are some of the main methods used in my rational-emotive therapy with my patients. In addition, some of the more conventional methods of psychotherapy, such as dream analysis, reflection of feeling, reassurance, and abreaction are also at times employed, but to a much lesser extent than they are used in most other forms of treatment. The main emphasis is ordinarily active-directive, confrontational, didactic, and philosophic. And the results, as I have shown elsewhere (Ellis, 1957; 1962a; 1962c), are significantly better, both in terms of improvements in patients and amount of therapeutic time required to achieve these improvements, than when I previously practiced classical analysis and psychoanalytically-oriented psychotherapy. It is also interesting to note that the unusual effectiveness of rational-emotive psychotherapy is duplicated by several other recent modes of therapy, particularly those reported by Berne (1957; 1962), Phillips (1956), Rosen (1953), Thorne (1957), and Wolpe (1958; 1961), all of which seem to have in common the element of an active-directive approach to the patient's problems.

Although the main emphasis in my type of psychotherapy is on analyzing and challenging the negative thinking of the patient, rather than on accentuating the positive aspects of their philosophy of life—as advocated by Coué (1923), Cowles (1954), Frankl (1955), Hart (1956), Maltz (1960), Peale (1952), and others—there are very specific positive implications of what I do in the therapeutic relationship. As noted above, I distinctly teach the patient that he *has* intrinsic value, or is a worthwhile human being to himself, as long as he is alive and can find *some* methods of enjoying himself during his lifetime. Several other positive goals of mental health are implicit or explicit in the teachings of rational-emotive psychotherapy. I have enumerated these goals in a recent paper (Ellis, 1962d):

1. *Self-interest.* The emotionally healthy individual should primarily be true to himself and not masochistically sacrifice himself for others. His kindness and consideration for others should be largely derived from the idea that he himself wants to enjoy freedom from unnecessary pain and restriction, and that he is only likely to do so by helping create a world in which the rights of others, as well as his own rights, are not needlessly curtailed.

2. *Self-direction.* The healthy individual should assume responsibility for his own life, be able independently to work out most of his problems, and while at times wanting or preferring the cooperation and help of others, he should not *need* their support for his effectiveness or well-being.

3. Tolerance. He should fully give other human beings *the right to be wrong*, and, while disliking or abhoring some of their behavior, still not blame *them*, as persons, for displaying this displeasing behavior. He should accept the fact that all humans are remarkably fallible, never unrealistically expect them to be perfect, and refrain from despising or punishing them when they make inevitable mistakes and errors (although he may at times objectively penalize them, in order to help them correct their mistakes).

4. Acceptance of uncertainty. The emotionally mature individual should completely accept the fact that we all live in a world of probability and chance, where there are not nor probably ever will be any absolute certainties; and he should realize that it is not at all horrible—indeed, in many ways it is fascinating and exciting—to live in such a probabilistic, uncertain world.

5. Flexibility. He should remain intellectually flexible, be open to change at all times, and unbigotedly view the infinitely varied people, ideas, and things in the world around him.

6. Scientific thinking. He should be sufficiently objective, rational, and scientific; and be able to apply the laws of logic and of scientific method not only to external people and events, but to himself and his interpersonal relationships.

7. Commitment. He should be vitally absorbed in something outside of himself, whether it be in people, things, or ideas; and should preferably have at least one major creative interest, as well as some outstanding human involvement, which are highly important to him, and around which he structures a good part of his life.

8. Risk-taking. The emotionally sound person should be able to take risks: to ask himself what he would really like to do in life, and then to try to do this, even though he has to chance defeat or failure. He should be adventurous (though not necessarily foolhardy); be willing to try almost anything once, just to see how he likes it; and look forward to some breaks in his usual life routines.

9. Self-acceptance. He should normally be glad to be alive, and to like himself just *because* he is alive, *because* he exists, and because he, as a living being, invariably has some power to enjoy himself, to create happiness and pleasure, and to ward off unnecessary pain. He should not equate his worth or value to himself on his extrinsic achievements, or on what *others* think of him, but on his personal existence: on *his* ability to think, feel, and act, and thereby to *make* some kind of an interesting, absorbed life for himself.

These are the kinds of more concrete positive or constructive goals that I am to help my patients achieve. As can easily be noted, many of these goals overlap significantly with those posited by such ancient and modern rational-minded philosophers and psychologists as Branden (1962a; 1962b), Epictetus (1899), Epicurus (1926), Freud (1924–1950; 1938), Marcus Aurelius (Hadas, 1961), Rand (1961), Russell (1950), Skinner (1962), and Spinoza (1901). Many of the psychotherapeutic goals that I keep in mind in regard to my patients also overlap significantly with the goals of mental health which are endorsed by an increasing number of existentialist and humanistic think-ers, including Angyal (1941), Braaten (1961), Goldstein (1954), Hartman (1959; 1962), Maslow (1962), May (1961), and Rogers (1961).

I still insist, however, that the more concrete constructive goals of psycho-therapy are derivatives of the two main goals that I outlined at the beginning of this paper: the minimization of the patient's anxiety and hostility. For as long as a human being is needlessly anxious or hostile, he simply is not going to achieve self-interest, self-direction, tolerance, acceptance of uncertainty, flexibility, scientific thinking, commitment, risk-taking, self-acceptance, or vir-tually any other road to positive mental health—for the simple reason that he will be ceaselessly consuming his time and energy in his anxious and hostile behavior, and will be sidetracked from doing almost anything else *but* being self-blaming and angry at others.

As I note in *Reason and Emotion in Psychotherapy* (1962a), it is un-fortunately all too easy for a person to cover up his underlying negative views about himself and others with some kind of "positive thinking" that will tempo-rarily divert him from his negative evalutions and make him "happy" despite his still holding such views. But sooner or later, if he mainly uses the tech-nique of diversion, his negative thinking will out, and will rise to smite him down. The only elegant and permanent solution to his basic neurosis or psycho-sis, therefore, is for him constantly to observe, challenge, question, and coun-terattack his self-defeating philosophies of life until they really go away, and he no longer is basically influenced by them.

This, therefore, remains my main goal as a psychotherapist: to induce the patient, as often as the results of his underlying disturbance (that is, his nega-tive emotions and the dysfunctional behavior to which they lead) arise, to *look* his fundamental philosophic premises straight in the eye, to *think* about them consciously and concertedly, to *understand* that they are based on illogical and inconsistent assumptions or deductions, and to *attack* them, by consistent verbal and motor activity, until they truly disappear or at least are reduced to minimal proportions. This method of persuading, cajoling, and at times literally forcing the patient to observe and to reappraise his *own* conscious and unconscious philosophies of life is the essence of rational-emotive psycho-therapy. I have found it to be, during the last decade, the most effective means I have ever discovered for permanently reducing and eliminating the anxiety and the hostility that seem to be the primary sources of almost all neurotic and psychotic symptoms, and which in their turn are created from the false and irrational philosophic assumptions that lie behind much of human behavior.

REFERENCES

Angyal, A. *Foundations for a science of personality.* New York: Commonwealth Fund, 1941.
Berne, E. Ego states in psychotherapy. *Amer. J. Psychother.*, 1957, **11**, 293–309.

Berne, E. *Transactional analysis in psychotherapy.* New York: Grove Press, 1962.

Braaten, L. J. The main theories of "existentialism" from the viewpoint of a psychotherapist. *Ment. Hyg.*, 1961, **45**, 10–17.

Branden, N. *Who is Ayn Rand?* New York: Random House, 1962.

Branden, N. Benevolence versus altruism. *Objectivist Newsltr.*, July, 1962, 27–28.

Coué, E. *My method.* New York: Doubleday, 1923.

Cowles, E. S. *Conquest of fatigue and fear.* New York: Holt, Rinehart and Winston, 1954.

Ellis, A. Outcome of employing three techniques of psychotherapy. *J. clin. Psychol.*, 1957, **13**, 334–350.

Ellis, A. *Reason and emotion in psychotherapy.* New York: Lyle Stuart, 1962. (a)

Ellis, A. Rational-emotive psychotherapy. Paper read at the Amer. Psychol. Ass. Convention, St. Louis, August 31, 1962. (b)

Ellis, A. The power of the printed, written, and recorded word in psychotherapy and counseling. Paper read at the Amer. Psychol. Ass. Convention, St. Louis, Sept. 3, 1962. (c)

Ellis, A. The case against religion: a psychotherapist's view. *The Independent*, Oct., 1962, 3–4. (d)

Ellis, A., and Harper, R. A. *Creative marriage.* New York: Lyle Stuart, 1961. (a)

Ellis, A., and Harper, R. A. *A guide to rational living.* Englewood Cliffs, N. J.: Prentice-Hall, 1961. (b)

Epictetus. *The works of Epictetus.* Boston: Little Brown, 1899.

Epicurus. *The extant remains.* London: Oxford University Press, 1926.

Frankl, V. E. *The doctor of the soul: an introduction to logotherapy.* New York: Knopf, 1955.

Freud, S. *Collected papers.* London: Imago Publishers, 1924–1950.

Freud, S. *Basic writings.* New York: Modern Library, 1938.

Goldstein, K. The concept of health, disease, and therapy. *Amer. J. Psychother.*, 1954, **8**, 745–764.

Hadas, M. (Ed.). *Essential works of stoicism.* New York: Bantam, 1961.

Hart, H. *Autoconditioning.* Englewood Cliffs, N. J.: Prentice-Hall, 1956.

Hartman, R. S. *The measurement of value.* Crotonville, N. Y.: General Electric Co., 1959.

Hartman, R. S. *The individual in management.* Chicago: Nationwide Insurance Co., 1962.

Maltz, M. *Psychocybernetics.* Englewood Cliffs, N. J.: Prentice-Hall, 1960.

May, R. *Existential psychology.* New York: Random House, 1961.

Maslow, A. H. *Toward a psychology of being.* Princeton: Van Nostrand, 1962.

Peale, N. V. *The power of positive thinking.* Englewood Cliffs, N. J.: Prentice-Hall, 1952.

Phillips, E. L. *Psychotherapy.* Englewood Cliffs, N. J.: Prentice-Hall, 1956.

Rand, Ayn. *For the new intellectual.* New York: Random House, 1961.

Rogers, C. R. *On becoming a person.* Boston: Houghton, Mifflin, 1961.

Rosen, J. N. *Direct analysis.* New York: Grune & Stratton, 1953.

Russell, B. *The conquest of happiness.* New York: Pocket Books, 1950.

Skinner, B. F. *Walden two.* New York: Macmillan, 1962.

Spinoza, B. *Improvement of the understanding, ethics, and correspondence.* New York: Dunne, 1901.

Thorne, F. C. An evaluation of eclectically-oriented psychotherapy. *J. consult. Psychol.*, 1957, **21**, 459–464.

Wolpe, J. *Psychotherapy of reciprocal inhibition.* Stanford: Stanford University Press, 1958.

Wolpe, J. The systematic desensitization treatment of neuroses. *J. nerv. ment. Dis.*, 1961, **132**, 189–203.

15

Goals of Psychotherapy

Rudolf Dreikurs, M.D.

An Introduction to the Person

by R. N. Lowe, Ph.D.

A half century ago the editor of the *Zentrablatt Für Psychoanalyse* (*Periodical for Psychoanalysis*) resigned. Alfred Adler, perhaps the most brilliant of the younger disciples of Sigmund Freud, publicly renounced his relationship with the founder of the New Science. At that time, Adler, together with a number of contemporaries, rejected the materialistic school of absolute causality to form the organization, the Free Psychoanalysts, later to become a school and movement designated by Adler as Individual Psychology, more recently identified as Adlerian Psychology.

Many of those associates, then and later, were to dedicate their thinking and activities to the furtherance of Adler's ideas. Foremost among those who came some time over a decade after Adler's break with Freud was Rudolf Dreikurs—medical doctor, psychiatrist, scholar, educator, innovator, and currently, in the writer's opinion, the leading exponent of modern Adlerian Psychology in this country if not the world.

Born of a successful merchant early in 1897 in Vienna, Dreikurs became, in his youth, active in an Austrian youth movement to which he attributed much of his current interest in social and political issues. A graduate of the Medical School of the University of Vienna, and always interested in psychiatry, he early became concerned with social psychiatry. During the mid-twenties he was one of the first to work toward rehabilitating alcoholics, an experience which undoubtedly provided the roots for his interest in group psychotherapy.

In 1937, the year of Adler's death, Dreikurs came to the United States, where he became a citizen and achieved distinction for his provocative position in the field of psychiatry and community mental health. In 1939 he established the first of a number of parent education clinics under the title Community Child Guidance Centers. These centers, now to be found in a number of communities in the country, may well prove to be Dreikurs' unique contribution to the mental health movement of this nation. In 1942 he received a professorship in psychiatry at the Chicago Medical School which has been followed in later years by a number of sustained visiting professorships in psychology and education throughout this and a number of foreign countries.

His publications, including professional articles and books, are in excess of 150, involving a number of fields: psychiatry, psychotherapy, juvenile delinquency, child development, human relations, and philosophy. In addition to being a pioneer in group and music therapy as well as in the preparation given to psychiatric social workers, he founded more than a decade ago what is now the *Journal of Individual Psychology* and the Chicago Alfred Adler Institute. He is a Fellow in the American Psychiatric Association and has held leading offices in the Society for Group Psychotherapy and Psychodrama, the Academy of Psychotherapy, the American Society of Adlerian Psychology, and the American Humanist Association.

THE question of the goals of psychotherapy has so far eluded any precise answer. One reason for this dilemma seems to lie in the term "therapy." Therapy, meaning treatment, implies cure. But do we really seek a "cure" of the patient who comes for treatment? Is the terminology, derived from the practice of medicine, really applicable to the field of psychological therapy? Furthermore, we not only disagree about the desirable outcome of the treatment, but also about the nature of the disease which we attempt to cure. In any other field of medicine the disease to be cured and the goal of the therapy is usually well defined. There may be a few controversial aspects, but neither the nature nor the desirable result of any specific therapy can be questioned as it can in a case of tuberculosis or heart failure.

What is responsible for the predicament which we encounter in the area of psychological treatment? It is primarily the confusion about the nature of neurosis and maladjustment. Only in this area is the goal of therapy uncertain and contested. If psychotherapeutic approaches are used as ancillary forms of treatment, let us say, in a case of chronic cardiac condition, then the goal is quite obvious and noncontroversial. A patient has to learn to live with his condition and to adjust to it. The goals of treatment in a case of psychosis are equally clear-cut, whether the therapy is medical or psychological. Recovery or amelioration of the psychotic process are the only possible objectives.

The target is by far less clear in cases of so-called emotional or character disorders. Is neurosis cured if the patient loses his symptoms? And what kind of changes are required to consider a character disorder as having been "cured"? Does it imply a total or only a partial change of personality? Is reconstruction of certain psychological mechanisms in the patient what is intended? If so, what are they? These are some of the questions for which there is still no generally accepted answer. Answers *have* been given, but they are often contradictory because they depend entirely on the orientation of the therapist. There is no possible agreement in sight as long as personality theories, concepts of neurosis, and therapeutic procedures and their rationales are as widely at variance as they are today.

Before presenting our own point of view, let us concern ourselves for a moment with the uncomfortable confu ion prevalent in the field of psychotherapy. The current dilemma of psychotherapy (Dreikurs, 1960) lies in the fact that psychotherapy implies more than a psychiatric and psychological technique. It is based on, and in turn fortifies, definite concepts of man, his nature, and his relationship to society. The founders of psychological schools created new concepts of man and reinforced them through the therapeutic practices which they established. They took concepts inherent in their cultural setting and made them popular in their efforts to understand and help their patients. Freud's model of man was in agreement with contemporary ideas, but it was he who made this model known and acceptable to wide circles through his technique of psychoanalysis. This holds equally true for Jung, Adler, Rogers, Frankl, and whoever developed new procedures and new rationales for therapy. Each practitioner operates within a chosen frame of reference, based on his ideas about man. In many cases he may not be aware of his own ideological premises. They may be vague, well defined, or even deceptive whenever his actions do not conform with his expressed ideas. Such confusion between theory and practice is frequent, and the failure to realize one's own premises is particularly evident amongst many so-called eclectics.

While each therapist operates on a definite, although often not conscious theory about personality, no personality theory can be scientifically validated at the present time. Social and behavioral sciences are still in a prescientific state (Argyle, 1957). The basic laws governing the relationship of individuals and groups are far from being recognized. Some are inclined to believe that such laws do not exist. Merton (1957) assumes that we will have to be satisfied with limited laws, while Frank (1957) expects a similar unification of social science as that found in physical science. This could only occur if a scientific approach could be found which would permit the grasp of "organized complexities" (Weaver, 1948).

Although scientists have failed to come up with a unified theory of human behavior, the practitioner dealing with human beings cannot wait. He has had to develop a working hypothesis by constructing a model of man according to which he governs his approaches. Since no theory of human behavior can be validated at present, each practitioner has to choose his own frame of reference. He then attempts to validate it by research which often is less scientific than circular. This writer has chosen the basic concepts which Alfred Adler developed in his Individual Psychology (H. L. Ansbacher and H. H. Ansbacher, 1956). From this point of view, the goals of psychotherapy and the methods by which one attempts to achieve them assume a distinctive pattern. Some of the ideas, conclusions, and techniques which the Adlerian psychotherapist has arrived at may be similar to those of others. Hall and Lindzey (1957) found that each theory of personality includes concepts which are shared by others. They introduced the notion of a cluster of concepts. Accordingly, some of our characteristic approaches may also appear in the practice of therapists who follow different schools of thought. Others are distinctively Adlerian.

One of the most characteristic and distinctive principles on which we operate is the teleo-analytic approach. It gives specific significance to our perception of the goal of therapy.[1] We see all behavior as being purposive, i.e., directed toward a goal. This is similar to the ideas of the early American pragmatism of Peirce and James, who postulated that the significance of behavior lies in its consequences. We have to recognize the movement of the patient at the beginning of therapy and compare it with his movements at the termination. We must distinguish the patient's goal from that of the therapist. These two may as often coincide as not, but we can assume, in the event of goal discrepancy, that the goal which the therapist has in mind may be more valid and more desirable. It is the goal which the therapist sets for his practice which is the subject of this discourse.

Let us first examine the goal of the patient. What brings him to the therapist's office in this particular phase of his life? Officially and verbally, he comes because he wants help. He suffers either from symptoms or from a subjective or objective evidence of deficiency and malfunction. He wants to change either how he feels or what he does. This is true for the vast majority of patients. Only few will openly admit that they come merely because someone else suggested that they need help. These are easy to deal with, provided one realizes that the therapeutic procedure implies always a change in goals.

Here the first therapeutic consideration has to be given to determining whether he needs help, and, if so, to convince him that he does need and can obtain it if he so desires. It is the first goal of our therapeutic effort to make the patient aware of what he is doing and what he needs to do. Our technique of exploration permits a rather quick diagnostic impression of his present functioning and his personality makeup. Therefore, we can offer him the possibility of exploring the situation to determine whether the opinion of those who suggested therapy was valid or not. If he wants to find out about himself, it can be done in a few interviews.

[1]The Adlerians are "teleoanalysts," as the Freudians are "psychoanalysts," and the Existentialists are "ontoanalysts."

Our first approach consists of a brief analysis of the patient's present life situation, his functioning at work, and his social and sexual relationships. Then we can explore his whole personality structure, the life style, through examination of his family Constellation, the dynamics within his family during his formative years, and his early recollections.[2] After these are analysed, we can confront the patient with his short-range and long-range goals in life—most of which are below his level of awareness. Then he is in a position to decide whether he wants to change or not. Even if he would not come for further treatment, an important goal of therapy has already been reached. The patient has been exposed to an experience where he can begin to understand himself. In most cases he becomes motivated for further therapy, since he knows now which changes are needed.

The situation is quite different when the patient seeks symptomatic relief. For him, getting well means losing his symptom or his incapacity. This quest is justified in the field of medicine. The patient comes for treatment because he feels sick and cannot function. He has the right to expect the doctor to help him get well. But can he expect the same from the psychotherapist, in regard to the variety of symptoms which bring him to his office? Here we must answer with a decisive "no." It has been generally accepted that psychotherapy does not have the prime purpose of freeing the patient from symptoms. The sad fact is that many psychiatrists and psychologists still consider neurotic or deficient patients as sick or "emotionally" disturbed.

As we see it, neurosis is not a disease. It is a pretense of being sick. The patient imitates the two cardinal aspects of any disease, i.e., suffering and loss of function. True enough, he is not functioning adequately and is suffering, but this is not due to any kind of illness. He is not the victim of a condition out of his control. He is, for whatever reason, merely unwilling to function. In order to obtain personal benefits, such as an escape from responsibility, the patient develops symptoms and suffers from them. It is therefore impossible to free him of these symptoms because he is busily, although unconsciously, engaged in maintaining them. In most cases he does not want to get well, although he may sincerely believe so. He wants to recover from his symptoms and his deficiencies, but in his given life situation he needs both. Therefore, symptomatic relief or removal of symptoms is no solution even if it were possible, since the patient is bound to find substitutes.

A hypnotist, by contrast, does not care what the problems are. He tries— often successfully—to impose his will on the patient, not without attempting to talk the patient into assuming that it is *he*, the patient, who produces the results. There may be other therapists who believe that they can "make" the patient well. We do not belong to this category. We know that we can help the patient only when he becomes willing to change his goals and movements in life. For this reason, one cannot consider mere relief from symptoms as indication of

[2]The meaning of these procedures and of the terms used is discussed later (pages 228–230).

successful therapy. We have seen patients who improved in order to avoid further treatment, to escape the painful experience of being confronted with themselves and their intentions, and the realization of their responsibility for what they were and did.

Sitting back and waiting for what the therapist can do is an attitude frequently assumed by the patient. Does he not do the same when he consults a general practitioner? Of course he takes medicines, but he is also willing to take pills from the therapist if this would be of help. As a matter of fact, he is often insulted and feels neglected if he does not get pills or other kinds of medical advice. That is the price which many psychotherapists have to pay for the widespread belief that a neurotic and disturbed patient is sick. The patient's intentions and movements are wrong, but this cannot be cured by any pill. He needs to "learn" about the facts of life and about the nature of his deviation in order to accept the goal of therapy, which is reeducation.

There is another and even more pernicious goal often encountered at the beginning of therapy. The patient does not believe that he can ever get well. In order to prove his good intentions, the patient indicates his willingness to do everything possible to aid in his recovery when, in reality, he is so sure that no one can help him that he resists any therapeutic effort. Here the difference between psychotherapy and medical therapy is most obvious. It is hard to believe that any physically sick patient would voluntarily consult a general practitioner with the intention to prove that he cannot be helped. In psychotherapy, however, this is more often the case than not.

The consequent work at cross-purposes is particularly damaging to a less experienced therapist. He may, first of all, be oblivious of the patient's intentions. If he does recognize them, he may try to persuade the patient that his pessimism is not justified. The patient may be right, unfortunately, because he has it in his power to defeat the best therapeutic efforts. He always can prove that his own pessimistic expectations were justified. A change of such an attitude is a therapeutic goal and must precede any further therapeutic endeavor. It cannot be achieved by fighting or arguing with the patient, nor by ignoring his schemes.

The first responsibility of the therapist is to establish a proper therapeutic relationship, which, in our terms, means a cooperative relationship. Resistance is merely the expression of noncooperation when the goals of the therapist and patient clash. Such an impasse can be overcome through therapeutic skill. It is always possible to find some course of action agreeable to patient and therapist. In our case, one of the means of establishing cooperation could be an effort to find out why and how the patient became so pessimistic. Another would be an examination of his personality structure in general. These and other suggestions on the part of the therapist can easily find acceptance from the patient and lead to a coordinated therapeutic procedure.

The final goal of any therapeutic or corrective effort is a change in the patient and his psychological makeup, but the nature of this change is a matter of controversy. In order to formulate the goals which we are setting for ourselves, we have to consider the basic assumptions on which we operate. We see man as a truly social being. Only within a group, in close cooperation with others, can the individual fulfill himself. He can only function as a member of the group to which he belongs. This sense of belonging can only occur when an individual considers himself equal to others. Only then can he be sure of his place and be willing to give his best for the benefit of all. Unfortunately, such certainty of one's place is rather rare in our contemporary neurotic society. In order to maintain our own worth and self-respect, we intimidate and discourage others, as we are discouraged and intimidated by them. The logic of social living, as Adler recognized it (1939), presupposes a state of equality, which we are approaching in our democratic era, but which still is a dream of the future. Only as an equal can the individual feel adequate and sure of his place. Only then can he fully develop his social interest, his feeling of belonging. If he feels inferior or inadequate, he limits his willingness and ability to contribute and to cooperate. Instead, he becomes more concerned with his compensatory effort toward self-elevation, or with defensive maneuvers to safeguard his endangered self-respect.

The extent to which he doubts his value and adequacy determines his social tolerance level. Inferiority feelings lower this level, as social interest increases it. Neurotic symptoms develop only in crisis situations when the individual no longer feels able to function adequately. Then he seeks an alibi or an excuse for withdrawal or escape. Symptoms, real or imagined deficiencies or inadequacies, are used for this purpose.[3] Consequently, the goal of therapy is a diminution of inferiority feelings and an increase in the extent and intensity of social feeling, of a feeling of belonging.

Another basic premise of our therapeutic efforts is man's ability to set his own goals and to decide the direction in which he moves. All his actions are movements within the social field. We can distinguish short-range and long-range goals. Behind the overt actions are cognitive processes, most of which do not take place on the conscious level. Whatever an individual does, it reveals his plans, his intentions, his goals. He evaluates every situation according to his private logic. He acts upon his concepts and beliefs in accordance with the value system which he has accepted for himself. He functions adequately as long as his movements are in line with the needs of any given situation, with the social requirements to which he is exposed. His subjective feeling of deficiency and failure arises in a crisis situation where he feels unable to function on his own premises. If he merely does not know how to meet specific contingencies, he may only need counseling to give him information

[3]The means by which the individual can choose his symptoms and develop and maintain them is well known. Creation and maintenance of symptoms require a conscious effort to suppress and stop them. If the patient is asked to produce or intensify a symptom, a process called "antisuggestion" (Dreikurs, 1944), it disappears temporarily.

about possible solutions to his problems; thus he may benefit from vocational, marital, or child-guidance counseling.

If a person, on the other hand, encounters a general impasse where he no longer can function in accordance with his basic concepts, he needs to examine and to reconsider the assumptions that form his life style. Psychotherapy then implies reconsideration, and, if necessary, change of basic assumptions and long-range goals. It leads to a change of the patient's concepts about himself, about life, and about his possibilities. Of particular significance is a change in his value system. It seems that one of the prime obligations of psychotherapy is to extricate the patient from the faulty values to which he is exposed in our society. In this sense, the goal of psychotherapy is not an "emotional" adjustment but actually a social adjustment, with all its implications.

Now let us look at the details of the goals which we have set for ourselves in our therapeutic tasks. The final result is a reorientation of the patient. This process of reorientation is the last of four phases which we can distinguish in the process of psychotherapy (Dreikurs, 1956). The first, as has been explained, is the establishment and maintenance of a proper therapeutic relationship. This is more than a therapeutic step. It implies a new experience and often a new relationship for the patient. Therefore, it is in itself a therapeutic goal. For many patients the relationship with the therapist is the first good and close relationship they have experienced. This type of relationship, with its give and take, its resilience in conflicts, and its endurance under the impact of hostility, can well form a pattern for future and more satisfactory relationships with others. Helping the patient to maintain such close and intimate cooperation constitutes a training for better interactions. This is almost an action experience because it goes beyond the verbal communications which form the major part of a therapeutic process.

The second phase in the process of psychotherapy is devoted to an analysis of the patient's present situation and his personality structure. While this phase does not have in itself any bearing on the goal of therapy, it is an indispensable prerequisite to the third phase. This phase consists of interpretation, providing the patient with insight and awareness of his basic assumptions, his movements, and their direction. Furthermore, our technique of exploring dynamic processes permits a clear definition of the patient's problems and the changes which are desirable and indispensable for an eventual better adjustment. It can also be employed in the terminal phase of therapy to determine the extent to which a reorientation has taken place.

Since the interpretation of the third step and the reorientation of the final phase are based to a large extent on the dynamics of the patient's life style, a short discussion of the concept of the life style and of the methods to determine it seems appropriate. During the formative years, in early childhood, the individual develops firm convictions about his place in the family, about methods and approaches which he finds effective, and about the meaning of social living as he perceives it. He starts off by trial and error, observing the effects of his actions, and reaching conclusions based on his subjective observations and interpretations. In order to meet the complexity of social living, he needs definite guiding lines for his conduct and therefore sets himself goals which will ensure him a place in the group. These goals become fixed and are directed toward long-range, fictitious goals of security. Within the given life style, the individual operates on immediate short-range goals which reflect his private logic. No one knows his own life style; it was developed without awareness as a result of the necessary and empirical search for a workable orientation. Even most of the immediate short-range goals do not come to our full awareness, because our private logic may conflict with our commonsense evaluations.

Adler provided a practical and relatively simple technique for a clear understanding of a person's basic personality pattern, i.e., his life style. It is impossible to comprehend a person's personality structure without information about his first four to six years of life. These are the formative years, for in this period each individual develops his concepts in his interaction with the other members of his family. Therefore, in order to understand the patient's life style, we must investigate his family constellation, the interactions within the family during his formative years. The investigation reveals his field of early experiences, the circumstances under which he developed his personal perspective and biases, his concepts and convictions about himself and others, and his fundamental attitudes and movements, not only in childhood, but throughout life. It is interesting to note that our understanding of the patient's life style is not based on the overt relationship between parents and children, or that between siblings; instead we explore the character, interests, successes, and failures of each child in the family. *They* indicate each one's movement, since behavior reflects the movement toward a specific goal. The competition and alliance between siblings can be revealed by their differences or similarities in interests, character traits, and activities. What the patient "was" as a child reveals clearly his movement toward others and his basic attitude toward life.

After the sociogram of the early family, the family constellation, has been clearly established, we solicit the early recollections of the patient. This fundamental and highly reliable projective test was described by Adler in 1913, but has not been universally used, mainly due to the opposition of Freud (1915) who called them irrelevant "concealing" memories. We all remember from the multitude of experiences during our early childhood only those incidents which fit into our outlook on life. From the incidents which the patient remembers from his early childhood one can accurately conclude what he thinks of himself and life. These early recollections are so reliable for the patient's outlook on life, that we can use this technique to clearly establish any change which occurred in the patient's basic concepts during the therapeutic process, or whether there are no changes, despite the disappearance of clinical symptoms. While this technique is relatively simple, its proper use requires training and skill. First, even the solicitation of incidents requires training. It is necessary to obtain with clarity all the details which the patient remembers. Then one has to distinguish between reports and true recollections. And finally, one has to be able to interpret recollections accurately, sensing the meaning which each detail has for the patient.

After we have obtained a clear picture of the patient's present movements and his basic concepts, which can be accomplished in a very few initial interviews, we begin immediately to interpret to him what we can see. We try to give him a picture of himself by confronting him with his intentions and goals, and with the mistaken ideas which direct his actions. Providing insight is an important, although an intermediate, goal since insight merely prepares the patient for the process of reorientation and can only be maintained under the constant supervision of the therapist. By making the patient aware of his self-determined goals, his intentions and decisions, we provide him with an opportunity to reconsider them and perhaps to change them for more adequate concepts and directions. After termination of therapy, the patient is again as little aware of what he intends to do in reality, of his private logic and of his basic goals, as he was before therapy. It seems that a psychological uncertainty principle (Dreikurs, 1963) makes it impossible for any individual to really know himself; if he could recognize his own bias, he would destroy it. After therapy, the patient cannot hope, any more than can any other individual, to understand himself. However, the difference is that after therapy he operates on the strength of sounder principles and more adequate concepts than before.

This brings us now to the final phase of therapy, the process of *reorientation*. Several questions arise: What kind of reorientation, if accomplished, indicates success of therapy? Is a permanent change of personality possible? If a permanent change of personality can be achieved, should we, in a particular case, attempt a total change of personality, or would a partial change be sufficient?

Various dynamic processes can effect a new orientation of the patient. Of greatest importance are the conclusions which the patient can draw from the insight which he may have gained. As he begins to see the purpose of his deficiencies and of his symptoms, he is in a position to reconsider his intentions. The kind of insight which we try to provide is different from that which usually can be obtained through introspection. Introspection usually implies recognition of past influences and present "feelings," and discovery of heretofore unknown deep-seated and unconscious mechanisms. This cannot possibly evoke the same motivation for change as the recognition of self-determined goals and purposes.

The neurotic particularly is in a conflict between his conscience and his rebellion. His symptoms are arrangements for the purpose of covering up his real intentions (Dreikurs, 1943). Bringing them to his attention is a powerful inducement to change. As Adler pointed out, one of the most effective therapeutic means is "spitting in the patient's soup." He can continue what he is doing, but it no longer "tastes so good." Even patients with a low tolerance for psychological insight, who either have intellectual difficulties or inner resistance, hardly ever fail to recognize their present and their basic goals. After all, we are not presenting to them abstract terms, but revealing to them their own inner logic, what they *really* think and believe. And if we are right, they respond.

We discuss with the patient his present decision as it is revealed by his actions and movements. By using his past history, we explain his present plans and intentions. He is not bound by the past, although he may "feel" shackled by it. The realization of one's own power to move in any chosen direction and the willingness to accept full responsibility for what one is doing are not merely requirements for a final reorientation, but lasting goals of therapy. They cannot be accomplished without a process of continued discussion, reexamination of the problems, discovery of alternatives, and learning about motivation, all leading to a new concept of man.

The most important factor in therapy as well as in any corrective endeavor is *encouragement*. One can well say that no effort which does not imply encouragement can have any lasting effect; conversely, wherever encouragement does take place, positive results ensue. The effects of any therapeutic or corrective procedure depend largely on the amount of encouragement given.

Such emphasis on encouragement may appear as exaggerated and unwarranted, unless one accepts two basic assumptions. One is related to the nature of deficiencies and maladjustment. From our point of view, they are the direct results of discouragement. It is so much easier and more satisfying to function well and adequately, to use one's resources and potentialities in a positive and constructive way, that no one would be willing to burden himself with all the tortures, suffering, and sacrifices which disfunction entails—unless he has lost his faith in himself. Only if he is discouraged does he switch to the "useless side" (Adler, 1927). This discouragement may occur in a crisis situation, or it may have originated in early childhood and be all-pervasive. All basic mistakes in a person's life style can be understood through the humiliations and frustrations which he experienced in his early childhood. Without encouragement, without restoring faith in himself, he can neither see his own abilities nor utilize them. Deliberate and persistent encouragement is needed to stimulate improvement, through the development of a better and more accurate self-picture. It counteracts the self-prejudice that characterizes every neurotic and deficient person. Discouragement underlies even the schizophrenic process and the character deficiencies of the psychopath; both schizophrenics and psychopaths succeed in covering up their inner bankruptcy through their characteristic psychopathological dynamics. For they too have lost their belief in finding their place in society through useful means.

We are dealing here with an essential aspect of Adlerian Psychology—its emphasis on inferiority feeling as a prime genetic factor of maladjustment. This emphasis has often been considered as farfetched and one-sided. How can a single dynamic factor explain all the varieties of deficiencies and maladjustment? To understand its significance, one must take into account the social constitution of man. The fundamental desire of every human being is to belong, to have status in the group of which he is a part. For this reason, the concern with status takes on pivotal significance. In our democratic society, the feeling of belonging presupposes the realization of being equal to others. While the concept of equality is difficult for many to understand, they experience a longing for it in their reaction to any situation where they feel inferior or suffer a loss in status, value, and significance. This fear of being inferior and, thereby, of being deprived of a significant place in the group, is almost universal and highly accentuated in our competitive society. The child is impressed with the fact that he amounts to nothing if he cannot successfully compete with others. Only superiority seems to guarantee a place in the group. This assumption, at least in certain areas, intensifies doubt and inferiority feelings and is often responsible for the declaration of bankruptcy which emotional and social maladjustment imply.

It then becomes obvious that the patient cannot change his self-concept unless he recognizes his own worth and value. He no longer is the same person when he overcomes his prejudice against himself and discovers that he is good enough as he is. For this reason, we feel justified in considering, as a primary goal of every therapy, helping the patient to restore faith in himself, to regain his self-respect, to recognize his inner strength instead of seeking constant new proof for his assumed weakness and disabilities. Rehabilitation implies the discovery of one's own dignity. These goals are implicit in every therapy, from faith healing to psychoanalysis, although they are not always openly acknowledged.

Since rehabilitation implies the discovery of one's own worth, overcoming inferiority feelings has far-reaching consequences on behavior. It removes all defense mechanisms, for the individual who is sure of his place in the group does not need to rebel against its demands. Social interest, based on a feeling of belonging, can only fully develop if inferiority feelings are absent. It is exactly this increased social interest which we consider as the basis for social and emotional improvement. The individual is stimulated to function well in a social setting, to take the vicissitudes of life in his stride without becoming frustrated, discouraged, demoralized, or sick. The courage to be imperfect is essential for full and uninhibited functioning. It brings about a high tolerance level which is in itself a goal of therapy.

Although encouragement is essential to psychotherapy, its crucial significance eludes those who look for more profound mechanisms. In our culture, where we are more prepared to discourage than encourage others, the processes and means of encouragement are often unknown. The technique of encouragement requires earnest study (Dinkmeyer and Dreikurs, 1963). It presupposes the ability to see the good in every human being and the skill to use this as a basis for growth. It requires faith in each patient that he can change, and faith in one's ability to stimulate a change. In the final analysis, encouragement depends less on what the therapist does than on the patient's response to it. Thus the process of encouragement is far from being a simple and superficial procedure, but constitutes an intricate and profound process affecting the intellectual, emotional, and moral functions of the patient.

This brings us to another aspect of psychotherapy. Concern with social values, with the "ironclad logic of social living" (Adler, 1929), characterizes the Adlerian approach to therapy. The value system on which the patient operates is our focal point. However, consideration of values during the psychotherapeutic process poses various problems. Are we in a position to determine which values are good for the patient and which not? Do we simply accept the standards of the surrounding community, of society, and help the patient to become adjusted by learning to conform? Or is there a yardstick by which we can measure the adequacy of value systems in various societies and can identify positive and negative, beneficial and detrimental values and standards?

Adler's concept of the "logic of social living" suggests the existence of basic laws for cooperation; it presents a normative formulation of social relationships. In this light, existing societies are not the final authority for the establishment of proper social values. Societies and their institutions can be evaluated as to their ability to create harmonious social functioning conducive to mental health. Adjustment, then, means not mere conformity to existing standards, but the movement towards an improved social attitude which will better fulfill the requirements for social living.

We may find normal reactions of normal people to abnormal conditions (Plant, 1937), or pathological reactions of people to either normal or abnormal conditions. We are concerned, therefore, with evaluating both individual reactions and the conditions under which people live. In psychotherapy we try to improve the abnormal reactions to reality, which includes partly normal, partly abnormal living conditions. While in our opinion the individual is not merely the product of circumstances, his environment does furnish probabilities for individual reaction. Certain prevalent social values are undesirable, because they restrict cooperation, which is indispensable for coping with the problems of life. Cooperation, since it is the basis for successful social relationships, is of primary concern in psychotherapy. Four attitudes are essential for cooperation. These attitudes, given with their antitheses, are: social interest—hostility; confidence in others—distrust and suspicion; self-confidence—inferiority feelings; courage—fear (Dreikurs, 1946).

As social interest is the basis for cooperation, so fear is one of the main obstacles to adequate social functioning in a democratic setting. It can be regarded as the sin of free man (Dreikurs, 1955). The climate of our communities is not conducive to the development of courage and self-confidence. A variety of contemporary standards, norms, and social conventions merit close scrutiny in their highly detrimental effects on cooperation, harmony, and mental health. In psychotherapy, we attempt to extricate patients from the mistaken social values in our present culture (Dreikurs, 1957).

Among the prominent mistaken and dangerous social stimulations is the assumed need for self-elevation. No one is ever told or given to understand that he is good enough as he is. On the contrary, such an assumption is considered as detrimental and dangerous for progress. Actually, the desire for self-elevation which is prevalent in our competitive society is by no means a prerequisite for growth and accomplishment. Much more reliable and less costly is the desire to be useful, which flows from a deep feeling of belonging, of a genuine interest in the welfare of others. The lust for glory, power, and self-aggrandisement may bring positive social achievements, but more often it brings collapse and failure. In therapy we try to help the patient to give up his movements on the "vertical plane" (Sicher, 1955) and to move on the horizontal plane of enthusiasm, love, interest, and enjoyment.

Another widely accepted social value reaps a terrific toll of human misery, despair, and failure. This is the goal of perfection which seems to be more emphasized today. Women, in their desire to become better than men, succumb easily to the mirage of perfectionism—and society supports the overwhelming desire to be good and right. Actually, most people who try so hard to be good, are not really interested in being good, but in being better—superior to others. Goodness and righteousness, as well as accomplishments, do not always express a sincere interest in the welfare of others. Many psychopathological conditions are intrinsically linked with this frustrated striving for perfection.

A related mistaken value fostered in our society and requiring consideration during therapy is the goal of ideal masculinity and femininity. Men suffer from the assumption that they are not enough of a man, and women strive desperately to achieve a feminine ideal. Both men and women often emulate the superior parent figures they saw as children. In therapy, we direct the patient's attention to general human values, independent from the incidental social implications of an imposed and changing sexual role. Instead of striving to be a "strong" man or "good" woman, we give the patient an interest in becoming a better human being. Freedom from sex-oriented behavior patterns is part of our therapeutic goal.

The basis for this search for perfection and superiority in our society is the fear of making mistakes. Our whole culture is mistake-centered. Our educational systems are dedicated to the prevention and correction of mistakes. This concern with possible future and past mistakes is universal and yet based on a fallacious assumption. Many believe that making a mistake is dangerous. But dangerous mistakes are rare, the exception rather than the rule. People also assume that lack of concern with mistakes may lead to carelessness. The opposite is true. The more afraid one is of making a mistake, the more one is prone to make it. One can be cautious and careful without fear of mistakes. Actually, making mistakes is unavoidable; and in most cases the mistake is less important than what is done afterwards. The mistake-centered orientation, detrimental and inadequate as it is, is partly a remnant of an outdated autocratic society in which doing wrong meant defiance of authority, and partly the result of our competitive striving, where making a mistake may mean humiliation and lower social status.

As the patient frees himself from his fear of being inferior and recognizes his worth and dignity, his apprehension decreases. Psychotherapy develops the courage to be imperfect, the ability to make mistakes graciously and to accept the ensuing predicament as a stimulation for corrective efforts. It is this courage to be imperfect which is essential for functioning as a free man, as an equal amongst equals.

This inner freedom permits the movement on the horizontal plane, toward people, toward cooperation. It does not entail either the sensation of personal success nor the torture of failure. The willingness to do one's best frees the patient from his dependency on the opinions of others. It frees him from the cultural tradition to establish yardsticks for measuring superiority and inferiority. Contrary to assumptions to which the patient is exposed in his environment, he can learn to trust his emotions, his unconscious processes, to accept his inevitable subjectivity, and to enjoy both the freedom and the obligation to choose and to decide. He stops trying to "control" himself as he has been advised to do since early childhood by realizing that he is doing only what he decides to do anyway, regardless of how much he may pretend not to be responsible for his actions.

It is obvious, therefore, that the mistaken social values which prevail today have great bearing on the neurotic inclination of most contemporaries. They overemphasize good and bad, right and wrong, up and down, without being able to do the good and avoid the bad. The therapeutic effect on the patient in moving toward usefulness, makes good and bad, up and down, parts of a normal pattern, like light and dark, harmony and discord. They belong together as alternating phases of a meaningful process. Absolute values disappear with the vanishing authority, and value judgments become personal choices and preferences rather than imposed shackles.

We are now in a position to answer some of the questions which were raised before. It is clear what kind of reorientation we consider necessary in a successful therapy. The change implies alteration in personal concepts and in social orientation. Therapy gives the patient an entirely new outlook. In certain stress situations he may fall back to his old pattern; but if the new trend is strong enough, it counteracts such tendencies. Whatever changes have been accomplished during therapy, they probably are less significant than those which occur after termination. The patient finds himself moving in a different direction. The final result of the therapeutic experience is the extent and the nature of the new trend. Therapy may have been terminated successfully, and still a relapse may ensue. Or conversely, a relatively insignificant change in a prematurely terminated therapy may lead to a far-reaching and permanent reorientation of the patient.

Does a patient's personality really change in therapy? About this we have no doubt. He is not the same individual before and after therapy. And this change is often permanent, regardless of temporary relapses or even recurrences of symptoms. We are today in a position to assess clearly whether, and to what extent, there has been any change in the personality structure of the patient. This can be determined by the evidence or absence of characteristic changes in early recollections. These changes are evidenced either in a different type of events which are now remembered, or in recollecting different details of the same event reported before, or—mostly dramatically—in the conviction that the incident which had been recorded before had never occurred. In one case, where the change of personality had been achieved within a few months, the patient could remember that he had told the therapist about a certain incident, but he could no longer remember nor visualize it.

The question whether a total change of personality is needed or whether a partial change is satisfactory seems meaningless. Any change in the basic concepts, even a minor one, implies a total change since the individual is no longer what he was. A change of all fundamental concepts and aspects of the personality is neither necessary nor possible. The correction of any basic mistaken concept is progress. Whether the extent of change is sufficient for future adequate living, only time can tell. In many instances, relatively minor changes in concepts and approaches prove to be sufficient. The patient, encouraged by his "success," learns to believe in himself, in his strength, and grows with the new experience of his ability to change and improve.

This, in our opinion, is the final outcome of a successful therapy. It is neither the question of one's capability, nor the extent of one's improvement. No change will create a perfect human being. The patient's ability to accept himself as he is, and his recognition that he is master of his own fate, is the basis for utilizing his ability to make the best decisions possible. This is the freedom which seems to be the optimal result of psychotherapy: to devote one's energies and resources to the tasks at hand and not to prove one's own value and significance.

REFERENCES

Adler, A. *Understanding human nature.* New York: Greenberg, 1927.

Adler, A. *The science of living.* New York: Greenberg, 1929.

Adler, A. *Social interest: a challenge to mankind.* New York: Putnam, 1939.

Ansbacher, H. L., and Ansbacher, R. R. *The individual psychology of Alfred Adler.* New York: Basic Books, 1956.

Argyle, M. *The scientific study of social behavior.* New York: Philosophical Library, 1957.

Dinkmeyer, D., and Dreikurs, R. *Encouraging children to learn: the encouragement process.* Englewood Cliffs, N. J.: Prentice-Hall, 1963.

Dreikurs, R. Neurosis, a challenge to medicine. *Chic. Med. Sch. quart.*, 1943, **4**, 4–6, 30–32.

Dreikurs, R. The technique of psychotherapy. *Chic. Med. Sch. quart.*, 1944, **5**, 4–7, 35.

Dreikurs, R. *The challenge of marriage.* New York: Duell, Sloan & Pearce, 1946.

Dreikurs, R. The religion of democracy. *The Humanist*, 1955, **15**, 210–215, 266–273.

Dreikurs, R. Adlerian psychotherapy. In F. Fromm-Reichmann and J. L. Moreno

(Eds.), *Progress in psychotherapy.* New York: Grune & Stratton, 1956. Pp. 111–118.

Dreikurs, R. Psychotherapy as correction of faulty social values. *J. indiv. Psychol.*, 1957, **13**, 150–158.

Dreikurs, R. The current dilemma in psychotherapy. *J. exist. Psychiat.*, 1960, **1** (2), 187–206.

Dreikurs, R. The psychological uncertainty principle. *Topic. Probl. Psychother.*, 1963, **4**, 23–31.

Frank. L. K. Research for what? *J. soc. Issues*, 1957, Supplement No. 10.

Hall, C. S., and Lindzey, G. *Theories of personality.* New York: Wiley, 1957.

Merton, R. K. *Social theory and social structure.* New York: Free Press, 1957.

Plant, J. S. *Personality and the culture pattern.* New York: Commonwealth Fund, 1937.

Sicher, L. Education for freedom. *Amer. J. indiv. Psychol.*, 1955, **11**, 97–103.

Weaver, W. Science and complexity. *Amer. Scient.*, 1948, **36** (4), 536–544.

16

A Psychology of the Optimal Man

George A. Kelly, Ph.D.

An Introduction to the Person

by George G. Thompson, Ph.D.

As student and in his productive professional career George A. Kelly has consistently reflected outstanding initiative and courage. Among the first to found a psychological clinic for service and training when the majority of American psychologists saw little future in this direction, he was also a leader among that small group of psychologists who effectively demonstrated during World War II that clinical psychology could make a unique contribution to the maximum utilization of human resources. Further, he had the courage to propose a theoretical alternative to the positivism and logical empiricism clearly favored by the majority of American psychologists. He "constructed" his own theory of human behavior to rationalize and systematize his views of man's creative efforts to understand himself and his relationships with others.

George Alexander Kelly was born in Kansas in 1905. In 1926, after three years at Friends University and one at Park College, he received a B.A. degree at the latter institution in physics and mathematics. His interest, however, had begun to shift to social problems, partly because of experience in intercollegiate debates. Therefore, he enrolled in educational sociology at the University of Kansas, with minor studies in labor relations and sociology. His master's thesis was a study of Kansas City workers' distribution of leisure time activities.

Kelly then taught part time in a labor college in Minneapolis, conducted classes in speech for the American Bankers Association, and taught an Americanization class for prospective citizens. After teaching in Iowa, and at the University of Minnesota, and a few months as an aeronautical engineer in Wichita, he went to Edinburgh on an exchange fellowship. There he received the Bachelor of Education degree in 1930; his thesis, under the direction of Sir Godfrey Thomson, dealt with the prediction of teaching success. Returning home, he enrolled in psychology for the first time, at the State University of Iowa, and the following June received a Ph.D. degree with a dissertation on common factors in speech and reading disabilities.

After a summer's teaching at the State University of Iowa he moved to Kansas, where he taught in the Fort Hays Kansas State College until receiving a commission in the Navy as an aviation psychologist during World War II. At Hays he found little occasion to pursue his recent interest in the physiological approaches to psychology, but there was need for clinical psychology, especially in the schools of the state. Soon he received some legislative support for a program of traveling clinics that let him and his students develop new approaches to clinical problems while in close contact with persons in distress.

At the beginning of the war in Europe George Kelly was placed in charge of the local civilian pilot training program and later was placed on duty in the Aviation Psychology Branch of the Navy's Bureau of Medicine and Surgery in Washington. In 1945, he was appointed to an associate professorship at the University of Maryland and from 1946 to 1951 was Professor and Director of Clinical Psychology at the Ohio State University, resuming these responsibilities from 1963 to 1965. He is currently the Riklis Professor of Behavioral Science at Brandeis University.

Other academic appointments were at Ohio State University, University of Chicago, University of Nebraska, Southern California, Northwestern University, and Brigham Young. In 1954, he directed an educational television research project at the Montclair State Teachers College in New Jersey, and in 1962 was a visiting professor at the City College of New York. In 1964, he taught at the University of New Hampshire, and in 1966 at Stanford University. He has also taught and delivered lectures at many universities in the Caribbean area and in South America.

George Kelly has been president of the Clinical and the Consulting Divisions of the American Psychological Association and of the American Board of Examiners in Professional Psychology. His best known scholarly contribution has been the development of a personality theory, the psychology of personal constructs, and the publication in 1955 of a two-volume work describing the theory and its clinical implications.

During the year 1960-61 he and his wife traveled around the world on a project financed by the Human Ecology Fund in an effort to apply the construct theory to certain international problems, and he lectured in Europe and Russia.

Psychologist, scholar, and scientist, George Kelly is a man of warmth and daring, with broad and penetrating views of the better world that man may someday be able to construct for himself.

ANY discussion of the goals of psychotherapy is likely to proceed in both of two directions. First it will lead its participants to speculate about the kind of creature man ought to make of himself. Then against this ideal, often so vaguely formulated that it provides no clear guidelines for continuing the discourse, the participants usually feel they must turn about and assess as realistically as they can those internal limitations of man that may prevent the attainment of this or any other human objective.

While these are the directions such a discussion ordinarily takes, there are many twists and turns that may be attempted in order to avoid or reshape the two issues. Among these is the especially attractive argument that man need seek only to become himself. By taking this position some psychologists attempt to resolve both matters at once—the question of what man should become and the question of what there is about his own self that blocks the fulfillment of his aspirations. Their stand, they hope, permits them to go on and say that psychotherapy needs no direction other than that spontaneously taken by their clients. Psychotherapy is something to be encouraged but never directed.

Although this posture of absolute respect for human nature in all its present forms appears to remove the onus of deciding what man should do with himself—and along with it the awful sense of responsibility for what is happening in human affairs everywhere—it seems to me to beg the question each of us asks himself sooner or later. In the end, man the person is left wondering in his loneliest hours what on earth he has been doing with himself, and man the psychotherapist, who has acquired an easy virtue with his clients by lapsing into permissiveness, will come to hold himself no less accountable for the outcome of his efforts.

This is the way I see it. Before this chapter is finished I may find myself accused of using this same psychological dodge. I shall not, however, accede to the charge!

PSYCHOTHERAPY AS AN ONTOLOGICAL VENTURE

The statement "to become oneself" makes sense only if you believe that man is presently something that he has not yet managed to become. The reasoning is a little tricky, for it requires that we distinguish between what is existing in some active state of being and what exists only latently, and, therefore, remains to be realized. The whole of oneself is presumed to include both levels of reality, but "being," in its strictly ontological sense, refers only to the former, to what is actually now existing.

The teleological construct of a human potentiality that has no actual "being," yet manages to serve as the sole activator of human destiny—and therefore as the infallible guide to psychotherapy as well—is more than a mite confusing. At worst, it encourages us to go around peering into dark corners looking for something which, by our own definition, is not there. At best, it sets us out in pursuit of something we would not be able to see even if we were lucky enough to catch up with it.

Now there is no harm in talking about things that cannot be seen. We do it all the time. But when we do it we are depending on inferences rather than direct observations. Even the modern materialists, with all their emphasis upon keeping one's eyes open to what is going on, are caught "observing" their inferences now and then, as if, like the dachshund who chased a "strange animal" around a tree, they had bumped into their own constructs. Indeed, if they, or any of us for that matter, were to take full account of themselves from beginning to end they too would likely come to the conclusion that their "direct observations" follow hard on the heels of their own adventures. Thus, in some degree, the observations of the most wide-eyed observer must be regarded as inferential—and therefore constructive—in nature.

It is when we forget this psychological fact that our inferences get in the way of our efforts, for constructs need to be evaluated not so much in terms of their visibility as in terms of what they lead us to do. It is against this criterion that the notion of a guiding human potentiality does us a disservice. We are tempted to go around looking for a certain golden key which, once it has been discovered, will unlock the door to all of human destiny.

Instead of arguing that man's potentialities are the guiding force behind his achievements, it seems more forthright to turn the proposition around and say that man is continually in the process of redefining his potentialities through the sheer audacity of his achievements. Having put the proposition in this way we can take a good look at what man has accomplished thus far and then venture to say something about what generally happens to human hopes and how it is that man's presumed limitations can so effectively block his efforts.

After looking at the unfolding record of man's achievement, one thing we can say is that whatever the range of human potentialities may ultimately turn out to be, there are probably a lot more of them than any individual can, even in his most expansive moments, reasonably hope to exploit in a lifetime. Some possibilities, therefore, have to be abandoned outright. Then there are some talents that one never suspects, although they might have been inferred from his achievements. Or if he does suspect them, they are conceived too late in life for him to do anything about them. Then again, besides these, some objectives are pretty likely to get in the way of others. Any attempt to achieve them negates the contrary ones. This forces the abandonment of still more of one's potentialities. In the end, even if a man carefully defines his objectives in terms of what seem to be his emerging potentialities, there still are limiting choices to be made.

Who is to make them? Stephen Leacock's man, who mounts his horse to ride off in all directions, will eventually find that some of his choices have been made by his horse. In the course of his headlong ride he, willy-nilly, abandons some of his brightest prospects in his galloping pursuit of the obvious. This is a common tragedy, as many a man past sixty-five realizes now that he has taken the time to think about it.

Ever since Eden it has been clear that man has capacities for both good and evil, and with them the burdensome yet exciting responsibility of distinguishing between the two, as well as between a lot of more transitive alternatives. The post-Eden man is held responsible even for the decisions of his horse. Most people, I am sure, are more or less convinced of this, in spite of the empathic amorality of their psychotherapists.

But the ontological decision that man must make, the decision to be something, need not be hemmed in by what he presumes are his potentialities, any more than it can be foreordained by them. Just how broad his field of choice is man will never know until he assails the impossible. One thing is sure, if he starts his venture into reality by circumscribing himself with prior assumptions about potentialities, or lack of them, nothing very exciting is going to happen. Rather, the initial question—the point of departure for the genuinely adventuresome person—is, What should he try to be? Or simply, What ought he to be?

I am well aware of the allergy psychologists have for "oughts." This is because many of them regard all commitments as coercive. Perhaps in too many cases their own early commitments proved to be intolerable. But to state our problem the way we have is far less coercive than to argue that man can aspire to nothing more than to be himself. The "ought" we propose is a venturesome "ought," an audacious one. It becomes coercive only when one surrenders his right to state the predicates of his sentences and resigns himself to the "oughts" that others impress upon him. In any case, the initiative in man's enterprises lies with decision and commitment rather than with impulse and fulfillment.

Psychotherapeutic movement can thus be said to get under way when a man starts questioning for himself what his immediate objectives may be and is thus led to initiate actions that challenge whatever previous notions he may have held as to what his limitations were. This is the first step in redefining his potentialities. He sets out to be what he is not.

The long-range objective of the psychotherapeutic effort is an extension of this first step. It, as well as that of any other worthwhile human undertaking, is not to conform to oneself, whole or fragment; or to society, lay or ordained; or to nature, whatever the latest version of that happens to be. This objective is for man continually to determine for himself what is worth the price he is going to end up paying for one thing or another anyway, to keep moving toward what he is not—surmounting obstacles as best he can—and to keep on doing both as long as he has anything to invest. To render and utilize technical aid in this ontological venture is the special transaction we call "psychotherapy."

EXPERIENCE AND VITALITY

The human enterprise does not follow a Euclidian line from point A to point B. No matter how carefully a man lays his plans and no matter how earnestly he announces his commitments, both plans and commitments are, almost from the very moment they are initiated, subject to reappraisal. An adolescent seeking to become a man, or a student aspiring to become a scholar, will change his notions about manhood or scholarship many times before he attains much of the status of either. This is not to say that his original plans were futile or that he must be unfaithful to his commitments. Even a plan which is abandoned outright may have served a purpose in leading one to the point where he could see more clearly what he should have planned instead.

So also with a commitment. A person who, from experience, knows what it means to be dedicated to a cause—even a bad one—may thus come to judge for himself what on earth is worth the ultimate price he must pay, that price being, of course, his own life. It is hard to say this of one who has never ventured to have the experience of commitment, although he too will certainly end up paying the same ultimate price, whether he wants to or not. And suppose, from his vantage point, the experienced man sees for the first time what lies beyond his original objectives and then commits himself to that instead, thus discarding the ill-phrased literalisms of his earlier commitments. Can it be said that he has proved disloyal to his undertakings? I think not.

I am not saying that it is experience that changes man, but rather, that man changes himself through a process called experience. Nor would I want to say, as the stimulus-response psychologists do, that external events shape the man. That denies human vitality altogether and reduces life to a prolonged reverberation of outside occurrences.

Psychotherapy needs to be understood as an experience, and experience, in turn, understood as a process that reflects human vitality. Thus to define psychotherapy as a form of treatment—something that one person does to another—is misleading. Psychotherapy takes place when one person makes constructive use of another who has offered himself for that purpose. The professional skills of the therapist, as well as much of his repertory as an experienced human being, are brought into the transaction. He offers as much of both as he thinks can be used. But it is the client who weaves them into the fabric of his own experience.

Just as human progress, as we have said, follows a circuitous course rather than a Euclidian line, so should personal experience be regarded as a circuitous affair. The teacher who had had only one year of experience—repeated twenty-nine times—had indeed made little headway in life. Human progress is not accomplished so much by the persistence of effort along a single line as by the exploration of paths leading to fresh vantage points from whence one may chart and rechart his course.

Experience, then, is not measured by years or the accumulation of events all handled in the same way, but by the revisions of one's outlook, revisions, of course, that take into account the outcomes of prior commitments. If one merely vacillates without taking into account what has occurred as a result of his previous ventures, or if he fails to put forth any serious effort to gain new perspectives, he may, to be sure, acquire some interesting scars to show his grandchildren, but he will end up surrendering his life without ever having experienced it.

What we have said about experience and the essential role of human vitality goes for psychotherapy too. Being a form of experience, it, too, follows an exploratory course, with many reappraisals based on the outcomes of yesterday's commitments. Goals get changed and changed again. Yesterday's useful insights become today's stubborn resistances and tomorrow's trivial cliches. The enterprise into which the client plunged himself last week may mark a crucial turning point in his life, long awaited by his therapist, yet it may be something that ought never to be repeated. Indeed, some of life's most precious moments ought never to be repeated. This, too, is one of the considerations to be kept in mind in any attempt to state the goals of psychotherapy.

HISTORICISM IN THE PSYCHOLOGY OF THE OPTIMAL MAN

To put it simply, it is not what the past has done to a man that counts so much as it is what the man does with his past. The psychotherapist can scarcely fail to be amazed at how differently two of his clients may make use of what has happened to them. If he is alert he will be aware of wide differences in the way they make use of him too. Men are not so much shaped by events—including what the psychotherapist says during interviews—as they are shaped by the meaning they ascribe to such noises. This is not to say that one is perfectly free to ignore what is going on. He is not. But man is always free to reconstrue that which he may not deny.

It is true that events of the past intrude themselves into our present and that to some extent, what we experience at any one moment is only the current phase of a process that began a long time ago, and will be likely to continue for a long time to come. But more and more, man takes a hand in directing the course the process takes. The history of things that happened before he was born may point to the circumstances in which one now finds himself, but they do not dictate what he may do about them. What a man does with his history and its legacies is up to his own ingenuity and whether or not he wishes to exercise it.

The phenomenological psychologists, of whom I certainly am not one, usually take the view that it is only the experience of the passing instant that is of essential psychological significance. But I would argue that it is the whole story of mankind that is of greatest psychological significance. It is significant, not because it tells us what has happened to man, but because it tells us what has happened by the hand of man. I am talking about a history that tells us what man has done, not one that claims to say what he was made to do. Once history is interpreted in this way we need not limit ourselves to the phenomenal moment in order to see man in dynamic perspective.

While the historical record provides us with a version of what man has actually done, it does not set the limits on what he could have done, nor on what he can do, nor on what he will do. The story of all science, for example, is, as I see it, a story of man's past psychological efforts unfolded in vast perspective. Those efforts produced, among other great things, what we know as the body of science, in itself an amazing display.

But this is not the most exciting part of the story that history has to tell us. This is only prologue. Infinitely more exciting is what potentiality these audacious feats suggest is locked up in the unrealized future of man. While the man of yesterday was developing a physicalistic science that tested itself by experiments and its ability to predict their outcomes, he was, without intending to do so, stating the basic postulates of a psychology for the man of tomorrow. Slowly he demonstrated not merely that events could be predicted, but, what was vastly more important, that *he was a predictor*. It was not only that hypotheses could be generated, experiments controlled, anticipations checked against realizations, and theories revised, but that he—man—was a hypothesizer, an experimenter, an anticipator, a critical observer, and an artful composer of new systems of thought. What he did, physically, portrayed what he was, psychologically.

Out of the saga of human achievement we can shape a postulate for a massive psychology of man. It runs like this: *a person's processes are psychologically channelized by the ways in which he anticipates events.* The bold pursuit of inferences that follow upon this postulate can serve to trace for us the outlines of a theory of personality we may call *the psychology of personal constructs.*

None of this is to say that the factual substance of our present day science draws any outer boundaries around man's capabilities, nor does it convince me that the scientists I know are optimal men. On the contrary, if examined closely, what man has accomplished in science, and in other forms of scholarly enterprise, points to the presence of psychological processes that have never been fully unleashed. The history of mankind, whether particularly scientific or generally literary, throws psychological light on the processes of man; it is not an iron chain of events that binds him forever to what he is—to that, and no more.

Some students, impressed by the accomplishments of scientists, try to make the most of themselves by acting like their heros. Acting like a scientist is child's play. What one observes in scientific effort is not something to be imitated outright, but rather something to be examined and construed. Properly construed, it may open new vistas that no scientist has yet envisioned.

As one abandons childlike imitation of scientists and launches into the exploration of the horizons opened up by them he is not likely to be regarded as a fellow scientist. Especially is he not likely to be so regarded by the psychologists of our day who are themselves still pretty much in the imitative stage of their mental development. But no matter; whatever one does that turns out well in the end is likely to be claimed by the "scientists" eventually.

Making use of the record of past events, whether in one's own biography or in the history of human progress, is not, then, a matter of looking for something to imitate, any more than it is a matter of reading the writing on the wall. The value of the record lies in its being subject to construction, for it is by construing events, not by subordinating oneself to them, that light is thrown on human possibilities not yet envisioned.

In psychotherapy, particularly, it makes a great deal of difference how the historical past is used. A therapist who is aware of the sweep of man's accomplishments, as well as what particular men have done about their handicaps, will envision the goals of his efforts quite differently from one who thinks in terms of disease entities, childhood traumata, or the closed economies of psychodynamic systems. As for the client, if he is one who regards his past as the successively emerging phases of his personal experience, each leading to a new outlook, he will make use of his therapeutic opportunities in a much different way than will one who recounts his past only to show what it has done to him and who looks at other men only to see who can tell him what to do.

THEORIES OF PSYCHOLOGISTS AND MEN

So far what has been said is that the goals of psychotherapy cannot be taken as self-evident, that man must determine them for himself, that they are subject to continual revision, even during the course of the interview series, and that, in any effort to reach goals, the past is something to be utilized rather than to be undone. This is background for saying next that the goals of psychotherapy cannot be entirely separated from the human processes and stages through which they are to be pursued. But in saying this we have simply elaborated our basic postulate: *a person's processes are psychologically channelized by the ways in which he anticipates events.*

Perhaps it is clear by now that we see no valuable distinction between the theorizing of psychologists, who may want to be seen as scientists, and their clients, who usually prefer to be seen as human. Both may be regarded as scientists, if you please, as well as men, for both seek to anticipate events. Both have their theories, in terms of which they attempt to structure the on rush of occurrences. Both hypothesize. Both experiment. Both observe. Both reluctantly revise their predictions in the light of what they observe, on the one hand, and the extent of their theoretical investment, on the other.

Nor do we see psychotherapists as *applied* scientists, in the sense of exploiting what the pure scientists have found out, i.e., using science in an unscientist-like manner. For us the course of therapy, like the course of all human enterprise, including scientific enterprise, is essentially exploratory, both for the therapist and for his client. This means that therapy is fraught with revisions, revisions that are undertaken by both client and therapist and by the two of them together. In short, psychotherapy is itself a form of experience, as we have defined experience.

Thus it is that the objectives of the psychotherapist must include the skillful facilitation of those human processes upon which all of us, scientist and client alike, depend as we move from stage to stage in the great human adventure. Goals, processes, and stages are often indistinguishable from each other. Indeed, the initiation and continuation of a lifetime effort to conjure up ever-fresh visions of what is worthwhile is itself a goal of psychotherapy. This is not the kind of goal at which you can hope to arrive and then stop looking further. It is, instead, a continuing series of commitments and revisions of commitments. Most of all it is a commitment to experience, with the stock-taking that honest experience requires. The person who profits from the therapeutic transaction is one who has started to make headway in this ceaseless enterprise.

Furthermore, it is probably futile, without due allowance for the circuitous routes man must follow, to specify the ultimate goals he hopes to attain, except, possibly, in some such imprecise terms as "heaven," "brotherhood of man," or "Utopia." Who knows where man will eventually arrive? Certainly not the certified therapists! Thus for man, whether he is seen as on his own or as clutching the hand of his somewhat befuddled therapist, ends and means often turn out to be indistinguishable from each other.

The tangible end of therapy is to implement the means by which the ultimate and intangible end of mankind's efforts can hope to be achieved. This is to say that while the therapist cannot quite put his finger on what his client should eventually achieve, he can at least put his finger on the processes by which his client might hope to achieve it. And he can implement those processes without knowing their ultimate outcome. To do this much is a perfectly tangible end of his psychotherapeutic effort. For what kind of a therapist would claim he knew where the ultimate end of man lies, or even what epitaph should be written on his client's tombstone? At best, all the wise therapist can hope to say is, "There, at last I think my client and I are hot on the trail of something." As for the client, at the end of his last psychotherapeutic session he can hope to say little more than something like this himself. Indeed, if he tries to say too much more than this, he probably needs to schedule some further sessions—with another therapist.

So the way a person lives his life cannot be divorced from how he anticipates the future (our basic postulate again), and vice versa. A man spends his time making as much money as he can. What does it mean? Perhaps he is trying to insure his family against every conceivable hazard, or himself from the haunting fear of disclosing his own insufficiency. Whatever it is, his money-making makes sense only in the light of his anticipations. But it also works the other way around. He may end up his life as a wealthy, grasping man, himself his family's worst hazard and, as a person, revealed as insufficient in more ways than when he started. The goal he so faithfully pursued turns out to be defined, not only by his ambition, but also by what he did to fulfill it. So for us all! The events we attempt to anticipate may turn out to be contaminated by what we did to anticipate them. In the words of our fundamental postulate, a person's processes are channelized by the ways in which he anticipates events.

The same goes for psychologists, who are known to have human characteristics too. Two therapists may state their goals in a similar way, yet have little in common, either in their methods or in what they eventually accept as confirming their predictions. For example, one American psychologist I know places primary psychological value on human "efficiency," while another says he hopes to aid in the fruition of a "fully functioning person." The two statements appear to be similar. Yet from listening to the two men I am convinced that what they would do to achieve their goal and when they would think they had reached it differ vastly. Indeed, what one would do to his client would, I am sure, be considered unconscionable by the other, and, perhaps, vice versa. My point, therefore, is that psychotherapeutic goals have to be understood as part of the psychologist's functional involvement with a theoretical position in which his working assumptions about the nature of mankind, and of his client, have been made to stand out as clearly as possible. What I am saying about understanding the psychotherapist is very similar to what I said about understanding man in general.

So how shall we state the objectives of psychotherapy? It is obvious by now that I do not intend to make up a list of "goals" to be checked off against the names of my colleagues who also write about psychotherapy, though from other points of view. Without a clear understanding of their theoretical positions it is impossible to know what they mean when they recite their own lists. So also for me and my client. Without some clear understanding of the fellow's outlook, that is to say, without some notion of the way he personally construes events of his past and present, it is uncertain what he will be doing to attain the goals either he or I envision, and what contaminated meaning those goals will eventually come to have. Goals can be distorted in the most grotesque ways by the means one employs in his effort to achieve them.

ONE PSYCHOLOGIST'S ASSUMPTIONS

We turn now to the things that must be said before any further statement of my own therapeutic goals can be fully understood. I believe that everything man does follows lines laid down in his effort to anticipate what will happen. We have already stated this as our basic postulate, though in somewhat different words.

Since this is our logical point of departure it is important that there be no misunderstanding about what such a statement means to us. One's anticipation of the onrush of events may not be expressed definitively; it may be expressed as a posture toward the future, possibly a future we would prefer not to portray too clearly or too realistically. A friend of mine, while driving her car, customarily closes her eyes when she gets caught in a tight spot. This is an anticipatory act; she suspects something may happen that she would prefer not to see. So far, it hasn't happened, though it is hard to understand why. Fortunately, in recent years she has given up driving a car; and that, too, is an anticipatory posture. Neither of her postures can be said to be very practical, but it would be hard to say neither of them was anticipatory in nature. As a matter of fact they seem very clearly to me to be anticipatory.

Most people anticipate death in a somewhat similar manner. This certainly does not mean that they go shopping for bargains in coffins. But in some persons especially we can see a great deal of what they do and say as an anticipatory posture toward death. Like my friend, they seem both to invite it to come and get them and to try to postpone it as long as possible, even to the extent of denying themselves the full life.

If we press this part of our theorizing into areas at the fringe of psychology's normal range of convenience we can say that contractions of the stomach, the beating of the heart, or the drooling of Pavlov's dog can easily enough be regarded as anticipatory. There is no reason to limit the notion of anticipation to what can be verbally communicated or logically projected.

We can, if we wish, extend this construct of anticipation to some other frontiers. We can speculate about the implications of saying that anticipation is one of the characteristic features of man, or saying that man is such and such a creature who does his best to cement the future to the past and thus grasp time in his own two fists, a Herculean task if there ever was one!

Some people are led to believe that man, in letting himself be guided by his ways of anticipating events, renders himself subservient to things that have not happened yet. But this is not true. Events do not control man's behavior before they occur, any more than they do afterward. The control of his behavior remains man's own prerogative, though limited, of course, by the amount of ingenuity he brings into play. If events, either past or expected, appear to manipulate a man it is only because, so far, he has figured out only one way to cope with them. He will continue to dance to the tune he thinks he hears them play until he contrives some other way of listening for the succession of notes.

Man never *waits* to see what will happen; he always *looks* to see what will happen. Even my motorist friend is looking for something, though she shuts her eyes to do it. Many of us close our eyes when we are looking for something, though not usually when we are looking for an opening in freeway traffic.

While man always looks to see what will happen, he is occasionally surprised out of his wits by what turns up. But if he had merely waited I doubt that he could ever have been surprised—not even faintly amused. Sometimes, to be sure, he is caught looking intently in the wrong direction. And there is many a time when he fails to be surprised because he overlooks what is going on under his nose.

All of this is, of course, my own particular assumption about the nature of man. Moreover, it is the way I, too, look to see what will happen, for, unlike most psychologists I know, who view themselves as scientists and their subjects as something else, my theory of personality applies to me as well as to people I don't like. It is the way I look to see what is going on in psychotherapy. It works moderately well, so far. I anticipate it will work better after I have explored its implications further.

While right now this anticipatory approach seems like a particularly reasonable way to go about the job of being a psychologist, especially a psychotherapist, undoubtedly I will change my mind in some ways, for changing one's mind as a result of pursuing his commitments is, as I have already said, an essential feature of honest human experience. Just where I will end up with this business I cannot foresee, but at least, as the reader may all too readily agree, my posture is one of anticipating some changes I cannot yet spell out. But if I am to describe the goals of psychotherapy as I see them today, it is imperative that the reader know something about my present assumptions, tentative though they may be, and that he not accuse me of failing to make any commitment to these assumptions. I am determined to see where they lead, and, having seen where they lead, I am equally determined to modify or abandon them in the light of what my quest reveals.

A PSYCHOLOGICAL DEFINITION OF LIFE

While our topic is the psychology of the optimal man, with particular reference to the goals of psychotherapy, it will do no harm to extend ourselves for a few moments and talk about life. This takes us outside the range of our assignment, and perhaps outside the range of psychology. But if we can venture a definition of life, whether human or otherwise, perhaps we can introduce an assumption of such far-reaching significance that what we attempt to say later about man in particular will be enhanced and clarified.

Let us start out with a definition, or an assumption, if you prefer, though all definitions are assumptions. Let us say that life is a way of using the present to link the future with the past in some original fashion. Now that we have started, let us pursue the implications of what we have said. We can say next that without life the present makes no difference in the future; only the past governs what will happen. Since, without life, there is no active anticipation of the future, the notion of a future does not even stand for anything until after it is too late to call it "future" any more. And without a future the present makes no sense either, for what is the present but the boundary between past and future. No future, no present! And without a present there is no point of observation from which to differentiate time.

Already we can see some psychotherapeutic implications of these extra-psychological inferences. Some clients do make only minimal use of the present for anticipating their future. Most psychotherapists have dealt with such a client. He seems to have only the most precarious foothold on this vantage point for looking out on what goes on. He is disengaged from reality. Even his life appears to be held in a state of suspension.

But to return to our extra-psychological discussion of the nature of life. We could define it otherwise. We could describe it, as many psychologists describe man's behavior, simply as the outcome of past events. But to do this is to lose one's grip on the future, particularly the future of human affairs, and, through the concurrent loss of the present, to deny oneself the vantage point for viewing or doing anything at all. I do not like the idea of giving up all this, not even to be called a scientist. It is too much like giving up the human enterprise in order to make of man something utterly predictable. But if the human enterprise is to be abandoned to the sequellae of past events, why bother to predict anything? If I am to give up one or the other, I would prefer to give up stimulus-response psychology, except, possibly, for explaining trivialities, or in those moments when I am in too much of a hurry to pay attention to what I am saying.

Everything we try to say about life seems to reflect upon psychology. Let us continue, therefore, to speculate about life. Suppose we were to take our fundamental postulate, the one we intended as a starting point for a psychology of man, and make a biological postulate out of it. Let us have a try. We shall then say something like this: *It is the nature of life to be channelized by the ways events are anticipated.* While I am not prepared to defend this assumption with great skill or the weight of much evidence, it does intrigue me and I cannot help but wonder where we would be led if we ventured to start from such a premise. Particularly, I wonder what a psychotherapist would be led to do or what goals he would envision for the outcomes of his efforts.

Salivation, for example, takes place in a manner that suggests the anticipation of food, or perhaps hunger—I am not sure which. Perhaps what is anticipated is an activity we call eating. Whatever it indicates, Pavlov seems to have demonstrated it and there is no reason we should not be grateful even though we are not quite sure what it was he demonstrated. The momentary rest the heart takes between beats can be construed as preparing it for its next effort. That, also, is consistent with observation.

But we must keep it clear in our minds, as long as we are following the implications of our tentative biological postulate, that it is not the impending event that makes a creature's mouth water or its heart rest up. It is the beast itself which does those things, and it does them as it does because this is in line with its particular ways of anticipating events. If the events were anticipated differently its heart and glands might very well function differently. Whether the anticipated events actually do take place later or not, e.g., whether the food arrives or the next beat occurs, is another matter.

This is not the place to press any argument about "lower order processes" in great detail, or to answer the frequently asked question, "But does personal construct theory have any practical application to rats?" It is sufficient for a paper dealing with the goals of psychotherapy merely to suggest the notion that possibly, quite apart from psychology, life itself is essentially an anticipation of events to come. This is a more venturesome postulate than the one from which the psychology of personal constructs was launched. But from it may spring some additional ideas about the whole of psychology, as well as about the goals of psychotherapy.

It follows, for example, from such a super-assumption that an overall technical goal of psychotherapy might be to enhance this essential feature of life by making the most of man's moment-to-moment expectations. This is to say that psychotherapy should make one feel that he has come alive. This, presumably, would be a good thing to have happen. But the expression really does not mean much unless behind it lies some assumption about the nature of life, such as is embodied in the biological postulate we have suggested.

One may, of course, question the appropriateness of our assumption on the grounds that it does not seem to correspond to our personal experience. For example, what about those rare and delectable hours when we can lie in the grass and look up at the fleecy summer clouds. Do we not then take life, savoring each moment as it comes without rudely trying to outguess it? Does one not feel very much alive on such occasions? Certainly! But this, too, is an anticipatory posture. To be sure, it is not the frantic apprehension of popping little events. It is rather a composed anticipation of a slowly drifting universe of great and benign proportions.

Still, what we have managed to say about the anticipatory nature of life, and the goal of therapy it implies, remains much too general. Perhaps the specifics it embraces will become clearer after we have returned to the line of inference stemming directly from our psychological postulate.

CRITERIA FOR A GOOD THEORY: SCIENTIFIC OR PERSONAL

A theory is a useful device, useful because one can derive from it all sorts of consistent notions about how to proceed in a variety of situations. Everybody has at least one tucked away somewhere, although many are reluctant to exhibit them, and some even deny that they have them, insisting instead that all their notions are revealed to them by direct observation of nature. I suppose one could regard this claim as itself a theory, but I intend to avoid any dispute that might ensue from pressing the point.

Generally it is supposed that a theory must be a comprehensive formulation; that is to say, it should be a statement of the essential feature of a large family of assumptions. There is some difference of opinion as to whether these assumptions all have to be logically inescapable in the theoretical formulation, or if the theory need serve only to provoke a fresh lot of semieducated guesses about the nature of things, without coming right out and saying precisely what these guesses should be.

But whatever the opinion, the fact of the matter is that every theory, scientific or personal, has embedded in it a great many assumptions that are not initially apparent to those who read it—or even very clear at first to the person who formulates it. These embedded assumptions are likely to have much to do with what eventually happens to the theory and the people who use it; this is true whether it is a theory used publicly by a group of scientists or a personal one used intuitively by a certain man in managing his daily affairs. All of this makes one of the objectives of psychotherapy the exploration of hidden assumptions in the client's construct system.

It is tempting to say that the foremost requirement of a good theory is that it should be true. But, in any literal sense, this is an impractical specification. We already know that most of the theories formulated in the past have served their times and proponents only to be displaced by others which, at some later juncture in the course of human thought, seemed better. We have reason to suspect, therefore, that almost any theory we formulate today is going to end up like its predecessors and, sooner or later, be supplanted. If we rejected all theories that were not known to be accurate portrayals of bedrock truth we would find ourselves with nothing to live by.

This is not quite the same as saying there is no truth. It is, rather, grounds for the stand that, whatever the truth is, no one, least of all a scientifically trained psychotherapist, ought to claim that he has quite caught up with it yet. Even if we don't catch up with it, however, each of us can gain on it. And that, too, is something that may hopefully be said of personal theories as well as scientific ones. Clients approach truth by the same kind of successive approximations that scientists employ. Psychotherapy helps them do it.

Good theorizing does not unwind itself endlessly without being checked. To test a theory one acts in accordance with its implications to see what will happen. In a broad sense, this is what we mean by scientific experimentation, though to be good science we think there should also be appropriate controls to discipline the conclusions we draw. If, under the aegis of a certain new theory, events become more predictable and many desirable things can be made to happen that failed to occur before, we are justified in saying the theory has a good measure of truth in it.

But experimentation is no special prerogative of the accredited scientist. It is, first of all, man's device. And because it is a human technique for getting closer to truth—employed more or less by all of us—it becomes the concern of any proper psychotherapeautic effort.

A theory, then, scientific or personal, ought to cover a lot of situations, to be fertile with coherent practical suggestions about what one might do in those situations, to be a reasonable approximation to the truth, serving the person at his present stage of development, and should always lead to constructive experimentation and revision. When we say specifically that these are the criteria of a good personal theory we are establishing some further objectives for psychotherapy to attain.

It should be noted that we have not said that *insight* is a goal of psychotherapy. That implies catching up with the truth. Too often, when such a notion is impressed upon a client, he functions well enough for a while after "completion" of his analysis, but eventually bogs down in some orthodoxy.

PSYCHOTHERAPEUTIC GOALS AND PSYCHOLOGICAL PROCESSES

Already the point has been made that psychotherapeutic goals cannot be appraised independently of the processes by which one seeks to attain them. Nor can either processes or goals be fully understood apart from the deeply underlying constructions employed by the client and his therapist. We have therefore discussed the underlying theories that men live by, whether they claim to be scientists or not. Then we discussed our own, and the emphasis it places upon anticipatory processes, very broadly conceived, in the life of man. And we have mentioned, too, the part that experimentation plays in checking one's construction of events, whether that construction is scientific or personal.

But our discussion has necessarily been very general, for when one brings up the matter of goals in psychotherapy he immediately involves himself in making value judgments and these tend to be more philosophical than technical in nature. Nevertheless, to understand what goals I value most, it should be helpful to mention more of the particular processes through which I think these goals can be attained.

In generating the theory of the psychology of personal constructs out of its basic postulate we are led by a series of inferences that need not be detailed here to say that one's ways of anticipating events can be regarded as his personal constructs. Each construct is a two-ended affair, i.e., it is a reference axis rather than a punctate designation of an object or an entity. When events are plotted against such an axis or within a system of such personal axes alternatives become identified and it becomes possible for a person to make some choices between them.

Only within his personal system is one ever free to make a choice in his own behalf, and only along the coordinate lines he himself has managed to erect is he ever free to initiate movement. Man's freedom, then, can be said to have ontological meaning only within the anticipatory framework he has devised; his personal construct system defines the only liberties he is ever able to claim. Adam and his girl friend found this out when they decided to look into the matter of good and evil. They shifted the basis of their actions from obedience to knowledge, thus achieving freedom and all the responsibilities that go with it.

There is no sense in prodding a client toward the choice of a therapeutic goal that does not yet fall within his coordinate system of personal constructs, any more than it would have made sense before The Fall to drag Adam and Eve off to a revival meeting—they wouldn't have known what all the shouting was about. One of the intermediate goals of psychotherapy, then, is to help the client devise a construct system through which he is free to move toward something worthwhile.

Given a pair of alternatives adequately defined within a client's personal construct system, how does one know which he will choose? It may seem doubtful at first, but I am inclined to believe he will always make what may be called the "elaborative choice." That is to say he will choose that alternative, aligned to one of his construct dimensions, which appears to provide the greater opportunity for the further elaboration of his anticipatory system.

Two men will not necessarily make the same choice, even though they may construe the alternatives the same way, nor will one man make the same choice at one time that he makes at another. It is still the man that makes the choice, not the alternatives that dictate it to him. At a certain stage in one's development it may be more promising to choose to do something that will help him define his position more clearly and thus consolidate his gains, just as a military commander who has seized the initiative must often pause to consolidate his position. But at other times one will choose to extend his system so it will embrace more of the unknown and bring more of the future within his grasp. The two kinds of action, because they are both efforts to develop the anticipatory system, are really not so different. Both are examples of the psychological principle of the elaborative choice. Of course, it seems that some clients are always consolidating their positions and others are always overextending them. But these are differences in strategy; the basic process remains the same.

Another process question is, Finding himself caught up in shifting circumstances, how does one decide what to do? This is the fix that most clients are in when they come running for psychological assistance. But in a less spectacular way it is a fix in which each of us finds himself a thousand times a day. The first step, of course, is to construe what we see. To do this we go through a *circumspection* phase, sometimes in a split second, without actually spelling out anything to ourselves, and sometimes in a period unduly prolonged by see-saw efforts to define the issue. This is a period of "trying on for size" the various constructs available in our personal repertory.

If one does not have many constructs circumspection may not take long, and he may achieve the somewhat enviable reputation of being "a man of action." If circumstances appear to be changing faster than he can keep up with them one may plunge through this phase of his *decision cycle*. This is the way to get the reputation of being impulsive. The Hamlets of this world, with their complex repertories, may not be able to tolerate the delay a full exploration of their repertories would require, and sometimes they may unexpectedly act on impulse before their complex circumspection process has finished weighing the issues.

In any case, the next step in the decision cycle is *preemption*. One construct is allowed to preempt the situation and define the pair of alternatives between which the person must make his choice. From then on, unless he backs up, the issue appears—whatever else may have some applicability to the situation—to be "this and this only."

Finally comes the commitment, and at this point the principle of the elaborative choice takes over. The whole decision cycle may be called the *C-P-C Cycle*, after the terms we have used for its phases: Circumspection, Preemption, and Choice. One of the intermediate objectives of psychotherapy is to help the client make appropriate use of this cycle whenever important action is required.

NEW CONSTRUCTS FOR OLD

New constructs are obviously invented, not discovered. But how? There are several ways, but one of the most interesting is through a process we have termed the *creativity cycle*. Here a warning is in order. If one defines construing as a process that follows conventional principles of logic and conceptualization, or if he has already classified the psychology of personal constructs in his own mind as "a cognitive theory," what follows won't make much sense.

Some construing is consistent. It may not be logical but it can still be consistent. Of two objects one is always construed as darker than the other, or heavier, or more beautiful; that is to say, whenever the construct dimension is applied to a pair of objects the outcome is the same. This is *tight* construction. Language labels, for example, once they are pinned on constructs, tend to tighten their usage. Mathematics is a particular language system that seems to have the maximum tightening effect. Of course, mathematics is supposed to be logical, too, but that is another matter. Tightening may or may not be a good thing. So may language. Certainly there are moments in psychotherapy when the conventionalities of language get in the way of the client's efforts, and there are other moments when they establish just the base he needs for extending his probe of the unknown.

But there is *loosened* construction too. The inconsistency of the dreams one tries to recall in the morning is a good example. Language may play a part in such dreams but it usually fails to keep their construction tight. Some of us don't have to be asleep to construe loosely. We can even make our spoken words clatter along with our loose construction in a way that would give Noah Webster the jitters.

Actually, construction can be tight or loose, regardless of whether words are tied to constructs or not. Many of the so-called physiological processes, which follow construction to our way of thinking just as much as the so-called conscious processes do, involve very tight construing—the regular beating of the heart, for example. On the other hand, free association, a supposedly conscious verbal process, has a loosening effect that many of us have found quite helpful in our short-sighted moments.

When we construe tightly we can subject our constructs to experimentation and to various other kinds of tests, but it is very hard to rotate them into new positions so as to get any new slant on our personal affairs. A tight construct tends to be brittle, and it stands firm or is shattered by the outcome of the predictions it invokes. It is almost impossible to test a loose construct, or, to put it better, a construct loosely used. In an elastic sort of way it seems to apply to almost everything—or to almost nothing—that happens. That, too, can be good, for if every idea we ever laid hold of remained rigid and either stood firm or collapsed in the face of every test it got, mental process would all be guesswork and any progress that happened to take place in human thinking would depend on the sheer accident of hitting on something useful.

The creativity cycle we envision is one that employs both loosening and tightening in a coordinated fashion. The cycle starts with a loosened phase in which construction is vague, elastic, and wavering. Out of this fertile chaos shapes begin to emerge and one seeks patiently to give them definite form until they are tight enough to talk about and to test. This notion of creativity does not suggest that one simply alternates between loose thinking and tight thinking, as he may appear to alternate between nighttime thinking and daytime thinking. These are not simply two separate exercises, but phases of the same creative process, just as I am convinced dreaming and alert critical thinking are essential phases of the basic process by which we keep ourselves from ending up as schizophrenics or automatons. It is when man tries too hard to separate his loosened construction from his tightened construction that he becomes unhinged and loses his ability to live creatively.

None of this has anything much to do with "creativity" as a particular trait possessed by "gifted" people, or that stultifying preoccupation which has been misnamed "the psychology of individual differences." We are talking about a human process, not about discriminable classes of mankind. Of course, we are willing to concede that some of us reach further into the outer chaos that surrounds us, and some further into the cosmos we have carved for ourselves, than others. And it is true, we know, that some go "loose" and stay that way, as, for example, those patients of early psychoanalytic technique who succumbed to its persistent loosening demands. It is true, also, that some of us get so tight and literal that when our thinking is finally shattered by its predictive failures we collapse into a protective looseness from which we dare not recover. But these are not traits; these are predicaments. They are some of the unfortunate outcomes of the psychological process all of us invoke when we try to solve our problems.

One of the important interim goals of psychotherapy is to help the client make optimal use of his ability to think both loosely and tightly and to employ those two phases of the creativity cycle in a proper relationship to each other. Moreover, therapy should enable a person to span an optimal range of loosening and tightening without breaking up the process into disjunctive thinking.

ORCHESTRATION OF PSYCHOTHERAPEUTIC TECHNIQUES

Unlike most personality theories, the psychology of personal constructs does not limit itself to any pet psychotherapeutic technique. More than any other theory, it calls for an orchestration of many techniques according to the therapist's awareness of the variety and nature of the psychological processes by which man works toward his ends.

In presenting the goals of psychotherapy as we see them we have laid initial stress on man as a creature who forges his own destiny rather than allowing himself to drift with the tide of human affairs. The term "personal constructs" refers to the guidelines by which he pinpoints anticipated events and along which he establishes the dimensions of the freedom he hopes to exercise and the pathways of movement he seeks to follow. There are many interesting processes man uses in reaching his ends, some of which we have attempted to describe. All of them fall within the purview of the technically versatile psychotherapist.

Man uses many kinds of resources too in attaining his goals. One such resource which men occasionally find useful is a psychotherapist. In addition to the goals that his client ought to seek, however, the therapist needs to have a goal of his own which he ought to try to use well.

17

The Goals and Families of Psychotherapy: Summary

Alvin R. Mahrer, Ph.D.

The purposes of this chapter are (1) to propose a summary of the general goals and ultimate aims of psychotherapy, and (2) to describe three families of psychotherapeutic personality models, together with their associated goals.

I. GENERAL GOALS OF PSYCHOTHERAPY

The contributors' statements about the goals of psychotherapy are open to a number of groupings. In proposing one such organization, two criteria served as guides. First, each goal is to be representative of the general body of contributors, even though it is recognized that no single goal received unanimous endorsement and that over time there may be changes in the agreement with any given goal. Second, the meaningfulness and representativeness of these goals is enhanced by using the specific phrasings and concrete meanings of each of the contributors. These, then, are the general goals of psychotherapy:

Reduction of Psychopathology

Psychotherapy reduces a psychopathological condition or state. The patient is characterized by a disease process, an emotional illness, psychological difficulties, and psychic disabilities which are remedied, reduced, alleviated, or treated by psychotherapy. There are two hallmarks in the reduction of psychopathology:

a. Reduction of symptomatology. Positive symptom reduction and improvement in symptomatology are major manifestations of reduced psychopathology. Symptoms encompass concrete behavior (e.g., eye tics, skin eruptions, nail biting) as well as global life patternings (e.g., lifelong searchings for the lost mother figure, insatiable drives to achieve sexual dominance).

b. Reduction of defenses. Psychotherapy reduces defenses and brings the patient to a state in which defenses and defensive behavior are no longer required. Avoidant mechanisms are minimized, together with "existentially untrue" actions and attitudes.

Reduction of Psychological Pain and Suffering

Psychotherapy reduces psychological pain and suffering. This is a generalized state with at least three components:

a. Reduced anxiety. The goal includes reduced anxiety, dread, distress, inner turmoil, and feelings of internal disintegration. Disabling anxiety is minimized.

b. Reduced hostility. Psychotherapy reduces hostility as well as rage, anger, aggression, and like emotions.

c. Reduced meaninglessness. The goal is a reduced feeling of meaninglessness, aloneness, separation from oneself and the world, distance from life, and of an existence without meaning or value.

Increased Pleasure

The goal includes self-fulfillment, enjoyment, fulfilled needs and desires, a sense of health, "expecting" well, and a positive feeling about life. Pleasure is also attendant upon creature comforts and biopsychological needs, especially in regard to sexual pleasure and enjoyment.

Increased Experiencing

The goal is to feel alive each moment, to experience the concrete process of living and feeling, to have a vital sense of being. There is an openness to experience and to change, a constantly changing commitment to the flow of experience.

Enhanced Self-relationship

Psychotherapy enhances the relationship with oneself. This is altered in two ways:

a. Increased self-acceptance. Acceptance of oneself increases, as does self-respect, self-tolerance, sense of personal equality, awareness of one's worth, sense of identity, and acceptance of one's dynamic existence. Self-acceptance pertains both to one's gifts and limitations, to the desirable and undesirable aspects of personality. Another component is a sense of inner peace, harmony, and internal integration.

b. Increased internal directedness. Psychotherapy enables one to experience an increased internal directedness, a turning to one's inner world, a living more richly within oneself, a greater enjoyment of solitude, a meaningful involvement in one's inner life.

Enhanced External Relationships

Relationships with and toward the external world are enhanced. There are at least four aspects of this goal:

a. Increased closeness of interpersonal relationships. The goal is to have an unimpaired ability to form attachments, to have improved external relationships. There is an enhanced ability to give and receive love, and an enhanced sense of unity and oneness, integration and harmony with others.

b. Increased competence of functioning. Psychotherapy improves functioning in terms of greater competency and efficiency in the carrying out of normal activities. This includes increased assertiveness, self-confidence, self-direction, freedom to make one's own decisions, to set one's own goals, and to determine for oneself. It also includes an ability to anticipate events, to hypothesize, to predict, to experiment, and to possess an adequate system of ideas, constructs, and assumptions which facilitate thinking with objectivity and rationality.

c. Increased ability to adjust. Psychotherapy increases the ability to adjust to the external world, to confront effectively the demands and limitations of life, to adjust life goals to limitations, to be realistic, to conform within the limits of social tolerance, to handle ordinary psychological conflicts and reasonable reality stresses, to bear unavoidable suffering, and to accept uncertainty.

d. Increased social commitment. The goal is to relate to and to become a part of the social order, with increased social responsibility and interest in social welfare and cultural development. There is increased productivity and achievement, social interest and belonging, and an ability to commit oneself to ideas and ideals.

The above is representative of the group of contributors taken as a whole. As such, the list is offered as an outline and summary of ultimate goals of psychotherapy in general. In addition to certain goals possessing representativeness and high frequency, the goals appeared to fall into three major clusters or families which may be termed *biopsychological developmental psychotherapies, psychological actualization psychotherapies,* and *reconstructive psychotherapies.* Our purpose is not to recategorize existing systems and schools of psychotherapy, nor is it to propose a firm, organized, threefold system of psychotherapies. Rather, we intend to move toward an understanding of psychotherapies solely from the point of view of their functions and their goals. If psychotherapies are looked at and understood from this point of view, our thesis is that some of the goals cluster together and are associated with a set of underlying theoretical conceptions about personality. We find three such families in attempting to understand the discussions of goals in this book, although the data contained herein are certainly open to other forms of organizations and it is questionable how extensively our threefold organization may apply to other psychotherapeutic goals and other underlying personality conceptions.

II. BIOPSYCHOLOGICAL DEVELOPMENTAL PSYCHOTHERAPIES

Intrinsic Capacities and Lines of Natural Development

The psychological personality derives from and is built upon a base of biological, physiological, and constitutional factors and processes. The "developmental" family rests upon this assumption (Fine, Greenblatt and Levinson, Raimy, Rosen, Whitehorn, Wolberg, and Wolpe).

The biophysio-constitutional foundations equip personality with at least three sets of intrinsic processes or factors *which it is the goal of psychotherapy to facilitate or assist:*

a. Personality contains a potential "natural" line or sequence of development and growth (Fine, Greenblatt and Levinson, Saul, Whitehorn, and Wolberg). This is a normal personality growth-developmental process which is roughly analogous to the organism's biological and neurophysiological stages of growth and development. This maturational line of development is the hallmark of this family of psychotherapies.

b. The biophysio-constitutional foundations provide personality with intrinsic natural healing powers, biological potentialities for recovery and health, and built-in healing processes (Greenblatt and Levinson, Whitehorn).

c. Associated with the biologically-given developmental-growth forces are intrinsic capacities for normality, for healthy normal behavior and normal functioning (Fine, Greenblatt and Levinson, Saul, Whitehorn, Wolberg; Raimy, Wolpe, and Rosen). (Raimy, Wolpe, and Rosen especially highlight this third biologically intrinsic factor.)

Blocks and Interferences to Biologically Intrinsic Capacities and Lines of Development

Difficulties (psychopathology) arise largely when factors block and interfere with the biophysio-constitutional lines of developmental growth and with the intrinsic capacities and potentialities for healthy, normal functioning (Greenblatt and Levinson, Saul, Whitehorn, Wolberg; Raimy, Wolpe, and Rosen).

The nature of the blocks and interferences range from broad to specific. Toward the broad end are such factors as the disease or illness itself (Wolpe). general threats to early attachments (Saul), global fixations, intrapsychic conflicts (Whitehorn), damage from trauma (Saul, Wolberg), and maladaptive interpersonal attitudes (Whitehorn). Toward the specific end are such blocks and interferences as: (a) a superego, acquired specifically from the early maternal environment and unassimilable by the ego, which blocks and interferes with integration among id, ego, and superego (Rosen); (b) a specific conviction about the self, with resultant disabling anxiety blocking and interfering with the emergence of the biologically intrinsic capacity for normal functioning (Raimy); and (c) persistent habits of unadaptive behavior, acquired by learning in an anxiety-generating situation, blocking the production of biologically intrinsic potentials for normal functioning (Wolpe).

Regardless of the nature of the block or interference, psychotherapy aims at their removal, reduction, elimination, or disengagement. Thus the blocks and interferences constitute one of the major targets of the psychotherapeutic process. Removal of the blocks and interferences permits the release of the growth-developmental process and the emergence of biologically-given normal functioning.

Normal, Healthy Functioning

The biophysio-constitutional foundation invests personality with a potential state of normal, healthy, mature functioning. Some family members emphasize the state of normal functioning as the culmination of a developmental process (Fine, Greenblatt and Levinson, Saul, Whitehorn, Wolberg), whereas others emphasize biophysio-constitutional intrinsic capacities for normal, healthy functioning (Rosen, Raimy, Wolpe).

The goal of psychotherapy is to attain mature, healthy, normal functioning described in terms of the general goals of psychotherapy proposed earlier.

Secondarily and to a limited degree it features reduced meaninglessness as a component of reduced psychological pain and suffering; increased experiencing; and enhanced self-relationship, including increased self-acceptance and increased internal directiveness.

Mature, Healthy, Normal Functioning as a Social-philosophical Value

The desirable state of affairs and the preferred way of being refer to the parameters and characteristics of mature, healthy, normal functioning. Inherent in this goal is a value judgment of the "goodness" attached to normality, health, and maturity (Greenblatt and Levinson, Fine, Raimy, Rosen, Saul, Whitehorn, and Wolpe). Proceeding a step further, some family members distinctly elevate health, maturity, and normal functioning by investing the concepts with philosophical good and religious value and acknowledging them as part of a secular philosophy of the good life (cf. Fine).

A goal of psychotherapy is to reach or approximate mature, healthy normality as a preferred mode of being and a desirable mode of functioning; mature, healthy normality may or may not serve as a distinct social-philosophical system of values.

Mediating Goals

The therapeutic process moves in the direction of more ultimate goals by utilizing subgoals, instrumental goals, working goals, and goals which serve as the pathways toward the more ultimate goals. These may be referred to as *mediating goals* (Parloff). To a large extent, their primary function is to remove or alleviate the blocks and interferences, thereby mediating the therapeutic process in the direction of the ultimate goals. *The psychotherapeutic process aims at mediating goals which appear to fall into three clusters:*

a. Correction of injurious "traumas." Some sort of maladjustive or deleterious influence has occurred, generally in the formative years. The nature of the experience may range from a trauma, in the traditional sense, to more broadly defined, ongoing, traumatic-like influences. The mediating goal is the correction of the injurious consequences of these traumas, consequences such as anxiety (Whitehorn, Raimy, Wolpe), maladjustive attitudes, learned ways of responding (Saul, Wolpe), and unadaptive emotional habits (Wolpe).

A number of working techniques are utilized in achieving this mediating goal. These include providing corrective emotional experiences (Saul, Whitehorn), helping the patient to identify with the "good foster mother" (Rosen), after-education (Saul), insight (Saul), weakening the bonds between stimuli and anxiety by means of "unlearning" techniques (Wolpe), the learning of anxiety-inhibiting habits (Wolpe), "counter-conviction" evidence (Raimy), and other techniques aimed at correcting the injurious impacts and consequences of the traumatic experiences.

b. Removal of repressions. A second cluster of mediating goals is termed the removal of repressions, the achievement of conscious awareness, the lifting of repressions, or the providing of insight. As the unconscious becomes conscious, the blocks and interferences are alleviated and the therapeutic process is mediated toward the ultimate goals.

c. Resolution of intrapsychic conflict. Blocks and interferences are also alleviated through the resolution of intrapsychic conflicts (Fine, Rosen, Whitehorn). This mediating goal serves as a pathway toward the more ultimate goals and is itself achieved through such working techniques as the reduction of the malevolent influence of the superego (Rosen) and, once again, the Protean insight.

These three clusters of mediating goals involve changes in behavior, actions, and feelings rather than changes in ideation, constructs, cognitions, or premises.

III. PSYCHOLOGICAL ACTUALIZATION PSYCHOTHERAPIES

Fundamental Psychological Processes and Personality Roots

The basic, fundamental structure of personality resides in and is derived from *psychological* processes, variables, and properties (Gendlin, Mahrer, van Kaam), with no presumption of a substratum composed of some other kinds of processes, variables, or properties (e.g., biological, genetic, physiological, or constitutional). *The goal of psychotherapy is to actualize these basic personality properties:*

a. Most prominently, there is a capacity for experiencing, for the concrete process of living and feeling, for actualizing the outward thrust of needs into experience, for accepting each moment of life, and for experiencing fully one's own dynamic existence (Gendlin, Mahrer, van Kaam).

b. Personality contains psychological drives, needs, motives, value-conclusions, impulses, feelings. These are fundamental psychological processes, part of the base of personality (Gendlin, Mahrer, van Kaam).

c. There is a capacity or property of self-acceptance, of coming to terms with the unique constellation of basic drives, of integration among the basic needs, of cohesion and fundamental harmony among basic parts of the personality (Gendlin, Mahrer, van Kaam).

Interferences and Blocks to Personality Processes, Variables, and Properties

Difficulties occur in the form of interferences and blocks to the capacity for experiencing, to the actualization of basic drives, needs, motives, and feelings, and to the capacity for integrative self-acceptance.

The following are among the significant blocks and interferences:

a. Any factor constitutes a block or an interference if it tends to inhibit, stop, narrow, or restrict the ongoingness of life and the concrete process of living, feeling, and experiencing (Gendlin).

b. Mediating, secondary needs stand between, buffer, inhibit, and block the direct, open experiencing of basic needs (Mahrer).

c. Disintegrative relationships among needs tend to interfere and block the capacity for oneness, internal peace, and integration (Mahrer).

d. A series of factors block and interfere with the achievement of dynamic existence, with the actualization of one's fundamental capacities and potentialities, and with the capacity to live honestly and comfortably with one's basic personality; these include fixations on one's neurotic guilt, a belief in unchangeability, forces which pull away from finding one's own individuality, deep anxiety at revealing oneself, and overly binding attachments (van Kaam).

One of the major targets of the psychotherapeutic process is to remove, alter, eliminate, or disengage these blocks and interferences to basic personality capacities, properties, and processes, thereby facilitating their actualization.

Optimal Functioning

The basic personality contains a potential for an optimal mode of functioning. The structure and the properties of the base of personality include a capacity for experiencing; a set of needs, motives, value-conclusions; and a capacity for self-acceptance and integration. When the blocks and interferences are removed or disengaged, the therapeutic process is able to develop the available, potential capacity for optimal functioning.

The goal is to attain optimal functioning described in terms of the general goals of psychotherapy as proposed earlier (see above).

Secondarily important are reduced hostility as a component of reduced psychological pain and suffering; and by increased competence of functioning, increased ability to adjust, as components of enhanced external relationships.

Social-philosophical Values and Optimal Functioning

Optimal functioning is far more than a neutral but desirable state. It is invested with philosophical good, and constitutes "the good life," complete with a value system (Gendlin, Mahrer, and van Kaam). Its attainment or approximation is a goal of therapy.

Mediating Goals

Another goal is the achievement of mediating goals. To a large extent, their primary function is to remove or alleviate blocks and interferences, thereby *mediating the therapeutic process in the direction of the ultimate goals.* By and large, the mediating goal consists of guided therapeutic experiencing of felt meanings, needs, value-conclusions, and feelings (Gendlin, Mahrer). The mediating goal is one of unfolding felt meanings, of uncovering needs, of differentiating value-conclusions, of penetrating feelings, of carrying forward, of progressive release and emergence, and of sequentially actualizing what lies within (Gendlin, Mahrer).

A number of working techniques are used to accomplish these mediating goals. They include, for example, the action-implied words of the therapist, focusing upon and living out the contained feeling of the moment, utilizing the therapist-patient interaction to carry the experiential process along, and detailed living through of inner feelings (Gendlin, Mahrer).

Such a mediating process involves changes in behaviors, actions, and feelings rather than changes in ideation, constructs, cognitions, or premises.

IV. RECONSTRUCTIVE PSYCHOTHERAPIES

The Fundamental Conceptual System

The roots of personality consist of a conceptual system of constructs, basic premises, fundamental ideas, and basic life assumptions. This conceptual system is the central determining factor behind psychological functioning, operations, and behavior; *a therapeutic goal is the alteration and reconstruction of that system.* The ideational system, as the fundamental stratum of personality, determines the nature of behavioral functioning, the personal-social life goals, and the mode of functioning. (Dreikurs, Ellis, Kelly).

This ideational-conceptual system is open to change or reconstruction along the contours of an altered set of basic assumptions, personal constructs, basic premises, or social goals (Dreikurs, Ellis, Kelly).

Reconstructing the Conceptual System

Within this framework it is assumed that man is able to achieve a significant degree of freedom from the determining conceptual system, to gain self-determination and self-direction, to attain a sense of freedom in setting one's own goals (Dreikurs, Ellis, Kelly). *This kind of reconstruction is a major therapeutic aim.*

A poor or inadequate ideational-conceptual system leads to impaired functioning, irrational behavior, deleterious personal-social life goals, and restricted or improper modes of anticipating events. Such a problematical system need not stand as a block or interference to any assumed set of intrinsic capacities or inherent potentialities (as in the previous two families of therapy). The system may be reconstructed or realigned along the contours of a more optimal life philosophy, an improved set of personal-social goals, and more optimal modes of anticipating events (Dreikurs, Ellis, Raimy). *A goal of psychotherapy is such reconstruction.*

Optimal Functioning

Optimal functioning depends upon a reconstructed system of personal constructs, basic assumptions and premises, and personal-social life goals. This reconstructed system leads to a sense of freedom, self-determination, and self-direction (Dreikurs, Ellis, Kelly). It also leads to an improved mode of channeling and anticipating events (Kelly).

In addition, the nature of optimal functioning depends upon the nature of the new, altered, or reconstructed conceptual system itself. Thus, optimal functioning may be dictated by a particular system of social values (Dreikurs), an existentially-oriented life philosophy (Ellis), or a changing outlook and commitment to moment-to-moment experience (Kelly).

The goal is to move toward optimal functioning which may be described in terms of the general goals of psychotherapy as proposed earlier (see above). Optimal functioning is, however, characterized secondarily and to a limited degree by reduced meaninglessness as a component of reduced psychological pain and suffering, and by enhanced self-relationship, including increased self-acceptance and increased internal directiveness.

Social-philosophical Values and Optimal Functioning

Optimal functioning refers to a useful and well-functioning conceptual system to which has been added a reconstructed extrinsic system of values. This reconstructed system of values stands as a distinct guide to a valued way of living. This reconstruction counts heavily on a revised, definite social-philosophical value system.

The goal of psychotherapy is to reach or approximate optimal functioning, a mode of being and functioning which is offered as a distinct social-philosophical system of values.

Mediating Goals

The primary function of the mediating goals is to provide the pathway toward altering, revising, and reconstructing the system of personal constructs, assumptions, premises, and social goals (Dreikurs, Ellis, Kelly).

The mediating goals include, for example, reorienting the early developed social goals (Dreikurs), changing the style of life (Dreikurs), instituting a social value system (Dreikurs), confronting and attacking irrational basic premises (Ellis), elaborating and changing the system of personal constructs (Kelly), and changing convictions about the self (Raimy). These serve as means of mediating the therapeutic process in the direction of the ultimate goals.

The mediating goals in turn are reached by a number of working techniques and subgoals. These include, for example, the establishment of a good therapeutic relationship, allowing the therapist to be used in helping the patient change himself through experience (Kelly), using the therapist as a model (Ellis), analysis of the patient's present personality structure (Dreikurs), providing an existentially-oriented philosophy (Ellis), substituting new constructs for old (Kelly), explaining and teaching the nature of the development of psychopathology (Ellis, Raimy), loosening and tightening the patient's construct system (Kelly), acting counter to the basic premises (Ellis), "trying on" various constructs (Kelly), presenting evidence counter to the held phrenaphobic conviction (Raimy), and interpretation, insight, and awareness (Dreikurs, Ellis).

These mediating goals involve changes in ideas, constructs and assumptions, as contrasted with changes in behavior, actions, and feelings.

CONCLUSIONS

A summary outline of the general goals of psychotherapy is offered as representative of the total of contributors' statements about psychotherapeutic aims.

While the goals of psychotherapy and underlying personality notions are open to other modes of conceptualization, our purpose is to propose one way in which psychotherapies may be organized, i.e., on the basis of their functions (their goals).

Psychotherapeutic goals may be described as forming three major families, each with its own model of personality. These are termed *biopsychological developmental psychotherapies, psychological actualization psychotherapies, and reconstructive psychotherapies.*

(A separate issue, to be discussed in Chapter 19, is the extent to which the developmental, actualization, and reconstructive families correspond to the Freudian, client-centered-existential, and learning theory systems respectively.)

18

The Goals and Families of Psychotherapy: Discussion

Alvin R. Mahrer, Ph.D.

The previous chapter proposed a set of general psychotherapeutic goals representative of the total offered by contributors. It was also proposed that the goals formed three families of psychotherapeutic approaches. The purpose of the present chapter is to discuss each proposed goal of psychotherapy from the point of view of each family or approach. The thesis is that goals vary with the nature of the associated psychotherapeutic family or "personality model." Goals vary in their "fit" with underlying personality conceptions, so that any given goal will be conceptually relevant or irrelevant, meaningful or nonmeaningful, depending upon the given psychotherapeutic family or personality model.

FACILITATING BIOPHYSIO-CONSTITUTIONALLY GROUNDED LINES OR STAGES OF DEVELOPMENTAL GROWTH

The developmental family assumes that psychological variables are rooted in a constitutional, biological, physiological, genetic foundation. There is a biopsychological developmental process growing out of this foundation, complete with stages of growth and identifiable sequences of biopsychological development. The developmental model is intimately associated with the above goal.

Neither the actualization nor the reconstructive families attribute such a foundation to psychological processes or constructs. Thus, in neither family is there a concept of a biophysio-constitutional developmental process with genetically predetermined stages of growth, sequences of development, or genetic unfoldings. The above goal is not appropriate for the actualization or reconstructive families.

Concepts of Fixation, Regression, and Developmental Arrests

The developmental assumption carries with it corollary concepts of fixations and developmental arrests. These refer to failures or difficulties in progressing from stage to stage of developmental growth. In addition, a developmental assumption would carry with it the concept of reverting to an earlier developmental stage or mode of functioning, or "regression."

Within a developmental framework, it is appropriate that a negative valence surround what may be termed "lack of proper development," "immaturity," "fixations," or "regressive behavior," since they are evidence of the failure to move appropriately from one developmental stage to another.

Since neither the actualization nor the reconstructive families include a basic assumption of biophysio-constitutionally grounded lines of genetic development and stages of growth, for these families the concepts of "fixated development," "regression," or "arrests in the developmental process" are far less relevant. Nor is there necessarily a negative valence attached to what may be described as immature behavior, "regressive" behavior, or lack of proper development.

ASSISTING BIOPHYSIO-CONSTITUTIONALLY GROUNDED, INTRINSIC HEALING POWERS, BIOLOGICAL POTENTIALITIES FOR RECOVERY AND HEALTH, AND BUILT-IN HEALING PROCESSES

Developmental psychotherapies accept the assumption of a biological, physiological, constitutional, genetic foundation to personality. Personality is equipped with biophysio-constitutional capacities and potentialities, among which are natural healing powers, biological potentialities for recovery and health, and built-in healing processes. The role of the therapeutic agent is to assist, supplement, and facilitate these healing-recovery forces which may be counted upon to carry a portion of the therapeutic burden.

Neither the actualization nor the reconstructive families accept the origins and foundations of personality as residing in a biological, physiological, constitutional, genetic base. Therefore, these families do not include biophysio-constitutionally derived capacities and potentialities for recovery, natural healing, and the like, nor is this goal appropriate for them, though it is for the developmental families.

Personality "Strength"

A "strong" personality is, in part, one well-endowed with biophysio-con-stitutionally grounded capacities for the regaining of health. The organism is constitutionally equipped to cope with, withstand, and recover from pressures from both the internal and the external world. Conceptual structural compo-nents of personality (e.g., *ego*) are therefore describable along a dimension of strength-weakness, partly in line with the healing-recovery capacity to with-stand stresses. A "strong" personality is constitutionally able to withstand and to recover; a "weak" one cannot.

The above picture is consistent with the developmental family; it is more or less foreign to the actualization and reconstructive families which do not include a conceptual set of biophysio-constitutionally derived capaci-ties for recovery and natural healing. The latter families do not call upon such biological or constitutional factors in accounting for their meanings of "strength."

FACILITATING BIOPHYSIO-CONSTITUTIONALLY GROUNDED, INHERENT POTENTIALITIES FOR MATURITY, HEALTH, AND NORMAL FUNCTIONING

The essence of a developmental approach is the (genetic) development of growth toward maturity, health, and normal functioning. Personality con-tains the endowed potential for maturity, health, and normal functioning which is produced as the culmination of the developmental process or is latent in the foundation of personality, ready to be released. Given the "right" conditions of growth and development, mature, healthy, normal functioning will result. The growth conditions might vary with different external experiences (e.g., dif-ferent familial, social, cultural milieus), but the essential core of mature, healthy normality lies latent within the constitutional foundation of personality. Thus this goal is most appropriate for the developmental families.

Neither the actualization nor the reconstructive families include biophysio-constitutional developmental or growth processes arising out of the genetic, biological foundation of personality, and culminating in mature, healthy nor-mality. Nor are there biologically endowed, intrinsic potentials for mature, healthy, normal functionings. Thus, neither of these therapies is as equipped for the above goal.

Sickness, Illness, and Abnormality

Concepts of health and normality imply companion concepts of sickness and abnormality, all within a biophysio-constitutional framework. There are appropriate, "healthy," "normal," and inappropriate, "sick," or "abnormal" modes of functioning at given stages and sequences of development. These concepts are most often associated with developmental psychotherapies, much less so with the actualization and reconstructive families.

ACTUALIZING THE BASIC PERSONALITY CAPACITIES, PROPERTIES, AND PROCESSES, WHICH INCLUDE THE CAPACITY FOR EXPERIENCING, BASIC DRIVES, NEEDS, AND MOTIVES-FEELINGS, AND A CAPACITY FOR INTEGRATIVE SELF-ACCEPTANCE

Both the actualization and the developmental families assume basic potentials in the personality. Therapy is to "bring out" or "move along" what is available within the basic layer of personality. Both the process of actualization and the process of development have this characteristic in common.

It is in the nature of the basic potentials and capacities that the two families differ markedly. For the actualization family, one of the basic characteristics of personality is the potential for the concrete process of living and feeling, for experiencing fully one's own dynamic existence. The developmental family does not attribute the same critical role to this property of personality. For the actualization family, the set of basic needs, motives, value-conclusions, feelings, and drives are *psychologically* derived rather than having a biological, physiological, genetic, constitutional foundation. Therefore, there is more fundamental importance to peaceful, harmonious, integrated relationships among needs, feelings, and basic drives. Thus, the above goal is more appropriate to the actualization family than to the developmental family.

The reconstructive family not only rejects the assumption of a set of basic potentials and capacities latent within the personality, but it treats these as invented products of our own theorizing and "construing." The therapeutic thrust of the reconstructive family is to alter, change, elaborate on, and reconstruct the basic assumptions, premises, social goals, and constructs, not to "bring them out" or "actualize" them. Finally, the reconstructive family assumes a qualitatively different set of basic properties of personality than does the actualization family. There are no capacities for experiencing basic drives or needs, nor is there a capacity for integrative self-acceptance. For this reason too, then, the above goal is far more appropriate to the actualization family than to the reconstructive family.

ALTERING AND RECONSTRUCTING THE DETERMINING CONCEPTUAL SYSTEM OF PERSONAL CONSTRUCTS, BASIC LIFE ASSUMPTIONS, FUNDAMENTAL PREMISES, AND SOCIAL GOALS

Only in the reconstructive model is such a critically determining role assigned to basic assumptions, basic premises, personal constructs, and life goals. This conceptual system stands as the foundation of personality, the base of personality processes. In contrast, the developmental and the actualization psychotherapies assume different basic personality components. There are instincts, integrative forces, basic needs, drives, basic feelings, psychic forces, and others, all of a nature unlike the reconstructive family's basic premises or personal constructs. Thus, the above goal is associated with a reconstructive family rather than with either the developmental or the actualization families.

The goal of changing, replacing, or reconstructing the basic personality factors is consistent primarily with the reconstructive family. There, basic premises are to be attacked and changed; basic personal constructs are to be elaborated and changed, old ones for new; basic life goals are to be reoriented. In the developmental and actualization families, the components of the foundations of personality are to be brought out, developed, and actualized. This difference between "reconstructing" and "developing-actualizing" ties the above goal to the reconstructive family alone.

REMOVING, ALTERING, OR DISENGAGING BLOCKS AND INTERFERENCES WITH BIOPHYSIO-CONSTITUTIONALLY GROUNDED LINES OF DEVELOPMENT AND INTRINSIC CAPACITIES FOR NORMAL, HEALTHY FUNCTIONING, OR WITH BASIC PERSONALITY CAPACITIES, PROPERTIES, AND PROCESSES, THEREBY FACILITATING THEIR ACTUALIZATION

The developmental and actualization families assume basic needs, drives, inner potentials, impulses, instincts, psychic forces, and pressing motives. These are opposed by a variety of factors which exert an impact of blocking, stopping, inhibiting, fixing, keeping down, restricting, buffering, interfering, and narrowing. Thus, both families are equipped for the above therapeutic goal. In contrast, the reconstructive model has no conception of blocked inner psychic forces, no instincts, no pressing drives, needs, basic feelings or the like; thus, the above goal is not as appropriate to it.

Impacts of Blocks During the Early Formative Years

Blocks and interferences have two impacts which are unique to the developmental model. First, they impair the line of development and the sequence of stages of growth, so that within this family it is meaningful to speak of developmental arrests, fixated development, and other consequences of interference with normal growth. Secondly, the biological foundation of personality gives rise to early formative years in which the developing organism is especially susceptible to deleterious influences. Blocks and interferences which occur during these early formative years thus have an especially damaging and long-term impact upon the developing personality.

The reconstructive family does not include lines of development, dynamic, pressing inner impulses-needs, blocks and interferences, or the biophysio-constitutional foundations of personality. Thus, it does not accept notions of developmental arrests and fixations, or of early heightened susceptibility to damage caused specifically by blocks and interferences. The actualization family does not include the biophysio-constitutional foundation of personality, and therefore does not accept the idea of developmental arrests and fixations, or the idea of a biologically forming organism especially vulnerable to the damage caused by blocks and interferences occurring during its formative years. Further, blocks and interferences are not of this nature in the actualization family.

RECONSTRUCTING THE BASIC SYSTEM OF PERSONAL CONSTRUCTS, LIFE PREMISES, AND LIFE GOALS TOWARD AN ENHANCED SENSE OF FREEDOM, SELF-DIRECTEDNESS, AND SELF-DETERMINATION, AND TOWARD A MORE OPTIMAL LIFE PHILOSOPHY, SET OF PERSONAL-SOCIAL LIFE GOALS, AND MODE OF ANTICIPATING EVENTS

In the reconstructive model, the basic system of constructs, assumptions, and life goals is open to change, elaboration, or reconstruction. It is possible to free oneself of this basic ideational system and to determine one's own way of viewing the world. One may achieve a sense of freedom in determining one's own personal and social goals and life style, and a large component of self-directiveness in channeling one's own psychological processes. Thus, the assumption of changeability and reconstructability of the basic ideational system equips the reconstructive model for goals of this meaning of freedom, self-directiveness, and self-determination.

In the other two models, the basic determining forces are far less open to replacement or reconstruction. The foundations of personality are composed of relatively immutable developmental growth processes, basic drives and needs, instincts, and motives. A goal of achieving freedom from the basic determining forces, of achieving the freedom to set one's own system in order and define one's own life movement is therefore somewhat less appropriate for the developmental and actualization psychotherapies.

The reconstructive model includes basic constructs, premises, and life goals which call for change because they lead the person into difficulties. The basic system does not contain the seeds of optimal functioning nor any particular potential for good or for a desirable way of being. In contrast, the actualization and the reconstructive models include foundations of personality which contain desirable potentials for an optimal way of being, i.e., are "good." Therefore, the above goal is more suited to the reconstructive model because of the difference in potential value of the foundation of personality.

If the basic ideas, constructs, premises, and goals may be reconstructed, the way is open for bold new directions. The reconstructive model is built to accept new life philosophies, fundamentally altered life styles, and changed commitments and ways of being. The challenge is to reconstruct fundamental personality components, and the challenge carries with it a spiritedness and an ambitiousness. In contrast, neither the actualization nor the developmental models are structured to reconstruct their fundamental stratum of personality along the above lines. The reconstructive model, primarily, is built to accept such radically new life philosophies as are implied in the above goal.

REDUCTION OF PSYCHOPATHOLOGY

The general meaning of "psychopathology" refers to a condition or state characterized by problems and difficulties. Something is wrong which psychotherapy aims at reducing, eliminating, or alleviating. At this general level of meaning, all three families of psychotherapy find the above goal appropriate and significant.

In the reconstructive model, the state of psychopathology refers to problems and difficulties arising out of poor or inadequate life styles, construct systems, irrational premises, and the like. In the actualization model, it refers to problems and difficulties attendant on poor or inadequate relations between and among personality structural components, and arising from the blocking of the basic needs, value-conclusions, and intrastructure of personality. In the developmental model, psychopathology has still a third meaning, closer to a condition of illness and disease as given below. Thus, each family accepts the goal of reducing psychopathology in the broad sense, though each has its own more technical interpretation of the term.

Illness and Disease

The biophysio-constitutional foundation of the developmental model provides the basis for identifying a set of psychopathologies analogous to traditional physical conditions or states, which may therefore be considered as "illnesses," "diseases," or "sicknesses." Each of the illnesses, diseases, or sicknesses theoretically possesses an identifiable set of symptoms signifying a particular underlying psychopathology and an identifiable natural course of development and natural history.

When the "reduction of psychopathology" is taken to mean the curing of illness, disease, or sickness, only the developmental model possesses the requisite biophysio-constitutional foundations. It alone is fitted to a "standard nomenclature of illnesses and diseases." Neither the actualization nor the reconstructive model possesses such a biophysio-constitutional base, and therefore, neither includes a goal of curing an illness, a disease, or a sickness.

Reduction of Symptomatology

For both the actualization and the reconstructive models, therapy aims at the reduction of poor, inadequate, and problematical functionings and ways of being. The manifest behavior of the patient is a prime target of the psychotherapeutic process. For the developmental model, there is likewise a focus upon the actual clinical functionings and the reduction of poor, inadequate, and problematical behaviors and actions. The developmental family may interpret these bits of actual clinical functionings as signs of the underlying psychopathological illness or disease. Nevertheless, within a broad meaning of symptomatology, the above goal is appropriate to all three models.

Reduction of Defenses

Defenses refer to barriers, to a broad array of mechanisms of avoidance, to what might be termed "indirections," to a moving away from life experience, and to any personality maneuver which subverts or runs from the threat associated with a pathological process. Each model includes some version of defenses, and the above goal is quite appropriate for each family of psychotherapies.

REDUCTION OF PSYCHOLOGICAL PAIN AND SUFFERING

For each model, psychological pain and distress are the accompaniments of a state of "psychopathology." Their reduction is the goal of each family of psychotherapies.

The actualization model emphasizes the bringing out into the realm of experience and the opening up of an awareness of one's existence, including the problems, difficulties, and sufferings. Although this family aims at the reduction of psychological pain and suffering, it further proposes that the direct, open experiencing of the authentic pain and suffering significantly modifies its meaning and impact. In addition, this model attempts to bring a measure of internal peace and integration to basic personality components. Basic suffering is not reduced or eliminated, but a dimension of self-acceptance, and internal integration is added. Thus, not only does this family accept the above goal, but it adds another dimension to our understanding of pain and suffering, a dimension which modifies the quality and significance of raw pain itself.

Varying Characteristics of Pain and Suffering

Each family has complex modes of understanding pain and suffering. Nevertheless, each seems to have certain defining characteristics, so that it is possible to draw three pictures of pain and suffering. In the developmental family, this includes (a) the pain and hurt of arrested development, of being fixated and blocked in normal growth processes, of being painfully infantile, and (b) the agony and threat of disrupted early attachments, of fundamental rejections. In the actualization family, the picture is of (a) a painful separation, and a distancing of the patient from his own needs and feelings, from existing and experiencing the ongoingness of life, and (b) the terrible inner strife and turmoil of basic parts at war, of being disintegrated. The reconstructive mood includes (a) the pain of inability to determine things for oneself, being unable to set one's own goals, being unable to predict, to change, to experiment with oncoming events, and (b) feelings of being limited, anxious, and angry with strong feelings of personal or social inferiority and lack of belonging.

Reduction of Anxiety

Each model places a premium on the reduction of anxiety, especially when anxiety refers to undue fear, dread, disabling tension, habits acquired in an anxiety-generating situation, disharmony, disintegration, and the inability to cope with danger or deal with anticipated events.

Anxiety Reduction and the Emergence of Normal Functioning

The developmental model includes a biological potential for normal, healthy, mature adjustive functioning. A subgroup within the developmental family not only aims at reduction of anxiety in its own right (as an ultimate goal), but assumes that this paves the way for the emergence of biological potentials for normal, healthy, mature, adjustive functioning.

Reduction of Hostility

Both the developmental and the reconstructive families include the reduction of hostility as a paramount therapeutic goal, especially when hostility is a general term encompassing anger, rage, aggression, and the like. Reasons for the presence of hostility range from frustration of biopsychological drives, in the developmental model, to anger as an accompaniment of irrational basic premises, in the reconstructive model.

For the actualization model, the reduction of hostility is only a secondary goal, one of limited extent. The process of releasing, actualizing, of opening up feelings to vital experiencing may unfold hostility as the "next" feeling, drive, value-conclusion, or need. In this sense, especially if it is drained of the pain of disintegration and of disruption among internal needs, "hostility" may occur as a therapeutic goal. This context may give hostility a qualitatively different meaning and significance than the hostility which is referred to in the developmental and reconstructive families.

Reduction of Meaninglessness

This goal refers to the sense of awful meaninglessness which accompanies separation from oneself and the world, a distance from life, an existence without meaning or value. Such a goal is of paramount importance in the actualization family; in the other two families the goal stands as not at all a *necessary* first-order goal. The actualization model is uniquely fitted for such a goal because of its particular emphasis upon experiencing the vital meaning of living. Meaninglessness, in the above sense, arises from the stopping or blocking of this fundamental characteristic of personality. Since this picture of personality is not characteristic of either the developmental or the reconstructive models, this goal is not paramount in these two families.

INCREASE IN PLEASURE

Each psychotherapeutic family accepts the goal of increased pleasure. Within the developmental and the actualization families, pleasure accompanies the fulfillment of needs and desires, the healthy expression of drives and impulses, the experiencing of feelings and needs. Pleasure is attendant on "creature" comforts, especially in regard to sexual pleasure and enjoyment.

The reconstructive model does not include such an array of forces pressing to be brought out; pleasure, therefore, has a different meaning. It refers to a well-functioning system which allows the person to anticipate and expect well, to operate easily and well. In addition, the reoriented and rebuilt constructs, basic premises, and personal-social goals include new philosophies of life, new psychological channels, and new life styles which heighten the sense of pleasure. Thus, the meaning and significance of pleasure may vary, but all three families aim for this central goal.

INCREASE IN EXPERIENCING

Experiencing refers to the concrete process of living and feeling, the vital sense of being and the awareness of one's existence, an openness and receptivity to internal and external stimuli, an "in touchness" with flux and with constantly changing commitments to the flow of experiences. The mode and manner of functioning may be maximally open to experiencing; as a process of functioning, it pervades "content" areas of functioning (e.g., sexual, vocational, social areas of functioning).

The experiencing of inner needs, feelings, and drives is perhaps the hallmark of therapeutic goals in the actualization model. One of the major basic properties of personality is the capacity for the concrete process of living and feeling, for the actualizing of the outward thrust of needs and feelings into experience, and for experiencing fully one's own dynamic existence. The above goal is central to this family.

Within the reconstructive family, the importance of the above goal depends upon the nature of the reconstructed system of personal constructs, basic premises, personal-social life goals, etc. Experiencing is not a basic property of personality but the reconstructed ideational system may emphasize the existential awareness of a modified life philosophy.

The state of health, within the developmental family, has a component of the good feeling of aliveness. However, the above goal is not central to this family. Experiencing in the above sense is neither a basic property of personality nor a component of a revised and reconstructed ideational system.

ENHANCED SELF-RELATIONSHIP

Three characteristics of the actualization model particularly equip this model for the above goal. First, this model places an exceedingly heavy emphasis upon one's own inner feelings and upon the personal full experiencing of one's own dynamic existence. The highest premium is placed on the internal locus of the broad process of experiencing. It is the inward (self) turning and the internal (self) locus which especially suits the actualization model for the above goal.

Second, the actualization model highlights the sense of internal peace and basic integration which flows out of the optimal alignment of basic personality elements. This sense of internal peace depends only to some extent upon the person's external relationships or involvements. Its locus is the internal self.

Third, the actualization model assumes a basic personality, an inner self. The person is offered the opportunity of becoming what he basically is. The critical liaison is between the person and his fundamental personality or his inner self.

Both the developmental and the reconstructive models aim moderately and to some extent toward an inward posture, with an enhanced self-relationship. However, neither places relatively as high a premium upon (a) the internal locus of experiencing; (b) internal integration of basic personality components; and (c) an accepting, loving, unified relationship between the person and his basic self.

The structure of the actualization model especially orients it toward the above goal. In contrast, the structure of the reconstructive model allows it to replace premises and assumptions with a new set whose content is that of a philosophy which may or may not be inner-directed or self-oriented.

Increase in Self-acceptance

As indicated above, the actualization model assumes an inner self, a basic personality, and the person's relationship with this inner self is a critical focus of psychotherapy. In addition, the elements of the basic personality (the self) are to be realigned in the direction of integration, acceptance, and harmony. Within the other two families, there is less of an emphasis upon the "self," and therefore, this goal is held only secondarily. Once again, however, the degree to which the reconstructive family includes this goal depends upon the nature of the reconstructed ideational system. It may well emphasize a "self-acceptance" set of premises, assumptions, or personal-social philosophy.

Increase in Inner-directedness

The increase in inner-directedness is a component of the general goal of an enhanced relationship with one's inner "self." Thus the three factors which particularly equip the actualization model to move toward an enhanced relationship with the inner self also account for the highlighting of a greater internal orientation. In the developmental and reconstructive families, the lesser importance of the internal locus of experiencing, the internal integration of basic personality components, and an accepting-integrated relationship between the person and his inner self, account for the limited premium placed upon the above goal.

ENHANCED EXTERNAL RELATIONSHIPS

"Enhanced external relationships" is a broad goal composed of four areas.

Increase in Close Interpersonal Relations

In the developmental family, normal, mature, healthy functioning includes a prominent component of warm, close, meaningful interpersonal relationships. These include loving-sexual relations. The developmental model pictures a mature organism separate from, but interacting with, an external environment. The nature of this ideal, mature, interactive relationship is characterized by closeness.

The actualization model emphasizes optimal basic need-drive relations in terms of harmony, oneness, unity, love-acceptance, and integration. The state of optimal basic need-drive relations is the paradigm for relationships between the individual and the external world, so that these interpersonal relations are likewise characterized by closeness, warmth, unity, oneness, love, and integration. The other therapeutic thrust toward experiential actualization likewise gives interpersonal relations candidness and genuineness as other aspects of the general goal of close interpersonal relations.

For the reconstructive model, the structure of the construct-premise-goal system does not lead *necessarily* to increased closeness of interpersonal relations. The appropriateness or inappropriateness of this goal is determined by the nature of the revised and reconstructed system. Thus, the content of the revised and elaborated personal-social goals may or may not emphasize belonging, closeness, and warmth in interpersonal relations.

Increase in Competent Functioning

The goal of competent functioning is so central to the developmental model that it almost serves as the defining property of mature, normal, healthy development. Competent functioning includes carrying out normal functioning, being able to hold a job, gain work satisfaction, be productive in work, and to function with spontaneity, assertiveness, and self-confidence.

The reconstructive system likewise invests its version of competent functioning with extremely high value as a therapeutic goal. The structure of the model permits the gaining of freedom from poor or inadequate basic constructs and premises; this orients the system toward competent functioning. The structure permits reconstruction toward enhanced anticipation of events; this also facilitates competent functioning. Finally, the system permits the addition of new constructs, premises, and life goals whose content and nature facilitate increased competency in functioning. Thus, the reconstructive family highlights competency as self-determined, self-directed functioning, heightened logical thinking, and refurbished processes of anticipation.

The actualization model does not include competent functioning as a defining property of normal, healthy, mature development, nor does it include the competence which grows out of the freedom from poor or inadequate basic constructs-premises. It lacks the structure for more competent anticipatory processes, and excludes the option of altering a determining system toward heightened competency of functioning.

Furthermore, that model inclines away from the notion of an external world so separated from the individual that one may deal with this separated entity in a competent fashion. Instead, what occurs as competent functioning in the other two models is meaningful here primarily in terms of the individual's *experiencings* during the concrete process of "competent" functioning. The activity may thus be accompanied with a vital aliveness and a keen sense of experiencing. But competent functioning *per se* achieves only secondary and limited importance as a therapeutic goal within the actualization family. Competent functioning should occur as a necessary epiphenomenon of the therapeutic process rather than its central target.

Increase in the Ability to Adjust

At least three features of the developmental model equip it for the goal of adjustment to external demands and to unavoidable frustrations and pressures. First, the fate of the developing personality (cf. ego) depends, to a large extent, upon its ability to adjust and to cope with libidinal impulses, basic biophysio-constitutional drives, and the psychic forces of the id. The necessity to adjust to and cope with separated (foreign) forces which threaten to endanger and overwhelm is reflected in the goal of being able to confront the demands of life and to adjust realistically.

Second, the model includes an initially weak developing organism, especially vulnerable to deleterious blocks and interferences from the external world's repertoire of potential traumas, especially serious threats to early attachments. The normal, mature personality must be able to adjust to the external threats and pressures.

Third, the biophysio-constitutional grounding of the basic personality processes invests them with the property of being fulfilled and gratified or frustrated and deprived (by the external world). The organism is thereby dependent upon the external world, and therefore it is involved in continuous processes of dealing with and adjusting to the shifting demands, threats, opportunities, and availabilities of fulfillment and gratification in the external environment. The importance of the goal of adjusting to the external world is thereby insured.

The reconstructive model is likewise structured for the goal of adjusting to the external world. First, the external world is understood in terms of its presenting a flow of events to the individual. In dealing with or adjusting to this flow, the person's processes (asserts one family member) are psychologically channeled by the ways in which he anticipates these events. Second, in this model the external world may be invested with a property of constant fluctuation, thus making it necessary to adjust to the external world by accepting uncertainty, being open to flexibility, and being able to predict and anticipate in relation to these external circumstances. Third, this family emphasizes self-determination and freedom from the rule of poor or inadequate determining constructs, basic premises, or life goals. Effective adjustment calls for a coping with the external world's efforts to determine and direct; the individual himself is to achieve the steering mechanism by gaining self-direction and self-determination for himself. Thus, the reconstructive model also orients therapy toward the goal of adjusting to the external world.

The actualization model is not built to support a *primary* goal of adjusting to the external world. The personality of the child is not open to (biophysio-constitutional) forces or instincts which must be coped with or adjusted to in some adequate manner, nor is this struggle the paradigm for coping with and adjusting to external forces which likewise threaten to overwhelm and damage. The personality is not like a newborn biological organism, vulnerable to developmental arrests from the traumatic influence of external forces. Basic motivations and needs are not biophysiological to the extent of requiring fulfillment and satisfaction from or being open to deprivation from the external world; biological tissue needs are not the paradigm. The person is not understood as adjusting to a flow of separated, external events, shifting and changing as they impinge upon the individual, nor is there a struggle to achieve self-determination. In general, the actualization model lacks the necessary structure to highlight the *primary* goal of "adjusting" to the external world.

Reality adjustment. In the actualization model, the larger measure of reality encompasses the inner world. What is "true" or "real" is anchored to the person's inner feelings, inner felt-meanings, authentic drives, impulses, and wishes. Adjustment to reality refers to the internal reality, to what has been termed "psychic reality." Thus, the criteria for what is "really" occurring is found within the realm of the person's own feelings, felt-meanings, and authentic drives. The goal becomes one of adjusting to the internal, real, meaningful world.

For the actualization model, the internal locus of reality invests external events with at least two meanings: (a) External events exert significance by touching off something within, by "meaning" something to the individual, by "reaching" him. (b) Fragments and aspects of the person himself occur as that person, but are localized outside in the external world. Thus, "adjusting to reality" is an adjustment to the deeper, inner "psychic reality" which gives meaning and significance to the external events.

For the developmental and reconstructive models, reality refers to the contours of the external world. Adjusting to reality stands as a primary goal involving the patient's relationship with the true, real aspects of what is "out there."

Increase in Social Commitment

In the developmental family, the package of normal, mature, healthy functioning includes meaningful achievement, increased social responsibility, increased interest in social welfare and cultural development, increased productiveness, and an increased commitment to the social order. Thus, the developmental family accepts the above goal.

For the reconstructive family, the relevancy and appropriateness of the above goal depends upon the nature of the reconstructed determining system. If the reconstructed system features constructs, premises, and life styles of social belonging and heightened social interest, for example, then the above goal becomes highly meaningful and appropriate.

In the actualization family, increased social commitment is a facet of openness to experience, to what is going on about the individual. In addition, the movement toward integration among basic personality elements calls for commitment to and involvement with the social order.

The structures of each of the models thus converge on the meaningfulness and appropriateness of the above goal.

ACHIEVING MEDIATING GOALS WHICH SERVE AS PATHWAYS TOWARD THE ULTIMATE GOALS OF PSYCHOTHERAPY

The goals described above stand as the more final, ultimate directional goals of the therapeutic process. Each of the three families possesses a set of means or methods (mediating goals) of accomplishing these ultimate goals.

Achieving the Mediating Goals of Correction of the Injurious Impacts of Traumas, Removal of Repressions, and the Resolution of Intrapsychic Conflict Through a Variety of Subgoals such as Corrective Emotional Experiences, Identification, After-education, Interpretation, Unlearning, and Adaptive Learning

In the developmental model, the developmental processes and intrinsic capacities for normal, healthy functioning set the stage for blocks and interferences to these biophysio-constitutional processes and capacities. Thus, elimination of these blocks and interferences is the function of the mediating goals.

One mediating goal within the developmental family is the *correction of the injurious impacts of traumas*. This mediating goal in turn is accomplished through such subgoals and working techniques as after-education, enabling and guiding the patient to undergo a corrective emotional experience, using techniques of unlearning the deleterious effects of early traumas and providing insight into traumatic influences. This mediating goal fits well with the developmental model because of its concepts of traumatically blocked growth-developmental forces and inherent normal functioning which may be released when the trauma and its impacts are removed or corrected, its concept of an initially weak organism (cf. ego) excessively vulnerable to the pressures of an alien external world, and because of other similar ideas.

A second mediating goal is the *removal of repressions, the providing of insight, and "making the unconscious conscious."* In the developmental model, the way is paved for this mediating goal by releasing the blocked forces, potentialities, and impulses through the removal of the repressions. Repression-removal, like correction of the injurious impacts of traumas, eliminates blocks and interferences to growth-developmental processes, and is especially fitted to this family.

A third means of removing blocks and interferences to growth-developmental processes is through the *resolution of intrapsychic conflicts*. The developmental model accommodates such a mediating goal by accepting the concept of a basic personality with elements in potential conflict with one another (cf. id-ego-superego conflicts). Variations on the more classic developmental model place less emphasis upon concepts of natural healing powers, built-in growth potentials, biological potentials for recovery, intrinsic maturational processes, or biologically-given healthy lines of development. The variation highlights the biologically intrinsic capacities for normal, healthy functioning. Thus, there would be less reason for dealing with traumatic arrestings of a growth process. On the other hand, the resolution of intrapsychic conflicts would be an important means of removing blocks and interferences with the latent biological capacities for normal functioning. In one instance, for example, this was to be accomplished by reducing the malevolent influence of the superego, encouraging the patient to identify with the "good foster mother" (i.e., the therapist). This tends to bring about a state of psychic cohesion.

The structure of the developmental model appears to accommodate the mediating goals of correcting the injurious impacts of traumas, removal of repressions, and resolving of intrapsychic conflicts. These share the function of eliminating blocks and interferences. (In the actualization family, resolving intra-psychic disintegrations is an ultimate goal, not a block-eliminating mediating goal.)

Achieving the Mediating Goal of Progressive, Sequential Therapeutic Experiencing of Feelings, Needs, and Felt Meanings

As in the developmental model, the actualization model provides a set of basic processes and variables which are blocked and whose release is interfered with by another set of variables. The function of mediating therapeutic goals is similarly the elimination of the blocks and interferences. In the actualization model, the nature of the basic processes and variables, the blocks and modes of removing those blocks differ from those of the developmental model. The nature and content of the mediating goals, too, differ; however, the function of the two sets of mediating goals is quite similar.

In contrast to the developmental model, the actualization model's set of mediating goals involves the progressive, sequential therapeutic experiencing of the patient's feelings, needs, and felt meanings. Therapeutic movement is toward the concrete unfolding of experiencings, involving the penetration of felt meanings, the opening up of the inner world of partly experienced, hidden, incompleted acts, fantasies, behaviors, and relationships. It involves a process of differentiating value-conclusions, therapeutic experiencing of increasingly deeper needs and feelings, and an existential confronting of one's own authentic personality.

The actualization model requires such goals on the basis of its fundamental capacity for experiencing, an assumption of needs-feelings-felt meanings-drives organized in progressively deeper strata, and a concept of basic needs-feelings-motivations available for actualization. The structure of that model appears to accommodate the mediating goal of a progressive, sequential therapeutic experiencing of feelings, needs, and felt meanings which share the function of removing blocks and interferences.

Achieving the Mediating Goal of Reorienting Social Goals, Elaborating and Changing Personal Constructs, and Revising Attitudes and Convictions

In contrast to the functions of mediating goals in the developmental and actualization models, the aim in the reconstructive family is not one of removing blocks or interferences to underlying processes, drives, or forces. In contrast, it is to reorganize and reconstruct the determining system of ideas, premises, constructs, and attitudes.

An extremely broad array of techniques and subgoals feeds into the mediating goals. The content and nature of many of these techniques and subgoals are similar to those found in the developmental and actualization model, but their function is directed toward reconstruction of the determining system of constructs, premises, and social goals. These techniques and subgoals vary from establishing a proper therapeutic relationship, insight, and analysis of the patient's present personality structure, to loosening and tightening constructs, and presenting evidence counter to the patient's previous attitudes.

Thus, the structure of the reconstructive model appears to accommodate the mediating goals of reorienting social goals, elaborating and changing personal constructs, and revising attitudes and convictions. These share the function of reorganizing the determining ideational system.

Constructs and premises versus behaviors and feelings. To some degree, the mediating goals of each family involve the changing of ideas, cognitions, and attitudes, as well as the changing of the patient's behavioral, feeling ways of being. Mediating goals are means of achieving ultimate goals which consist of changes in ideas, constructs, and premises, as well as actions, feelings, and behaviors. Furthermore, mediating goals rest upon techniques and subgoals which include changes in ideas-constructs-premises as well as actions-feelings-behaviors. But in the reconstructive model, the burden of actual therapeutic change seems to be mediated through the changing of the constructs, ideas, attitudes, and social goals. In both the developmental and the actualization models, the burden of actual therapeutic change is mediated through the feeling-experiencing of needs, corrective "emotional" experiences, and the emotion-feeling components of wishes, drives, needs, impulses, and motivational forces.

CONCLUSIONS

1. Some goals of psychotherapy are shared by each family, even though they are described with different words, their meaning and significance may vary somewhat from family to family, and there are gross differences in the underlying rationales. For example, each family highlights such goals as the reduction of symptomatology, reduction of defenses, and reduction of anxiety.

2. The preponderance of psychotherapeutic goals is not shared by the three families. These goals may be relevant and meaningful for one psychotherapeutic family, while having less relevance or meaning within another.

3. Each psychotherapeutic family or personality model appears to be conceptually associated with a relatively unique set of psychotherapeutic goals. Thus, a meaningful association occurs between a given personality model and a particular set of goals.

19

The Goals and Families of Psychotherapy: Implications

Alvin R. Mahrer, Ph.D.

THE purpose of the present chapter is to discuss the implications of psychotherapeutic families and goals. The previous two chapters have considered the goals themselves, their organization, and their relationships with three proposed psychotherapeutic families. The present chapter considers the implications for the general area of psychotherapy.

UNIFORMITY OF GOALS IN PSYCHOTHERAPY RESEARCH

It is untenable to maintain that psychotherapists proceed toward uniform goals, yet this assumption underlies much of the research in the area of psychotherapy. Such research stands upon rather shaky methodological ground if the researcher assumes this, while the psychotherapists in his experiments actually are headed in inconsistent and often opposing directions. It is important for researchers to provide some means of assessing the degree to which the psychotherapists who are used in research share a uniformity of goals. Certain goals have a high likelihood of being generally adopted. For example, research on the therapeutic reduction of anxiety would be likely to find that psychotherapists generally shared this goal. However, if the research concerns other goals, the results might do little more than reflect the inconsistency in intent among the psychotherapists used in the research.

Researchers frequently group together psychotherapists on the basis of their avowed "school" or approach. Thus, there are Sullivanians, Freudians, behavior therapists, Adlerians, client-centered therapists, social learning therapists, and others. It is doubtful that the similarity existing within a "school" necessarily includes a similarity in the goals of therapy, for the characteristics which define any given school allegiance have no necessary bearing on the goals. Thus it is proposed that the degree of good variability or uniformity is a significant methodological variable in research on psychotherapy, one which must be controlled or studied in a well-designed investigation.

MEDIATING GOALS AS RESEARCH SUBSTITUTES FOR ULTIMATE GOALS

In research on psychotherapeutic change, it is tempting to focus on mediating goals either as a substitute for ultimate goals or on the assumption that a change in the mediating goal implies a change in the ultimate goal. For example, the achievement of insight may serve as a significant mediating goal toward more ultimate goals of psychotherapy. However, it is unwise to assume that increased insight necessarily carries with it correlated increases in the achievement of the ultimate goals of psychotherapy; this assumption calls for research investigation. Also, it is misleading to identify insight or any other mediating goal as an ultimate therapeutic goal. For research purposes, it is helpful to distinguish mediating from ultimate goals and to study the extent to which achievement of the former necessarily implies the achievement of the latter.

FUNCTIONAL SIMILARITY OF MEDIATING GOALS

Perhaps the primary feature of a mediating goal is its functionality. Mediating the therapeutic process toward the ultimate goals invests these mediating goals with a purpose. Organized on the basis of their *function*, a number of mediating goals become similar, even though superficially they seem quite different in *content*. Likewise, those similar in surface appearance may mediate quite different ultimate goals.

According to the reconstructive approach, interpretation, insight, and awareness may be used to loosen the hold of certain irrational basic premises or personal-social goals as the therapeutic process moves toward instituting a more desirable life style or life philosophy. Within the developmental approach, the phenotypically similar interpretation, insight, and awareness may serve as a means of resolving intrapsychic conflict, thereby removing a block to normal, healthy functioning.

Mediating goals with similar content and surface appearance are grossly different in function. On the other hand, in all three families mediating goals with grossly dissimilar phenotypic appearance may be identical in their function. Both the mediating goal of using the therapist as a model and the mediating goal of acting counter to basic irrational premises have the function of attacking certain premises and facilitating new ones, according to the reconstructive model. It seems most sensible to understand, study, and classify mediating goals on the basis of their function (purpose or aim) rather than their surface content or appearance.

INSIGHT AS A MEDIATING GOAL

Insight is one of the chief mediating goals and may be understood on the basis of the multiplicity of its functions within each psychotherapeutic family. It is used to uncover the patient's basic personality, to remove repressions and help make the unconscious conscious, to free and build the ego. A means of learning and unlearning adaptive and unadaptive behaviors, it also facilitates identification with the "good parent," i.e., the therapist, and aids in bringing about corrective emotional experiences. It is used to change critical convictions and to reduce disabling anxiety and intrapsychic conflict, and to change a patient's life style and basic life assumptions. Insight helps a patient comprehend that his present behavior has antecedents and that his presently maintained beliefs are important, so that he may forcibly attack the basic irrational premises.

Without exhausting the list, it seems clear that a study of the functions of insight would yield many grossly different types. For research, teaching, and training purposes and for understanding both the concept and techniques of insight, these various types should not be lumped into a single category; rather, insight should be carefully analyzed from the point of view of its functions.

LEARNING AS A MEDIATING GOAL

Many mediating goals may be broadly conceptualized as "learning." A partial list would include reeducating, providing corrective emotional experiences, serving as a (learning) model for the patient, teaching the patient, changing behavior and life styles, differentiating meaning, reinforcing the therapeutic process, helping the patient to grow, to learn and unlearn unadaptive emotional habits, to acquire responses, change convictions, and others. Indeed, the psychotherapeutic process itself may be described as a grand process of learning. As a mediating goal, learning is an extremely broad enterprise.

Learning in the Developmental Family

In the developmental family, learning procedures and techniques aim at the blocks and interferences to normal functioning, the disease, malfunction, disabling condition, or problem. Once these are removed or alleviated, the therapeutic process moves toward normal, healthy, mature functioning. The desirable mode of functioning is not learned directly; blocks and interferences cannot be sidestepped.

Learning in the Reconstructive Family

In the reconstructive family, the broad scope of learning procedures is likewise employed to attack and alleviate the problem, the poor or disruptive elements (constructs, premises, life goals). However, in contrast to the developmental model, optimal functioning here is open to direct learning. Learning processes are used to bring about a new way of life, add new goals, append a new life philosophy, accrue a new set of personal constructs, and, in short, to "learn" directly the optimal mode of functioning. Thus, the functions of learning differ in the two families.

Learning is used so broadly that it encompasses the entire psychotherapeutic process. One challenge is to classify the various learning techniques on the basis of their functions. For example, in the developmental model, learning is a means of clearing blocks and paving the way for normal, healthy functioning. The reconstructive model not only utilizes learning methods to clear away problems, but also directly to bring about optimal functioning. With regard to the broad area of learning as a mediating goal in psychotherapy, the second challenge is to utilize specific learning techniques and processes for specific mediating purposes within each family.

UNIFORMITY VERSUS HETEROGENEITY AMONG APPROACHES

One contention is that the various psychotherapies are basically quite uniform; differences are more manufactured than real, and consist largely of differences in vocabulary. The opposite contention maintains that differences are real and that various psychotherapies are heterogeneous. One way of studying similarities or differences is to analyze the purposes, aims, and functions of each school or therapeutic approach. Our own investigation of the three proposed families revealed both similarities and differences in goals.

The uniformity across the three families is concretely identifiable. By and large, each of our proposed families accepted the following goals: the reduction of psychopathology (as defined earlier); of symptomatology (broadly defined); of defenses (broadly defined); of psychological pain and suffering; of anxiety; the increase in pleasure and social commitment; and the achievement of mediating goals which serve as pathways toward the more ultimate goals of psychotherapy.

Although each family may invest the above goals with its own style, particular meaning, and theoretical rationale, these goals remain as distinctive points of similarity. With regard to all other therapeutic goals, there are more significant differences in degrees of acceptance by all families. Some are second-order goals, and some become optional within a given family. It appears, therefore, that our three families reveal certain similarities as well as meaningful differences, at least with regard to therapeutic goals. It is in-

accurate to assert that the approaches are either uniform or totally heterogeneous or that various approaches use different means (mediating goals)
to attain the same end results (ultimate goals).

"Bad" States or Conditions

Each family labels certain conditions or states as "bad," undesirable,
problematical, or pathological. Regardless of the exact label, the goal is to
reduce or resolve them. In general, the three families agree that a particular
condition is bad, undesirable, problematical, or pathological on the basis of
two factors:

(a) They prevent, interfere with, or block the achievement of whatever the
model considers to be "good" or desirable, healthy or optimal. (b) They involve psychological pain. Although each family has its own version of such
pain, the common theme is that such a state exists and should be eliminated
or reduced.

One or both of these two factors accounts for each family's repertoire of
"bad" states or conditions and underlies such a broad spectrum of bad, undesirable, problematical, or pathological states as the following: being neurotic or psychotic, having an emotional illness, being maladaptive, being sick,
having a disease, being abnormal, being deviate, lacking normal functioning,
being immature, being hindered in experiencing, having a tight construct
system, lacking identification, being unable to face authentic guilt, having a
malevolent superego, being unable to set one's own life goals, being basically
disintegrated, or having any of a myriad of symptoms, difficulties, or patholo-
gies.

THE DATA OF PSYCHOTHERAPY

The patient presents the psychotherapist with highly complex sets of
data. These include postures, intonations, conversations, historical material,
interactions, topical changes, complaints, anecdotes, pauses, feelings, thoughts,
and ideas. Each personality model encompasses all these ongoing data, selecting the particular parts to be emphasized as the referential data for psychotherapy.

The reconstructive model highlights the ongoing conceptual, thinking, and
cognitive processes with the most important data consisting of systems of
constructs, concepts, and premises. The flow of psychotherapeutic material reveals the nature of the conceptual system. In addition, the construct system
may be shown to be limited, or basic premises irrational.

In the actualization model, the patient is coping, feeling, reaching, behaving, experiencing. Here, the flow of data reveals the ongoingness of the
present, the nature of present feelings and behavior, and the beginnings of what
is within, ready to be experienced and enacted next.

The developmental model stresses the nature of personality functioning, the manifestations of personality structure. The therapist is attuned to a highly threatening superego, narcissism, healthy ego functioning, indications of defense mechanisms, and the initial stages of transference.

"DEEP" PSYCHOTHERAPY

A popular assumption is that certain psychotherapies are "deeper" than others, i.e., involve more pervasive reorganization of the fundamental strata of personality and bring about more profound personality changes. Our data permit no systematic conclusions on this issue, but a few observations are in order.

One aspect of "depth" lies in the nature of therapeutic goals. Presumably, "deeper" psychotherapies would aim at "deeper" goals. Accordingly, it is proposed that the study of the depth of any given psychotherapy utilizes a systematic outline of goals for purposes of comparison. The hypothesis would be that deeper psychotherapies (e.g., Freudian psychoanalysis) would be associated with unique and "deeper" goals than those of a "less deep" therapeutic approach. Our own analysis of the three families reveals differences in goals. However, even on the basis of an acknowledged difference in goals, there is no basis for identifying one of our three families as being "deeper" than the others.

It may be that the difference in depth refers to the nature of the mediating goals. Interpretation of the transference neurosis (in the developmental family) may be deeper than encouraging the patient to behave counter to his premises (in the reconstructive family). On the other hand, the replacement of the basic elements of the foundation of personality (in the reconstructive family) may be deeper than removing blocks to relatively unalternable bio-physio-constitutional forces and processes (in the developmental family).

All in all, it appears that our three families do not differ in depth, although the general issue of deeper schools or approaches to psychotherapy is not directly touched upon.

The Resolution of Basic Problems

The personality models imply another dimension to the depth of the psychotherapy, viz., the attitude toward resolution of the basic problems. One attitude is that the truly basic personality is an intact unit, essentially unalterable. Therapy aims at helping the patient to accept and live with the basic problems. The attitude toward and relationship with the basic personality, then, are modifiable. Gross changes, however, may be accomplished at the behavioral level, so that the patient's functioning is open to significant modification. Each of the three personality models may accommodate this attitude.

The other attitude is that the fundamental elements of personality are open to change. They arise out of dynamic fields which are still accessible to psychotherapy. Conceivably, the patient may be freed of these problems; it is not a matter of accepting them or learning to live wisely with them. This attitude, too, may be held by any of our three families.

Although a given personality model may incline toward or away from the former or latter attitude, there are no clearcut differences among the three models: the above attitudes cut across the models rather than being identified with a given one. Thus, it cannot be said that the models differ in depth of psychotherapy when depth refers either to (1) the nature of the therapeutic goals, (2) the use of "deeper" mediating goals, or (3) the probability of resolving basic ("deeper") problems.

UNIQUE PERSONALITY MODELS UNDERLYING PSYCHO-THERAPY

Every personality theory, from psychoanalysis to client-centered, from those rooted in sociology to those derived from computer mathematics, will find that our three proposed models (developmental, actualization, and reconstructive) fail to appreciate or reflect the conceptual refinements, theoretical richness, and complexity of their particular concepts. These personality theories may contain profound bodies of knowledge about human personality, and psychotherapy *ought* to be based on and reflect these complex realms of understanding. However, our contention is that traditional bodies of knowledge about human personality, motivation, personality development, psychopathology, and behavioral change do not, in fact, bear a direct, systematic relationship to the actual theory and practice of psychotherapy in operation. Regardless of their similarity to or difference from the three proposed in this book, it is contended that unique personality models underlie actual psychotherapeutic processes.

Thus, the therapist may enter the practice of psychotherapy well schooled in Freudian psychoanalysis, Adlerian Psychology, or behavioral models based upon animal research or studies of laboratory responses in standardized psychological test situations; nevertheless, it is proposed that other as yet undefined models underlie therapists' actual operations in the psychotherapeutic situation. Furthermore, the therapist's mode of understanding the patient, his clinical description of the case, is probably based upon one personality conceptualization, while other conceptualizations actually underlie the ongoing processes of treatment.

Once a personality theory acquires stature, its vocabulary dominates psychotherapeutic practices and operations. In the course of time, qualitative changes may occur in the theoretical principles and in the personality models actually used in psychotherapy, even though the original vocabulary is retained. Thus, the continuation of the old terms gives the illusion that the original personality model still holds, when in fact, new and as yet undefined personality models are in operation.

Two implications arise from the assumption that unique personality models underlie the actual psychotherapeutic process, one pertaining to research and one to teaching-training.

Research Implication

To the extent that improvement in psychotherapeutic methods is tied to improvement in psychotherapeutic personality models, it is suggested that research inquiry be addressed toward the uncovering and identification of the actual personality models which operate in actual therapeutic operations. For example, experienced and "effective" psychotherapists may be studied in live operation, with the aim of learning the principles and theoretical constructs which guide their movements, words, and interactions.

Teaching-training Implication

A most important part of the early teaching and training of a student therapist lies in identifying and understanding the student's highly personal personality conceptions and personality models which reveal themselves in his actual therapeutic operations. Ordinarily, it is not only inaccurate and misleading, but also damaging to the learning of psychotherapy to presume that the student's avowed theoretical allegiance, the theoretical orientation of his academic institution, or the particular vocabulary he chooses to use in publicly discussing psychotherapy have a great deal to do with the personality model which determines his actual therapeutic operations. The data for such an analysis include the nature of the patient-therapist relationship, the methods by which the therapist attempts to alter behavior, the topics to which the therapist attends, counter-transference, etc. In short, every aspect of the therapeutic process will reflect the therapist's underlying theoretical psychotherapeutic model.

PERSONALITY MODELS AND PROFESSIONAL TRAINING

In addition to the value of extracting the student's guiding personality model, there are broader implications for the training of psychotherapists. Our thesis is that there is not one kind of psychotherapy, but rather at least three distinct families with three associated optimal professional training programs. Professional squabbling over "the best" kind of professional training is based, in part at least, on the untenable assumption that there is only one (best) psychotherapeutic personality model.

The developmental model is intimately tied to foundations of biology, neurology, physiology, anatomy, and the fabric of "medical" tradition. A full appreciation of the critical determining forces and variables in psychotherapy calls for thorough training in these basic fields. At the present time, this training is most available at medical schools, psychiatric residencies, and psychoanalytic institutes.

The actualization family calls for different training. Within this model the basic foundations of personality are psychological rather than medical or biophysio-constitutional. There is a strictly psychological understanding of the wellsprings of personality, of personality change, of the structure of personality, of motivation, and of the principles of psychotherapy. At the present time, training is found in university graduate departments of psychology.

The reconstructive model calls for professional training within the tradition of psychology's world of constructs, cognitions, attitudes, and theoretical systems of premises. Its underlying philosophy and theoretical model of personality lie essentially within the realm of psychology. Such training is best sought in university graduate departments of psychology.

Progress in Professional Training

This progress involves continual improvement in each of the theoretical conceptualizations of personality and its associated training programs. Within medical schools, psychiatric residencies, and psychoanalytic institutes, the mainstream of tradition conceptualizes psychotherapy as a means of treating and healing disease and illness. Thus, progress within the developmental family would involve continual enrichment with the fullness and knowledge of the medical tradition and medical research.

However, medical training for psychotherapy is inadequate and inappropriate when one abandons the developmental model, and along with it the biophysio-constitutional grounding and the conception of psychotherapy within the medical model of treating and healing an illness or a disease. Progress in training for psychotherapy within the framework of the actualization and reconstructive families rests essentially upon psychological research, improvements in university graduate departments of psychology and their professional training programs, and the growth and development of psychological theories of personality and principles of psychotherapy.

PERSONALITY MODELS AND INDIVIDUAL PSYCHO-THERAPISTS

It is likely that the major theoretical emphasis of any given psychotherapist would fall largely within one major psychotherapeutic family, with, however, offshoots into other families. Although the families were derived from the several contributors to this book (and reflect only the chapters in this book rather than their previous writings), it is certainly neither intended nor expected that the family serve as a cell, completely containing the theoretical ideas of a contributor or of any given psychotherapist.

Although the fact highlights the inadequacy of our proposed three-family category system, experienced, effective therapists in actual operation probably borrow from each of the three families *and* from the concepts of individual psychology, ego psychology, Freudian psychoanalysis, character analysis, learning theories, client-centered psychotherapy, and so on. If the working personality conceptions and models of these psychotherapists seem confused and inconsistent viewed through the eyes of any given category system, then perhaps research should search for deeper consistencies and newer categories.

PERSONALITY MODELS AND THE INDIVIDUAL PATIENT

The three proposed personality models represent three conceptions of the human being, his personality structure, his psychological base, his capacity for modification, and his potential way of functioning. Although each family of personality conceptions implicitly assumes the universal applicability of its particular model, it is conceivable that human beings represent a variety of personality structures. More practically, each personality model may have its own "range of convenience" as George Kelly puts it. Each personality model may, therefore, offer the best way of understanding certain categories of patients, may offer them the most efficacious mode of treatment; and would dovetail most appropriately with their particular therapeutic capacities and readiness.

If given personality models have their own ranges of convenience and applicability, both in terms of effectiveness of understanding and in terms of treatment, then one may conceive of a pretherapeutic evaluation designed to provide the best "fit" between the particular patient and the most appropriate therapeutic family.

The Likelihood of Improvement Without Psychotherapy

As a special case, personality models differ on the issue of "spontaneous" improvement in the course of life experiences, without the benefit of psychotherapeutic "intervention." It would appear that the developmental model's concept of natural healing processes enables that model to encompass such changes. Thus, the organism would have a distinct capacity for recovering from setbacks, for healing itself, and for dealing "naturally" with external stresses. The presence of this concept inclines the model toward the likelihood of improvement, recovery, and beneficial change without psychotherapy. Even though it is recognized that many other factors contribute to the likelihood of improvement without psychotherapy, it can be seen that the presence or absence of such concepts helps to incline the model either toward or away from such an expectation.

PERSONALITY MODELS AND PROGRESS IN PSYCHOTHERAPY

Psychotherapeutic operations are, in large measure, tied to the underlying personality conceptions and models. The strong implication, then, is that truly effective progress in psychotherapy depends upon progress in the field of personality theory and personality model-building. There are at least two avenues of development.

The first refers to the systematic unfolding of the psychotherapeutic techniques and operations which are contained within present personality models. This calls for a process of systematic, logical deduction from established personality models, which have not been drained of their therapeutic implications by any means. For each model, then, the appropriate question is the nature of psychotherapeutic processes which are implied and which may be derived.

The second course of development refers to the creative development of personality models. As new understanding of personality arises, and as research points toward the need for modification in the theoretical understanding of personality, personality models will be pressured to change. There must be a willingness on the part of psychotherapists to accept changes in the underlying personality model, with consequent changes in psychotherapeutic operations.

Learning Theories

Throughout this book, there is a striking tendency to use the vocabulary of learning theories. It may be that these theories will offer a medium of communication among psychotherapists from a variety of schools and approaches. The trend may be toward a common "learning" language. In addition, each of the three proposed families include mediating goals derived in large part from learning theories.

Although these are substantial contributions, the larger question is the extent to which learning theory models of personality will prove meaningful and effective. This issue is beyond the scope of this book, but progress in the field of psychotherapy will undoubtedly rest upon the resolution of this issue.

Correspondence with Contemporary Schools of Psychotherapy

Developmental psychotherapies may perhaps be identified as Freudian psychoanalytic psychotherapy; actualization psychotherapies as client-centered-existential psychotherapies; reconstructive psychotherapies as a form of learning theory psychotherapies. It is beyond the scope of this book to identify the proposed goals and underlying families of psychotherapies as "Freudian," "Jungian," "Sullivanian," "Adlerian," or whatever. Such an investigation calls for a sensitive knowledge of the many variations and derivatives of, for example, Freudian psychoanalysis as a body of personality conceptions and a system of psychotherapy. The many variations and derivatives of learning theories and behavior modification psychotherapies would make such a task a delicate and gigantic undertaking. Our purpose has been to inquire what sorts of families of personality conceptions emerge from a study of psychotherapeutic functions or goals, rather than to study the similarities and differences in the goals of our established schools of psychotherapy.

PSYCHOTHERAPY AS A POSITIVE PROCESS

In general, psychotherapy is associated with the negative side of life, with problems, illness, and suffering. Even though the goal is to eliminate or reduce problems and unhappiness, the content remains essentially negative. On the other hand, the summary and outline of general goals indicates that psychotherapy might well become a highly positive venture, with positive feelings, good aspects, and happier, less negative components to the process. To a large extent, at least one of the determinants lies within the nature of the personality model: a given personality model may incline the therapy toward dealing with essentially negative contents rather than toward more positive contents and goals.

When the patient and therapist both tacitly or explicitly move toward termination, it may be that the negative component of psychotherapy is coming to an end. At that point the personality model may or may not open up the possibility of a new vista of positive goals. Therapy may really begin at the point where most therapies leave off. A critical analysis is needed of the theoretical structure of personality models with a view to either accepting limited negative goals or to progressing toward more positive uses of the psychotherapeutic process.

CREATIVITY

The goals of psychotherapy select various components of creativity, rather than treating it as a single, unitary concept. Some kinds or components are increased, others decreased, by the psychotherapeutic process.

What appears as creativity may really be a symptom of psychopathology indicative of an emotional illness or a condition of psychic discomfort. Since the goal of treatment is the elimination of psychopathology, symptoms should disappear and there should be a reduction in this false creativity. Such false creativity may also really be a defense, avoiding and masking the drives, needs, or impulses at a deeper personality level; the general elimination of defenses will probably carry with it this defense, too.

Creative expression is a part of generalized feelings of pleasureful fulfillment, enjoyment, satisfaction, and the positive enjoyment of health, and therefore the therapeutic process should enhance and facilitate this component of creativity. Another goal of treatment is to increase the expression of life's ongoingness, an essential ingredient in the experiential process, and a component of creativity.

Creative expression is a mark of the person's willingness to enter into his inner world; this increases as psychotherapy opens up the person to himself. On the other hand, unimpaired creative functioning is also a sign of increased competence, signifying a more efficient involvement with the external world, and should increase as psychotherapy frees energy toward the external world. Creativity is a part of the increased productiveness which accompanies a heightened commitment to the society about oneself. Increased achievement often involves increased creativity. Thus psychotherapy enhances certain components of creativity while acting to reduce others.

SOCIAL-PHILOSOPHICAL VALUE SYSTEMS

Each of the three proposed families of psychotherapy has its own version of "the good life," the ideal or optimal way of living and being in the world. For the developmental model what is philosophically "good" is tantamount to what is "natural" biologically and genetically. Thus, its philosophical values are tied to concepts of maturity, health, and normal functioning. The other models turn to other realms for the theoretical foundations of their social-philosophical value systems.

The therapist maintains a distinct set of values associated with whatever personality model guides his operations. Value may be placed upon "health," "maturity," or some other set of concepts linked with psychotherapeutic goals, but the investment of philosophical value remains. When one cautions the therapist to separate his own personal set of morals, values, ideals, and the like from his psychotherapy, it must nevertheless be acknowledged that he operates within a larger set of psychotherapeutic values and philosophical "goods." This philosophical system is maintained even though there is, perhaps, no intrusion of the therapist's concrete attitude toward specific topics such as divorce, deviate sexuality, psychopathic behavior, and the like.

PSYCHOTHERAPY AND SOCIAL CHANGE

Implied in the ultimate goals of psychotherapy are conceptions of optimal social communities and methods of bringing about broad social change. Each family of psychotherapies possesses the means of moving toward optimal living for collective individuals. However, the major social contribution of psychotherapy may not lie in its ultimate goals; instead, psychotherapy may offer society the means of bringing about effective change through mediating goals.

Psychological methods of achieving mediating psychotherapeutic goals would not be limited to the treatment of an emotional illness. Instead, they may be incorporated into means for achieving broader social change and more positive social goals. As described by Reuben Fine, therapeutic groups may provide the instruments of moving toward effective social change, or psychological principles and techniques of mediating therapeutic change may be adapted for use in individual self-analysis, again as a means of bringing about broader social change. It is conceivable that collective individuals can come to understand and use the methods and techniques of undergoing corrective emotional experiences, resolving intrapsychic conflict, gaining self-understanding, acquiring adaptive habits, differentiating their own value-conclusions, attacking their own irrational basic premises, and changing their own construct system. Whether on a group or individual basis, psychotherapeutic (mediating) methods may hold promise as means of achieving social change.